Illustrative Student Essa

Research Coverage

Why Do You Need This New Edition?

If you are wondering why you should buy this new edition of Literature, here are 7 good reasons!

1. **NEW MLA Document Maps:** These visual representations help students locate key information for frequently cited sources such as books and Web sites.
2. **NEW Visualizing Genres:** Fiction, poetry, and drama each feature a section devoted to images that represent key literary principles or visual-based media within the genre. In fiction, a comic strip and graphic novel are featured; in poetry, shaped poetry is highlighted; and in drama, two different production photos of *Hamlet* are used to compare and contrast different staging techniques.
3. **NEW Design:** The entire book has been redesigned to make key features and selections easier to find and read.
4. **NEW Fiction Selections:** Eleven new works, including James Baldwin, "Sonny's Blues," Joyce Carol Oates, "Where Are You Going, Where Have You Been?" and Ernest Hemingway, "Hills Like White Elephants."
5. **NEW Poetry Selections:** Forty-five new works, including Pablo Neruda, "If You Forget Me," Gwendolyn Brooks, "The Mother," and Yusef Komunyakaa, "Facing It."
6. **NEW Drama Selection:** August Wilson, *Fences*
7. **NEW Poetic Careers:** Four varied poetic careers are now highlighted:
   - **Emily Dickinson,** including "Because I could not stop for Death."
   - **Robert Frost,** including "Stopping by Woods on a Snowy Evening."
   - **Langston Hughes,** including "Harlem 1951."
   - **Sylvia Plath,** including "Daddy."

Literature

An Introduction to Reading and Writing
Ninth Edition
EDGAR V. ROBERTS

Hallmark and New Features of **Literature, Ninth Edition**

Writing

The Ninth Edition features fully integrated coverage of writing about literature.

Every chapter covering a literary element includes:

- Writing about the element
- Strategies for organizing ideas
- Illustrative student essays in MLA style with commentary
- Special topics for writing and arguing about the element

36 MLA-style *Illustrative Student Essays* provide student models for every element in the book.

Second Illustrative Student Essay (Allegory)

Underlined sentences in this paper *do not* conform to MLA style and are used solely as teaching tools to emphasize the central idea, thesis sentence, and topic sentences throughout the paper.

Murphy 1

Heather Murphy
Professor Thomas
English 2B
5 February 2008

The Allegory of Hawthorne's "Young Goodman Brown"°

Nathaniel Hawthorne's "Young Goodman Brown" is a nightmarish narrative. [1] It allegorizes the process by which something good--religion--becomes a justification for intolerance and prejudice. The major character, Young Goodman Brown of colonial Salem, begins as a pious and holy person, but he takes a walk into a nearby darkening forest of suspicion. The process is portrayed by Hawthorne as something created by the devil himself, who leads Goodman Brown into the increasingly evil and sinful night. By the end of the allegory, Brown is transformed into an unforgiving, antisocial, dour, and dreary misanthrope.

°This story appears on pages 385–92.

Part I, *The Process of Reading, Responding to, and Writing About Literature*, provides detailed coverage of the writing process, including multiple drafts of a student paper with annotations to demonstrate the process.

Research

Three chapters on research—one each for fiction, poetry, and drama—feature full MLA-style research papers annotated to point out research information specific to each genre.

Chapter 10A features full coverage of the research process, including paraphrasing material, avoiding plagiarism, and citing sources.

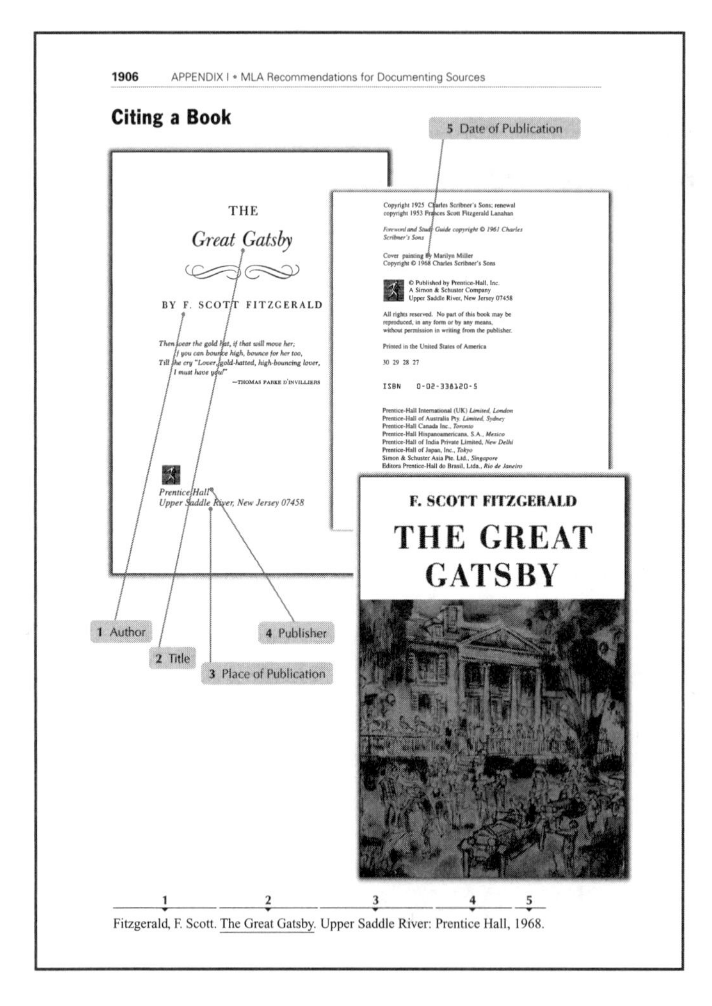

NEW—Highly visual MLA document maps help students locate key information on frequently cited sources such as books and Web sites.

Visuals

An engaging color insert features works of art and connects them to various pieces of literature throughout the book. These images help reinforce the themes found in the literature.

NEW—The Ninth Edition boasts a fresh new design that makes key features and selections easier to find and read.

NEW—Visualizing genres sections for fiction, poetry, and drama include images representing key literary principles or visual-based media within the genre. For example, in drama two different versions of *Hamlet* are presented to demonstrate costuming and staging differences.

Additional Resources

NEW—The Ninth Edition features new inside front cover references. The inside front cover includes a chart detailing where to find writing and research coverage in the book along with all the student papers. The inside back cover offers alphabetical and chronological lists of all authors included in the anthology.

Chronological List of Authors Included in *Literature*, Ninth Edition

Aesop, ca. 600 BCE
Sophocles, 496–406 BCE
Petronius (Gaius Petronius Arbiter), d. 66 CE
St. Luke, fl. ca. 90 CE.
Sir Thomas Wyatt, 1503–1542
Queen Elizabeth I (Elizabeth Tudor), 1533–1603
Sir Walter Ralegh, 1552–1618
Christopher Marlowe, 1564–1593
William Shakespeare, 1564–1616
John Donne, 1572–1631
Ben Jonson, 1573–1637
Robert Herrick, 1591–1674
Henry King, 1592–1669
George Herbert, 1593–1633
Edmund Waller, 1606–1687
John Milton, 1608–1674
Anne Bradstreet, 1612–1672
Andrew Marvell, 1621–1678
Molière (Jean Baptiste Poquelin), 1622–1673
John Dryden, 1631–1700
Jonathan Swift, 1667–1745
Alexander Pope, 1688–1744
Thomas Gray, 1716–1771
William Cowper, 1731–1800
Phillis Wheatley, 1754–1784
William Blake, 1757–1827
Robert Burns, 1759–1796
William Wordsworth, 1770–1850
Samuel Taylor Coleridge, 1772–1834
Cornelius Whur, 1782–1853
Friedrich Rückert, 1788–1866
Percy Bysshe Shelley, 1792–1822
William Cullen Bryant, 1794–1878
John Keats, 1795–1821
Ralph Waldo Emerson, 1803–1882
Nathaniel Hawthorne, 1804–1864
Elizabeth Barrett Browning, 1806–1864
Henry Wadsworth Longfellow, 1807–1882
John Greenleaf Whittier, 1807–1892
Edgar Allan Poe, 1809–1849
Abraham Lincoln, 1809–1865
Alfred, Lord Tennyson, 1809–1892
Robert Browning, 1812–1889
Emily Brontë, 1818–1848
Arthur Hugh Clough, 1819–1861
Herman Melville, 1819–1891
Walt Whitman, 1819–1892
Matthew Arnold, 1822–1888
Frances E. W. Harper, 1825–1911
Henrik Ibsen, 1828–1906
Emily Dickinson, 1830–1886
Christina Rossetti, 1830–1894
Lewis Carroll, 1832–1898
Mark Twain (Samuel Clemens), 1835–1910
Thomas Hardy, 1840–1928
Ambrose Bierce, 1842–1914?
Gerard Manley Hopkins, 1844–1889
William Ernest Henley, 1849–1903
Emma Lazarus, 1849–1887
Guy de Maupassant, 1850–1893
te Chopin, 1851–1904
nrad, 1857–1924

George William Russell (Æ), 1867–1935
Edwin Arlington Robinson, 1869–1935
Stephen Crane, 1871–1900
Paul Lawrence Dunbar, 1872–1906
Robert Frost, 1874–1963
Amy Lowell, 1874–1925
Rainer Maria Rilke, 1875–1926
John Masefield, 1878–1967
Carl Sandberg, 1878–1967
Wallace Stevens, 1879–1955
Abbie Huston Evans, 1881–1983
Susan Glaspell, 1882–1948
James Joyce, 1882–1941
Franz Kafka, 1883–1924
William Carlos Williams, 1883–1963
D. H. Lawrence, 1885–1930
Ezra Pound, 1885–1972
Frances Cornford, 1886–1960
Siegfried Sassoon, 1886–1967
Robinson Jeffers, 1887–1962
Marianne Moore, 1887–1972
T. S. Eliot, 1888–1965
Katherine Mansfield, 1888–1923
Eugene O'Neill, 1888–1953
John Crowe Ransom, 1888–1974
Alan Seeger, 1888–1916
Anita Scott Coleman, 1890–1960
Claude McKay, 1890–1948
Katherine Anne Porter, 1890–1980
Archibald MacLeish, 1892–1982
Edna St. Vincent Millay, 1892–1950
Wilfred Owen, 1893–1918
Dorothy Parker, 1893–1967
E. E. Cummings, 1894–1962
Jean Toomer, 1894–1967
Robert Graves, 1895–1985
John Chipman Farrar, 1896–1974
Eugenio Montale, 1896–1981
Louise Bogan, 1897–1970
William Faulkner, 1897–1962
Herman J. Mankiewicz, 1897–1953
Chief Dan George, 1899–1981
Ernest Hemingway, 1899–1961
Robert Francis, 1901–1987
Salvatore Quasimodo, 1901–1968
Arna Bontemps, 1902–1973
Langston Hughes, 1902–1967
Ogden Nash, 1902–1971
Stevie Smith, 1902–1971
John Steinbeck, 1902–1968
Frank O'Connor, 1903–1966
Richard Eberhart, 1904–2005
C. Day Lewis, 1904–1972
Pablo Neruda, 1904–1973
W. H. Auden, 1907–1973
A. D. Hope, 1907–2000
Louis MacNeice, 1907–1963
Theodore Roethke, 1907–1963
Josephine Jacobsen, 1908–2003
Miklós Radnóti, 1909–1944
Sir Stephen Spender, 1909–1995
Eudora Welty, 1909–2001
Elizabeth Bishop, 1911–1979
Tennessee Williams, 1911–1983
Irving Layton, 1912–2006
Anne Ridler, 1912–2001

Randall Jarrell, 1914–1965
Dudley Randall, 1914–2000
Henry Reed, 1914–1986
William Stafford, 1914–1993
Dylan Thomas, 1914–1953
Tom Whitecloud, 1914–1972
Ray Durem, 1915–1963
Isabella Gardner, 1915–1981
Arthur Miller, 1915–2005
Americo Parédes, 1915–1999
Orson Welles, 1915–1985
Gwendolyn Brooks, 1917–2000
Robert Lowell, 1917–1977
Arthur Laurents, b. 1918
Shirley Jackson, 1919–1965
May Swenson, 1919–1989
Amy Clampitt, 1920–1994
Howard Nemerov, 1920–1991
Hayden Carruth, b. 1921
James Emanuel, b. 1921
Mona Van Duyn, 1921–2004
Richard Wilbur, b. 1921
Elizabeth Brewster, b. 1922
Philip Larkin, 1922–1985
Mari Evans, b. 1923
Denise Levertov, 1923–1998
James Baldwin, 1924–1987
Jimmy Carter, b. 1924
Edward Field, b. 1924
Lisel Mueller, b. 1924
Brian W. Aldiss, b. 1925
Donald Justice, 1925–2004
Carolyn Kizer, b. 1925
Flannery O'Connor, 1925–1964
Gerald Stern, b. 1925
Robert Creeley, 1926–2005
Allen Ginsberg, 1926–1997
David Wagoner, b. 1926
Galway Kinnell, b. 1927
W. S. Merwin, b. 1927
Phyllis Webb, b. 1927
James Wright, 1927–1980
Maya Angelou, b. 1928
Edward Albee, p. 1928
Peter Davison, 1928–2004
Philip Levine, b. 1928
Cynthia Ozick, b. 1928
Anne Sexton, 1928–1974
John Hollander, b. 1929
X. J. Kennedy, b. 1929
Maurice Kenny, b. 1929
Adrienne Rich, b. 1929
Gary Snyder, b. 1930
Alice Munro, b. 1931
Judith Viorst, b. 1931
Joanne Greenberg, b. 1932
Linda Pastan, b. 1932
Sylvia Plath, 1932–1963
John Updike, b. 1932
Jack Agüeros, b. 1934
Wendell Berry, b. 1934
Leonard Cohen, b. 1934
Audre Lorde, 1934–1992
N. Scott Momaday, b. 1934
Marge Piercy, b. 1934
Sonia Sanchez, b. 1934
Mark Strand, b. 1934
Paul Zimmer, b. 1934
Betty Keller, b. 1935
Mary Oliver, b. 1935
Lucille Clifton, b. 1936
Andre Dubus, 1936–19

Michael S. Harper, b. 1938
Joyce Carol Oates, b. 1938
Margaret Atwood, b. 1939
Carl Dennis, b. 1939
Stephen Dunn, b. 1939
Elaine Terranova, b. 1939
Toni Cade Bambara, 1939–1995
Raymond Carver, 1939–1989
Seamus Heaney, b. 1939
Ted Kooser, b. 1939
John Chioles, b. 1940
William Heyen, b. 1940
Robert Pinsky, b. 1940
Billy Collins, b. 1941
Robert Hass, b. 1941
Simon Ortiz, b. 1941
Tino Villanueva, b. 1941
Marilyn Hacker, b. 1942
Mora, Pat, b. 1942
Sharon Olds, b. 1942
Dave Smith, b. 1942
Nikki Giovanni, b. 1943
Louise Glück, b. 1943
Susan Griffin, b. 1943
Jim Northrup, b. 1943
James Tate, b. 1943
Ellen Bryant Voigt, b. 1943
Peter Ulisse, b. 1944
Alice Walker, b. 1944
Daniel Halpern, b. 1945
August Wilson, 1945–2005
Thomas Lux, b. 1946
Tim O'Brien, b. 1946
Brenda Serotte, b. 1946
Jane Kenyon, 1947–1995
Yusef Komunyakaa, b. 1947
Liz Lochhead, b. 1947
Molly Peacock, b. 1947
Wyatt Prunty, b. 1947
Jane Shore, b. 1947
David Lehman, b. 1948
Alan Lightman, b. 1948
Heather McHugh, b. 1948
Leslie Marmon Silko, b. 1948
Shelly Wagner, b. 1948
Lynn Emanuel, b. 1949
Jamaica Kincaid, b. 1949
Bruce Weigl, b. 1949
Carolyn Forché, b. 1950
Chase Twichell, b. 1950
Bart Edelman, b. 1951
Jorie Graham, b. 1951
Joy Harjo, b. 1951
Beth Henley, b. 1952
Dorianne Laux, b. 1952
Judith Ortiz Cofer, b. 1952
Naomi Shihab Nye, b. 1952
Alberto Rios, b. 1952
Gary Soto, b. 1952
Amy Tan, b. 1952
Charles Harper Webb, b. 1952
Edward Hirsch, b. 1953
Jane Hirshfield, b. 1953
Gjertrud Schnackenberg, b. 1953
David Wojahn, b. 1953
Sandra Cisneros, b. 1954
Carolina Hospital, b. 1957
Li-Young Lee, b. 1957
Lorrie Moore, b. 1957
Daniel Orozco, b. ca. 1957
Daniel Tobin, b. 1958

In the literary criticism chapter, criticism in the manner of each school is applied to *Young Goodman Brown* and one additional selection, to help students understand the distinct characteristics of each school.

The Ninth Edition retains the helpful quick-reference materials found in previous editions. A glossary of terms, chronological and alphabetical listings of authors, and a thematic table of contents help students easily access the material they need.

Frontmatter

This section provides you with the following materials from the full book:

- **Brief Table of Contents:** Highlights chapter names and major sections of the book.
- **Detailed Table of Contents:** Lists all the chapters, main topics, sections and selections featured in the book.
- **Topical and Thematic Table of Contents:** Arranges all the selections in the book into various themes and topics for an alternative to the genre approach.
- **Preface:** Details all changes to the new edition; provides explanations for the book's organization and rationale; and lists all relevant book-specific and generic supplements available with the book.

The following new authors and selections have been added to the Ninth Edition:

Fiction

James Baldwin, "Sonny's Blues"
Raymond Carver, "Cathedral"
Joseph Conrad, "The Secret Sharer"
Stephen Crane, "The Open Boat"
Joanne Greenberg, "And Sarah Laughed"
Thomas Hardy, "The Three Strangers"
Ernest Hemingway, "Hills Like White Elephants"
Joyce Carol Oates, "The Cousins"; "Where Are You Going, Where Have You Been"
Daniel Orozco, "Orientation"
Luigi Pirandello, "War"

Poetry

Gwendolyn Brooks, "The Mother"
Judith Ortiz Cofer, "Latin Women Pray"
Robert Frost, "Pan With Us"
Dan Georgakis, "Hiroshima Crewman"
Allen Ginsberg, "A Further Proposal"
Nikki Giovanni, "Poetry"

George Gordon, Lord Byron, "She Walks in Beauty"

George Herbert, "Colossians III"

Langston Hughes, "Bad Man"; "Cross"; "Dead in There"; "Dream Variations"; "Madam And Her Madam"; "125th Street"; "Po' Boy Blues"; "Silhouette"; "Subway Rush Hour"; "The Weary Blues"

David Ignatow, "The Bagel"

Ben Jonson, "On My First Daughter"

Yusef Komunyakaa, "Facing It"

Katherine Larson, "Statuary"

Robert Lowell, "Memories of West Street and Lepke"; "Skunk Hour"

Eugenio Montale, "English Horn (Corno Inglese)"; "Buffalo (Buffalo)"

Marianne Moore, "The Fish"; "Poetry"

Pat Mora, "La Migra"

Pablo Neruda, "Every Day You Play"; "If You Forget Me"

Dorothy Parker, "Résumé"

Sylvia Plath, "Ariel"; "The Colossus"; "Cut"; "Daddy"; "Edge"; "The Hanging Man"; "Lady Lazarus"; "The Rival"; "Song for a Summer's Day"

Miklós Radnóti, "Forced March"

Christina Rossetti, "Echo"

Gary Snyder, "Milton by Firelight."

David Wojahn, "'It's Only Rock and Roll, but I Like It"

Drama

August Wilson, *Fences*

Literature

Literature

An Introduction to Reading and Writing

NINTH EDITION

Edgar V. Roberts

Emeritus, Lehman College
The City University of New York

New York San Francisco Boston
London Toronto Sydney Tokyo Singapore Madrid
Mexico City Munich Paris Cape Town Hong Kong Montreal

Senior Acquisitions Editor: Vivian Garcia
Director of Development: Mary Ellen Curley
Development Editor: Katharine Glynn
Executive Marketing Manager: Joyce Nilsen
Senior Supplements Editor: Donna Campion
Production Manager: Savoula Amanatidis
Project Coordination, Text Design, and Electronic Page Makeup: Nesbitt Graphics, Inc.
Cover Design Manager: John Callahan
Cover Image: Mark Klein/New England Rural Images
Senior Manufacturing Buyer: Dennis J. Para
Printer and Binder: Quebecor World Book Services—Taunton
Cover Printer: Phoenix Color Corporation

For permission to use copyrighted material, grateful acknowledgment is made to the copyright holders on pp. XXX–XXX, which are hereby made part of this copyright page.

Library of Congress Cataloging-in-Publication Data

[CIP Data T/K]

Please visit us at www.pearsonhighered.com

ISBN-13: 978-0-13-604099-6; ISBN-10: 0-13-604099-3 (Student Edition)
ISBN-13: 978-0-13-604102-3; ISBN-10: 0-13-604102-7 (Marketing Sampler)

1 2 3 4 5 6 7 8 9 10—QWT—11 10 09 08

Brief Contents

Contents

STORIES FOR STUDY 228

 SANDRA CISNEROS ***The House on Mango Street* 228**
"I knew then that I had to have a house."

 JOSEPH CONRAD ***The Secret Sharer* 253**
What goes on in the mind of a person, insecure in his own position, when he makes a difficult moral judgment which may prove disastrous?

 JOANNE GREENBERG ***And Sarah Laughed* 253**
The wife and mother in a family of hearing-impaired people learns to understand and appreciate their difficulties.

 JAMES JOYCE ***Araby* 262**
An introspective boy learns much about himself when he tries to keep a promise.

 CYNTHIA OZICK ***The Shawl* 266**
Can a mother in a Nazi concentration camp save her starving and crying baby?

Writing About Setting 269 • *Illustrative Student Essay: The Setting of Conrad's "The Secret Sharer"* 271

Writing Topics About Setting 274

5 STRUCTURE: THE ORGANIZATION OF STORIES 275

Formal Categories of Structure 275

Formal and Actual Structure 277

STORIES FOR STUDY 278

 RALPH ELLISON ***Battle Royal* 278**
An intelligent black student, filled with hopes and dreams, is treated with monstrous indignity.

 THOMAS HARDY ***The Three Strangers* 287**
The natives of Higher Crowstairs make a major decision about right and wrong even though they are more concerned about other matters.

 JAMAICA KINCAID ***What I Have Been Doing Lately* 300**
Life develops from the repetition and recirculation of dreams and fantasies.

 JOYCE CAROL OATES ***Where Are You Going, Where Have You Been?* 302**
A teenage girl is visited by an aggressive stranger who does not accept "no" for an answer.

 TOM WHITECLOUD ***Blue Winds Dancing*** ***313***
A Native American student leaves college in California to spend Christmas in his hometown in Wisconsin.

Writing About Structure in a Story 317 • ***Illustrative Student Essay: Conflict and Suspense in Hardy's "The Three Strangers"*** ***318***

Writing Topics About Structure 323

6 TONE AND STYLE: THE WORDS THAT CONVEY ATTITUDES IN FICTION 324

Diction: The Writer's Choice and Control of Words 324

Tone, Irony, and Style 328

Tone, Humor, and Style 329

STORIES FOR STUDY 331

 KATE CHOPIN ***The Story of an Hour*** ***331***
Louise Mallard is shocked and grieved by news that her husband has been killed, but she is about to have an even greater shock.

 WILLIAM FAULKNER ***Barn Burning*** ***333***
A young country boy grows in awareness, conscience, and individuality despite his hostile father.

 ERNEST HEMINGWAY ***Hills Like White Elephants*** ***344***
While waiting for a train, a a man and woman reluctantly discuss an urgent situation.

 ALICE MUNRO ***The Found Boat*** ***347***
After winter snows have melted in a small Canadian community, young people start making discoveries about themselves.

 FRANK O'CONNOR ***First Confession*** ***354***
Jackie as a young man tells about his first childhood experience with confession.

 DANIEL OROZCO ***Orientation*** ***359***
A new employee is introduced to the rather unusual and surprising situations in the office.

 JOHN UPDIKE ***A & P*** ***363***
As a checkout clerk at the A & P near the local beaches, Sammy learns about the consequences of a difficult choice.

Writing About Tone and Style 367 • ***Illustrative Student Essay: Frank O'Connor's Control of Tone and Style in "First Confession"*** 370

Writing Topics About Tone and Style 374

7 Symbolism and Allegory: Keys to Extended Meaning 375

Symbolism 375

Allegory 377

Fable, Parable, and Myth 378

Allusion in Symbolism and Allegory 379

STORIES FOR STUDY 380

AESOP ***The Fox and the Grapes*** **380**
What do people think about things that they can't have?

ANONYMOUS ***The Myth of Atalanta*** **381**
In ancient times, how could a superior woman maintain power and integrity?

ANITA SCOTT COLEMAN ***Unfinished Masterpieces*** **382**
Worthiness cannot rise when it is depressed by poverty and inequality.

NATHANIEL HAWTHORNE ***Young Goodman Brown*** **385**
In colonial Salem, Goodman Brown has a bewildering encounter that changes his outlook on life.

FRANZ KAFKA ***A Hunger Artist*** **393**
Public interest wanes even in a unique person.

LUKE ***The Parable of the Prodigal Son*** **399**
Is there any limit to what a person can do to make divine forgiveness impossible?

GABRIEL GARCÍA MARQUEZ ***A Very Old Man with Enormous Wings*** **400**
How do simple villagers respond to a miraculous visitor who appears in their town?

KATHERINE ANNE PORTER ***The Jilting of Granny Weatherall*** **405**
At the end nears, Granny Weatherall has her memories and is surrounded by her loving adult children.

JOHN STEINBECK *The Chrysanthemums* 411
As a housewife on a small ranch, Elisa Allen experiences changes to her sense of self-worth.

Writing About Symbolism and Allegory 417 • 📄 *Illustrative Student Essay (Symbolism): Symbols of Light and Darkness in Porter's "The Jilting of Granny Weatherall"* 421 • 📄 *Illustrative Student Essay (Allegory): The Allegory of Hawthorne's "Young Goodman Brown"* 425

Writing Topics About Symbolism and Allegory 430

8 IDEA OR THEME: THE MEANING AND THE MESSAGE IN FICTION 432

Ideas and Assertions 432

Ideas and Issues 432

Ideas and Values 433

The Place of Ideas in Literature 434

How to Find Ideas 435

STORIES FOR STUDY 438

 NEW **JAMES BALDWIN** *Sonny's Blues* 438
A devoted brother describes how his brother, Sonny, is hurt by racial prejudice, and how Sonny finds fulfillment through love of music.

 TONI CADE BAMBARA *The Lesson* 457
When a group of children visit a toy store for the wealthy, some of them draw conclusions about society and themselves.

 ANTON CHEKHOV *The Lady with the Dog* 462
Bored with life, Dmitri Gurov meets Anna Sergeyevna and discovers previously unknown emotions and extremely new problems.

 D. H. LAWRENCE *The Horse Dealer's Daughter* 471
Dr. Jack Fergusson and Mabel Pervin find, in each other's love, a new reason for being.

 AMERÍCO PAREDES *The Hammon and the Beans* 482
Is American liberty restricted to people of only one group, or is it for everyone?

Writing About a Major Idea in Fiction 486 • 📄 *Illustrative Student Essay: D. H. Lawrence's "The Horse Dealer's Daughter" as an Expression of the Idea that Loving Commitment is Essential in Life* 488

Writing Topics About Ideas 492

12 Words: The Building Blocks of Poetry 653

22A Writing Research Essays on Poetry

PART IV

Reading and Writing About Drama 1203

23 The Dramatic Vision: An Overview 1204

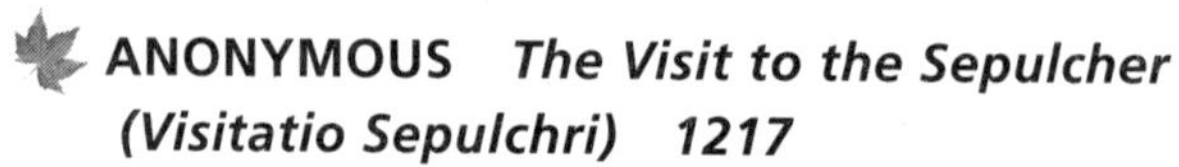

Topical and Thematic Contents

For analytical purposes, the following topical and thematic contents groups the selections into twenty-six categories. The idea is that the topical categories will facilitate a thematic and focused study and comparison of a number of works (see Chapter 30). Obviously each of the works brings out many other issues than are suggested by the topics. For comparison, however, the topics invite analyses based on specific issues. Thus, the category "Women" suggests that the listed works may profitably be examined for what they have to say about the lives and problems specifically of women, just as the category "Men" suggests a concentration on the lives and problems specifically of men. The topical headings are suggestive only; they are by no means intended to mandate interpretations or approaches. For emphasis, I will repeat this, and also I will italicize, underline, and boldface it: ***The subject headings are suggestive only; they are by no means intended to mandate interpretations or approaches.*** I have accordingly assigned a number of works to two and sometimes even more categories. Ibsen's *A Dollhouse,* for example, is not easily classified within a single category.

Because entries for the topical and thematic contents are to be as brief as possible, I use only the last names of authors and artists, although for authors with the same last names (e.g., Phyllis Webb, Charles Harper Webb; Beth Henley, W. E. Henley; Flannery O'Connor, Frank O'Connor), I supply the complete name. In listing works I shorten a number of longer titles. Thus I refer to *Let America* (Hughes) rather than *Let America Be America Again,* and to *That Time of Year* (Shakespeare) rather than *That Time of Year Thou May'st in Me Behold,* and so on, using such recognizable short titles rather than the full titles that appear in the regular table of contents, in the text itself, and in the index. Of course, some titles are already brief, such as *Reconciliation* (Whitman), *Eating Poetry* (Strand), *Edge* (Plath), and *A Worn Path* (Welty). Obviously, such titles are included in their entirety.

Continued from the earlier editions are references to works of art that are included in the plates. I hope that these will be usefully consulted for comparative purposes and that such comparisons will enhance the discussions of the various topics.

AMERICA IN PEACE, WAR, AND TRIBULATION

Stories

Poems

Plays

Art

ART, LANGUAGE, AND IMAGINATION

Stories

Poems

Art

CONFORMITY AND REBELLION

Stories

Plays

Art

THE INDIVIDUAL AND SOCIETY

Stories

Poems

Plays

Art

INNOCENCE AND EXPERIENCE

Stories

Poems

Plays

Art

LIFE'S VALUES, CONDUCT, AND MEANING

Stories

Poems

Plays

Art

LOVE AND COURTSHIP

Stories

Poems

Plays

Art

MEN

Stories

Poems

Plays

Plays

Art

RACE, ETHNICITY, AND NATIONALITY

Stories

Poems

Play

REALITY AND UNREALITY

Stories

Poems

Plays

Art

RECONCILIATION AND UNDERSTANDING

Stories

Poems

Play

Art

SALVATION AND DAMNATION

Stories

Poems

Art

WAR AND VIOLENCE

Stories

Poems

Plays

Art

WOMEN

Stories

Poems

Plays

Art

WOMEN AND MEN

Stories

Poems

Plays

Art

YOUTH AND AGE

Stories

Poems

Plays

Art

Preface to the Ninth Edition

In the seventeenth century, John Dryden used the phrase "Here is God's Plenty" when he described Chaucer's *Canterbury Tales.* The same, I think, is applicable to the more than 500 separate works contained in this anthology. But the book is more than a collection. Its bedrock idea is that actual student writing deepens student understanding and appreciation of great literature. Many former students who long ago left our classrooms remember many works well because they once wrote essays about them in our literature-and-composition classes. To adapt a phrase from Joseph Joubert (1754–1824), it is axiomatic that students learn twice when they write about literature, for as they develop their thinking and writing skills they also solidify their understanding of what they have read. If speaking makes us ready, as Bacon said, writing makes us exact, and writing is therefore essential in the study of literature, or of any other discipline. It is the finished product of reading and thinking. *Literature: An Introduction to Reading and Writing* is dedicated to this idea.

Because writing reinforces reading so strongly, the ninth edition presents more than fifty illustrative writing examples embodying the strategies and methods described in the various chapters and appendixes. These full essays and paragraphs are intended as specimens to illustrate what students *might* do (not what they *must* do) with a particular topic. The goal of the essays is to show that the creation of thought does not take place until writers are able to fuse their reading responses with particular topics and issues (e.g., the symbolism in a poem, the main idea in a story, the use of stage directions in a play).

The illustrative essays are comparatively short and not as long as some instructors might assign, on the grounds that when responding to longer assignments about literature, many of our students, alas, inflate their papers with needless summary. It is clear that without a guiding, argumentative point, we don't have thought, and that without thought we cannot have a good essay. A simple summary of a work does not qualify as good writing.

In the major chapters, following each of the illustrative essays, there are analytical discussions (titled "Commentary on the Essay") that point out how the topics have served as the basis of the writer's thought. Graphically, the format of underlining thesis and topic sentences in the illustrative essays is a way of emphasizing the connections, and the format is thus a complementary way of fulfilling an essential aim of the book.

A logical extension (and a major hope) of this combined approach is that the techniques students acquire in studying literature as a reading and also a writing undertaking will help them in every course they may ever take, and in whatever professions or occupations they may follow. Students will always *read*—if not the authors contained here, then other authors, and certainly newspapers, letters, legal documents, memoranda, directions, instructions, magazine articles, technical and nontechnical reports, business proposals, Internet communications, and much more. Although as students advance into their working years they may never again need to write about topics such as setting, imagery, or symbolism, they will certainly always find a future need to *write.*

Most of the works anthologized in this edition are by American, British, and Canadian authors, but there has also been an increase in the number of ancient and medieval writers, along with later writers who lived in or came from Australia, France, Germany, Hungary, Italy, Norway, Poland, Russia, and South America, with authors who represent the diverse backgrounds of African American, American Indian, Latino, and Chinese cultures. In total, 296 authors are represented here, including five anonymous authors. Slightly below sixty-one percent of the authors—180—were born after 1900. Of the eighty-three writers born since 1935, forty-two are women, or just slightly above fifty percent. If one counts only the number of authors born since the ending of World War II (1945), the percentage of women writers rises close to sixty percent.

The ninth edition includes a total of 519 separate works—fifty-nine stories, 442 poems (including some short portions of very long poems), and eighteen plays. Each work is suitable for discussion either alone or in comparison with other works. Ten stories, one play, and forty-six poems are added here that were not included in the eighth edition. For purposes of analytical comparison, the works in two genres by seven writers are included—specifically Crane, Glaspell, Hughes, Oates, Poe, Shakespeare, and Updike. In addition, there are two plays by Shakespeare—a tragedy and a comedy—and there are two or more poems by a number of poets. A new feature, for more intensive study, is the addition of an increased number of poems in Chapter 21, "Four Major American Poets." To the twenty-five poems of Dickinson in this edition, and the eighteen by Frost, both of whom were represented in the eighth edition in detail, there are ten new poems by Hughes and nine by Plath, thus bringing the number of Hughes's poems to fifteen, and of Plath's to thirteen.

An additional feature is new in the ninth edition. This is the "visualizing" sections on fiction, poetry, and drama, which are to be found in Chapters 1, 11, and 23. Commentators have often observed that today's students are more visually oriented than students of the past—most likely because of the ever-present influence of television and computers in the home, and also because of the many other graphic forms in which the American public is introduced to facts and ideas. This aspect of our culture is often deplored, but it seems more fruitful to accept it as a fact of life and then go ahead to bring it to bear on the imaginative reading of literary works. What is important here is the development of the capacity

to think,
to follow through on ideas,
    and
to imagine—

in short, to exercise the mind totally in the interpretation of literature, and in any intellectual endeavor that our students will ever undertake. The study of fiction in the ninth edition is augmented by a discussion about the relationship between graphic narratives and verbal narratives. In poetry, the connection is made between traditional closed-form poetry, on the one hand, and visual poetry and prose poems, on the other. Of the three genres, the study of drama has traditionally been the most visual, for students can make connections between their own reading and the experiences they have had with plays on the stage or on film. The idea of these parallel sections is to provide students with an additional armament in their comprehension, their thought, and their emotional responses.

A Brief Overview of the Ninth Edition

The ninth edition reaffirms a principle to which *Literature: An Introduction to Reading and Writing* is dedicated—flexibility. The earlier editions have been used for introduction-to-literature courses, genre courses, and both composition and composition-and-literature courses. Adaptability and flexibility have been the keys to this variety. Instructors can use the book for classroom discussions, panel discussions, essay- or paragraph-length writing and study assignments, and questions for special topics not covered in class.

FICTION. The "Reading and Writing About Fiction" section, the first in the book following the Introduction, consists of eleven chapters. Chapter 1 presents a general introduction to fiction, and Chapters 2 through 8—the topical chapters vital in each section of the book—introduce students to important subjects such as structure, character, point of view, symbolism, and idea. Chapter 9 includes four stories by Edgar Allan Poe, and for intensive study these are accompanied by a number of critical readings on Poe. Chapter 10 contains seven stories for additional enjoyment and study.

Readers will note that some of the eleven newly added stories are classic—such as those by Baldwin, Conrad, Crane, and Hemingway. The new stories complement the forty-eight stories that are retained from the eighth edition, such as those by Bierce, Faulkner, Gilman, Hawthorne, Joyce, Lawrence, Porter, and Twain.

Following Chapter 10 is Chapter 10A, the eleventh of the fiction chapters, which is devoted to research connected with fiction. Parallel discussions are Chapters 22A and 28A, which are about research in poetry and drama. These chapters have been added to reflect increased emphasis in research in the college teaching of literature, as noted by many observers of current practices in American colleges. Note that in Chapter 10A there is an extensive discussion of plagiarism and its avoidance. There has been great demand for this discussion on behalf of students, for as emphasis is placed on studying literature with the aid of research, comparable emphasis must also be placed on the judicious and ethical use of secondary sources.

POETRY. The thirteen poetry chapters are arranged similarly to the fiction chapters. Chapter 11 is introductory. Chapters 12 through 20 deal with topics such as diction, imagery, tone, and symbolism. Chapter 21 presents the possibility of more intensive study of four major American poets, consisting of extensive selections by Dickinson, Frost, Hughes, and Plath. Chapter 22 contains 116 poems for additional enjoyment and study. Chapter 22A is the companion of Chapters 10A and 28A. Brief biographies of the anthologized poets are included in a separate section at the back of the book.

Poetry selections range from late medieval times to contemporary works, including poems published in the early years of the twenty-first century. Representative poets are Wyatt, Queen Elizabeth I, Shakespeare, Donne, Dryden, Pope, Wordsworth, Keats, Tennyson, Hopkins, Pound, Yeats, Eliot, Layton, Amy Lowell, Nye, and Clifton. Forty-six poems are new to the ninth edition. They represent a variety of poets, most of whom are widely recognized. Ginsberg, Hughes, Ignatow, Komunyakaa, Robert Lowell, Eugenio Montale, Mora, Neruda, Radnóti, Snyder, and Plath come readily to mind. Along with the poems included for the first time, the ninth edition retains 394 poems that were included in the eighth edition. The writers of two of these—Lincoln and Carter—were American presidents. Recent poets with many distinctions are Agüeros, Forché, Harjo, Hirshfield, Hospital, and Peacock. Of special note is the inclusion here of a number of nineteenth-century poets who were chosen for poems illustrating noteworthy aspects of American life. These are Bryant, Emerson, Ingham, Lincoln, Melville, and Whittier. (See the first category in the Topical and Thematic Table of Contents).

DRAMA. The drama section contains eighteen titles. New in the ninth edition is the critically acclaimed play *Fences* by August Wilson. Eight of the longer plays that were in the eighth edition have been kept in the ninth because of their independent significance (*Death of a Salesman, A Dollhouse, The Glass Menagerie, Hamlet, Love Is the Doctor, A Midsummer Night's Dream, Mulatto, Oedipus the King*). The total of full-length plays is now nine. These representative full plays make the ninth edition useful for instructors who wish to illustrate the history of drama. In an anthology of this scope, the nine shorter works (*The Sandbox, Am I Blue, The Bear, Before Breakfast, Tea Party, Visitatio Sepulchri,* and *Trifles,* together with the two film scenes—from *Citizen Kane* and *The Turning Point*) are valuable not only in themselves but also because they may be covered in no more than one or two classroom periods. The shorter plays may be enlivened by having parts read aloud and acted by students. Indeed, the anonymous *Visitatio Sepulchri* and Keller's *Tea Party* are brief enough to permit both classroom reading and discussion in a single period.

Additional Features

TABLE OF CONTENTS. The table of contents lists all the works and major chapter discussion heads in the book. A feature that has been well received are the many accompanying sentences that contain brief descriptions or impressions of the stories, plays, and a number of poems. It is hoped that these guiding sentences and questions will continue to interest students in approaching, anticipating, and reading the works.

TOPICAL AND THEMATIC TABLE OF CONTENTS. To make the ninth edition as flexible as possible, I have continued the topical and thematic table of contents, which is organized around a number of topics, such as *Hope and Renewal; Women; Men; Women and Men; Conformity and Rebellion; Endings and Beginnings; Innocence and Experience;* and *Race, Ethnicity, and Nationality.* Under these topics, generous numbers of stories, poems, and plays (and also comparable works of art) are listed (many in a number of categories), to aid in the study and comparison of topical or thematic units.

A special word seems still in order for the category *America in Peace, War, and Tribulation,* which is included first in the topical and thematic table of contents. After the attacks on the United States on September 11, 2001, it is fitting that a category of uniquely American topics be included for student analysis and discussion. Obviously there cannot be a full and comprehensive examination of the background and thought to be considered in extensive courses in American Literature, but a selection of works that bear on American life and values seems now to be deeply important. Some works in the category reflect an idealized America, but many also shed light on problems and issues that the United States has faced in the past and is continuing to face today. A few of the works concern our country at its beginning; some reflect the life of the frontier and the Civil War; others introduce issues of minority culture; still others introduce subjects such as war, misfortune, personal anguish, regret, healing, relationships between parents and children, the symbolic value of work, nostalgia, love, prejudice, and reverence for the land. It is my hope that students will study the listed works broadly, as general human issues that also deal with the complexity of life in the United States today.

QUESTIONS. Following each anthologized selection in the detailed chapters are study questions designed to help students in their exploration and understanding of literature. Some of these questions are factual and may be answered quickly. Others provoke extended thought and classroom discussion, and may also serve for both in-class and out-of-class writing assignments. At the ends of twenty chapters I include a number of more general assignments, offering students writing topics about character, symbolism, tragedy, etc. Many of these are comparison-contrast topics, and a number of them—at least one in each chapter—are assignments requiring creative writing (for example, "Write a poem," or "Compose a short scene"). Unique about these topics is that students are asked not only to write creatively and argue cogently, but also to analyze their own creative processes.

DATES. To place the various works in historical context, I provide the life dates for all authors, to the degree that these dates have been established. Because some contemporary authors are private and elusive, however, it has proved necessary to make a very small number of estimates of their dates. All the authors, except for the anonymous ones, are listed chronologically (and also alphabetically) on the inside covers. Along with the title of each anthologized work, I include its date of publication. Sometimes, however, a work was not published until long after the author actually wrote it, as with most of Emily Dickinson's poems. In such cases I have included the date of composition, if known, parenthetically.

NUMBERING. For convenient reference, I have adopted a regular style of numbering the selections by fives:

Stories:	*Every fifth paragraph.*
Poems:	*Every fifth line.*
Poetic plays:	*Every fifth line, starting at 1 with each new scene and act.*
Prose plays:	*Every fifth speech, starting at 1 with each new scene and act.*

GLOSSES AND EXPLANATORY FOOTNOTES. For poetry and poetic plays, brief marginal glosses are provided wherever they are needed. When a fuller explanation is required—for stories, poems and plays—I supply explanatory footnotes. Words and phrases that are footnoted or glossed are highlighted by a raised degree sign (°). Footnotes are located according to line, paragraph, or speech numbers.

GLOSSARY. In the introductory discussions in the various chapters, significant terms and concepts are boldfaced. These are gathered alphabetically and explained briefly in the extensive glossary following the appendixes, with references locating page numbers in the text where the terms are considered more fully. Although the glossary is based on the chapters of the ninth edition, it is in fact comprehensive enough to be useful for general purposes.

BOXED DISCUSSIONS WITHIN THE CHAPTERS. In a number of chapters, separately boxed and shaded sections signal brief but essential discussions of a number of significant matters. The topics chosen for this treatment—such as the use of tenses in discussing a work, the use of authorial names, explanations of how to refer to parts of plays, and the concept of decorum—were based on the recommendations of instructors and students. Users of previous editions have found these boxed discussions interesting and helpful.

SPECIAL WRITING TOPICS. In the ninth edition I have retained the section titled "Special Writing Topics about Literature," which follows the drama section. This section contains three chapters (29– 31) that at one time were appendixes, but that on the advice of many readers are now presented as a major section of the book. These chapters are arranged for emphasis on recent critical theory together with practical guides for writing comparison-contrast essays on literature and writing examinations on literature.

PHOTOGRAPHS AND ART REPRODUCTIONS. To encourage the comparison of literary art with fine art and photography, a number of art reproductions and photographs are included, some within the chapters, and many in a full-color insert. Most of these artworks are considered directly in the introductions to the various chapters. I hope that the reproductions, together with others that instructors might wish to add during the course of teaching, will encourage comparison-and-contrast discussions and essays about the relationship of literature and art. As already noted, the Topical and Thematic Table of Contents lists relevant artworks along with literary works.

DRAMATIZATIONS ON VIDEOTAPE AND DVD. To strengthen the connections between fiction and drama, a number of stories are included that are available on videocassettes and also DVDs, which can be used as teaching tools for support and interpretation. References to a number of the available dramatizations are included in the Instructor's Manual. In the introductions to many of the plays there is a listing of many of the cassette and DVD versions that can be brought into the classroom.

Revisions

There is little throughout the ninth edition that has not been reexamined, revised, or rewritten. Extensive revisions have been made in the general introduction, the introductions to all the genres, and especially the introductory sections on Dickinson, Frost, Hughes, and Plath together with innumerable changes and, I hope, improvements throughout the text.

The two appendixes have also been changed and updated. Many of the current MLA recommendations for documenting electronic sources, for example, are helpfully illustrated in Appendix I. The poet biographies in Appendix II have been updated to include new poets and up-to-date information. The glossary has been amended and rewritten throughout, as it has been improved regularly throughout the various editions of *Literature: An Introduction to Reading and Writing.*

In all the chapter discussions, the feature of subheads as sentences rather than topics has been retained from past editions. It is my hope that clearly defining headings will enable students to assimilate the following content easily. Of special importance in each of the main chapters are the sections "Questions for Discovering Ideas" and "Strategies for Organizing Ideas," which have been revised in light of the continuing goal to help students focus on their writing assignments.

Reading and Writing Now and in the Future

The more effectively students write about literature when taking their literature courses, the better they will be able to write later on—no matter what the topic. It is axiomatic that the power to analyze problems and make convincing written and oral presentations is a major characteristic of leadership and success in all fields. To acquire the skills of disciplined reading and strong writing is therefore the best possible preparation that students can make for the future, whatever it may hold.

While I stress the value of the ninth edition as a teaching tool, I also emphasize that literature is to be enjoyed and loved. Sometimes we neglect the truth that study and delight are complementary, and that intellectual stimulation and emotional enjoyment develop not only from the immediate responses of pleasure, involvement, and sympathy, but also from the understanding, contemplation, and confidence generated by knowledge and developing skill. I therefore hope that the selections in the ninth edition of *Literature: An Introduction to Reading and Writing* will teach students about humanity; about their own perceptions, feelings, and lives; and about the timeless patterns of human existence. I hope they will take delight in such discoveries and become engaged as they make them. I see the book as a stepping-stone to lifelong understanding, future achievement, and never-ending joy in great literature.

Supplementary Material for Instructors and Students

An extensive package of supplements accompanies this edition of *Literature: An Introduction to Reading and Writing* for both instructors and students. Any one of the student supplements is available at no additional cost when packaged, except where noted. To create a package, contact your local Pearson representative.

Instructor Materials

INSTRUCTOR'S MANUAL (0-13-604100-0). This comprehensive instructor's manual prepares you to teach any of the works contained in the text and also helps you in making assignments and comparing individual works with other works. Each of the chapters in the manual begins with introductory remarks and interpretive comments about the works (stories, poems, plays) within the chapter of the book. These are followed by detailed suggestions for discussing every study question. The instructor's manual also provides detailed discussion of works contained in the book, reviews of videotape and DVD performances of a number of stories in the book, and references to audio clips of poetry. Writing assignments and workshops with suggested guidelines for student editors help students to write about literature effectively.

THE LONGMAN ELECTRONIC TESTBANK FOR LITERATURE—CD ROM VERSION (0-321-14314-0). This testbank features various objective questions on the major works of fiction, short fiction, poetry, and drama. A versatile and handy resource, this easy-to-use testbank can be used for all quizzing and testing needs. This product is also available in print.

MYLITERATURELAB FACULTY TEACHING GUIDE (0-321-33213-X). This helpful resource gives instructors step-by-step advice for integrating the features of MyLiteratureLab into their classroom, including detailed instructions in how to use Exchange, an electronic instructor/peer feedback tool.

TEACHING LITERATURE ONLINE, SECOND EDITION (0-321-10618-0). Concise and practical, *Teaching Literature Online* provides instructors with strategies and advice for incorporating elements of computer technology into the literature classroom. Offering a range of information and examples, this manual provides ideas and activities for enhancing literature courses with the help of technology.

Technology/Mulitmedia

The following supplements represent technology that is book-specific to Roberts, *Literature,* Ninth Edition.

COMPANION WEB SITE. The Companion Web Site offers a multitude of resources at <www.pearsonhighered.com/roberts>. Here you will find a chapter-by-chapter guide to this text, as well as online quizzes that include instant scoring. The Web site also features author bios, annotated links for further study, a literary walking tour, and an interactive timeline. There is also an abundance of Web links to research specific authors, famous works written during numerous literary periods, and online literary journals. Students are invited to practice their writing about literature with writing activities, essay questions, writing workshops that show multiple drafts of student papers with commentary on each draft, and exclusive *Writers on Writing* interview videos.

LITERARY VISIONS PROGRAM. Literary Visions is a video instructional series on literary analysis for college and high school classrooms and adult learners. Noted critics, authors, scholars, and actors enliven this exploration of literature and literary analysis. Dramatizations, readings, and discussions build skills in critical thinking and writing. Illuminating excerpts of short fiction, poetry, plays, and essays—both classic and contemporary—highlight standard literary forms and devices including plot, myth, setting, and character. This course, containing twenty-six half-hour videocassettes, can be used as a complete college-level course; as supplementary material in courses in literature, composition, poetry, or drama, or those focusing on specific topics and genres within literature; as an offering for adult or continuing education students; as an important addition to library video collections; and as enrichment material for advanced high school curricula. For more information, visit <www.learner.org/resources/series41.html>.

Our *Literary Visions Study Guide,* an accompanying study guide for the Literary Visions program, contains information about lessons, objectives, goals, lesson assignments, a viewing guide, formal and informal writing exercises, self-tests, additional reading activities, and an overview of each video lesson. Several of the works covered in the videos and study guide are found in the ninth edition of *Literature: An Introduction to Reading and Writing.* This study guide is available at an additional cost.

The following supplements represent generic technology supplements that work with any of our introductory literature anthologies.

MYLITERATURELAB (WWW.MYLITERATURELAB.COM). MyLiteratureLab is a Web-based, state-of-the-art, interactive learning system designed to enhance introductory literature courses. It adds a whole new dimension to the study of literature with Longman Lectures, which are evocative, richly illustrated audio readings that include advice on how to read, interpret, and write about literary works from our own roster of Longman authors. This powerful program also features Diagnostic Tests, Interactive Readings with clickable prompts, student sample papers, Literature Timelines, Avoiding Plagiarism research aid, Grade Tracker, and Exchange, an electronic instructor/peer feedback tool.

ART OF LITERATURE CD-ROM (0-13-189103-0). This CD-ROM offers your students an extensive and interactive reference featuring video and audio clips of dramatic reenactments of selections, including Ernest Hemingway's "A Clean, Well-Lighted Place" and Gwendolyn Brooks' "We Real Cool"; In-depth sections for fiction, poetry, and drama offer further analysis and interactive activities for select works; Visuals for Study provide artwork related to literature pieces and photos of featured artists, and other literary resources.

VIDEO PROGRAM. For qualified adopters, an impressive selection of videotapes is available to enrich students' experience of literature. Contact your local representative. You may find your local representative by going to www.pearsonhighered.com and clicking *Find Your Rep.*

Course-Related Supplements

PENGUIN DISCOUNT NOVEL PROGRAM. In cooperation with our sister company Penguin Putnam, Inc., Pearson is proud to offer a variety of Penguin paperbacks at a significant discount—almost sixty percent off the retail price—when packaged with any Pearson title. To review the list of titles available for other disciplines, visit the Pearson/Penguin Putnam Web site at www.pearsonhighered.com/penguin.

Sourcebooks Shakespeare

Pearson Publishers, in conjunction with Sourcebooks, Inc., proudly offers The Sourcebooks Shakespeare. This revolutionary new book and CD format offers the complete text of the play with rich illustrations and extensive explanatory and production notes. An accompanying audio CD, narrated by acclaimed actor Sir Derek Jacobi, features recordings of key scenes from memorable productions to allow students to compare different interpretations of the play and its characters.

ANALYZING LITERATURE: A GUIDE FOR STUDENTS, SECOND EDITION (0-321-09338-0). This supplement provides critical reading strategies, writing advice, and sample student papers to help students interpret and discuss literary works from a variety of genres. Suggestions for collaborative activities and online research topics are also featured as well as numerous exercises and writing assignments.

EVALUATING A PERFORMANCE (0-321-09541-3). Writing by Michael Greenwald and perfect for the student assigned to review a local production, this supplement offers specific prompts and suggestions for evaluating a production. Designed to look like a Playbill, it provides students with a convenient place to record their evaluation of the play's acting, directing, staging, lighting, costuming, and so on.

A GLOSSARY OF LITERARY AND CRITICAL TERMS (0-321-12691-2). This easy-to-use glossary includes definitions, explanations, and examples for over a hundred literary and critical terms that students commonly encounter in their readings or hear in their lectures and class discussions. In addition to basic terms related to form and genre, the glossary also includes terms and explanations related to literary history, criticism, and theory.

THE LONGMAN LITERATURE TIMELINE (0-321-14315-9). Prepared by Heidi L. M. Jacobs, this laminated four-page timeline provides students with a chronological overview of major literary works. In addition, the timeline lists major sociocultural and political events to provide students with historical and contextual insights into the impact historical events have had on writers and their works and vice versa.

RESPONDING TO LITERATURE: A WRITER'S JOURNAL (0-321-09542-1). This beautiful spiral-bound journal, by Daniel Kline, provides students with their own space for recording their reactions to the literature they read. Guided writing prompts, suggested writing assignments, and overviews of literary terms provide students with the tools and ideas they need for responding to fiction, poetry, and drama.

WHAT EVERY STUDENT SHOULD KNOW ABOUT CITING SOURCES WITH MLA DOCUMENTATION (0-321-44737-9). Michael Greer's brief guide provides specific instructions on writing and documenting in Modern Language Association (MLA) style. It offers a comprehensive listing of in-text and works-cited models for a wide variety of print, electronic, and online sources. Also included are frequently asked questions about MLA style and guidelines for formatting research papers.

WHAT EVERY STUDENT SHOULD KNOW ABOUT AVOIDING PLAGIARISM (0-321-44689-5). This brief guide teaches students to take plagiarism seriously and understand its consequences. Here, source usage methods—summary, paraphrase and quotation—are explained, with examples. The most common types of plagiarism are discussed, from simple mistakes such as forgetting to use quotation marks when using someone else's exact words, to wholesale fraudulence, such as purchasing student papers from online sites and claiming them as one's own work. A brief essential guide to citing sources using both MLA and APA documentation styles is also included.

WHAT EVERY STUDENT SHOULD KNOW ABOUT RESEARCHING ONLINE (0-321-44531-7). David Munger and Shireen Campbell have written this brief guide that teaches students how to conduct research in the first place they will look: the Web. It provides details on how to use search engines and databases, how to evaluate sources, how to document borrowed materials, and how to avoid online plagiarism. Annotated screenshots of Web pages show students where to locate the information they need to create a proper citation; numerous examples of correctly cited online and electronic sources are also provided.

Acknowledgments

As this book goes into its ninth edition, I wish to acknowledge the many people who at various times have offered helpful advice, information, and suggestions. To name them, as Dryden says in *Absalom and Achitophel,* is to praise them. They are Professors Eileen Allman, Peggy Cole, David Bady, Andrew Brilliant, Rex Butt, Stanley Coberly, Betty L. Dixon, Elizabeth Keats Flores, Alice Griffin, Loren C. Gruber, Robert Halli, Leslie Healey, Catherine Heath, Rebecca Heintz, Karen Holt, Claudia Johnson, Matthew Marino, Edward Martin, Evan Matthews, Pearl McHaney, Daniel McNama, Ruth Milberg-Kaye, Nancy K. Miller, JoAnna Stephens Mink, Ervin Nieves, Glen Nygreen, Michael Paull, Norman Prinsky,

Bonnie Ronson, Dan Rubey, Margaret Ellen Sherwood, Beverly J. Slaughter, Donald Tuthill, Keith Walters, Chloe Warner, Scott Westrem, Mardi Valgemae, Matthew Winston, and Ruth Zerner, and also Christel Bell, Linda Bridgers, Catherine Davis, Jim Freund, Edward Hoeppner, Anna F. Jacobs, Eleanor Tubbs, Brooke Mitchell, April Roberts, David Roberts, Gary Brown, Diane Foster, Braden Welborn, and Eve Zarin. I give special recognition and thanks to Ann Marie Radaskiewicz and to Professor Robert Zweig. The skilled assistance of Jonathan Roberts has been essential and invaluable at every stage of all the editions.

A number of other people have provided sterling guidance for the preparation of the ninth edition. They are Catherine Heath and Gary Brown of Victoria College; Brian Boyle, Prairie State College; Angie Macri, Pulaski Technical College; Dorothy Minor, Tulsa Community College, NEC; Mary L. Simpson, Central Texas College; Brenda Cornell, Central Texas College; Crystal Clark, Columbus State Community College; Evelyn Beck, Piedmont Technical College; Joshua Dickson, Jefferson Community College; Howard Kerner, Polk Community College; Jim Richey, Tyler Junior College; Emily Cosper, Delgado Community College; David Plumb, Broward College; Diana Gatz, St. Petersburg College; Joseph Couch, Montgomery College; Mark Coley, Tarrant County College; and Bente Videbaek, SUNY, Stony Brook.

I wish especially to thank Vivian Garcia, Senior English Editor. She has been eminently creative, cheerful, helpful, and obliging during the time we have worked together. To Stephanie Magean, whose copy editing of the manuscript has been inestimably fine, I offer an extra salute of gratitude. Additional thanks are reserved for Lois Lombardo our production editor, who has devoted great knowledge, intelligence, diligence, good humor, and skill to the many tasks needed to bring a book of this size to fruition. Thanks are also due to Mary Dalton Hoffman for her superb work on securing permissions, Rona Tuccillo for research into the various photographs and illustrations, and to Joyce Nilsen, Executive Marketing Manager, Savoula Amanatidis, Production Manager, Donna DeBenedictis, Managing Editor, Dennis Para, Senior Manufacturing Buyer, and to Heather Vomero, Editorial Assistant. I also thank Carrie Brandon, Maggie Barbieri, Nancy Perry, Alison Reeves, Kate Morgan Jackson, Bill Oliver, and Paul O'Connell, earlier Prentice Hall English editors, for their imagination and foresight, and also for their patience with me and support of for their the years. Of major importance was the work of Ray Mullaney, Editor-in-Chief, Development, for his pioneering work with the text and for his continued support. I am also grateful to Gina Sluss, Barbara Muller, Marlane Miriello, Viqi Wagner, and Anne Marie Welsh for their work on earlier editions of the book.

Special acknowledgment is due to my associate, Professor Henry E. Jacobs (1946–1986) of the University of Alabama. His energy and creativity were essential in planning, writing, and bringing out the first edition of *Literature: An Introduction to Reading and Writing* back in 1986, but "fate and gloomy night" intervened to prevent our working together on subsequent revisions. *Vale.*

—Edgar V. Roberts

Part I

The Process of Reading, Responding to, and Writing About Literature

This first part provides an overview of literature, a discussion of active reading strategies, and a walkthrough of the writing process from brainstorming through a final student essay. By walking students through the process, the material in this part equips them with the tools they will need to become effective readers and writers.

Highlights of this part include:

What Is Literature, and Why Do We Study It?
This section provides an overall introduction to literature and uses Guy de Maupassant's "The Necklace" to teach active reading strategies.

Major Stages in Thinking and Writing About Literary Topics: Discovering Ideas, Preparing to Write, Making an Initial Draft of Your Essay, and Completing the Essay
As the title indicates, this section takes students from discovering ideas for writing about literature to a final draft of a student essay. The major topics in this section are listed below.

- Preparing to Write
- Making an Initial Draft of Your Essay
- Argument in Essays About Literature
- Illustrative Student Essay (First Draft)
- Revision
- Illustrative Student Essay (Final Draft)

A Short Guide to the Use of References and Quotations in Essays About Literature
This final section offers invaluable advice on using quoted material and references in writing about literature.

Part I

The Process of Reading, Responding to, and Writing About Literature

The chapters that follow introduce a number of analytical approaches important in the study of literature, along with guidance for writing informative and well-focused essays based on these approaches. The chapters will help you fulfill two goals of composition and English courses: (1) to write good essays and (2) to understand and assimilate great works of literature.

The premise of this book is that no educational process is complete until you can apply what you study. That is, you have not learned something—really *learned* it—*until you talk or write about it.* This does not mean that you retell a story, state an undeveloped opinion, or describe an author's life, but rather that you deal directly with intellectual and artistic issues about individual works. The need to write requires you to strengthen your understanding and knowledge through the recognition of where your original study might have fallen short. Thus, it is easy for you to read the chapter on point of view (Chapter 2), and it is also easy to read Shirley Jackson's story "The Lottery." Your grasp of point of view as a concept will not be complete, however, nor will your appreciation of the technical artistry of this story be complete, until you have prepared yourself to write about the technique. As you do so, you will need to reread parts of the work, study your notes, and apply your knowledge to the problem at hand; you must check facts, grasp relationships, develop insights, and try to express yourself with as much exactness and certainty as possible.

Primarily, then, this book aims to help you improve your writing skills through the use of literature as subject matter. After you have finished a number of essays derived from the chapters ahead, you will be able to approach just about any literary work with the confidence that you can understand it and write about it.

What Is Literature, and Why Do We Study It?

We use the word **literature,** in a broad sense, to mean compositions that tell stories, dramatize situations, express emotions, and analyze and advocate ideas. Before the invention of writing thousands of years ago, literary works were necessarily spoken or sung, and they were retained only as long as living people continued to repeat them. In some societies, the oral tradition of literature still exists, with many poems and stories designed exclusively for spoken delivery. Even in our modern age of writing, printing, and electronic communication, much literature is still heard aloud rather than read silently. Parents delight their children with stories and poems read aloud; poets and storywriters read their works directly before live audiences; plays and scripts are interpreted on stages and before movie and television cameras for the benefit of a vast public.

No matter how we assimilate literature, we gain much from it. In truth, readers often cannot explain why they enjoy reading, for goals and ideals are not easily articulated. There are, however, areas of general agreement about the value of systematic and extensive reading.

Literature helps us grow, both personally and intellectually. It opens doors for us. It stretches our minds. It develops our imagination, increases our understanding, and enlarges our power of sympathy. It helps us see beauty in the world around us. It links us with the cultural, philosophical, and religious world of which we are a part. It enables us to recognize human dreams and struggles in different places and times. It helps us develop mature sensibility and compassion for all living beings. It nurtures our ability to appreciate the beauty of order and arrangement—gifts that are also bestowed by a well-structured song, a beautifully painted canvas, or a skillfully-chiseled statue. It enables us to see worthiness in the aims of all people. It exercises our emotions through interest, concern, sympathy, tension, excitement, regret, fear, laughter, and hope. It encourages us to assist creative and talented people who need recognition and support. Through our cumulative experience in reading, literature shapes our goals and values by clarifying our own identities—both positively, through acceptance of the admirable in human beings, and negatively, through rejection of the sinister. It enables us to develop perspectives on events occurring locally and globally, and thereby it gives us understanding and control. It is one of the shaping influences of life. It makes us human.

Types of Literature: The Genres

Literature may be classified into four categories or *genres:* (1) prose fiction, (2) poetry, (3) drama, and (4) nonfiction prose. Usually the first three are classified as **imaginative literature.**

The genres of imaginative literature have much in common, but they also have distinguishing characteristics. **Prose fiction,** or **narrative fiction,** includes **myths, parables, romances, novels,** and **short stories.** Originally, *fiction* meant anything made up, crafted, or shaped, but today the word refers to prose stories based in the imaginations of authors. The essence of fiction is **narration,** the relating or recounting of a sequence of events or actions. Fictional works usually focus on one or a few major characters who change and grow (in their ability to make decisions, their awareness or insight, their intellect, their attitude toward others, their sensitivity, and their moral capacity) as a result of how they deal with other characters and how they attempt to solve their problems. Although fiction, like all imaginative literature, can introduce true historical details, it is not real history, for its main purpose is to interest, stimulate, instruct, and divert, not to create a precise historical record.

If prose is expansive, **poetry** tends toward brevity. It offers us high points of emotion, reflection, thought, and feeling in what the English poet Wordsworth called "narrow room[s]." Yet in this context, it expresses the most powerful and deeply felt experiences of human beings, often awakening deep responses of welcome recognition: "Yes, I know what that's like. I would feel the same way. That's exactly right." Poems make us think, make us reflect, and generally instruct us. They can also stimulate us, surprise us, make us laugh or cry, inspire us, exalt us. Many poems become our lifelong friends, and we visit them again and again for insight, understanding, laughter, or the quiet reflection of joy or sorrow.

Poetry's power lies not only in its words and thoughts, but also in its music, using rhyme and a variety of rhythms to intensify its emotional impact. Although poems themselves vary widely in length, individual lines are often short because poets distill the greatest meaning and imaginative power from their words through rhetorical devices such as **imagery** and **metaphor.** Though poetry often requires many **formal** and **metrical** restrictions, it is paradoxically the very restrictiveness of poetry that provides poets with great freedom. Traditionally important poetic forms include the fourteen-line **sonnet,** as well as **ballads, blank verse, couplets, elegies, epigrams, hymns, limericks, odes, quatrains, songs** or **lyrics, tercets** or **triplets, villanelles,** and the increasingly popular **haiku.** Many songs or lyrics have been set to music, and some were written expressly for that purpose. Some poems are long and discursive, like many poems by the American poet Walt Whitman. **Epic poems,** such as those by Homer and Milton, contain thousands of lines. Since the time of Whitman, many poets have abandoned rhymes and regular rhythms in favor of **free verse,** a far-ranging type of poetry growing out of content and the natural rhythms of spoken language.

Drama is literature designed for stage or film presentation by people—actors—for the benefit and delight of other people—an audience. The essence of drama is the development of **character** and **situation** through **speech** and **action.** Like fiction, drama may focus on a single character or a small number of characters, and it enacts fictional (and sometimes historical) events as if they were happening right before our eyes. The audience therefore is a direct witness to the ways in which characters are influenced and changed by events and by other characters. Although most modern plays use prose **dialogue** (the conversation of two or more characters), on the principle that the language of drama should resemble the language of ordinary people as much as possible, many plays from the past, such as those of ancient Greece and Renaissance England, are in poetic form.

Nonfiction prose consists of news reports, feature articles, essays, editorials, textbooks, historical and biographical works, and the like, all of which describe or interpret facts and present judgments and opinions. The goal of nonfiction prose is to present truths and conclusions about the factual world. Imaginative literature, although also grounded in facts, is less concerned with the factual record than with the revelation of truths about life and human nature. Recently another genre has been emphasized within the category of nonfiction prose. This is **creative nonfiction,** a type of literature that is technically nonfiction, such as essays, articles, diaries, and journals, but which nevertheless introduces carefully structured form, vivid examples, relevant quotations, and highly creative and imaginative insights.

Reading Literature and Responding to It Actively

Sometimes we find it difficult, after we have finished reading a work, to express thoughts about it and to answer pointed questions about it. But more active and thoughtful reading gives us the understanding to develop well-considered answers. Obviously, we need to follow the work and to understand its details, but just as importantly, we need to respond to the words, get at the ideas, and understand the implications of what is happening. We rely on our own fund of knowledge and experience to verify the accuracy and truth of situations and incidents, and we try to articulate our own emotional responses to the characters and their problems.

To illustrate such active responding, we will examine "The Necklace" (1884), by the French writer Guy de Maupassant. "The Necklace" is one of the best known of all stories, and it is included here with marginal notes like those that any reader might make during original and follow-up readings. Many notes, particularly at the beginning, are *assimilative;* that is, they record details about the action. But as the story progresses, the marginal comments are more concerned with conclusions about the story's meaning. Toward the end, the comments are full rather than minimal; they result not only from first responses but also from considered thought. Here, then, is Maupassant's "The Necklace."

GUY DE MAUPASSANT (1850–1893)

Henri-René-Albert-Guy de Maupassant (1850–1893) is considered one of the major nineteenth-century French naturalist writers. Scion of an aristocratic Norman family, he received his baccalaureate degree from a lycée at Le Havre, after which he began studying law. When the Franco–Prussian War broke out, he served in the French army, including battlefield duty. After leaving the military he became a minor bureaucrat, first in the Ministry of Marine and then in the Ministry of Education (also the workplace of Loisel, the husband of "The Necklace").

As a youth Maupassant was an energetic oarsman, swimmer, and boatman—a power that he also devoted to his career as a writer. During the 1870s in Paris, he had regularly submitted his literary efforts to the novelist Gustave Flaubert (1821–1880), a family friend who regarded him as a son and whose criticism both improved and encouraged him. In Maupassant's thirties, after the death of his mentor Flaubert, his career flourished. His first published volume was a collection of poems (Des Vers, 1880), which he had to withdraw after it created a scandal and a lawsuit because of its sexual openness. After this time, until his death in 1893, he produced thirty volumes—novels, poems, articles, travel books, and three hundred short stories. In addition to "The Necklace," a few of his better-known stories are "The Ball of Fat," "Mademoiselle Fifi," and "A Piece of String."

Maupassant was a meticulous writer, devoting much attention to the reality of everyday existence (hence his status as a naturalist writer). A number of his stories are about events occurring during the Franco–Prussian War. Some are about life among bureaucrats, some about peasant life in Normandy, and a large number, including "The Necklace," about Parisian life. His major stories are characterized by strong irony; human beings are influenced by forces they cannot control, and their wishes are often frustrated by their own defects. Under such circumstances, Maupassant's characters exhibit varying degrees of weakness, hypocrisy, vanity, insensitivity, callousness, and even cruelty, but those who are victimized are viewed with understanding and sympathy.

The Necklace (1884)

Translated by Edgar V. Roberts

She was one of those pretty and charming women, born, as if by an error of destiny, into a family of clerks and copyists. She had no dowry, no prospects, no way of getting known, courted, loved, married by a rich and distinguished man. She finally settled for a marriage with a minor clerk in the Ministry of Education.

"She" is pretty but poor, and has no chance in life unless she marries. Without connections, she has no entry into high society and marries an insignificant clerk.

She was a simple person, without the money to dress well, but she was as unhappy as if she had gone through bankruptcy, for women have neither rank nor race. In place of high birth or important family connections, they can rely only on their beauty, their grace, and their charm. Their inborn finesse, their elegant taste, their engaging personalities, which are their only power, make working-class women the equals of the grandest ladies.

She is unhappy.

A view of women who have no chance for an independent life and a career. In 1884, women had nothing more than this. Sad.

She suffered constantly, feeling herself destined for all delicacies and luxuries. She suffered because of her grim apartment with its drab walls, threadbare furniture, ugly curtains. All such things, which most other women in her situation would not even have noticed, tortured her and filled her with despair. The sight of the young country girl who did her simple housework awakened in her only a sense of desolation and lost hopes. She daydreamed of large, silent anterooms, decorated with oriental tapestries and lighted by high bronze floor lamps, with two elegant valets in short culottes dozing in large armchairs under the effects of forced-air heaters. She imagined large drawing rooms draped in the most expensive silks, with fine end tables on which were placed knick-knacks of inestimable value. She dreamed of the perfume of dainty private rooms, which were designed only for intimate tête-à-têtes with the closest friends, who because of their achievements and fame would make her the envy of all other women.

She suffers because of her cheap belongings, wanting expensive things. She dreams of wealth and of how other women would envy her if she could display finery. But such luxuries are unrealistic and unattainable for her.

When she sat down to dinner at her round little table covered with a cloth that had not been washed for three days, in front of her husband who opened the kettle while declaring ecstatically, "Ah, good old beef stew! I don't know anything better," she dreamed of expensive banquets with shining placesettings, and wall hangings portraying ancient heroes and exotic birds in an enchanted forest. She imagined a gourmet-prepared main course carried on the most exquisite trays and served on the most beautiful dishes, with whispered gallantries which she would hear with a sphinxlike smile as she dined on the pink meat of a trout or the delicate wing of a quail.

Her husband's taste is for plain things, while she dreams of expensive gourmet food. He has adjusted to his status. She has not.

She had no decent dresses, no jewels, nothing. And she loved nothing but these; she believed herself born only for these. She burned with the desire to please, to be envied, to be attractive and sought after.

She lives for her unrealistic dreams, and these increase her frustration. 5

She had a rich friend, a comrade from convent days, whom she did not want to see anymore because she suffered so much when she returned home. She would weep for the entire day afterward with sorrow, regret, despair, and misery.

She even thinks of giving up a rich friend because she is so depressed after visiting her.

Well, one evening, her husband came home glowing and carrying a large envelope.

A new section in the story.

"Here," he said, "this is something for you."

She quickly tore open the envelope and took out a card engraved with these words:

The CHANCELLOR OF EDUCATION *and*
MRS. GEORGE RAMPONNEAU
request that
MR. AND MRS. LOISEL
do them the honor of coming to dinner
at the Ministry of Education
on the evening of January 8.

An invitation to dinner at the Ministry of Education. A big plum.

Instead of being delighted, as her husband had hoped, she threw the invitation spitefully on the table, muttering:

It only upsets her. 10

"What do you expect me to do with this?"

"But honey, I thought you'd be glad. You never get to go out, and this is a special occasion! I had a lot of trouble getting the invitation. Everyone wants one. The demand is high and not many clerks get invited. Everyone important will be there."

Loisel really doesn't understand her. He can't sympathize with her unhappiness.

She looked at him angrily and stated impatiently:

"What do you want me to wear to go there?"

He had not thought of that. He stammered:

"But your theater dress. That seems nice to me . . ."

She declares that she hasn't anything to wear. 15

He tries to persuade her that her theater dress might do for the occasion.

He stopped, amazed and bewildered, as his wife began to cry. Large tears fell slowly from the corners of her eyes to her mouth. He said falteringly:

"What's wrong? What's the matter?"

But with a strong effort she had recovered, and she answered calmly as she wiped her damp cheeks:

"Nothing, except that I have nothing to wear and therefore can't go to the party. Give your invitation to someone else at the office whose wife will have nicer clothes than mine." 20

Distressed, he responded:

"Well, all right, Mathilde. How much would a new dress cost, something you could use at other times, but not anything fancy?"

Her name is Mathilde.

He volunteers to pay for a new dress.

She thought for a few moments, adding things up and thinking also of an amount that she could ask without getting an immediate refusal and a frightened outcry from the frugal clerk.

Finally she responded tentatively:

She is manipulating him.

"I don't know exactly, but it seems to me that I could get by on four hundred francs."

He blanched slightly at this, because he had set aside just that amount to buy a shotgun for Sunday lark-hunts the next summer with a few friends in the Plain of Nanterre.

The dress will cost him his next summer's vacation. (He doesn't seem to have included her in his plans.)

However, he said:

"All right, you've got four hundred francs, but make it a pretty dress."

As the day of the party drew near, Mrs. Loisel seemed sad, uneasy, anxious, even though her gown was all ready. One evening her husband said to her:

A new section, the third in the story. The day of the party is near. Tension is mounting.

"What's the matter? You've been acting funny for several days."

She answered:

"It's awful, but I don't have any jewels to wear, not a single gem, nothing to dress up my outfit. I'll look like a beggar. I'd almost rather not go to the party."

Now she complains that she doesn't have any nice jewelry. She is manipulating him again.

He responded:

"You can wear a corsage of cut flowers. This year it's all the rage. For only ten francs you can get two or three gorgeous roses."

She was not convinced.

"No . . . there's nothing more humiliating than looking shabby in the company of rich women."

She has a good point, but there seems to be no way out.

But her husband exclaimed:

"God, but you're silly! Go to your friend Mrs. Forrestier, and ask her to lend you some jewelry. You know her well enough to do that."

He proposes a solution: Borrow jewelry from Mrs. Forrestier, who is apparently the rich friend mentioned earlier.

She uttered a cry of joy:

"That's right. I hadn't thought of that."

The next day she went to her friend's house and described her problem.

Mrs. Forrestier went to her mirrored wardrobe, took out a large jewel box, opened it, and said to Mrs. Loisel:

"Choose, my dear."

Mathilde has her choice of her friend's jewels.

She saw bracelets, then a pearl necklace, then a Venetian cross of finely worked gold and gems. She tried on the jewelry in front of a mirror, and hesitated, unable to make up her mind about each one. She kept asking:

"Do you have anything else?"

"Certainly. Look to your heart's content. I don't know what you'd like best."

Suddenly she found a superb diamond necklace in a black satin box, and her heart throbbed with desire for it. Her hands shook as she picked it up. She fastened it around her neck, watched it gleam at her throat, and looked at herself ecstatically.

A "superb" diamond necklace. This is what the story has been building up to.

Then she asked, haltingly and anxiously:

"Could you lend me this, nothing but this?"

This is what she wants, just this.

"Why yes, certainly."

50

She jumped up, hugged her friend joyfully, then hurried away with her treasure.

She leaves with the "treasure" Things might be looking up for her.

The day of the party came. Mrs. Loisel was a success. She was prettier than anyone else, stylish, graceful, smiling and wild with joy. All the men saw her, asked her name, sought to be introduced. All the important administrators stood in line to waltz with her. The Chancellor himself eyed her.

A new section.

The party. Mathilde is a huge success.

She danced joyfully, passionately, intoxicated with pleasure, thinking of nothing but the moment, in the triumph of her beauty, in the glory of her success, on cloud nine with happiness made up of all the admiration, of all the aroused desire, of this victory so complete and so sweet to the heart of any woman.

Another judgment about women. Does the author mean that only women want to be admired? Don't men want admiration, too?

She did not leave until four o'clock in the morning. Her husband, since midnight, had been sleeping in a little empty room with three other men whose wives had also been enjoying themselves.

Loisel, with other husbands, is bored, while the wives are literally having a ball.

He threw, over her shoulders, the shawl that he had brought for the trip home—a modest everyday wrap, the poverty of which contrasted sharply with the elegance of her evening gown. She felt it and hurried away to avoid being noticed by the other women who luxuriated in rich furs.

Ashamed of her shabby everyday shawl, she rushes away to avoid being seen. She is forced back into the reality of her true situation. Her glamour is gone.

55

Loisel tried to hold her back:

"Wait a minute. You'll catch cold outdoors. I'll call a cab."

But she paid no attention and hurried down the stairs. When they reached the street they found no carriages. They began to look for one, shouting at cabmen passing by at a distance.

They walked toward the Seine, desperate, shivering. Finally, on a quay, they found one of those old night-going buggies that are seen in Paris only after dark, as if they were ashamed of their wretched appearance in daylight.

A comedown after the nice evening. They take a wretched-looking buggy home.

It took them to their door, on the Street of Martyrs, and they sadly climbed the stairs to their flat. For her, it was finished. As for him, he could think only that he had to begin work at the Ministry of Education at ten o'clock.

"Street of Martyrs" Is this name significant?

60

Loisel is down-to-earth.

She took the shawl off her shoulders, in front of the mirror, to see herself once more in her glory. But suddenly she cried out. The necklace was no longer around her neck!

SHE HAS LOST THE NECKLACE!

Her husband, already half undressed, asked:

"What's wrong?"

She turned toward him frantically:

"I . . . I . . . I no longer have Mrs. Forrestier's necklace."

65

He stood up, bewildered:

"What! . . . How! . . . It's not possible!"

And they looked in the folds of the gown, in the folds of the shawl, in the pockets, everywhere. They found nothing.

They can't locate it. It seems to be lost. What a horrible feeling. What a comedown.

He asked:

70 "You're sure you still had it when you left the party?"

"Yes. I checked it in the vestibule of the Ministry."

"But if you'd lost it in the street, we would've heard it fall. It must be in the cab."

"Yes, probably. Did you notice the number?"

"No. Did you see it?"

75 "No."

Overwhelmed, they looked at each other. Finally, Loisel got dressed again:

"I'm going out to retrace all our steps," he said, "to see if I can find the necklace that way."

And he went out. She stayed in her evening dress, without the energy to get ready for bed, stretched out in a chair, drained of strength and thought.

He goes out to search for the necklace.

Her husband came back at about seven o'clock. He had found nothing.

But is unsuccessful.

80 He went to Police Headquarters and to the newspapers to announce a reward. He went to the small cab companies, and finally he followed up even the slightest hopeful lead.

He really tries. He's doing his best.

She waited the entire day, in the same enervated state, in the face of this frightful disaster.

Loisel came back in the evening, his face pale and haggard. He had found nothing.

"You'll have to write to your friend," he said, "that you broke a clasp on her necklace and that you're having it fixed. That'll give us time to look around."

Loisel's plan to explain delaying the return. He takes charge, is resourceful.

She wrote as he dictated.

85 By the end of the week they had lost all hope.

Things are hopeless.

And Loisel, looking five years older, declared:

"We'll have to see about replacing the jewels."

Note that Loisel does not even suggest that they explain things to Mrs. Forrestier.

The next day they took the case which had contained the necklace and went to the jeweler whose name was inside. He looked at his books:

They hunt for a replacement.

"I wasn't the one, Madam, who sold the necklace. I only made the case."

90 Then they went from jeweler to jeweler, searching for a necklace like the other one, racking their memories, both of them sick with worry and anguish.

In a shop in the Palais-Royal, they found a necklace of diamonds that seemed to them exactly like the one they were looking for. It was priced at forty thousand francs. They could buy it for thirty-six thousand.

A new diamond necklace will cost 36,000 francs, a monumental amount.

They got the jeweler to promise not to sell it for three days. And they made an agreement that he would buy it back for thirty-four thousand francs if the original was recovered before the end of February.

They make a deal with the jeweler. (Is Maupassant hinting that things might work out for them?)

Loisel had saved eighteen thousand francs that his father had left him. He would have to borrow the rest.

It will take all of Loisel's inheritance . . .

He borrowed, asking a thousand francs from one, five hundred from another, five louis° here, three louis there. He wrote promissory notes, undertook ruinous obligations, did business with finance companies and the whole tribe of loan sharks. He compromised himself for the remainder of his days, risked his signature without knowing whether he would be able to honor it; and, terrified by anguish over the future, by the black misery that was about to descend on him, by the prospect of all kinds of physical deprivations and moral tortures, he went to get the new necklace, and put down thirty-six thousand francs on the jeweler's counter.

. . . plus another 18,000 francs that must be borrowed at enormous rates of interest.

Mrs. Loisel took the necklace back to Mrs. Forrestier, who said with an offended tone:

Mrs. Forrestier is offended and complains about Mathilde's delay. 95

"You should have brought it back sooner; I might have needed it."

She did not open the case, as her friend feared she might. If she had noticed the substitution, what would she have thought? What would she have said? Would she not have taken her for a thief?

Is this enough justification for not telling the truth? It seems to be for the Loisels.

Mrs. Loisel soon discovered the horrible life of the needy. She did her share, however, completely, heroically. That horrifying debt had to be paid. She would pay. They dismissed the maid; they changed their address; they rented an attic flat.

A new section, the fifth.

She learned to do the heavy housework, dirty kitchen jobs. She washed the dishes, wearing away her manicured fingernails on greasy pots and encrusted baking dishes. She handwashed dirty linen, shirts, and dish towels that she hung out on the line to dry. Each morning, she took the garbage down to the street, and she carried up water, stopping at each floor to catch her breath. And, dressed in cheap house dresses, she went to the fruit dealer, the grocer, the butcher's, with her basket under her arms, haggling, insulting, defending her measly cash penny by penny.

They suffer to repay their debts. Mathilde accepts a cheap attic flat, and does all the heavy housework herself to save on domestic help.

She pinches pennies and haggles with the local merchants.

They had to make installment payments every month, and, to buy more time, to refinance loans.

They struggle to meet payments. 100

The husband worked evenings to make fair copies of tradesmen's accounts, and late into the night he made copies at five cents a page.

Mr. Loisel moonlights to make extra money.

And this life lasted ten years.

At the end of ten years, they had paid back everything—everything—including the extra charges imposed by loan sharks and the accumulation of compound interest.

For ten years they struggle, but they endure.

Mrs. Loisel looked old now. She had become the strong, hard, and rude woman of poor households. Her hair unkempt, with uneven skirts and rough, red hands, she spoke loudly, washed floors with large buckets of water. But sometimes, when her husband was at work, she sat down near the window, and she dreamed of that evening so long ago, of that party, where she had been so beautiful and so admired.

Another new section, the sixth of the story.

The Loisels have successfully paid back the loans. They have been quite virtuous.

°*louis:* a gold coin worth twenty francs.

105 What would life have been like if she had not lost that necklace? Who knows? Who knows? Life is so peculiar, so uncertain. How little a thing it takes to destroy you or to save you!

Mrs. Loisel (why does the narrator not say "Mathilde"?) is roughened and aged by the work. But she has behaved "heroically" (paragraph 98) and has shown her mettle.

Well, one Sunday, when she had gone for a stroll along the Champs-Elysées to relax from the cares of the week, she suddenly noticed a woman walking with a child. It was Mrs. Forrestier, still youthful, still beautiful, still attractive.

Mrs. Loisel felt moved. Would she speak to her? Yes, certainly. And now that she had paid, she could tell all. Why not?

The point of the story? Small, uncertain things shape our lives; we hang by a thread.

She walked closer.

"Hello, Jeanne."

110 The other gave no sign of recognition and was astonished to be addressed so familiarly by this working-class woman. She stammered:

The seventh part of the story, a scene on the Champs-Elysées. Mathilde sees Jeanne Forrestier for the first time in the previous ten years.

"But . . . Madam! . . . I don't know. . . . You must have made a mistake."

"No. I'm Mathilde Loisel."

Her friend cried out:

"Oh! . . . My poor Mathilde, you've changed so much."

Jeanne notes Mathilde's changed appearance.

115 "Yes. I've had some tough times since I saw you last; in fact hardships . . . and all because of you! . . ."

"Of me . . . how so?"

"You remember the diamond necklace that you lent me to go to the party at the Ministry of Education?"

"Yes. What then?"

"Well, I lost it."

Mathilde tells Jeanne everything.

120 "How, since you gave it back to me?"

"I returned another exactly like it. And for ten years we've been paying for it. You understand this wasn't easy for us, who have nothing. . . . Finally it's over, and I'm damned glad."

Mrs. Forrestier stopped her.

"You say that you bought a diamond necklace to replace mine?"

"Yes, you didn't notice it, eh? It was exactly like yours."

125 And she smiled with proud and childish joy.

Mrs. Forrestier, deeply moved, took both her hands.

"Oh, my poor Mathilde! But mine was only costume jewelry. At most, it was worth only five hundred francs! . . ."

SURPRISE! The lost necklace was not made of real diamonds, and the Loisels have slaved for no reason at all. But hard work and sacrifice probably brought out better qualities in Mathilde than she otherwise might have shown. Is this the point of the story? Look again at paragraph 105.

Reading and Responding in a Computer File or Notebook

The marginal comments printed with "The Necklace" demonstrate the active reading-responding process you should apply to everything you read. Use the margins in your text similarly to record your comments and questions, but plan also to record your more lengthy responses in a notebook, on note cards, on separate sheets of paper, or in a computer file. Be careful not to lose anything; keep all your notes. As you progress from work to work, you will find that your written or saved comments will be immensely important to you as your record, or journal, of your first impressions together with your more carefully considered and expanded thoughts.

In keeping your notebook, your objective should be to learn assigned works inside and out and then to say perceptive things about them. To achieve this goal, you need to read the work more than once. Develop a good note-taking system so that as you read, you will create a "memory bank" of your own knowledge. You can make withdrawals from this fund of ideas when you begin to write. As an aid in developing your own procedures for reading and "depositing" your ideas, you may wish to begin with the following guidelines for reading. Of course, you will want to modify these suggestions and add to them as you become a more experienced and disciplined reader.

GUIDELINES FOR READING

1. **Observations for basic understanding**
   a. Explain words, situations, and concepts. Write down words that are new or not immediately clear. Use your dictionary, and record the relevant meanings in your notebook. Write down special difficulties so that you can ask your instructor about them.
   b. Determine what is happening in the work. For a story or play, where do the actions take place? What do they show? Who is involved? Who is the major figure? Why is he or she major? What relationships do the characters have with one another? What concerns do the characters have? What do they do? Who says what to whom? How do the speeches advance the action and reveal the characters? For a poem, what is the situation? Who is talking, and to whom? What does the speaker say about the situation? Why does the poem end as it does and where it does?
2. **Notes on first impressions**
   a. Make a record of your reactions and responses. What did you think was memorable, noteworthy, funny, or otherwise striking? Did you worry, get scared, laugh, smile, feel a thrill, learn a great deal, feel proud, find a lot to think about?
   b. Describe interesting characterizations, events, techniques, and ideas. If you like a character or an idea, explain what you like, and do the same for characters and ideas you don't like. Is there anything else in the work that you especially like or dislike? Are parts easy or difficult to understand? Why? Are there any surprises? What was your reaction to them? Be sure to use your own words when writing your explanations.
3. **Development of ideas and enlargement of responses**
   a. Trace developing patterns. Make an outline or a scheme: What conflicts appear? Do these conflicts exist between people, groups, or ideas? How are the conflicts resolved? Is one force, idea, or side the winner? How do you respond to the winner or to the loser?
   b. Write expanded notes about characters, situations, and actions. What explanations need to be made about the characters? What is the nature of the situations (e.g., young people discover a damaged boat, and themselves, in the spring; a prisoner tries to hide her baby from cruel guards, and so on)?

What is the nature of the actions (e.g., a mother and daughter go shopping, a series of strangers intrude upon the celebration of a christening, a woman is told that her husband has been killed in a train wreck, a group of children are taken to a fashionable toy store, and so on)? What are the people like, and what are their habits and customs? What sort of language do they use?

c. Memorize important, interesting, and well-written passages. Copy them in full on note cards, and keep these in your pocket or purse. When walking to class, riding public transportation, or otherwise not occupying your time, learn them by heart. Please take memorization seriously.

d. Always write down questions that come up during your reading. You may raise these in class, and trying to write out your own answers will also aid your own study.

Sample Notebook Entries on Maupassant's "The Necklace"

The following entries demonstrate how you can use the foregoing guidelines in your first thoughts about a work. You should try to develop enough observations and responses to be useful later, both for additional study and for developing essays. Notice that the entries are not only comments but also questions.

Early in the story, Mathilde seems to be spoiled. She and her husband are not well off, but she is unable to face her own situation.

She is a dreamer but seems harmless. Her daydreams about a fancy home, with all the expensive belongings, are not unusual. It would be unusual to find people who do not have such dreams.

She is embarrassed by her husband's taste for plain food. The storyteller contrasts her taste for trout and quail with Loisel's cheaper favorites.

When the Loisels get the invitation to the ball, Mathilde becomes difficult. Her wish for an expensive dress (the cost of Loisel's shotgun) creates a problem, and she creates another problem by wanting to wear fine jewelry.

Her change in character can be related to the places in the story: the Street of Martyrs, the dinner party scene, the attic flat. Also she fills the places she daydreams about with the most expensive things she can imagine.

Her success at the party shows that she has the charm the storyteller talks about in paragraph 2. She seems never to have had any other chance to exert her power.

The worst part of her personality is shown in rushing away from the party because she is ashamed of her ordinary and shabby shawl, which she had worn because the time of the story is January. It is Mathilde's unhappiness and unwillingness to adjust to her modest means that cause the financial downfall of the Loisels. This disaster is her fault.

Borrowing the money to replace the necklace shows that both Loisel and Mathilde have a strong sense of honor. Making up the loss is good, even if it destroys them financially.

There are some nice touches, like Loisel's seeming to be five years older (paragraph 86) and his staying with the other husbands of women enjoying themselves (paragraph 54). These are well done.

It's too bad that Loisel and Mathilde don't confess to Jeanne that the jewels are lost. Their pride or their honor stops them—or perhaps their fear of being accused of theft.

Their ten years of slavish work (paragraphs 98-102) show how they have come down in life. Mathilde does all her work by hand, so she really does pitch in and is, as the narrator says, heroic.

The attic flat is important. Mathilde becomes loud and frumpy when living there (paragraph 99), but she also develops strength. She does what she has to. The earlier apartment and the elegance of her imaginary rooms had brought out her limitations.

The setting of the Champs-Elysées also reflects her character, for she feels free there to tell Jeanne about the disastrous loss and the ten years of sacrifice (paragraph 121), producing the surprise ending. A curious point: Is it likely that Mathilde would not have had any contact with Mrs. Forrestier during that ten-year period?

The narrator's statement "How little a thing it takes to destroy you or to save you!" (paragraph 105) is full of thought. The necklace is little, and it makes a gigantic problem. This creates the story's irony.

Questions: Is this story more about the surprise ending or about the character of Mathilde? Is she to be condemned or admired? Does the outcome stem from the little things that make us or break us, as the narrator suggests, or from the difficulty of rising above one's economic class, which seems true, or both? What do the speaker's remarks about women's status mean? (Remember, the story was published in 1884.) This probably isn't relevant, but wouldn't Jeanne, after hearing about the substitution, give the full value of the necklace to the Loisels (or at least return the necklace to them), and wouldn't they then be pretty well off?

These are reasonable—and also fairly full—remarks and observations about "The Necklace." Use your notebook or journal similarly for all reading assignments. If your assignment is simply to learn about a work, general notes like these should be enough. If you are preparing for a test, you might write pointed observations more in line with what is happening in your class, and also write and answer your own questions (see Chapter 31, "Taking Examinations on Literature"). If you have a writing assignment, observations like these can help you focus more closely on your topic—such as character, idea, or setting. Whatever your purpose, always take good notes, and put in as many details and responses as you can. The notes will be invaluable to you as a mind refresher and as a wellspring of thought.

Major Stages in Thinking and Writing About Literary Topics: Discovering Ideas, Preparing to Write, Making an Initial Draft of Your Essay, and Completing The Essay

Finished writing is the sharpened, focused expression of thought and study. It begins with the search for something to say—an idea. Not all ideas are equal; some are better than others, and getting good ideas is an ability that you will develop the more you think and write. As you discover ideas and explain them in words, you will also improve your perceptions and increase your critical faculties.

In addition, because literature itself contains the subject material (though not in a systematic way) of philosophy, religion, psychology, sociology, and politics, learning to analyze literature and to write about it will also improve your capacity to deal with these and other disciplines.

Writing Does Not Come Easily—for Anyone

A major purpose of your being in college, of which your composition and literature course is a vital part, is to develop your capacity to think and to express your thoughts clearly and fully. However, the process of creating a successfully argued essay—the actual process itself of writing—is not automatic. Writing begins in uncertainty and hesitation, and it becomes certain and confident—accomplished—only as a result of great care, applied thought, a certain amount of experimentation, the passage of time, and much effort. When you read complete, polished, well-formed pieces of writing, you might assume, as many of us do, that the writers wrote their successful versions the first time they tried and never needed to make any changes and improvements at all. In an ideal world, perhaps, something like this could happen, but not in this one.

If you could see the early drafts of writing you admire, you would be surprised and startled—and also encouraged—to see that good writers are also human and that what they first write is often uncertain, vague, tangential, tentative, incomplete, and messy. Good writers do not always like their first drafts; nevertheless, they work with their efforts and build upon them. They reconsider their ideas and try to restate them, discard some details, add others, chop paragraphs in half and reassemble the parts elsewhere, throw out much (and then maybe recover some of it), revise or completely rewrite sentences, change words, correct misspellings, sharpen expressions, and add new material to tie all the parts together in a smooth, natural flow.

The Goal of Writing: To Show a Process of Thought

As you approach the task of writing, you should constantly realize that your goal should always be to *explain* the work you are analyzing. You should never be satisfied simply to restate the events in the work. Too often students fall easily into a pattern of retelling a story or play, or of summarizing the details of a poem. But nothing could be further from what is expected from good writing. **Good writing should be the embodiment of your thought; it should show your thought in action.** Thinking is an active process that does not happen accidentally. Thinking requires that you develop ideas, draw conclusions, exemplify them and support them with details, and connect everything in a coherent manner. Your goal should constantly be to explain the results of your thinking—your ideas, your play of mind over the materials of a work, your insights, your conclusions.

Approach each writing assignment in light of the following objectives: You should consider your reader as a person who has read the work, just as you have done. This person knows what is in the work, and therefore does not need you to restate what she or he already knows. Instead, your reader wants to learn from you what to think about it. Therefore, always, your task as a writer is to explain something about the work, to describe the thoughts that you can develop about it. Let us consider again Maupassant's "The Necklace." We have recognized that the main character, Mathilde Loisel, is a young Parisian housewife who is married to a minor clerk in the Ministry of Education. We know this, but if we are reading an essay about the story we will want to learn more. Let us then suppose that a first goal of one of your paragraphs is to explain the deep dissatisfaction Mathilde feels in the early part of the story. Your paragraph might go as follows:

> In the early part of the story Maupassant establishes that Mathilde is deeply dissatisfied with her life. Her threadbare furniture and drab walls are a cause of her unhappiness. Under these circumstances her daydreams of beautiful rooms staffed by "elegant valets," together with a number of rooms for intimate conversations with friends, multiply her dissatisfaction. The meager meals that she shares with her husband make her imagine sumptuous banquets that she feels are rightfully hers by birth but that are denied her because of her circumstances. The emphasis in these early scenes of the story is always on Mathilde's discontentment and frustration.

Notice that this paragraph does not simply go over the story's events, but rather refers to the events in order to explain to us, as readers, the causes for Mathilde's unhappiness. The paragraph illustrates your process of thought. Here is another way in which you might use a thought to connect the same materials:

> In the early part of the story Maupassant emphasizes the economic difficulty of Mathilde's life. The threadbare furniture and ugly curtains, for example, highlight that there is no money to purchase better things. The same sparseness of existence is shown by the meager meals that she shares with her husband. With the capacity to appreciate better things, Mathilde is forced by circumstances to make do with worse. Her dreams of sumptuous banquets are therefore natural, given her level of frustration with the life around her. In short, her unhappiness is an understandable consequence of her aversion to her plain and drab apartment and the tightness of money.

Here the details are substantially the same as in the first paragraph, but they are unified by a different idea—namely, the economic constraints of Mathilde's life. What is important is that neither paragraph tells only the details. Instead the paragraphs illustrate the goal of writing with a purpose. Whenever you write, you should always be trying, as in these examples, to use a dominating thought or thoughts to shape the details in the work you are analyzing.

For both practiced and beginning writers alike, there are four stages of thinking and writing, and in each of these there are characteristic activities. In the beginning stage, writers try to find the details and thoughts that seem to be right for eventual inclusion in what they are hoping to write. The next (or middle) stage is characterized by written drafts, or sketches—ideas, sentences, paragraphs. An advanced stage of writing is the forming and ordering of what has previously been done—the creation and determination of a final essay. Although these stages occur in a natural order, they are not separate and distinct, but merge with each other and in effect are fused together. However, when you think you are close to finishing your essay, you may find that you are not as close as you might have thought. You are now in the finishing or completing stage, when you need to include something else, something more, something different, and something to make things complete. At this point you can easily re-create an earlier stage to discover new details and ideas. You might say that your work is always tentative until you regard it as finished or until you need to turn it in.

Discovering Ideas ("Brainstorming")

With the foregoing general goal in mind, let us assume that you have read the work about which you are to write and have made notes and observations on which you are planning to base your thought. You are now ready to consider and plan what to include in your essay. This earliest stage of writing is unpredictable and somewhat frustrating because you are on a search. You do not know quite what you want, for you are reaching out for ideas and you are not yet sure what they are and what you might say about them. This process of searching and discovery, sometimes also called **brainstorming,** requires you to examine any and every subject that your mind can produce.

Just as you are trying to reach for ideas, however, you also should try to introduce purpose and resolution into your thought. You have to zero in on something specific, and develop your ideas through this process. Although what you first write may seem indefinite, the best way to help your thinking is to put your mind, figuratively, into specific channels or grooves, and then to confine your thoughts within these boundaries. What matters is to get your mind going on a particular topic and to get your thoughts down on paper or onto a computer screen. Once you can see your thoughts in front of you, you can work with them and develop them. The drawing on the next page can be helpful to you as an illustration of the various facets of a literary work, or ways of talking about it.

Consider the work you have read—story, poem, play—as the central circle, from which a number of points, like the rays of a star, shine out, some of them prominently, others less so. These points, or rays, are the various subjects, or topics,

that you might decide to select in exploration, discovery, and discussion. Because some elements in a work may be more significant than others, the points are not all equal in size. Notice also that the points grow larger as they get nearer to the work, suggesting that once you select a point of discussion you may amplify that point with details and your own observations about the work.

You can consider literary works in many ways, but for now, as a way of getting started, you might choose to explore (1) the work's characters, (2) its historical period and background, (3) the social and economic conditions it depicts, (4) its major ideas, (5) any of its artistic qualities, or (6) any additional ideas that seem important to you.[1] These topics, of course, have many subtopics, but any one of them can help you in the concentration you will need for beginning your essay (and also for classroom discussion). All you need is one topic, just one; don't try everything at the same time. Let us see how our illustration can be revised to account for these topics. In the drawing on the next page the number of points is reduced to illustrate the points or approaches we have just raised (with an additional and unnamed point to represent all the other approaches that might be used for other studies). These points represent your ways of discovering ideas about the work.

Study the Characters in the Work

You do not need to be a professional psychologist to discuss the persons or characters that you find in a work (see also Chapter 3). You need to raise only issues about the characters and what they do and what they represent. What are the

[1]Together with additional topics, these critical approaches are discussed in more detail in Chapter 29.

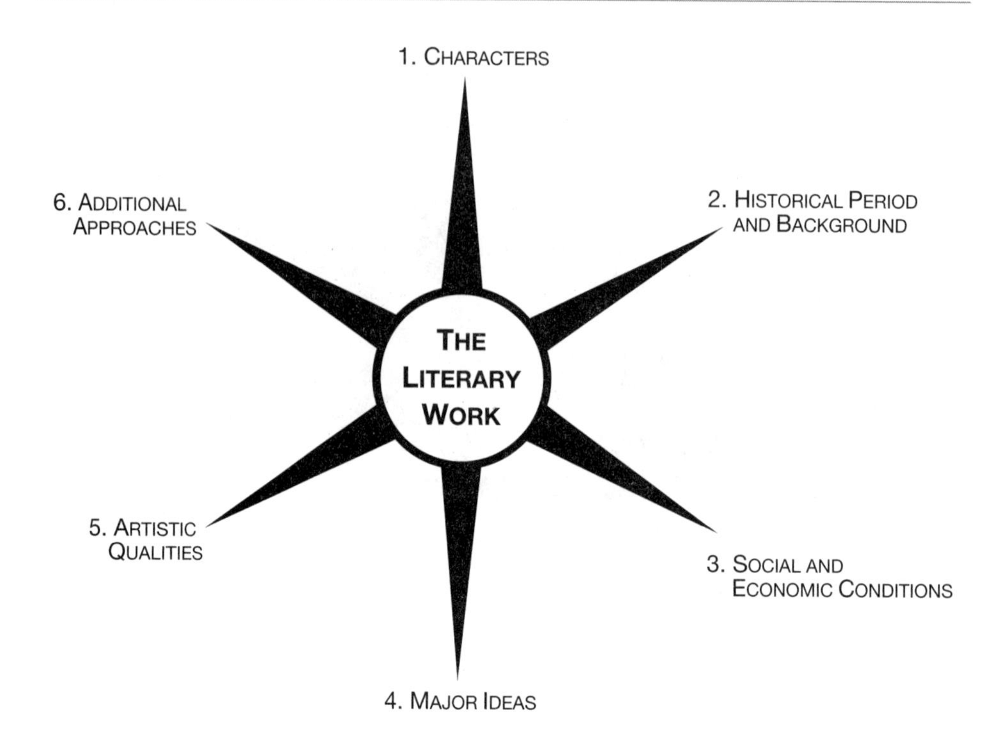

characters like at the beginning of the work? What happens to them? Do they do anything that causes them to change, and how are they changed? Are the changes for good or for bad? Why do the characters do the things they do? What do they do correctly? What do they do incorrectly? Why? For example, Mathilde is wrong not to tell Jeanne about the lost necklace. Such an immediate admission of truth would save her and her husband ten years of hardship and deprivation. But Mathilde does not tell the truth. Why not? What do we learn about her character because she avoids or ignores this admission? Is her avoidance understandable? Why?

In discussing character, you might also wish to raise the issue of whether the characters in the work do or do not do what might normally be expected from people in their circumstances. Do they correspond to type? The idea here is that certain attitudes and behaviors are typical of people at particular stages of life (e.g., children behaving like children, lovers dealing with their relationship, a young couple coping with difficult finances). Thus we might ask questions about whether the usual circumstances experienced by the characters affect them, either by limiting them in some way or by freeing them. What attitudes seem typical of the characters? How do these attitudes govern what the characters do, or do not do? For example, one of the most typical circumstances of life is marriage. According to the positive and ideal type of marriage, a husband and wife should be forthcoming with each other; they should tell each other things and should not conceal what is on their minds. If they have problems, they should discuss them and try to solve them together. In "The Necklace" we see that Mathilde and Loisel do not show these desired qualities, and their absence of communication can be seen as an element in their financial catastrophe. However, during their long years of trouble they work together; they eventually exhibit the quality of honesty, and in this respect they fulfill their role, or type, as a married couple.

An analysis of typical attitudes themselves can also furnish you with material for discussion. For example, Mathilde, who is a member of the lower commercial class, has attitudes that are more appropriate to the upper or leisure class. She cannot bridge this gap, and her frustration causes her to nag her husband to give her enough money to live out her dream, if only for a moment.

Determine the Work's Historical Period and Background

An obvious topic is the historical circumstances of the work. When was the work written? How well does it portray details about life at the time it appeared? What is historically unique about it? To what degree does it help you learn something about the past that you did not previously know? What actions in the work are like or unlike actions going on at the present time? What truthfulness to life do you discover in the work? In "The Necklace," for example, which was published more than a century ago, Mathilde's duty is to stay at home as a housewife—a traditional role—while her husband is the family breadwinner. After the loss of the necklace she can no longer afford domestic help, and she is compelled to do all her own housework and her own shopping. She has none of today's home conveniences—no dishwasher, microwave, refrigerator or car. Her husband, a clerk or secretary-copyist, spends his workday copying business records by hand, for at the period of the story there were few typewriters and absolutely no word processors. Discussing matters like these might also help you with works written during modern times, because our own assumptions, artifacts, and habits will bear analysis and discussion.

Analyze the Work's Economic and Social Conditions

Closely related to the historical period, an obvious topic to pursue in many works is the economic and social condition of the characters. To what level of life, economically, do the characters belong? How are events in the work related to their condition? How does their money, or lack of it, limit what they do? How do their economic circumstances either restrict or liberate their imaginations? How do their jobs and their apparent income determine their way of life? If we ask some of these questions about "The Necklace," as we have seen, we find that Mathilde and her husband are greatly burdened by their lack of money, and also that their obligation to repay their huge loan drives them into economic want and sacrifice.

An important part of the economic and social analysis of literature is the consideration of female characters and what it means to be a woman. This is the feminist analysis of literature, which asks questions like these: What role is Mathilde compelled to take as a result of her sex and family background? How does Jeanne's way of life contrast with that of Mathilde? What can Mathilde do with her life? To what degree is she limited by her role as a housewife? Does she have any chance of an occupation outside the home? How does her economic condition cause her to yearn for better things? What causes her to borrow the necklace? What is her contribution, as a woman, to the repayment of the loans? Should

Mathilde's limited life in "The Necklace" be considered as a political argument for greater freedom for women? Once you start asking questions like these, you will find that your thinking is developing along with your ideas for writing.

The feminist approach to the interpretation of literature has been well established, and it will usually provide you with a way to discuss a work. It is also possible, of course, to analyze what a work says about the condition of being a man, or being a child. Depending on the work, many of the questions important in a feminist approach are not dissimilar to those you might use if you are dealing with childhood or male adulthood.

One of the most important social and economic topics is that of race and ethnicity. What happens in the work that seems to occur mainly because of the race of the characters? Is the author pointing out any deprivations, any absence of opportunity, any oppression? What do the characters do under such circumstances? Do they succeed or not? Are they negative? Are they angry? Are they resolute and determined? Your aim in an inquiry of this type should be to concentrate on actions and ideas in the work that are clearly related to race.

Explain the Work's Major Ideas

One of the major ways of focusing on a work is to zero in on various ideas and values or issues to be discovered there. What ideas might we gain from the story of the lengthy but needless sacrifice and drudgery experienced by Mathilde and her husband? An obvious and acceptable idea is presented by the speaker—namely, that even the smallest, most accidental incident can cause immense consequences. This is an idea that we might expand and illustrate in an entire essay. Here are some other ideas that we might also pursue, all of them based on the story's actions:

- Many actions have unforeseeable and uncontrollable consequences.
- Lack of communication is a major cause of hardship.
- Adversity brings out a character's good qualities.
- Mutual effort enables people to overcome difficulties.

These ideas are all to be found in Maupassant's story. In other works, of course, we may find comparable ideas, in addition to other major ideas and issues.

Describe the Work's Artistic Qualities

A work's artistic qualities provide many possible topics for studying, but basically here you may consider matters such as the work's plan or organization and the author's narrative method, writing style, or poetic techniques. In "The Necklace," we thus observe that almost the entire story develops with Mathilde at the center (narrative method; see also Chapter 2, on point of view). At first, the story brings us close to Mathilde, for we are told of her dissatisfaction and impatience with her surroundings. As the story progresses, the storyteller/speaker presents her person and actions more objectively and also more distantly. Another artistic approach would be to determine the story's pattern of development—how, chronologically, the loss of the necklace brings financial misfortune to the Loisels. We might also look for the author's inclusion of symbols in the story, such as the name of the street where the Loisels originally live, their move to an attic flat, or the roughness of Mathilde's hands as a result of her constant housework. There are many other ways to consider the formal aspects of a literary work.

Explain Any Other Approaches that Seem Important

Additional ways of looking at a work such as "The Necklace" might occur to you beyond those just described. One reader might raise the issue that the story's speaker seems to exhibit a particularly patronizing attitude toward women. He draws attention to Mathilde's joy because of the party, and generalizes about how her "victory" was so "sweet to the heart of any woman" (paragraph 53). A writer might want to make more of this attitude. Another aspect of the story might be the way in which Mathilde's physical appearance undergoes change as a result of her dismissing the maid and taking on the household chores herself. Still another aspect is the attitude of Loisel and his relationship with Mathilde, which seems rather distant. The story tells nothing about his reactions to the misfortune beyond how he pitches in to restore the borrowed money, almost to the point of enslaving himself to the task. Would he never have uttered any reproachful words toward his wife? The point here is that additional ideas may suggest themselves to you, and that you should keep yourself open to explore and discuss any of these other ways of seeing and thinking.

Preparing to Write

By this time you will already have been focusing on your topic and will have assembled much that you can put into your essay. You should now aim to develop paragraphs and sketches of what you will eventually include. You should think constantly of the point or argument you want to develop, but invariably digressions will occur, together with other difficulties—false starts, dead ends, total cessation of thought, digressions, despair, hopelessness, and general frustration. Remember, however, that it is important just to start. Jump right in and start writing anything at all—no matter how unacceptable your first efforts may seem—and force yourself to deal with the materials. The writing down of ideas does not commit you. You should not think that these first ideas are untouchable and holy just because you have written them on paper or on your computer screen. You can throw them out in favor of new ideas, you can make cross-outs and changes, and you can move paragraphs or even sections around as you wish. However, if you do not start writing, your first thoughts will remain locked in your mind and you will have nothing to work with. You must learn to accept the uncertainties in the writing process and make them work *for* you rather than *against* you.

Build Ideas from Your Original Notes

You need to get your mind going by mining your notebook or computer file for useful things you have already written. Thus, let us use an observation in our original set of notes—"The attic flat is important"—in reference to the poorer rooms where Mathilde and her husband live while they are paying back their creditors. With such a note as a start, you might develop a number of ideas to support an argument about Mathilde's character, as in the following:

> The attic flat is important. Early in the story, in her apartment, Mathilde is dreamy and impractical. She seems delicate, but after losing the necklace, she is delicate no longer. She becomes a worker after they move to the flat. She does a lot more when living there.
>
> In the flat, Mathilde has to sacrifice. She gives up her servant, washes greasy pots, climbs stairs carrying buckets of water, sloshes water around to clean floors, and does all the clothes washing by hand.
>
> When living in the flat she gets stronger, but she also becomes loud and common. She argues with shopkeepers to get the lowest prices. She stops caring for herself. There is a reversal here, from incapable and well groomed to capable but coarse.

In this way, even in an assertion as basic as "The attic flat is important," the process of putting together details is a form of concentrated thought that leads you creatively forward. You can express thoughts and conclusions that you could not express at the beginning. Such an exercise in stretching your mind leads you to put elements of the work together in ways that create ideas for good essays.

Trace Patterns of Action and Thought

You can also discover ideas by making a list or scheme for the story or main idea. What conflicts appear? Do these conflicts exist between people, groups, or ideas? How does the author resolve them? Is one force, idea, or side the winner? Why? How do you respond to the winner or to the loser? Using this method, you might make a list similar to this one:

> At the beginning, Mathilde is a fish out of water. She dreams of wealth, but her life is drab and her husband is dull.
>
> Fantasies make her even more dissatisfied; she punishes herself by thinking of a wealthy life.
>
> When the Loisels get the dinner invitation Mathilde pouts and whines. Her husband feels discomfort when she manipulates him into buying her an expensive party dress.
>
> Her world of daydreams hurts her real life when her desire for wealth causes her to borrow the necklace. Losing the necklace is just plain bad luck.

These arguments all focus on Mathilde's character, but you may wish to trace other patterns you find in the story. If you start planning an essay about another pattern, be sure to account for all the actions and scenes that relate to your topic. Otherwise, you may miss a piece of evidence that could lead you to new conclusions.

THE NEED FOR THE ACTUAL PHYSICAL PROCESS OF WRITING

Thinking and writing are interdependent processes. If you don't get your thoughts into words that are visible to you on a paper or computer screen, your thinking will be impeded. It is therefore vital for you to use the writing process as the most significant means of developing your ideas. If you are doing an assignment in class—tests, or impromptu essays—write your initial responses on a single side of your paper. This strategy will enable you to spread your materials out to get an actual physical overview of them when you begin writing. Everything will be open to you; none of your ideas will be hidden on the other side of the paper.

Outside of class, however, when you are at home or otherwise able to use a computer, your machine is an indispensable tool for your writing. It will help you develop ideas, for it quickly enables you to eliminate unworkable thoughts and to replace them with others. You can move sentences and paragraphs into new contexts, test how they look, and move them somewhere else if you choose.

In addition, the ability to print initial and tentative stages of writing makes rewriting easier. Using the printed draft, you can make additional notes, corrections, and suggestions for further development. With the marked-up draft as a guide, you can go back to the word processor and fill in your changes and improvements, repeating this procedure as often as you can. You can also make edits directly to your draft and track changes to see your edits versus your original draft. This facility makes the machine an incentive for improvement, right up to your final draft.

Word processing also helps you in the final preparation of your essays. Studies have shown that errors and awkward sentences are frequently found at the bottoms of handwritten pages. The reason is that writers hesitate to make improvements when they get near the end of a page because they shun the dreariness of starting the page over. Word processors eliminate this difficulty completely. Changes can be made anywhere in the draft, at any time, without any ill effect on the final appearance of your essay.

Regardless of your writing method, you should always remember that unwritten thought is incomplete thought. You cannot lay everything out at once on the word processor's screen. You can see only a small part of what you are writing. Therefore, somewhere in your writing process, you need to prepare a complete draft of what you have written. A clean, readable draft permits you to gather everything together and to make even more improvements through revision.

Raise and Answer Your Own Questions

A habit you should always cultivate is to raise your own questions, and try to answer them yourself as you consider your reading. The guidelines for reading (pp. 13–14) will help you formulate questions, but you can raise additional questions like these:

- What is happening as the work unfolds? How does an action at the beginning of the work bring about later actions and speeches?

- Who are the main characters? What seems unusual or different about what they do in the work?
- What conclusions can you draw about the work's actions, scenes, and situations? Explain these conclusions.
- What are the characters and speakers like? What do they do and say about themselves, their goals, the people around them, their families, their friends, their work, and the general circumstances of their lives?
- What kinds of words do the characters use: formal or informal words, slang or profanity?
- What literary conventions and devices have you discovered, and how do these affect the work? (When an author addresses readers directly, for example, that is a convention; when a comparison is used, that is a device, which might be either a metaphor or a simile.)

Of course, you can raise other questions as you reread the piece, or you can be left with one or two major questions that you decide to pursue.

Put Ideas Together Using a Plus-Minus, Pro-Con, or Either-Or Method

A common and very helpful method of discovering ideas is to develop a set of contrasts: plus-minus, pro-con, either-or. Let us suppose a plus-minus method of considering the following question about Mathilde: Should she be "admired" (plus) or "condemned" (minus)?

PLUS: ADMIRED?	MINUS: CONDEMNED?
After she cries when they get the invitation, she recovers with a "strong effort"—maybe she doesn't want her husband to feel bad.	She wants to be envied and admired only for being attractive and intriguing, not for more important qualities. She seems spoiled and selfish.
She scores a great victory at the dance. She really does have the power to charm and captivate.	She wastes her time in daydreaming about things she can't have, and she whines because she is unhappy.
Once she loses the necklace, she and her husband become poor and deprived. But she does "her share . . . completely, heroically" (paragraph 98) to make up for the loss.	Even though the Loisels live poorly, Mathilde manipulates her husband into giving her more money than they can afford for a party dress.
Even when she is poor, she dreams about that marvelous, shining moment at the great ball. This is pathetic, because Mathilde gets worse than she deserves.	She assumes that her friend Jeanne would think her a thief if she admitted losing the necklace. Shouldn't she have had more confidence in Jeanne?
At the end, after everything is paid back, and her reputation is secure, Mathilde confesses the loss to Jeanne.	She becomes loud and coarse and haggles about pennies, thus undergoing a cheapening of her person and manner.

By putting contrasting observations side by side in this way, you will find that ideas will start to come naturally and will be helpful to you when you begin writing, regardless of how you finally organize your essay. It is possible, for example, that you might develop either column as the argumentative basis of an essay, or you might use your notes to support the idea that Mathilde is too complex to be either wholly admired or wholly condemned. You might also want to introduce an entirely new topic of development—for example, that Mathilde should be pitied rather than condemned or admired. In short, arranging materials in the plus-minus pattern is a powerful way to discover ideas—a truly helpful habit of promoting thought—that can lead to ways of development that you do not at first realize.

Originate and Develop Your Thoughts Through Writing

You should always write down what you are thinking for, as a principle, *unwritten thought is incomplete thought.* Make a practice of writing your observations about the work, in addition to any questions that occur to you. This is an exciting step in preliminary writing because it can be useful when you write later drafts. You will discover that looking at what you have written can not only enable you to correct and improve the writing you have done but also lead you to recognize that you need more. The process goes just about like this: "Something needs to be added here—important details that my reader will not have noticed, new support for my argument, a new idea that has just occurred to me, a significant connection to link my thoughts." If you follow such a process, you will be using your own written ideas to create new ideas. You will be advancing your own abilities as a thinker and writer.

The processes just described of searching for ideas, or brainstorming, are useful for you at any stage of composition. Even when you are fairly close to finishing your essay, you might suddenly recognize that you need to add something more (or subtract something you don't like). When that happens, you may return to the discovery or brainstorming process to initiate and develop new ideas and new arguments.

Making an Initial Draft of Your Essay

As you use the brainstorming and focusing techniques, you are also in fact beginning your essay. You will need to revise your ideas as connections among them become clearer and as you reexamine the work to discover details to support the argument you are making. By this stage, however, you already have many of the raw materials you need for developing your topic.

Base Your Essay on a Central Idea, Argument, or Statement

By definition, an essay *is an organized, connected, and fully developed set of paragraphs that expand on a* **central idea, central argument,** or **central statement.** All parts of an essay should contribute to the reader's understanding of the idea.

To achieve unity and completeness, each paragraph refers to the argument and demonstrates how selected details from the work relate to it and support it. The central idea helps you control and shape your essay, just as it also provides guidance for your reader.

A successful essay about literature is a brief but thorough (not exhaustive) examination of a literary work in light of topics like those we have already raised—from character, background, and economic conditions to circumstances of gender, major ideas, artistic qualities, and any additional topic such as point of view and symbolism. Central ideas or arguments might be (1) that a character is strong and tenacious, or (2) that the story shows the unpredictability of action, or (3) that the point of view makes the action seem "distant and objective," or (4) that a major symbol governs the actions and thoughts of the major characters. In essays on these topics, all materials must be tied to such central ideas or arguments. Thus, it is a fact that Mathilde in "The Necklace" endures ten years of slavish work and sacrifice as she and her husband accumulate enough money to repay their monumental debt. This we know, but it is not relevant to an essay on her character unless you connect it by a central argument showing how it demonstrates one of her major traits—her growing strength and perseverance.

Look through all of your ideas for one or two that catch your eye for development. In all the early stages of preliminary writing, the chances are that you have already discovered at least a few ideas that are more thought provoking, or more important, than the others.

Once you choose an idea you think you can work with, write it as a complete sentence that is essential to the argument of your essay. A simple phrase such as "setting and character" does not focus thought the way a sentence does. The following sentence moves the topic toward new exploration and discovery because it combines a topic with an outcome: "The setting of 'The Necklace' reflects Mathilde's character." You can choose to be even more specific: "Mathilde's strengths and weaknesses are reflected in the real and imaginary places in 'The Necklace.'"

Now that you have phrased a single, central idea or argument for your essay, you have also established a guide by which you can accept, reject, rearrange, and change the ideas you have been planning to develop. You can now draft a few paragraphs (which you may base on some of the sketches you have already made; always use as much as you can of your early observations) to see whether your idea seems valid, or you can decide that it would be more helpful to make an outline or a list before you do more writing. In either case, you should use your notes for evidence to connect to your central idea. If you need to bolster your argument with more supporting details and ideas, go once again to the techniques of discovery and brainstorming.

Using the central idea that the changes in the story's settings reflect Mathilde's character might produce a paragraph like the following, which presents an argument about her negative qualities:

> The original apartment in the Street of Martyrs and the dream world of wealthy places both show negative sides of Mathilde's character. The real-life apartment, though livable, is shabby. The furnishings all bring out her discontent. The shabbiness

THE NEED FOR A SOUND ARGUMENT IN ESSAYS ABOUT LITERATURE

As you write about literature, you should always try to connect your explanations to a specific argument; that is, you are writing about a specific work, but you are trying to prove—or argue—or demonstrate—a point or idea about it. This book provides you with a number of separate subjects relating to the study of literature. As you select one of these and begin writing, however, you are not to explain just that such-and-such a story has a character who changes and grows, or that such-and-such a poem contains the thought that nature creates great beauty. Rather, you should assert the importance of your topic to the work as a whole in relation to a specific point or argument. One example of an argument might be that a story's first-person point of view permits readers to draw their own conclusions about the speaker's character. Another argument might be that the poet's thought is shown in a poem's details about the bustling sounds and sights of animals in springtime.

Let us therefore repeat and stress that your writing *should always have an argumentative edge*—a goal of demonstrating the truth of your conclusions and clarifying and illuminating your idea about the topic and also about the work. It is here that the accuracy of your choices of details from the work, the soundness of your conclusions, and the cumulative weight of your evidence are essential. You cannot allow your main ideas to rest on one detail alone, but must support your conclusions by showing that the bulk of material leads to them and that they are linked in a reasonable chain of fact and logic. It is such clarification that is the goal of argumentation.

makes her think only of luxuriousness, and having one servant girl causes her to dream of having many servants. The luxury of her dream life heightens her unhappiness with what she actually has.

In such a preliminary draft, in which the purpose is to connect details and thoughts to the major idea, many details from the story are used in support. In the final draft, this kind of support is essential.

Create a Thesis Sentence as Your Guide to Organization

With your central idea or argument as your focus, you can decide which of the earlier observations and ideas can be developed further. Your goal is to establish a number of major topics to support your argument and to express them in a **thesis sentence** or **thesis statement**—an organizing sentence that contains the major topics you plan to treat in your essay. Suppose you choose three ideas from your discovery stage of development. If you put the central idea at the left and the list of topics at the right, you have the shape of the thesis sentence. Note that the first two topics below are taken from the discovery paragraph.

CENTRAL IDEA	TOPICS
The setting of "The Necklace" reflects Mathilde's character.	1. First apartment 2. Dream-life mansion rooms 3. Attic flat

This arrangement leads to the following thesis statement or thesis sentence.

> Mathilde's character growth is connected to her first apartment, her dream-life mansion rooms, and her attic flat.

You can revise the thesis sentence at any stage of the writing process if you find that you do not have enough evidence from the work to support it. Perhaps a new topic will occur to you, and you can include it, appropriately, as a part of your thesis sentence.

As we have seen, the central idea or central argument is the *glue* of the essay. The thesis sentence lists the parts to be fastened together—that is, the topics in which the central idea is to be demonstrated and argued. To alert your readers to your essay's structure, the thesis sentence is usually placed at the end of the introductory paragraph, just before the body of the essay.

As you write your first draft, you need to support the points of your thesis sentence with your notes and discovery materials. You can alter, reject, and rearrange ideas and details as you wish, as long as you change your thesis sentence to account for the changes (a major reason why many writers write their introductions last). The thesis sentence just shown contains three topics (it could be two, or four, or more) to be used in forming the body of the essay.

Begin Each Paragraph with a Topic Sentence

Just as the organization of the *entire essay* is based on the thesis, the form of each *paragraph* is based on its **topic sentence**—an assertion about how a topic from the predicate of the thesis statement supports the argument contained or implied in the central idea. The first topic in our example is the relationship of Mathilde's character to her first apartment, and the resulting paragraph should emphasize this relationship. If your topic is the coarsening of her character during the ten-year travail, you can then form a topic sentence by connecting the trait with the location, as follows:

> The attic flat reflects the coarsening of Mathilde's character.

Beginning with this sentence, the paragraph will present details that argue how Mathilde's rough, heavy housework changes her behavior, appearance, and general outlook.

Select Only One Topic—No More—for Each Paragraph

You should treat each separate topic in a single paragraph—one topic, one paragraph. However, if a topic seems especially difficult, long, and heavily detailed, you can divide it into two or more subtopics, each receiving a separate paragraph of its own—two or more subtopics, two or more separate paragraphs. Should you

REFERRING TO THE NAMES OF AUTHORS

As a general principle, for both men and women writers, you should regularly include the author's *full name* in the *first sentence* of your essay. Here are model first sentences.

> Shirley Jackson's "The Lottery" is a story featuring both suspense and horror.

> "The Lottery," by Shirley Jackson, is a story featuring both suspense and horror.

For all later references, use only last names, such as *Jackson, Maupassant, Lawrence,* or *Porter.* However, for the "giants" of literature, you should use the last names exclusively. In referring to writers like Shakespeare and Dickinson, for example, there is no need to include *William* or *Emily.*

In spite of today's informal standards, never use an author's first name alone, as in "*Shirley* skillfully creates suspense and horror in 'The Lottery.'" Also, do not use a courtesy title before the names of dead authors, such as "*Ms.* Jackson's 'The Lottery' is a suspenseful horror story," or "*Mr.* Shakespeare's idea is that information is uncertain." Use the last names alone.

As with all conventions, of course, there are exceptions. If you are referring to a childhood work of a writer, the first name might be appropriate, but be sure to shift to the last name when referring to the writer's mature works. If your writer has a professional or a noble title, such as "*Lord* Byron" or "*Queen* Elizabeth," it is not improper to use the title. Even then, however, the titles are commonly omitted for males, so that most references to Lord Byron and Alfred, Lord Tennyson, should be simply to "Byron" and "Tennyson."

Referring to living authors is somewhat problematical. Some journals and newspapers often use the courtesy titles *Mr.* and *Ms.* in their reviews. However, scholarly journals, which are likely to remain on library shelves and Web sites for many decades, follow the general principle of beginning with the entire name and then using only the last name for later references.

make this division, your topic then is really a section, and each paragraph in the section should have its own topic sentence.

Use Your Topic Sentences as the Arguments for Your Paragraph Development

Once you create a topic sentence, you can use it to focus your observations and conclusions. Let us see how our topic about the attic flat can be developed in a paragraph of argument:

> The attic flat reflects the coarsening of Mathilde's character. Maupassant emphasizes the burdens Mathilde endures to save money, such as mopping floors, cleaning greasy and encrusted pots and pans, taking out the garbage, and washing clothes and dishes by hand. This work makes her rough and coarse, an effect also shown by her giving up care of her hair and hands, wearing the cheapest dresses possible, haggling with the local shopkeepers, and becoming loud and penny-pinching. If at the beginning she is delicate and attractive, at the end she is unpleasant and coarse.

THE USE OF VERB TENSES IN THE DISCUSSION OF LITERARY WORKS

Literary works spring into life with each and every reading. You may thus assume that everything happening takes place in the present, and when writing about literature you should use the *present tense of verbs*. It is correct to say, "Mathilde and her husband *work* and *economize* [not *worked* and *economized*] for ten years to pay off the 18,000-franc loan they *take out* [not *took out*] to pay for the lost necklace."

When you consider an author's ideas, the present tense is also proper, on the principle that the words of an author are just as alive and current today (and tomorrow) as they were at the moment of writing, even if this same author might have been dead for hundreds or even thousands of years.

Because it is incorrect to shift tenses inappropriately, you may encounter a problem when you refer to actions that have occurred prior to the time of the main action. An instance is Bierce's "An Occurrence at Owl Creek Bridge" (Chapter 1), in which the main character, a Southern gentleman during the Civil War, is about to be hanged by Union soldiers because he tried to sabotage a strategically important bridge. The story emphasizes the relationship between cause (the attempted sabotage, occurring in the past) and effect (the punishment, occurring in the present). In discussing such a narrative it is important to keep details in order, and thus you can introduce the past tense as long as you make the relationship clear between past and present, as in this example: "Farquhar *is actually hanged* [present tense] by the Union soldiers. But his perceptions *turn him* [present tense] toward the past, and his final thoughts *dwell* [present tense] on the life and happiness he *knew* [past tense] at his own home with his dearest wife." This intermingling of past and present tenses is correct because it corresponds to the pattern of time brought out in the story.

A problem also arises when you introduce historical or biographical details about a work or author. It is appropriate to use the *past tense* for such details if they genuinely do belong to the past. Thus it is correct to state, "Shakespeare *lived* from 1564 to 1616," or that "Shakespeare *wrote* his tragedy *Hamlet* in about 1600–1601." It is also permissible to mix past and present tenses when you are treating historical facts about a literary work and are also considering it as a living text. Of prime importance is to keep things straight. Here is an example showing how past tenses (in bold) and present tenses (in italic) may be used when appropriate:

> Because *Hamlet* **was** first **performed** in about 1601, Shakespeare most probably **wrote** it shortly before this time. In the play, a tragedy, Shakespeare *treats* an act of vengeance, but more importantly he *demonstrates* the difficulty of ever learning the exact truth. The hero, Prince Hamlet, *is* the focus of this difficulty, for the task of revenge *is assigned* to him by the Ghost of his father. Though the Ghost *claims* that his brother, Claudius, *is* his murderer, Hamlet *is* not able to verify this claim.

Here, the historical details are in the past tense, while all details about the play *Hamlet*, including Shakespeare as the creating author whose ideas and words are still alive, are in the present.

As a general principle, you will be right most of the time if you use the present tense exclusively for literary details and the past tense for historical details. When in doubt, however, *consult your instructor*.

Here, details from the story are introduced to provide support for the topic sentence. All the subjects—the hard work, the lack of personal care, the wearing of cheap dresses, and the haggling with the shopkeepers—are introduced not to retell the story but rather to exemplify the argument the writer is making about Mathilde's character.

Develop an Outline as the Means of Organizing Your Essay

So far we have been creating a de facto **outline**—that is, a skeletal plan of organization. Some writers never use any outline but prefer informal lists of ideas; others always rely on outlines; still others insist that they cannot make an outline until they have finished writing. And then there are those writers who simply hate outlines. Regardless of your preference, your final essay should have a tight structure. Therefore, you should use a guiding outline to develop and shape your essay.

The outline we focus on here is the **analytical sentence outline.** This type is easier to create than it sounds. It consists of (1) an introduction, including the central idea and the thesis sentence, together with (2) topic sentences that are to be used in each paragraph of the body, followed by (3) a conclusion. When applied to the subject we have been developing, such an outline looks like this:

TITLE: *How Setting in "The Necklace" Is Connected to Mathilde's Character*

1. **Introduction**
   a. *Central idea*: Maupassant uses setting to show Mathilde's character.
   b. *Thesis statement*: Her character growth is brought out by her first apartment, her daydreams about elegant rooms in a mansion, and her attic flat.
2. **Body:** *Topic sentences* a, b, and c (and d, e, and f, if necessary)
   a. Details about her first apartment explain her dissatisfaction and depression.
   b. Her daydreams about mansion rooms are like the apartment because they too make her unhappy.
   c. The attic flat reflects the coarsening of her character.
3. **Conclusion** *Topic sentence*: All details in the story, particularly the setting, are focused on the character of Mathilde.

The *conclusion* may be a summary of the body; it may evaluate the main idea; it may briefly suggest further points of discussion; or it may be a reflection on the details of the body.

The illustrative essays included throughout this book are organized according to the principles of the analytical sentence outline. To emphasize the shaping effect of these outlines, all central ideas, thesis sentences, and topic sentences are underlined. In your own writing, you can underline or italicize these "skeletal" sentences as a check on your organization. Unless your instructor requires such markings, however, remove them in your final drafts.

Illustrative Student Essay (First Draft)

The following illustrative essay is a first draft of the subject we have been developing. It follows our outline, and it includes details from the story in support of the various topics. It is by no means, however, as good a piece of writing as it could be. The draft omits a topic, some additional details, and some new insights that are included in the second draft, which follows later (pp. 45–48). It therefore reveals the need to make improvements through additional brainstorming and discovery-prewriting techniques.

Underlined sentences in this paper *do not* conform to MLA style and are used solely as teaching tools to emphasize the central idea, thesis sentence, and topic sentences throughout the paper.

Deal 1

James Deal

Professor Smith

English 102

16 April 2008

How Setting in "The Necklace" Is Related
to the Character of Mathilde

Explain what setting is used for?

Does Mathilde's character grow or change?

More specific word needed

[1] In "The Necklace" Guy de Maupassant does not give much detail about the setting. He does not even describe the necklace itself, which is the central object in his plot, but he says only that it is "superb" (paragraph 47). Rather, he uses the setting to reflect the character of the central figure, Mathilde Loisel.* All his details are presented to bring out her traits. Her character growth is related to her first apartment, her dream-life mansion rooms, and her attic flat.†

Explain her reaction to this

Dissatisfaction is with husband or her life?

[2] Details about her first apartment explain her dissatisfaction and depression. The walls are "drab," the furniture "threadbare," and the curtains "ugly" (paragraph 3). There is only a simple country girl to do the housework. The tablecloth is not changed daily, and the best dinner dish is beef stew. Mathilde has no evening clothes, only a theater dress that she does not like. These details show her dissatisfaction about her life with her low-salaried husband.

*Central idea
†Thesis sentence

Deal 2

[3] Her dream-life images of wealth are like the apartment because they too make her unhappy. In her daydreams about life in a mansion, the rooms are large, filled with expensive furniture and bric-a-brac, and draped in silk. She imagines private rooms for intimate talks, and big dinners with delicacies like trout and quail. With dreams of such a rich home, she feels even more despair about her modest apartment on the Street of Martyrs in Paris.

Be more specific about her dream world

Quote from story?

[4] The attic flat reflects the coarsening of Mathilde's character. Maupassant emphasizes the burdens she endures to save money, such as mopping floors, cleaning greasy and encrusted pots and pans, taking out the garbage, and washing clothes and dishes by hand. This work makes her rough and coarse, a fact also shown by her giving up care of her hair and hands, wearing the cheapest dresses possible, haggling with local shopkeepers, and becoming loud and penny-pinching. If at the beginning she is delicate and attractive, at the end she is unpleasant and coarse.

What else does the attic flat indicate about Mathilde? (Her work ethic?)

Perhaps a paragraph about her walk on the Champs-Elysees

[5] Maupassant focuses everything in the story, including the setting, on the character of Mathilde. He does not add anything extra. Thus he says little about the big party scene, but emphasizes the necessary detail that Mathilde was a great "success" (paragraph 52). It is this detail that brings out some of her early attractiveness and charm, despite her more usual frustration and unhappiness. Thus in "The Necklace," Maupassant uses setting as a means to his end—the story of Mathilde and her unnecessary sacrifice.

Any other details that highlight Mathilde's character?

Good first draft. Work on more specific topic sentences and more details in body paragraphs. Make sure details in body paragraphs are related to topic sentences. You may wish to include another paragraph about the walk on the Champs-Elysees.

Deal 3

Work Cited

Maupassant, Guy de. "The Necklace." Literature: An Introduction to Reading and Writing, Ed. Edgar V. Roberts. 9th ed. New York: Pearson Longman, 2009. 5–12.

Completing the Essay: Developing and Strengthening Your Essay Through Revision

After finishing your first draft, like this one, you may wonder what more you can do. Things may seem to be complete as they are, and that's it. You have read the work several times, have used discovering and brainstorming techniques to establish ideas to write about, have made an outline of your ideas, and have written a full draft. How can you do better?

The best way to begin is to observe that a major mistake writers make when writing about literature is to do no more than retell a story or summarize an idea. Retelling a story shows only that you have read it, not that you have thought about it. Writing a good essay requires you to arrange a pattern of argument and thought.

Make Your Own Arrangement of Details and Ideas

One way to escape the trap of summarizing stories and to set up a pattern of development is to stress your own order when referring to parts of a work. Rearrange details to suit your own central idea or argument. It is often important to write first about the conclusion or middle. Should you find that you have followed the chronological order of the work instead of stressing your own order, you can use one of the preliminary writing techniques to figure out new ways to connect your materials. The principle is that you should introduce details about the work *only* to support the points you wish to make. Details for the sake of detail are unnecessary.

Use Literary Material as Evidence to Support Your Argument

When you write, you are like a detective using clues as evidence for building a case, or a lawyer citing evidence to support an argument. Your goal is to convince your readers of your knowledge and the reasonableness of your conclusions. It is vital to use evidence convincingly so that your readers can follow your ideas. Let us look briefly at two drafts of a new example to see how writing can be improved by the pointed use of details. These are from drafts of an essay on the character of Mathilde.

PARAGRAPH 1

The major flaw of Mathilde's character is that she seems to be isolated, locked away from other people. She and her husband do not talk to each other much, except about external things. He speaks about his liking for beef stew, and she states that she cannot accept the big invitation because she has no nice dresses. Once she gets the dress, she complains because she has no jewelry. Even when borrowing the necklace from Jeanne

PARAGRAPH 2

The major flaw of Mathilde's character is that she is withdrawn and uncommunicative, apparently unwilling or unable to form an intimate relationship. For example, she and her husband do not talk to each other much, except about external things such as his taste for beef stew and her lack of a party dress and jewelry. With such an uncommunicative marriage, one might suppose that she would be more open with her close friend,

Forrestier, she does not say much. When she and her husband discover that the necklace is lost, they simply go over the details, and Loisel dictates a letter of explanation, which Mathilde writes in her own hand. Even when she meets Jeanne on the Champs-Elysées, Mathilde does not say a great deal about her life but only goes through enough details about the loss and replacement of the necklace to make Jeanne exclaim about the needlessness of the ten-year sacrifice.

Jeanne Forrestier, but Mathilde does not say much even to her. This flaw hurts her greatly, because if she were more open she might have explained the loss and avoided the horrible sacrifice. This lack of openness, along with her self-indulgent dreaminess, is her biggest defect.

A comparison of these paragraphs shows that the first has more words than the second (157 compared to 120) but that it is more appropriate for a rough than a final draft because the writer does little more than retell the story. Paragraph 1 is cluttered with details that do not support any conclusions. If you try to find what it says about Maupassant's actual use of Mathilde's solitary traits in "The Necklace," you will get little help. The writer needs to revise the paragraph by eliminating details that do not support the central idea.

On the other hand, the details in paragraph 2 actually do support the declared topic. Phrases such as "for example," "with such," and "this lack" show that the writer of paragraph 2 has assumed that the audience knows the story and now wants to read an argument in support of a particular interpretation. Paragraph 2 therefore guides readers by connecting the details to the topic. It uses these details as evidence, *not* as a retelling of actions. By contrast, paragraph 1 recounts a number of relevant actions *but does not connect them to the topic.* More details, of course, could have been added to the second paragraph, but they are unnecessary because the paragraph develops the argument with the details used. Good writing has many qualities, but one of the most important is shown in a comparison of the two paragraphs: *In good writing, no details are included unless they are used as supporting evidence in a pattern of thought and argument.*

Always Keep to Your Point; Stick to It Tenaciously

To show another distinction between first- and second-draft writing, let us consider a third example. The following unrevised paragraph, in which the writer assumes an audience that is interested in the relationship of economics to literature, is drawn from an essay about the idea of economic determinism in Maupassant's "The Necklace." In this paragraph the writer is trying to argue the point that economic circumstances underlie a number of incidents in the story. The idea is to assert that Mathilde's difficulties result not from her character traits but rather from her financial restrictions.

> More important than chance in governing life is the idea that people are controlled by economic circumstances. Mathilde, as is shown at the story's opening, is born poor. Therefore she doesn't get the right doors opened for her, and she settles down to marriage with a

minor clerk, Loisel. With a vivid imagination and a burning desire for luxury, seeming to be born only for a life of ease and wealth, she finds that her poor home brings out her daydreams of expensive surroundings. She taunts her husband when he brings the big invitation, because she does not have a suitable (that is, "expensive") dress. Once she gets the dress it is jewelry she lacks, and she borrows that and loses it. The loss of the necklace means great trouble because it forces the Loisels to borrow heavily and to struggle financially for ten years.

This paragraph begins with an effective topic sentence, indicating that the writer has a good plan. The remaining part, however, shows how easily writers can be diverted from their objective. The flaw is that the material of the paragraph, while accurate, is not clearly connected to the topic. Once the second sentence is under way, the paragraph gets lost in a retelling of events, and the promising topic sentence is forgotten. The paragraph therefore shows that the use of detail alone will not support an intended meaning or argument. *As a writer, you must do the connecting yourself, and make sure that all relationships are explicitly clear.* This point cannot be overstressed.

Let us see how the problem can be treated. If the ideal paragraph can be schematized with line drawings, we might say that the paragraph's topic should be a straight line, moving toward and reaching a specific goal (the topic or argument of the paragraph), with an exemplifying line moving away from the straight line briefly to bring in evidence but returning to the line to demonstrate the relevance of each new fact. Thus, the ideal scheme looks like this, with a straight line touched a number of times by an undulating line:

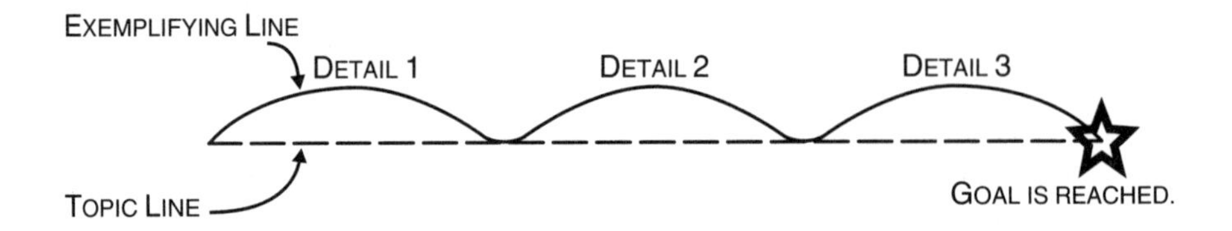

Notice that the exemplifying line, fluctuating to illustrate how documentation or exemplification is to be used, always returns to the topic line. A visual scheme for the faulty paragraph on "The Necklace," however, looks like this, with the line never returning but flying out into space.

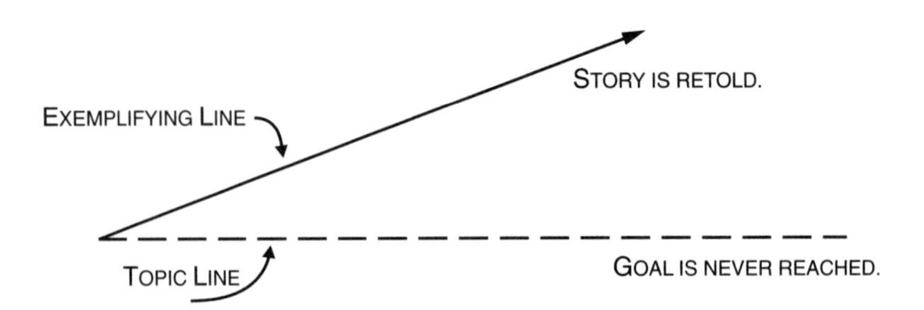

How might the faulty paragraph be improved? The best way is to remind the reader again and again of the topic and to use examples from the text in support.

As our model wavy-line diagram indicates, each time a topic is mentioned, the undulating line merges with the straight, or central-idea line. This relationship of argument to illustrative examples should prevail no matter what subject you write about, and you have to be tenacious in forming these connecting relationships. If you are analyzing *point of view*, for example, you should keep connecting your material to the speaker, or narrator, and the same applies to topics such as character, idea, or setting. According to this principle, we might revise the paragraph on economic determinism in "The Necklace" as follows. (Parts of sentences stressing the relationship of the examples to the topic sentence are underlined.)

> *More important than chance in governing life is the idea that people are controlled by economic circumstances.* As illustration, the speaker begins by emphasizing that Mathilde, the main character, is born poor. Therefore she doesn't get the right doors opened for her, and she settles down to marriage with a minor clerk, Loisel. In keeping with the idea, her vivid imagination and burning desire for luxury feed on her weakness of character as she feels deep unhappiness and depression because of the contrast between her daydreams of expensive surroundings and the poor home she actually has. These straitened economic circumstances inhibit her relationship with her husband, and she taunts him when he brings the big invitation because she does not have a suitable (that is, "expensive") dress. As a merging of her unrealistic dream life with actual reality, her borrowing of the necklace suggests the impossibility of overcoming economic restrictions. In the context of the idea, the ten-year sacrifice to pay for the lost necklace demonstrates that being poor keeps people down, destroying their dreams and their hopes for a better life.

The paragraph now successfully develops the argument promised by the topic sentence. While it has also been lengthened, the length has been caused not by inessential detail but by phrases and sentences that give form and direction. You might object that if you lengthened all your paragraphs in this way, your essays would grow too bulky. The answer is to reduce the number of major points and paragraphs, on the theory that *it is better to develop a few topics pointedly than to develop many pointlessly*. Revising for the purpose of strengthening central and topic ideas requires that you either throw out some topics or else incorporate them as subpoints in the topics you keep. To control your writing in this way can result only in improvement.

Check Your Development and Organization

It bears repeating over and over again that the first requirement of a good essay is to introduce a central idea or argument and then stick to it. Another major step toward excellence is to make your central idea expand and grow. The word *growth* is a metaphor describing the disclosure of ideas that were not at first noticeable, together with the expression of original, new, and fresh interpretations.

Try to Be Original

In everything you write, now and in the future, you should always try to be original. You might claim that originality is impossible because you are writing about someone else's work. "The author has said everything," might be the argument, "and therefore I can do little more than follow the story." This claim rests on the mistaken assumption that you have no choice in selecting material and no opportunity to have individual thoughts and make original contributions.

But you do have choices and opportunities to be original. You really do. One obvious area of originality is the development and formulation of your central idea. For example, a natural first response to "The Necklace" is "The story is about a woman who loses a borrowed necklace and endures hardship to help pay for it." But this response does not promise an argument because it refers only to events in the story and not to any idea. You can point the sentence toward an argument, however, if you call the hardship "needless." Just this word alone demands that you explain the differences between needed and unneeded hardships, and your application of these differences to the heroine's plight would produce an original essay. Even better and more original insights could result if the topic of the budding essay were to connect the dreamy, withdrawn traits of the main character to her misfortunes. A resulting central idea might be "People themselves create their own difficulties." Such an argument would require you to define not only the personal but also the representative nature of Mathilde's experiences, an avenue of exploration that could produce much in the way of a fresh, original essay about "The Necklace."

You can also develop your ability to treat your subject originally if you plan the body of the essay to build up to what you think is your most important and incisive idea. As examples of such planning, the following brief outline suggests how a central idea can be widened and expanded:

ARGUMENT: ***Mathilde Grows as a Character in "The Necklace"***

1. She has normal daydreams about a better life.
2. In trying to make her daydreams seem real, she takes a risk but then loses.
3. She develops by facing her mistake and working hard to correct it.

The list shows how you can enlarge a subject if you treat your exemplifying details in an increasing order of importance. In this case, the order moves from Mathilde's habit of daydreaming to her growing strength of character. The pattern shows how you can meet two primary standards of excellence in writing—organization and growth.

Clearly, you should always try to develop your central idea or argument. Constantly adhere to your topic, and constantly develop it. Nurture it and make it grow. Admittedly, in a short essay you will be able to move only a short distance with an idea or argument, but you should never be satisfied to leave the idea exactly where you found it. To the degree that you can learn to develop your ideas, you will receive recognition for increasingly original writing.

Write with Specific Readers as Your Intended Audience

Whenever you write, you must decide how much detail to discuss. Usually you base this decision on your judgment of your readers. For example, if you assume that they have not read the work, you will need to include a short summary as background. Otherwise, they may not understand your argument.

Consider, too, whether your readers have any special interests or concerns. If they are particularly interested in politics, sociology, religion, or psychology, for example, you may need to select and develop your materials along one of these lines.

Your instructor will let you know who your audience is. Usually, it will be your instructor or your fellow students. They will be familiar with the work and will not expect you to retell a story or summarize an argument. Rather, they will want you to explain and interpret the work in the light of your main assertions about it. Thus, you can omit details that do not exemplify and support your argument, even if these details are important parts of the work. What you write should always be based on your developing idea together with your assessment of your readers.

Use Exact, Comprehensive, and Forceful Language

In addition to being original, organized, and well-developed, the best writing is exact, comprehensive, and forceful. At any stage of the composition process, you should try to correct and improve your earliest sentences and paragraphs, which usually need to be rethought, reworded, and rearranged.

Try to make your sentences meaningful. First, ask yourself whether your sentences mean what you really intend, or whether you can make them more exact and therefore stronger. For example, consider these two sentences from essays about "The Necklace":

1. It seems as though the main character's dreams of luxury cause her to respond as she does in the story.
2. This incident, although it may seem trivial or unimportant, has substantial significance in the creation of the story; by this I mean the incident that occurred is essentially what the story is all about.

These sentences are inexact and vague and therefore are unhelpful. Neither of them goes anywhere. Sentence 1 is satisfactory up to the verb *cause*, but then it falls apart because the writer has lost sight of an argumentative or thematic purpose. It would be better to describe what the response *is* rather than to say nothing more than that some kind of response *exists*. To make the sentence more exact, we might try the following revision.

> Mathilde's dreams of luxury make her dissatisfied with her own possessions, and therefore she goes beyond her financial means to attend the big party.

With this revision, the writer could readily go on to consider the relationship of the early part of the story to the later parts. Without the revision, it is not clear where the writer might go.

Sentence 2 is vague because the writer has lost all contact with the main thread of argument. If we adopt the principle of trying to be exact, however, we can create more meaning and more promise:

> The accidental loss of the necklace, which is trivial though costly, supports the narrator's claim that major turns in life are produced not by earthshaking events but rather by minor ones.

In addition to working for exactness, try to make sentences—all sentences, but particularly thesis and topic sentences—complete and comprehensive. Consider the following sentence:

> The idea in "The Necklace" is that Mathilde and her husband work hard to pay for the lost necklace.

Although this sentence promises to describe an idea, it does no more than state the story's major action. It needs additional rethinking and rephrasing to make it more comprehensive, as in these two revisions:

1. In "The Necklace" Maupassant brings out the importance of overcoming mistakes through hard work and responsibility.
2. Maupassant's surprise ending in "The Necklace" symbolizes the need for always being truthful.

Both new sentences are connected to the action described by the original phrasing, "Mathilde and her husband work hard to pay for the lost necklace," although they point toward differing treatments. The first sentence concerns the virtue shown by the Loisels in their sacrifice. Because the second sentence includes the word *symbolizes*, an essay stemming from it would stress the Loisels' mistake in not confessing the loss. In dealing with the symbolic meaning of their failure, an essay developed along the lines of the second sentence would focus on the negative sides of their characters, and an essay developed from the first sentence would stress their positive sides. Both of the revised sentences, therefore, are more comprehensive than the original sentence and thus would help a writer get on the track toward a thoughtful and analytical essay.

Of course, creating fine sentences is never easy, but as a mode of improvement, you might use some self-testing mechanisms:

- *For story materials*. Always relate the materials to a point or argument. Do not say simply, "Mathilde works constantly for ten years to help pay off the debt." Instead, blend the material into a point, like this: "Mathilde's ten-year effort shows her resolution to overcome the horror of indebtedness," or "Mathilde's ten-year effort brings out her strength of character."
- *For responses and impressions*. Do not say simply, "The story's ending left me with a definite impression." What are you giving your readers with a sentence like this? They want to know what your impression is, and therefore you need to describe it, as in the following: "The story's ending surprised me and also made me sympathetic to the major character," or "The story's ending struck me with the idea that life is unpredictable and unfair."
- *For ideas*. Make the idea clear and direct. Do not say, "Mathilde lives in a poor household," but rather refer to the story to bring out an idea, as follows: "Mathilde's story shows that economic deprivation hurts a person's quality of life."
- *For critical commentary*. Do not be satisfied with a statement such as "I found 'The Necklace' interesting." All right, the story is interesting, but what does that tell us? Instead, try to describe *what* was interesting and *why* it was interesting, as in this sentence: "I found 'The Necklace' interesting because it shows how chance and bad luck may disrupt or even destroy people's lives."

Good writing begins with attempts, like these, to rephrase sentences to make them really say something. If you always name and pin down descriptions, responses, and judgments, no matter how difficult the task seems, your sentences can be strong and forceful because you will be making them exact and comprehensive.

Illustrative Student Essay (Improved Draft)

If you refer again to the first draft of the essay about Maupassant's use of setting to illustrate Mathilde's character (pp. 36–37), you might notice that several parts of the draft need extensive reworking and revising. For example, paragraph 2 contains a series of short, unconnected comments; and the last sentence of that paragraph implies that Mathilde's dissatisfaction relates mainly to her husband rather than to her general circumstances. Paragraph 4 focuses too much on Mathilde's coarseness and not enough on her sacrifice and cooperation. The first draft also ignores the fact that the story ends in another location—the fashionable Parisian street the Champs-Elysées, where Maupassant continues to demonstrate the nature of Mathilde's character. Finally, there is not enough support in this draft for the contention (in paragraph 5) that everything in the story is related to the character of Mathilde.

To discover how these issues can be more fully considered, the following revision of the earlier draft creates more introductory detail, includes an additional paragraph, and reshapes each of the paragraphs to stress the relationship of the central idea or argument to the topics of the various paragraphs. Within the limits of a short assignment, the essay illustrates all the principles of organization and unity that we have been discussing here.

Underlined sentences in this paper *do not* conform to MLA style and are used solely as teaching tools to emphasize the central idea, thesis sentence, and topic sentences throughout the paper.

Deal 1

James Deal

Professor Smith

English 102

16 April 2008

How Maupassant Uses Setting in "The Necklace" to Show the Character of Mathilde

[1] In "The Necklace" Guy de Maupassant uses setting to reflect the character and development of the main character, Mathilde Loisel.* As a result, his

*Central idea.

Deal 2

setting is not particularly vivid or detailed. He does not even describe the ill-fated necklace--the central object in the story--but states only that it is "superb" (paragraph 47). In fact he includes descriptions of setting only if they illuminate qualities about Mathilde. Her changing character can be connected to the first apartment, the dream-life mansion rooms, the attic flat, and a fashionable public street.†

[2] Details about the modest apartment of the Loisels on the Street of Martyrs indicate Mathilde's peevish lack of adjustment to life. Though everything is serviceable, she is unhappy with the "drab" walls, "threadbare" furniture, and "ugly" curtains (paragraph 3). She has domestic help, but she wants more servants than the simple country girl who does the household chores in the apartment. Her embarrassment and dissatisfaction are shown by details of her irregularly cleaned tablecloth and the plain and inelegant beef stew that her husband adores. Even her best theater dress, which is appropriate for apartment life but which is inappropriate for more wealthy surroundings, makes her unhappy. All these details of the apartment establish that Mathilde's major trait at the story's beginning is maladjustment. She therefore seems unpleasant and unsympathetic.

[3] Like the real-life apartment, the impossibly wealthy setting of her daydreams about owning a mansion strengthens her unhappiness and her avoidance of reality. All the rooms of her fantasies are large and expensive, draped in silk and filled with nothing but the best furniture and bric-a-brac. Maupassant gives us the following description of her dream world:

> She imagined a gourmet-prepared main course carried on the most exquisite trays and served on the most beautiful dishes, with whispered gallantries that she would hear with a sphinxlike smile as she dined on the pink meat of a trout or the delicate wing of a quail. (paragraph 4)

With such impossible dreams, her despair is complete. Ironically, this despair, together with her inability to live with reality, brings about her undoing. It makes her agree to borrow the necklace (which is just as unreal as her

† **Thesis sentence.**

Deal 3

daydreams of wealth), and losing the necklace drives her into the reality of giving up her apartment and moving into the attic flat.

[4] Also ironically, the attic flat is related to the coarsening of her character while at the same time it brings out her best qualities of hard work and honesty. Maupassant emphasizes the drudgery of the work Mathilde endures to maintain the flat, such as walking up many stairs, washing floors with large buckets of water, cleaning greasy and encrusted pots and pans, taking out the garbage, washing clothes by hand, and haggling loudly with local shopkeepers. All this reflects her coarsening and loss of sensibility, also shown by her giving up hair and hand care and by wearing cheap dresses. The work she performs, however, makes her heroic (paragraph 98). As she cooperates to help her husband pay back the loans, her dreams of a mansion fade, and all she has left is the memory of her triumphant appearance at the Minister of Education's party. Thus the attic flat brings out her physical change for the worse at the same time that it also brings out her psychological change for the better.

[5] Her walk on the Champs-Elysées illustrates another combination of traits--self-indulgence and frankness. The Champs-Elysées is the most fashionable street in Paris, and her walk to it is similar to her earlier indulgences in her daydreams of upper-class wealth. But it is on this street where she meets Jeanne, and it is her frankness in confessing to Jeanne that makes her completely honest. While the walk thus serves as the occasion for the story's concluding surprise and irony, Mathilde's being on the Champs-Elysées is totally in character, in keeping with her earlier reveries about luxury.

[6] Other details in the story also have a similar bearing on Mathilde's character. For example, the story presents little detail about the party scene beyond the statement that Mathilde is a great "success" (paragraph 52)--a judgment that shows her ability to shine if given the chance. After she and Loisel accept the fact that the necklace cannot be found, Maupassant includes details about the Parisian streets, about the visits to loan sharks, and about the

Deal 4

jewelry shops in order to bring out Mathilde's sense of honesty and pride as she "heroically" prepares to live her new life of poverty. Thus, in "The Necklace," Maupassant uses setting to highlight Mathilde's maladjustment, her needless misfortune, her loss of youth and beauty, and finally her growth as a responsible human being.

Deal 5

Work Cited

Maupassant, Guy de. "The Necklace." Literature: An Introduction to Reading and Writing. Ed. Edgar V. Roberts. 9th ed. New York: Pearson Longman, 2009, 5–12.

Commentary on the Essay

Several improvements to the first draft are seen here. The language of paragraph 2 has been revised to show more clearly the inappropriateness of Mathilde's dissatisfaction. In paragraph 3, the irony of the story is brought out, and the writer has connected the details to the central idea in a richer pattern of ideas, showing the effects of Mathilde's despair. Paragraph 5—new in the improved draft—includes additional details about how Mathilde's walk on the Champs-Elysées is related to her character. In paragraph 6, the fact that Mathilde is able "to shine" at the dinner party is interpreted according to the central idea. Finally, the conclusion is now much more specific, summarizing the change in Mathilde's character rather than saying simply that the setting reveals "her needless misfortune." In short, the second draft reflects the complexity of "The Necklace" better than the first draft. Because the writer has revised the first-draft ideas about the story, the final essay is tightly structured, insightful, and forceful.

Essay Commentaries

Throughout this book, the illustrative essays are followed by short commentaries that show how the essays embody the chapter instructions and guidelines. For each essay that has a number of possible approaches, the commentary points out which one is used; and when an essay uses two or more approaches, the commentary makes this fact clear. In addition, each commentary singles out one of the paragraphs for more detailed analysis of its argument and use of detail. The commentaries will hence help you develop the insights necessary to use the essays as aids in your own study and writing.

A Summary of Guidelines

To sum up, follow these guidelines whenever you write about a story or any kind of literature:

- Do not simply retell the story or summarize the work. Bring in story materials only when you can use them as support for your central idea or argument.
- Throughout your essay, keep reminding your reader of your central idea.
- Within each paragraph, make sure that you stress your topic idea.
- Develop your subject. Make it bigger than it was when you began.
- Always make your statements exact, comprehensive, and forceful.
- And this bears repeating: Do not simply retell the story or summarize the work.

Writing Topics About the Writing Process

1. Write a brainstorming paragraph on the topic of anything in a literary work that you find especially good or interesting. Write as the thoughts occur to you; do not slow yourself down in an effort to make your writing seem perfect. You can make corrections and improvements later.
2. Using marginal and notebook notations, together with any additional thoughts, describe the way in which the author of a particular work has expressed important ideas and difficulties.
3. Create a plus-minus table to list your responses about a character or ideas in a work.
4. Raise questions about the actions of characters in a story or play in order to determine the various customs and manners of the society out of which the work is derived.
5. Analyze and explain the way in which the conflicts in a story or play are developed. What pattern or patterns do you find? Determine the relationship of the conflicts to the work's development, and fashion your idea of this relationship as an argument for a potential essay.
6. Basing your ideas on your marginal and notebook notations, select an idea and develop a thesis sentence from it, using your idea and a list of possible topics for an argument or central idea for an essay.
7. Using the thesis sentence you write for exercise 6, develop a brief analytical sentence outline that could help you in writing a full essay.

A Short Guide to the Use of References and Quotations in Essays About Literature

In establishing evidence for the points you make in your essays and essay examinations, you constantly need to refer to various parts of stories, plays, and poems. You also need to include shorter and longer quotations and to keep the time sequences straight within the works you are writing about. In addition, you may need to refer to biographical and historical details that have a bearing on the work or works you are studying. So that your own writing may flow as accurately and naturally as possible, you must be able to integrate these references and distinctions of time clearly and easily.

Integrate Passages and Ideas into Your Essay

Your essays should reflect your own thought as you study and analyze the characteristics, ideas, and qualities of an author's work. In a typical discussion of literature, you constantly need to introduce brief summaries, quotations, general interpretations, observations, and independent applications of everything you are discussing. It is not easy to keep these various elements integrated and to keep confusion from arising.

Distinguish Your Thoughts from Those of Your Author

Often a major problem is that it is hard for your reader to figure out when *your* ideas have stopped and your *author's* have begun. You must therefore arrange your sentences to make the distinctions clear, but you must also blend your materials so that your reader may follow you easily. Let us see an example of how such problems may be handled. Here, the writer being discussed is the Victorian poet Matthew Arnold (1822–1888). The passage moves from reference to Arnold's ideas to the essay writer's independent application of the ideas.

> [1] In his poem "Dover Beach," Arnold states that in past times religious faith was accepted as absolute truth. [2] To symbolize this idea he refers to the ocean, which surrounds all land, and the surf, which constantly rushes onto the earth's shores. [3] According to this symbolism, religious ideas are as vast as the ocean and as regular as the surf, and these ideas at one time constantly and irresistibly replenished people's lives. [4] Arnold's symbol of the flowing ocean changes, however, to a symbol of the ebbing ocean, thus illustrating his idea that belief and religious certainty were falling away. [5] It is this personal sense of spiritual emptiness that Arnold is associating with his own times, because what he describes, in keeping with the symbolism, is that in the present time the "drear" shoreline has been left vacant by the "melancholy long withdrawing roar" of retreat and reduction (lines 25–27).

This specimen paragraph combines but also separates paraphrase, interpretation, and quotation, and it thereby eliminates any possible confusion about the origin of the ideas and also about who is saying what. In the first three sentences the writer uses the phrases "Arnold states," "To symbolize this idea," and "According to this symbolism" to show clearly that interpretation is to follow. Although the fourth sentence marks a new direction of Arnold's ideas, it continues to separate restatement from interpretation. The fifth sentence indicates, through the phrase "in keeping with the symbolism," what seems to the writer to be the major idea of "Dover Beach."

Integrate Material by Using Quotation Marks

It is often necessary, and also interesting, to use short quotations from your author to illustrate and reinforce your ideas and interpretations. Here the problem of separating your thoughts from the author's is solved by quotation marks. In such an internal quotation, you may treat prose and poetry in the same way. If a poetic quotation extends from the end of one line to the beginning of another, however, indicate the line break with a virgule (/), and use a capital letter to begin the next line, as in the following:

> In "Lines Written in Early Spring" Wordsworth describes a condition in which his speaker is united with the surrounding natural world. Nature is a combination of the "thousand blended notes" of joyful birds (line 1) and the sights of "budding twigs" (line 17) and the "periwinkle" (line 10). In the exact words of the speaker, these "fair works" directly "link / The human soul that through me ran" (lines 5 and 6).

Blend Quotations into Your Own Sentences

The use of internal quotations still creates the problem of blending materials, however, for quotations should never be brought in unless you prepare your reader for them in some way. *Do not*, for example, use quotations in the following manner:

> Wordsworth states that his woodland grove is filled with the sounds of birds, the sights of flowers, and the feeling of the light wind, making for the thought that creatures of the natural world take pleasure in life. "The birds around me hopped and played."

This abrupt quotation throws the reader off balance because it is not blended into the previous sentence. It is necessary to prepare the reader to move from your discussion to the quotation, as in the following revision:

> Wordsworth claims that his woodland scene is made joyful by the surrounding flowers and the gentle breeze, causing his speaker, who states that "The birds around me hopped and played," to conclude that the natural world has resulted from a "holy plan" created by Nature.

Here the quotation is made an actual part of the sentence. This sort of blending is satisfactory, provided that the quotation is brief.

Indent Long Quotations and Set Them in Block Format

You can follow a general rule for incorporating quotations in your writing: Do not quote within a sentence any passage longer than twenty or twenty-five words (but consult your instructor, for the allowable number of words may vary). Quotations of greater length demand so much separate attention that they interfere with your own sentence. It is possible but not desirable to conclude one of your sentences with a quotation, but you should never make an extensive quotation in the *middle* of a sentence. By the time you finish such an unwieldy sentence, your reader will have lost sight of how it began. When your quotation is long, you should make a point of introducing it and setting it off separately as a block.

The physical layout of block quotations should be this: Double-space the quotation (like the rest of your essay), and indent it ten spaces from your left margin to distinguish it from your own writing. You might use fewer spaces for longer lines of poetry, but the standard should always be to create a balanced, neat page. After the quotation, resume your own discourse at the left margin or with a new paragraph. Do not leave extra lines of space above or below the quotation. Here is a specimen, from an essay about Wordsworth's "Lines Written in Early Spring":

> In "Lines Written in Early Spring" Wordsworth develops an idea that the world of nature is linked directly to the moral human consciousness. He speaks of no religious systems or books of moral values. Instead, he derives his ideas directly from his experience, assuming that the world was made for the joy of the living creatures in it, including human beings ("man"), and that anyone disturbing that power of joy is violating "Nature's holy plan" itself. Wordsworth's moral criticism, in other words, is derived from his faith in the integrity of creation:
>
> If this belief from heaven be sent,
If such be Nature's holy plan,
Have I not reason to lament
What man has made of man?
(lines 21–24)
>
> The concept that morality and life are joined is the most interesting and engaging aspect of the poem. It seems to encourage a live-and-let-live attitude toward others, however, not an active program of direct outreach and help.

When quoting lines of poetry, always remember to quote them *as lines*. Do not run them together as though they were continuous prose. When you create such block quotations, as in the preceding example, you do *not* need quotation marks.

Today, computer usage is the established means of preparing papers, and therefore computer styling has become prominent in the handling of the matters discussed here. If you have style features in your menu, such as "Poem Text" or

"Quotation," each of which sets block quotations apart from "Normal" text, you may certainly make use of the features. Be sure to explain to your instructor what you are doing, however, to make sure that your computer's features correspond to the styles that are required for your class.

Use an Ellipsis to Show Omissions

Whether your quotation is long or short, you will often need to change some of the material in it to conform to your own sentence requirements. You might wish to omit something from the quotation that is not essential to your point or to the flow of your sentence. Indicate such omissions with an ellipsis (three spaced periods), as follows (from an essay about Bierce's "An Occurrence at Owl Creek Bridge"):

> Under the immediate threat of death, Farquhar's perceptions are sharpened and heightened. In actuality there is "swirling water . . . racing madly beneath his feet," but it is his mind that is racing swiftly, and he accordingly perceives that a "piece of dancing driftwood . . . down the current" moves so slowly that he believes the stream is "sluggish."

If your quotation is very brief, however, do not use ellipses as they might be more distracting than helpful. For example, do not use them in a quotation like this:

> Keats asserts that ". . . a thing of beauty . . ." always gives joy.

Instead, make your quotation without the ellipses:

> Keats asserts that "a thing of beauty" always gives joy.

Use Square Brackets to Enclose Words that You Add Within Quotations

If you add words of your own to integrate the quotation into your own train of discourse or to explain words that may seem obscure, put square brackets around these words, as in the following passage:

> In "Lines Written in Early Spring," Wordsworth refers to a past experience of extreme happiness, in which Nature seemed to "link/The human soul that through . . . [him] ran." He is describing a state of mystical awareness in which "pleasant thoughts/Bring [him] sad thoughts," and make him "lament" moral and political cruelty (lines 2–8).

Be Careful Not to Overquote

A word of caution: *Do not use too many quotations*. You will be judged on your own thought and on the continuity and development of your own essay. It is tempting to include many quotations on the theory that you need to use examples from the text to illustrate and support your ideas. Naturally, it is important to introduce examples, but you should understand that too many quotations can disturb the flow of your own thought. If your essay consists of many illustrations linked together by no more than your introductory sentences, how much thinking have you actually shown? Try, therefore, to create your own discussion, using appropriate examples to connect your thought to the text or texts you are analyzing.

Preserve the Spellings in Your Source

Always reproduce your source exactly. Sometimes the works of British authors may include words like *tyre, defence, honour,* and *labour*. Duplicate these as you find them. Although most anthologies, such as this one, modernize the spelling of older writers, you may often encounter "old-spelling" editions in which all words—such as *entring, Shew, beautie, ore* (for "over"), *witte* (for "wit"), *specifick, 'twas, guaranty* (for "guarantee"), or *determin'd*—are spelled and capitalized exactly as they were centuries ago. Your principle should be *to duplicate everything exactly as you find it,* even if this means spelling words like *achieve* as *atchieve, music* as *Musick,* or *joke* as *joak*. A student once changed the word *an* to "and" in the construction "an I were" in a Shakespeare play. The result was misleading, because in introductory clauses *an* really meant *if* (or *and if*) and not *and*. Difficulties like this one are rare, but you can avoid them if you reproduce the text as you find it. Should you think that something is either misspelled or confusing as it stands, you may do one of two things:

1. Clarify or correct the confusing word or phrase within brackets, as in the following:

   In 1714, fencing was considered a "Gentlemany [i.e., gentlemanly] subject."

2. Use the word *sic* (Latin for *thus,* meaning "It is this way in the text") in brackets immediately after the problematic word or obvious mistake:

   He was just "finning [sic] his way back to health" when the next disaster struck.

Chapter 1

Fiction: An Overview (Sample Literary Element Chapter)

Every literary element chapter in the anthology follows the same pattern to reinforce learning.

- A description of the element and definition of key terms
- In-chapter table of contents of all featured selections
- Selections that serve as models of the element
- Author headnotes and photos (except poetry where only select photos and portraits appear and biographies of poets are included in an end-of-book appendix)
- Questions following each selection
- Writing about the literary element
    - Discovering ideas for writing about the element
    - Strategies for organizing ideas about the element
    - Illustrative student essay that models how to write about the element
    - Commentary on the essay detailing how the essay follows good form
    - Suggestions for writing topics about the element

Visualizing Genres

This sample chapter also highlights one of our key new features—Visualizing Genres—which provides a visual representation of the literary genre. In this sample chapter, a comic strip *Bizarro* is featured as well as an excerpt from the graphic novel *Maus*. In poetry, our visualizing section highlights shaped poetry whereas in drama the images provide a comparison/contrast of two different filmed versions of *Hamlet*.

Part II

Reading and Writing About Fiction

Chapter 1

Fiction: An Overview

Fiction originally meant anything *made up* or *shaped.* As we understand the word today, it refers to *short or long prose stories*—and it has retained this meaning since 1599, the first year for which we have a record for it in print. Fiction is distinguished from the works it imitates, such as *historical accounts*, *reports*, *biographies*, *autobiographies*, *letters*, and *personal memoirs* and *meditations.* Although fiction often resembles these forms, it has a separate identity because it originates not in historical facts but in the imaginative and creative powers of the author. Writers of fiction may include historically accurate details, but their overriding goal is to tell a story and say something significant about life.

The essence of fiction, as opposed to drama, is **narration,** the recounting or telling of a sequence of events or actions. The earliest works of fiction relied almost exclusively on narration, with speeches or dialogue being reported rather than quoted directly. Much recent fiction includes extended passages of dialogue, thereby becoming more *dramatic* even though narration is still the primary mode.

Fiction is rooted in ancient legends and **myths.** Local priests told stories about their gods and heroes, as shown in some of the narratives of ancient Egypt. In the course of history, traveling storytellers would appear in a court or village to entertain listeners with tales of adventure in faraway countries. Although many of these were fictionalized accounts of events and people who may not ever have existed, they were largely accepted as fact or history. An especially long tale, an **epic,** was recited during a period of days. To aid their memories and to impress and entertain their listeners, the storytellers chanted their tales in poetry, often accompanying themselves on a stringed instrument.

Legends and epics also reinforced the local religions and power structures. Myths of gods like Zeus and Athena (Greece), Jupiter and Minerva (Rome), and Baal and Ishtar (Mesopotamia) abounded, together with stories of famous men and women like Achilles, Aeneas, Atalanta, David, Helen of Troy, Hercules, Joseph, Odysseus, Oedipus, Penelope, Ruth, Romulus and Remus, and Utu-Napishtim. The ancient Macedonian king and general Alexander the Great (356–323 BCE) developed many of his ideas about nobility and valor from *The Iliad,* Homer's epic about the Trojan War—and, we might add, from discussing the epic with his tutor, the philosopher Aristotle.

Perhaps nowhere is the moralistic-argumentative aspect of ancient storytelling better illustrated than in the **fables** of Aesop, a Greek who wrote in the sixth century BCE, and in the parables of Jesus as told in the Gospels of the New Testament (see Chapter 7). In these works, a short narrative provides an illustration of a religious, philosophic, or psychological conclusion.

Starting about eight hundred years ago, storytelling in Western civilization was developed to a fine art by writers such as Marie de France, a Frenchwoman who wrote in

England near the end of the twelfth century, Giovanni Boccaccio (Italian, 1313–1375), and Geoffrey Chaucer (English, c. 1340–1400). William Shakespeare (1564–1616) drew heavily on history and legend for the stories and characters in his plays.

Modern Fiction

Fiction as we understand the word today did not begin to flourish until the seventeenth and eighteenth centuries, when an alteration in the perception of human nature developed. For many centuries the idea had prevailed that human beings were in a fallen moral state—a state of "total depravity"—and that by themselves they needed the controlling hands of monarchy and church to keep them moral, peaceful, and pious. During the Renaissance, however, thinkers began to claim that humanity should be viewed within a perspective of greater and broader latitude. Some people were fallen, yes, but many others were not; and they could become moral through their own efforts without the control of political and moral authorities. It was this analysis that underlay the development of the democratic theory of government that has been accepted in much of modern society.

In literature, it thus became possible to view human beings of all social stations and ways of life as important literary topics. As one writer put it in 1709, human nature is by no means simple, for it is governed by many complex motives such as "passion, humor, caprice, zeal, faction, and a thousand other springs."[1] Observations such as this were the basis of the individual and psychological concerns that characterize fiction today. Indeed, fiction is strong because it is so real and personal. Characters have both first and last names; the countries and cities in which they live are visualized as real places, with real influences on the inhabitants; and their actions and interactions are like those that readers themselves have experienced, could experience, or could readily imagine themselves experiencing.

Along with attention to character, fiction is also concerned with the significance of place or environment on the lives of people. In the simplest sense, location is a backdrop or setting within which characters speak, move, and act. But more broadly, environment comprises the social, economic, and political conditions that affect the outcomes of people's lives. Fiction is primarily about the interactions among people, but it also involves these larger interactions—either directly or indirectly. Indeed, a typical work of fiction includes many forces, both small and large, that influence the ways in which characters meet and deal with their problems.

The first true works of fiction in Europe, however, were less concerned with society or politics than adventure. These were the lengthy Spanish and French **romances** of the sixteenth and seventeenth centuries. In English the word **novel** was borrowed from French and Italian to describe these works and to distinguish them from medieval and classical romances as something that was *new* (the meaning of *novel*). In England the word *story* was used along with *novel* in reference to the new literary form.

The increased levels of education and literacy in the eighteenth century facilitated the development of fiction. During the times of Shakespeare and John Dryden

[1] Anthony Ashley Cooper, Third Earl of Shaftesbury, "Sensus Communis," III, 3.

(1631–1700), the only way a writer could make a living from writing was either to be a member of the nobility or have a subsidy from a member of the nobility, or else to have a play accepted at a theater and then receive either a direct payment or the proceeds of an "author's benefit." The paying audiences, however, were limited to people who lived within a short distance of the theater or who had the leisure and money to stay in town and attend the plays during the theater season.

Once great numbers of people could read for themselves, the paying audience for literature expanded. A writer could write a novel and receive money for it from a publisher, who would then profit from a wide sale. Readers could start reading the book when they wished, and they would finish it when it was convenient to do so. Reading a novel could even be a social event, for people would gather together and read to each other as a means of sharing the reading experience. Quite often, as tastes for fiction developed, the writers would publish monthly installments of their novels. When the mail brought these new episodes and chapters, the principal activity would quickly focus on circles of listeners, who would listen eagerly while an expressive reader would bring the stories to life. Often these episodes would extend for many months, and the fiction-consuming public would discuss the latest experiences, and speculate about what would be happening next. With this wider audience of people whom authors would never see or know, it became possible for writers to develop a legitimate career out of their trade. Lengthy fictional stories had arrived as a major genre of literature.

The Short Story

Because novels were long, they took a long time to read—hours, days, even weeks. The early nineteenth-century American writer Edgar Allan Poe (1809–1849) addressed this problem and developed a theory of the **short story,** which he described in a review of Nathaniel Hawthorne's *Twice-Told Tales*. Poe was convinced that "worldly interests" prevented people from gaining the "totality" of comprehension and response that he believed reading should provide. A short, concentrated story (he called it "a brief prose tale" that could be read at a single sitting) was ideal for producing such a strong impression.

In the wake of the taste for short fiction after Poe, many writers have worked in the form. Today, stories are printed in many periodicals, such as *Harper's Magazine*, *The Atlantic Monthly*, and *Zoetrope*, and in many collections, such as *American Short Story Masterpieces*. Some of the better-established writers—William Faulkner, Ernest Hemingway, Shirley Jackson, Flannery O'Connor, Joyce Carol Oates, John Updike, Alice Walker, and Eudora Welty, to name only a small number—have published their stories in separate volumes.

Elements of Fiction I: Verisimilitude and *Donnée*

Fiction, along with drama, has a basis in **realism** or **verisimilitude.** That is, the situations or characters, although they are the invention of writers, are similar to those that many human beings experience, know, or think. Even fantasy, the creation of events that are dreamlike or fantastic, is anchored in the real world, however

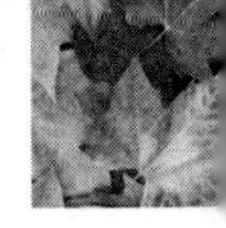

remotely. This connection of art and life has led some critics to label fiction, and also drama, as an art of imitation. Shakespeare's Hamlet states that an actor attempts to portray real human beings in realistic situations (to "hold a mirror up to Nature").

The same may also be said about writers of fiction, with the provisos that reality is not easily defined and that authors can follow many paths in imitating it. What matters in fiction is the way in which authors establish the ground rules for their works, whether with realistic or nonrealistic characters, places, actions, and physical and chemical laws. The assumption that authors make about the nature of their story material is called a postulate or a premise—what the American novelist Henry James called a ***donnée*** (something given). The *donnée* of some stories is to resemble the everyday world as much as possible. Eudora Welty's "A Worn Path" is such a story. In it we follow the difficult walk of an elderly woman as she goes from home to a medical office in Natchez, Mississippi, and we also learn of the virtually hopeless futility of her mission. The events of the story are not uncommon; they could happen in life just as Welty presents them.

Once a *donnée* is established, it governs the directions in which the story moves. Jackson's "The Lottery" (Chapter 2), for example, contains a premise or *donnée* that may be phrased like this: "Suppose that a small, ordinary town held a lottery in which the prize was not something good but instead was something bad." Everything in Jackson's story follows from this premise. At first we seem to be reading about innocent actions in a rural American community. By the end, however, in accord with the premise, the story enters the realm of nightmare.

In such ways authors may lead us into remote, fanciful, and symbolic levels of reality, as in Gilman's "The Yellow Wallpaper" (Chapter 10), in which we readers become drawn in to the disoriented world of a narrator who has totally lost her grip on the actuality of the situations around her. In Poe's "The Masque of the Red Death" (Chapter 9), the phantasmagoric *donnée* is that Death may assume a human but sinister shape. Literally nothing is out of bounds as long as the author makes clear the premise for the action.

Scenes and actions such as these, which are not realistic in our ordinary sense of the word, are normal in stories *as long as they follow the author's own stated or implied ground rules*. You may always judge a work by the standard of whether it is consistent with the premise, or the *donnée*, created by the writer.

In addition to referring to various levels of reality, the word *donnée* may also be taken more broadly. In *futuristic* and *science fiction*, for example, there is an assumption or *donnée* of certain situations and technological developments (e.g., interstellar space travel) that are not presently in existence. In a *love story*, the *donnée* is that two people meet and overcome an obstacle of some sort (usually not a serious one) on the way to fulfilling their love. Interesting variations of the love story are James Joyce's "Araby" (Chapter 4), D. H. Lawrence's "The Horse Dealer's Daughter" (Chapter 8), and Alice Munro's "The Found Boat" (Chapter 6).

There are, of course, other types. A *growth* or *apprenticeship story*, for example, is about the development of a major character, such as Jackie in Frank O'Connor's "First Confession" (Chapter 6). In the *detective story*, a mysterious event is posited, and then an individual draws conclusions from the available evidence, as in Susan Glaspell's "A Jury of Her Peers" (Chapter 3), in which the correct detective work is done by two women, not by the legally authorized police investigators.

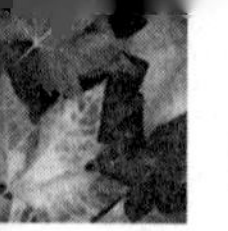

In addition to setting levels of reality and fictional types, authors may use other controls or springboards as their *données*. Sometimes an initial situation may be the springboard of the narrative, such as the orientation speech in Daniel Orozco's "Orientation" (Chapter 6). Or the key may be a pattern of behavior, such as the boy's reactions to the people around him in O'Connor's "First Confession," or the solution of a mystery about a community icon, as in Faulkner's "A Rose for Emily." A shaping force, or *donnée*, always guides the actions, and often a number of such controls operate at the same time.

Elements of Fiction II: Character, Plot, Structure, and Idea or Theme

Works of fiction share a number of common elements. For reference here, the more significant ones are *character*, *plot*, *structure*, and *idea* or *theme*.

Character Brings Fiction to Life

Stories, like plays, are about characters, who are *not* real people but who are nevertheless *like* real people. A **character** may be defined as a reasonable facsimile of a human being, with all the good and bad traits of being human. Most stories are concerned with characters who are facing a major problem that develops from misunderstanding, misinformation, unfocused ideals and goals, difficult situations, troubled relationships, and generally challenging situations. The characters may win, lose, or tie. They may learn and be the better for the experience or may miss the point and be unchanged.

As we have stated, modern fiction has accompanied the development of a psychological interest in human beings. Psychology itself has grown out of the philosophical and religious idea that people have many inborn capacities—some of them good and others bad. People encounter many problems in their lives, and they make many mistakes; they expend much effort in coping and adjusting. But they nevertheless are important and interesting and are therefore worth writing about, whether male or female; young or old; white, black, tan, or yellow; rich or poor; worker or industrialist; traveler or resident; doctor, librarian, mother, daughter, homemaker, prince, ship captain, bartender, or army lieutenant.

The range of fictional characters is vast: A married couple struggling to repay an enormous debt, a young man learning about the nature of his desires, a woman recalling many conflicts with her mother, two close relatives speculating about the loss of their past, a woman surrounded by her insensitive and self-seeking brothers, a man making triumphs out of his blunders, an unmarried couple dealing with the serious issue of what to do about the possibility of future childbirth, a woman feverishly recollecting her long experience without a man whom she had loved—all these, and more, may be found in fiction just as they may also be found in all levels and conditions of life. Because we all share the same capacities for concern, involvement, sympathy, happiness, sorrow, exhilaration, and disappointment,

we are able to find endless interest in such characters and their ways of coping with their circumstances.

Plot Is the Plan of Fiction

Fictional characters, who are drawn from life, go through a series of lifelike actions or incidents, which make up the story. In a well-done story, all the actions or incidents, speeches, thoughts, and observations are linked together to make up an entirety, sometimes called an **organic unity.** The essence of this unity is the development and resolution of a **conflict**—or conflicts—in which the **protagonist,** or central character, is engaged. The interactions of causes and effects as they develop sequentially or chronologically make up the story's **plot.** (See the section on writing on pp. 119–125) That is, a story's actions follow one another in time as the protagonist meets and tries to overcome opposing forces. Sometimes plot has been compared to a story's *map, scheme,* or *blueprint.*

Often the protagonist's struggle is directed against another character—an **antagonist.** Just as often, however, the struggle may occur between the protagonist and opposing groups, forces, ideas, and choices—all of which make up a collective antagonist. The conflict may be carried out wherever human beings spend their lives, such as a kitchen, a hotel, a railway station bar, a restaurant, a town square, a schoolroom, an ordinary living room, a church, an exclusive store, a vacation resort, a café, or a battlefield. The conflict may also take place internally, within the mind of the protagonist.

Structure Is the Knitting Together of Fiction

Structure refers to the way a story is assembled. Chronologically, all stories are similar because they move from beginning to end in accord with the time needed for *causes* to produce *effects.* But authors choose many different ways to put their stories together. Some stories are told in straightforward sequential order, and a description of the plot of such stories is identical to a description of the structure. Other stories, however, may get pieced together through out-of-sequence and widely separated episodes, speeches, secondhand reports, vague recollections, accidental discoveries, dreams, nightmares, periods of delirium, fragments of letters, overheard conversations, and the like. In such stories, the plot and the structure diverge widely. Therefore, in dealing with the structure of stories, we emphasize not chronological order but the actual *arrangement* and *development* of the stories as they unfold, part by part. Usually we study an entire story, but we may also direct our attention toward the structure of a smaller aspect of arrangement such as an episode or passage of dialogue.

Idea or Theme Is the Vivifying Thought of Fiction

The word **idea** refers to the result or results of general and abstract thinking. A **theme** is an enactment or embodiment of an idea—an idea in movement, a recurrent idea. Often the two words are used interchangeably. Either directly or indirectly, fiction embodies ideas and **themes** that underlie and give life to stories and novels.

Writers do not need to state their ideas in specific words, but the strength of their works depends on the power with which they exemplify ideas and make them clear. Thus, writers of comic works are committed to the idea that human difficulties can be treated with humor. More serious works often show characters in the throes of difficult moral choices—the idea being that in a losing situation the only winners are those who maintain honor and self-respect. Mystery and suspense stories develop from the idea that problems have solutions, although the solutions at first may seem remote or impossible. Even stories written for entertainment alone, some of which may at first seem devoid of ideas, stem out of an idea or position that the work itself makes clear. Writers may deal with the triumphs and defeats of life, the admirable and the despicable, the humorous and the pathetic; but whatever their goal, they are always expressing ideas about human experience. We may therefore raise questions such as these as we look for ideas in fiction:

- What does this mean?
- Why does the author include it?
- What idea or ideas does it show?
- Why is it significant?

Many works can be discussed in terms of the *issues* that they raise. An **issue** may involve a work's characters in direct or implicit argument or opposition, and it may also bring out crucially important moments of decision about matters of private or public concern. In addition to the issues that the characters face, the works themselves may be considered for their more general issues.

Fictional ideas can also be considered as major themes that tie individual works together. Often an author makes the theme obvious, as in the Aesop fable in which a man uses an ax to kill a fly on another man's forehead. The theme of this fable might loosely be expressed in the sentence "The cure should not be worse than the disease." A major theme in Maupassant's "The Necklace" (p. 5) is that people may be destroyed or saved by the most minor of unforeseeable but sometimes unlucky events.

The process of determining and describing the themes or ideas in stories is never complete; there is always another theme that we can discuss, another issue that may be explored. Thus in Maupassant's "The Necklace," we might note the additional themes that adversity brings out worth, that telling the truth is better than concealing it, that envy often produces ill fortune, that people may build their lives on incorrect assumptions, and that good fortune is never recognized until it is lost. Indeed, one of the ways in which we judge stories is to determine the degree to which they embody a number of valid and important ideas.

Elements of Fiction III: The Writer's Tools

Narration Creates the Sequence and Logic of Fiction

Writers have a number of modes of presentation, or "tools," that they use in their stories. The principal tool (and the heart of fiction) is **narration,** the reporting of actions in sequential order. The object of narration is to *render* the story, to make it

clear and to bring it alive to the reader's imagination through the movement of sentences through time. Unlike works of painting and sculpture, the reading and comprehension of a narration cannot be done in a single view. Jacques-Louis David's painting "The Death of Socrates" (p. I–10), for example, is like a narrative because it tells a story—an actual historical occurrence. As related by Plato in the dialogue *Phaedo,* Socrates takes the cup of hemlock, which he will drink as the means of carrying out his own execution. David does include details that tell the story visually. In the rear of the painting some of Socrates' friends have said good-bye and are sorrowfully mounting stairs to leave. Two of the remaining men hold their heads in grief, and two turn toward a wall in despair. The jailer avoids looking at Socrates as he offers the cup of hemlock. Also, on the bed are the unlocked manacles that might have held Socrates, thus emphasizing that he was, all the time, free to walk away had he so chosen. In fact, however, it is only the moment just before Socrates drinks the hemlock that David is able to capture in his painting. As a contrast, the writer of a narrative may include details about the many events leading up to and following such a moment, for a narration moves in a continuous line, from word to word, scene to scene, action to action, and speech to speech. As a result of this chronological movement, the reader's comprehension must necessarily also be chronological.

VISUALIZING FICTION

Cartoons, Graphic Narratives, Graphic Novels

David's painting is in the artistic tradition of "History Painting," which portrays a famous subject, such as *The Death of Socrates,* or *The Thracian Girl Carrying the Head of Orpheus on His Lyre* (see pp. I–10 and I–1). A closely connected type of painting is "Genre Painting," which features scenes of ordinary life, such as Brueghel's *Peasants' Dance* (see p. I–18). A modern popular development of such art is the single line-drawn cartoon together with a caption, brought to perfection by the many cartoonists who provided comic panels for *The New Yorker* and also the innumerable other publications that have flourished right up to the present time. The point about most of the cartoons is that they are based in narrative, as are the history and genre painting traditions. In no more than a single picture drawing, clever cartoonists supply the graphic means by which viewers are able to infer how a situation has developed, and how it will conclude.

Whereas the painting traditions featured realistic or semirealistic visions of humanity, however, the cartoonists developed caricatures in their portrayal of their human and animal subjects. One of the many cartoons done for *The New Yorker* by Charles Addams (1912–1988), shows the Addams family, in their characteristically ghoulish garb and appearance, high on a terraced area of their ghostly house, preparing to pour boiling oil down on a group of Christmas choristers. One may easily imagine both the history and future of this event. The Addams cartoons, in this comically macabre vein, were so popular that a series of films and TV programs were successfully developed that dramatized

various actions of the family. One of the most popular of modern cartoonists has been Gary Larson (b. 1950), who created thousands of panels for "The Far Side," the title of the syndicated cartoons he drew to popular acclaim from 1980 to 1995. Many of Larson's devoted followers expressed great regret when he gave up these cartoons. As his narrative technique, Larson created a situation that is easily followed because of both the various signs and also demonstrative actions of his characters, many of whom are not just caricatures of doughy and distorted human beings, but also of alien travelers, cows, ducks, dogs, snakes, spiders, ocean monsters, bears, deer, rhinoceroses, and comparable creatures. Even though there is no more than just a single picture in the typical Larson cartoon, Larson skillfully supplies a comic caption and the artistic narrative details from which readers may easily infer both the beginning and the ending.

Closely connected to the single panel cartoon, another major popular mode of narrative presentation is the comic strip, which became a part of regular daily newspapers in the twentieth century. Usually the comics were printed in three or four panels during each day of the week, and then on Sundays there was a color strip, usually involving as many as a dozen narrative cartoon panels. Often there was a continuous story in these strips that held the interest of readers for a number of months. From 1933 until 1987, for example, a strip featuring "Brick Bradford" continued regularly. The story, mainly science fiction, was played out both on a global and universal scale. One interesting adventure involved Brick and company taking a trip in a uniquely compressing and expanding spaceship, which reduced them to such an infinitely small degree that they could engage in an adventure on one of the atoms within the eye of a Lincoln-head penny. Other extremely popular comics featured Dick Tracy, a prominent detective concerned with solving crimes and capturing criminals (still regularly published), and *Terry and the Pirates* (1934–1973), a strip that took its readers to those wars in Asia that led up to and included American involvement in the Pacific Theater of operations during World War II. So popular were these comic strips that quarterly publications were soon issued, in which crime fighters like Superman, Batman, and The Specter would be the heroes of as many as four separate and complete adventure narratives.

Following World War II, many writers, collaborating with cartoonists, went beyond the traditional comic book limitations and started to adapt the comic book format for more serious and systematic novels. Well-known literary works first reached many readers through this medium, and many readers became so interested that they actually went on to read and appreciate the originals. In addition, many writers and cartoonists worked to create new graphically based works, often called "graphic novels." Perhaps the most famous of these is *Maus,* by Art Spiegelman, the winner of a Special Pulitzer Prize award in 1992. *Maus* is a work in the comic/graphic format that describes the horror and brutality of the German concentration camps, as witnessed by his father, during World War II (see p. 66). The form has proliferated and has reached the level of its own narrative/dramatic type. A number of separate "Sin City yarns" by Frank Miller (b. 1957), for example, has been used as the basis for popular films. In 2007, a graphic novel originally by Miller, with Lynn Varley, was *300,* which was made into a film dramatizing the story of the ancient battle between Greeks and Persians at Thermopylae.

DAN PIRARO Cartoon from *Bizarro*

Dan Piraro is a multitalented and prize-winning cartoonist, who was born in the latter twentieth century and educated in Oklahoma. He was especially artistic, and when working in the advertising department at Neiman-Marcus he would sketch out unique cartoons that fascinated and entertained his co-workers. With such material, he successfully began syndicating his work in 1985, just five years after Gary Larson first syndicated his The Far Side. *Piraro named his cartoons* Bizarro *because of the closeness in sound to his own name, and also because of the obvious closeness to the Italian word* bizzarro *and our own word* bizarre. *His devoted followers, who look forward eagerly to his daily* Bizarro *cartoons which appear in many newspapers throughout the country, have termed his work as "surreal," "ascerbic," "oddball," and "off the wall." In addition to being a cartoonist, Piraro has also developed his skills as a speaker and a showman. He continues to do fine art, and to date has published eleven separate books, two of which are the recent* The Three Little Pigs Buy the White House *(2004) and* Bizarro and Other Strange Manifestations of the Art of Dan Piraro *(2006).*

QUESTIONS

1. How does Piraro establish the narrative situation of this cartoon? On what very famous work of art does the drawing depend? What is the narrative in the original work? What is the narrative in Piraro's cartoon? How is the cartoon narrative particularly modern?
2. Why would the cartoon not be as funny as it is if we did not recognize the original from which the cartoon is derived?
3. On the basis of the contrast between the story in the cartoon and the story in the original to which it alludes, what principles of humor can you develop and describe?

ART SPIEGELMAN Page from *Maus*

Art Spiegelman (b. 1948) was born in Sweden and came to the United States with his parents. When in high school, he became fascinated with the art of cartooning and made that his profession. For more than twenty years he worked at designing popular products, including such things as candy wrappers. He also spent a number of years teaching at the School for Visual Arts in New York, and he founded a comic magazine, Raw. *His most accomplished work is his graphic novel* Maus, *a page of which is included here as an illustration of the subject and technique. Another of Spiegelman's honors was a Guggenheim Fellowship.*

Style Is the Author's Skill in Bringing Language to Life

The medium of fiction and of all literature is language, and the manipulation of language—the style—is a primary skill of the writer. A mark of a good style is the use of active verbs and nouns that are specific and concrete. Even with the most

active and graphic diction possible, writers can never render their incidents and scenes exactly, but they may be judged on how vividly they tell their stories.

Point of View Guides What We See and Understand in Fiction

One of the most important ways in which writers knit their stories together, and also an important way in which they try to interest and engage readers, is through the careful control of **point of view**—the *voice* of the story, the speaker who does the narrating. It is the way the story establishes authenticity, either in reality or unreality. It may be regarded as the story's *focus*, the *angle of vision* from which things are not only seen and reported but also judged.

Basically, there are two kinds of point of view, but there are many, many variations, sometimes obvious and sometimes subtle. In the first-person point of view, a fictitious observer tells us what he or she saw, heard, concluded, and thought. This viewpoint is characterized by the use of the pronoun *I,* as the speaker refers to his or her position as an observer or commentator. The speaker or narrator—terms that are interchangeable—may sometimes seem to be the author speaking directly using an authorial voice. More often, however, the speaker is an independent character—a persona with characteristics that separate her or him from the author.

In common with all narrators, the first-person narrator establishes a clearly defined relationship to the story's events. Some narrators are deeply engaged in the action and are major movers; others are only minor participants or observers; still others have had nothing to do with the action but are transmitting the reports of others who were more fully involved. Sometimes the narrator uses the *we* pronoun if he or she is or has been part of a group that has witnessed the action or participated in it. Often, too, the narrator might use *we* when referring to ideas and interpretations shared with the reader or listener—the idea being to draw readers into the story as much as possible.

The third-person point of view uses third-person pronouns (*she, he, it, they, her, him, them,* etc.).[2] The third-person point of view may be (1) **limited,** with the focus being on one particular character and what he or she does, says, hears, thinks, and otherwise experiences; (2) **omniscient,** with the possibility that the activities and thoughts of all the characters are open and fully known by the speaker; or (3) **dramatic, or objective,** in which the story is confined *only* to the reporting of actions and speeches, with no commentary and no revelation of the thoughts of any of the characters unless the characters themselves express their thoughts dramatically.

Understanding point of view usually requires subtlety of perception—indeed, it may be one of the most difficult of all concepts in the study of fiction. In fuller perspective, therefore, we may think of it as the *total position* from which things are viewed, understood, and communicated. The position might be simply physical: *Where was the speaker located when the events occurred? Does the speaker give us a close or distant view of the events?* The position might also be personal or philosophical: *Do the events illustrate a personal opinion* (Maupassant's "The Necklace" [Part I p. 6]), *embody a philosophical judgment* (Hawthorne's "Young Goodman Brown"

[2] The possibilities of a second-person point of view are discussed in Chapter 2, p. 132.

[Chapter 7]), or *argue a theological principle* (St. Luke's "The Parable of the Prodigal Son" [Chapter 7])?

Point of view is one of the major ways by which authors make fiction vital. By controlling point of view, an author helps us make reasonable inferences about the story's actions. Authors use point of view to raise some of the same questions in fiction that perplex us in life. We need to evaluate what fictional narrators as well as real people tell us, for what they say is affected by their limitations, attitudes, opinions, and degree of candidness. The first-person narrator of James Joyce's "Araby" (Chapter 4) describes a series of boyhood incidents leading up to his memory that he had deceived himself with vain desires. In other words, he emphasizes what he considers to be his own shortcomings. But we might also realize that this narrator is unwittingly showing that it was not he who was at fault, but rather the religious and moral structure of which he was a part. For readers, the perception of a fictional point of view can be as complex as life itself, and it may be as difficult—in fiction as in life—to evaluate our sources of information.

Description Creates the World of Fiction

Together with narration, a vital aspect of fiction is **description**—those words that cause readers to imagine or re-create the scenes and actions of a story. Description can be both physical (places and persons) and psychological (an emotion or set of emotions). Because excessive description sometimes interrupts or postpones a story's actions, many writers include only as much as is necessary to provide locations for what is happening in the story.

Mood and atmosphere are important aspects of descriptive writing, and to the degree that descriptions are evocative, they may reach the level of **metaphor** and **symbolism.** These characteristics of fiction are a property of all literature, and you will also encounter them whenever you read poems and plays.

Dialogue Creates Interactions Among Fictional Characters

Another major tool of the writer of fiction is **dialogue.** By definition, dialogue is the conversation of two people, but more than two characters may also participate. It is of course the major medium of the playwright, and it is one of the means by which fiction writers bring vividness and dramatic tension to their stories. Straight narration and description can do no more than make a secondhand assertion ("hearsay") that a character's thoughts and responses exist, but dialogue makes everything firsthand and real.

Dialogue is hence a means of *showing* or *actualizing* rather than *reporting*. If characters feel pain or declare love, their own words may be taken as the expression of what is on their minds. Some dialogue may be terse and minimal. Other dialogue may be expanded, depending on the situation, the personalities of the characters, and the author's intent. Dialogue may concern any topic, including everyday and practical matters, personal feelings, reactions to the past, future plans, changing thoughts, sudden realizations, and ideas—be they political, social, philosophical, or religious.

The language of dialogue indicates the intelligence, articulateness, educational levels, or emotional states of the speakers. Hence the author might use *grammatical mistakes, faulty pronunciation*, or *slang* to show a character of limited or disadvantaged background or a character who is trying to be seen in that light. *Dialect* shows the region from which the speaker comes, just as *accent* indicates a place of national origin. *Jargon* and *cliché* suggest self-inflation or intellectual limitations—usually reasons for laughter. The use of *private or intimate expressions* clearly shows people who are close to each other emotionally. Speech that is interrupted by *voiced pauses* (for example, "er," "ah," "um," "y'know") or speech characterized by *inappropriate words* might show a character who is unsure or not in control. There are many possibilities in dialogue, but no matter what qualities you find, writers include dialogue to enable you to know their characters better.

Tone and Irony Guide Our Perceptions of Fictional Works

In every story we may consider **tone**—the ways in which authors convey attitudes toward readers and also toward the work's subjects. One of the major components of tone—**irony**—refers to language and situations that seem to reverse normal expectations. *Word choice* is the characteristic of **verbal irony,** in which what is meant is usually the opposite of what is said, as when we *mean* that people are doing badly even though we *say* that they are doing well. Broader forms of irony are situational and dramatic. **Situational irony** refers to circumstances in which bad things happen to good people, or in which rewards are not earned because forces beyond human comprehension seem to be in total control, making the world seem arbitrary and often absurd. In **dramatic irony** characters have only a nonexistent, partial, incorrect, or misguided understanding of what is happening to them, while both readers and other characters understand the situation more fully. Readers hence become concerned about the characters and hope that the characters will develop understanding quickly enough to avoid the problems bedeviling them and the pitfalls endangering them.

Symbolism and Allegory Relate Fiction to the Larger World

In literature broadly, as in fiction narrowly, even apparently ordinary things may be seen as **symbols**—everyday objects, occurrences, speeches, actions, and characters that may be understood to have meaning (or meanings) in excess of their obvious function and texture. Some symbols are widely recognized and therefore are considered as **cultural** or **universal.** Water, flowers, jewels, aspects of topography, the sun, certain stars, the flag, altars, and minarets are examples of cultural symbols. Other symbols are **contextual;** that is, they take on symbolic meaning only in their individual works, as when in Maupassant's "The Necklace" (Part I), Mathilde and her husband move into an attic flat so that they may save money. This action may be taken as representative or symbolic of their loss of economic and social status.

When a complete story, in addition to maintaining its own narrative integrity, can be applied point by point to a parallel set of situations, it is an **allegory.** Many stories are not complete allegories, however, even though they may contain sections having allegorical parallels. For instance, the Loisels' long servitude in Maupassant's "The Necklace" is similar to the lives and activities of many people who perform tasks for mistaken or meaningless reasons. "The Necklace," therefore, has allegorical overtones even though it is not, in totality, an allegory.

Commentary Provides Us with an Author's Thoughts

Writers may also include **commentary,** analysis, or interpretation, in the expectation that readers need insight into the characters and their actions. When fiction was new, authors often expressed such commentary directly. Henry Fielding (1707–1754) divided his novels into "books" and included a chapter of personal and philosophical commentary at the beginning of each of these. In the next century, George Eliot (1819–1880) included many extensive passages of commentary in her novels.

Later writers have kept commentary at a minimum, preferring instead to concentrate on direct action and dialogue, thereby allowing readers to draw their own conclusions about meaning. In first-person narrations, however, we may expect the narrators to make their own personal comments. Such observations may be accepted at face value, but we should recognize that anything the speakers say is also a mode of character disclosure and therefore just as much a part of the total story as the narrative incidents.

The Elements Together Are Present in Works of Fiction

These, then, are the major tools of fiction, which authors usually employ simultaneously in their works. Thus the story may be told by a character who is a witness, and thus it has a *first-person point of view*. The major *character,* the *protagonist,* goes through a series of actions as a result of a carefully arranged *plot*. Because of this plot, together with the author's chosen method of *narration,* the story will follow a certain kind of arrangement, or *structure,* such as a straightforward sequence or a disjointed series of episodes. The action may demonstrate the story's *theme* or central *idea*. The writer's *style* may be manifested in ironic expressions. The description of the character's actions may reveal *irony of situation,* while at the same time this situation is made vivid through *dialogue* in which the character is a participant. Because the plight of the character is like the plight of many persons in the world, this character may be considered as a *symbol,* and the various actions of his story may be considered as an *allegory*.

Throughout each story we read, no matter what characteristics we are considering, it is most important to realize that a work of fiction is an entirety, a unity. Any reading of a story should be undertaken not to break things down into parts but to understand and assimilate the work *as a whole*. The separate analysis of various topics is thus a *means* to that end, *not* the end itself. The study of fiction, like the study of all literature, is designed to foster our growth and to increase our understanding of the human condition.

Stories for Study

AMBROSE BIERCE (1842–1914?)

Bierce was a native of Ohio, the youngest of nine children in the highly religious family of a poor farmer. When the Civil War began, he enlisted in the Union army as a drummer boy and rose to the rank of major by the war's end. After the war he went to San Francisco to begin a career in journalism. At various times he reported, edited, and wrote reviews for papers such as the San Francisco Examiner *and the* San Francisco News-Letter. *After he married, he and his wife spent five years in England, but eventually she left him and their two children died—events that had an embittering effect on him. In 1913 he traveled to Mexico, and nothing further is known about him; he is presumed to have died in revolutionary fighting there in 1914. Bierce published his first story in 1871 and later published two volumes of stories:* In the Midst of Life *(1892, originally published in 1891 as* Tales of Soldiers and Civilians, *which included "An Occurrence at Owl Creek Bridge"), and* Can Such Things Be? *(1893). He is perhaps best known for his sometimes cynical* The Devil's Dictionary *(1911). He favored the short story as a form over the novel on much the same grounds as Poe—namely, that the story could be designed to produce a single effect. He believed that fiction should be realistic and should build to concluding twists and surprises—goals that are seen in "An Occurrence at Owl Creek Bridge." His complete works, which he edited himself, appeared in twelve volumes from 1909 to 1912.*

 An Occurrence at Owl Creek Bridge (1891)

A man stood upon a railroad bridge in northern Alabama, looking down into the swift water twenty feet below. The man's hands were behind his back, the wrists bound with a cord. A rope closely encircled his neck. It was attached to a stout cross-timber above his head and the slack fell to the level of his knees. Some loose boards laid upon the sleepers supporting the metals of the railway supplied a footing for him and his executioners—two private soldiers of the Federal army, directed by a sergeant who in civil life may have been a deputy sheriff. At a short remove upon the same temporary platform was an officer in the uniform of his rank, armed. He was a captain. A sentinel at each end of the bridge stood with his rifle in the position known as "support," that is to say, vertical in front of the left shoulder, the hammer resting on the forearm thrown straight across the chest—a formal and unnatural position, enforcing an erect carriage of the body. It did not appear to be the duty of these two men to know what was occurring at the center of the bridge; they merely blockaded the two ends of the foot planking that traversed it.

Beyond one of the sentinels nobody was in sight; the railroad ran straight away into a forest for a hundred yards, then, curving, was lost to view. Doubtless there was an outpost farther along. The other bank of the stream was open ground—a gentle acclivity topped with a stockade of vertical tree trunks, loopholed for rifles, with a single embrasure through which protruded the muzzle of a brass cannon commanding the bridge. Midway of the slope between the bridge and fort were the spectators—a single company of infantry in line, at "parade rest," the butts of the rifles on the ground, the barrels inclining slightly backward against the right shoulder, the hands crossed upon the stock. A lieutenant stood at the right of the line, the point of his sword upon the ground, his left hand resting upon his right. Excepting the group of four at the center of the bridge, not a man moved. The company faced the bridge, staring stonily, motionless. The sentinels, facing the banks of the stream, might have been statues to adorn the bridge. The captain stood with folded arms, silent, observing the work of his subordinates, but making no sign. Death is a dignitary who when he comes announced is to be received with formal manifestations of respect, even by those most familiar with him. In the code of military etiquette silence and fixity are forms of deference.

The man who was engaged in being hanged was apparently about thirty-five years of age. He was a civilian, if one might judge from his habit, which was that of a planter. His features were good—a straight nose, firm mouth, broad forehead, from which his long, dark hair was combed straight back, falling behind his ears to the collar of his well-fitting frock coat. He wore a mustache and pointed beard, but no whiskers; his eyes were large and dark gray, and had a kindly expression which one would hardly have expected in one whose neck was in the hemp. Evidently this was no vulgar assassin. The liberal military code makes provision for hanging many kinds of persons, and gentlemen are not excluded.

The preparations being complete, the two private soldiers stepped aside and each drew away the plank upon which he had been standing. The sergeant turned to the captain, saluted and placed himself immediately behind that officer, who in turn moved apart one pace. These movements left the condemned man and the sergeant standing on the two ends of the same plank, which spanned three of the cross-ties of the bridge. The end upon which the civilian stood almost, but not quite, reached a fourth. This plank had been held in place by the weight of the captain; it was now held by that of the sergeant. At a signal from the former the latter would step aside, the plank would tilt and the condemned man go down between two ties. The arrangement commended itself to his judgment as simple and effective. His face had not been covered nor his eyes bandaged. He looked a moment at his "unsteadfast footing," then let his gaze wander to the swirling water of the stream racing madly beneath his feet. A piece of dancing driftwood caught his attention and his eyes followed it down the current. How slowly it appeared to move! What a sluggish stream!

5 He closed his eyes in order to fix his last thoughts upon his wife and children. The water, touched to gold by the early sun, the brooding mists under the banks at some distance down the stream, the fort, the soldiers, the piece of driftwood—all had distracted him. And now he became conscious of a new disturbance. Striking through the thought of his dear ones was a sound which he could neither ignore nor understand, a sharp, distinct, metallic percussion like the stroke of a blacksmith's hammer upon the anvil; it had the same ringing quality. He wondered what it was, and whether immeasurably distant or near by—it seemed both. Its recurrence was regular, but as slow as the tolling of a death knell. He awaited each stroke with impatience and—he knew not why—apprehension. The intervals of silence grew progressively longer; the delays became maddening. With their greater infrequency the sounds increased in strength and sharpness. They hurt his ear like the thrust of a knife; he feared he would shriek. What he heard was the ticking of his watch.

He unclosed his eyes and saw again the water below him. "If I could free my hands," he thought, "I might throw off the noose and spring into the stream. By diving I could evade the bullets and, swimming vigorously, reach the bank, take to the woods and get away

home. My home, thank God, is as yet outside their lines; my wife and little ones are still beyond the invader's farthest advance."

As these thoughts, which have here to be set down in words, were flashed into the doomed man's brain rather than evolved from it the captain nodded to the sergeant. The sergeant stepped aside.

II

Peyton Farquhar was a well-to-do planter, of an old and highly respected Alabama family. Being a slave owner and like other slave owners a politician he was naturally an original secessionist and ardently devoted to the Southern cause. Circumstances of an imperious nature, which it is unnecessary to relate here, had prevented him from taking service with the gallant army that had fought the disastrous campaigns ending with the fall of Corinth,° and he chafed under the inglorious restraint, longing for the release of his energies, the larger life of the soldier, the opportunity for distinction. That opportunity, he felt, would come, as it comes to all in war time. Meanwhile he did what he could. No service was too humble for him to perform in aid of the South, no adventure too perilous for him to undertake if consistent with the character of a civilian who was at heart a soldier, and who in good faith and without too much qualification assented to at least a part of the frankly villainous dictum that all is fair in love and war.

One evening while Farquhar and his wife were sitting on a rustic bench near the entrance to his grounds, a gray-clad soldier rode up to the gate and asked for a drink of water. Mrs. Farquhar was only too happy to serve him with her own white hands. While she was fetching the water her husband approached the dusty horseman and inquired eagerly for news from the front.

"The Yanks are repairing the railroads," said the man, "and are getting ready for another advance. They have reached the Owl Creek bridge, put it in order and built a stockade on the north bank. The commandant has issued an order, which is posted everywhere, declaring that any civilian caught interfering with the railroad, its bridges, tunnels or trains will be summarily hanged. I saw the order." 10

"How far is it to the Owl Creek bridge?" Farquhar asked.

"About thirty miles."

"Is there no force on this side of the creek?"

"Only a picket post half a mile out, on the railroad, and a single sentinel at this end of the bridge."

"Suppose a man—a civilian and student of hanging—should elude the picket post and perhaps get the better of the sentinel," said Farquhar, smiling, "what could he accomplish?" 15

The soldier reflected. "I was there a month ago," he replied, "I observed that the flood of last winter had lodged a great quantity of driftwood against the wooden pier at this end of the bridge. It is now dry and would burn like tow."

The lady had now brought the water, which the soldier drank. He thanked her ceremoniously, bowed to her husband and rode away. An hour later, after nightfall, he repassed the plantation, going northward in the direction from which he had come. He was a Federal scout.

III

As Peyton Farquhar fell straight downward through the bridge he lost consciousness and was as one already dead. From this state he was awakened—ages later, it seemed to him—by the pain of a sharp pressure upon his throat, followed by a sense of suffocation. Keen,

---

° *Corinth:* In the northeast corner of Mississippi, near the Alabama state line, Corinth was the site of a battle in 1862 won by the Union army.

poignant agonies seemed to shoot from his neck downward through every fiber of his body and limbs. These pains appeared to flash along well-defined lines of ramification and to beat with an inconceivably rapid periodicity. They seemed like streams of pulsating fire heating him to an intolerable temperature. As to his head, he was conscious of nothing but a feeling of fulness—of congestion. These sensations were unaccompanied by thought. The intellectual part of his nature was already effaced; he had power only to feel, and feeling was torment. He was conscious of motion. Encompassed in a luminous cloud, of which he was now merely the fiery heart, without material substance, he swung through unthinkable arcs of oscillation, like a vast pendulum. Then all at once, with terrible suddenness, the light about him shot upward with the noise of a loud plash; a frightful roaring was in his ears, and all was cold and dark. The power of thought was restored; he knew that the rope had broken and he had fallen into the stream. There was no additional strangulation; the noose about his neck was already suffocating him and kept the water from his lungs. To die of hanging at the bottom of a river!—the idea seemed to him ludicrous. He opened his eyes in the darkness and saw above him a gleam of light, but how distant, how inaccessible! He was still sinking, for the light became fainter and fainter until it was a mere glimmer. Then it began to grow and brighten, and he knew that he was rising toward the surface—knew it with reluctance, for he was now very comfortable. "To be hanged and drowned," he thought, "that is not so bad; but I do not wish to be shot. No; I will not be shot; that is not fair."

He was not conscious of an effort, but a sharp pain in his wrist apprised him that he was trying to free his hands. He gave the struggle his attention, as an idler might observe the feat of a juggler, without interest in the outcome. What splendid effort—what magnificent, what superhuman strength! Ah, that was a fine endeavor! Bravo! The cord fell away; his arms parted and floated upward; the hands dimly seen on each side in the growing light. He watched them with a new interest as first one and then the other pounced upon the noose at his neck. They tore it away and thrust it fiercely aside, its undulations resembling those of a water snake. "Put it back, put it back!" He thought he shouted these words to his hands, for the undoing of the noose had been succeeded by the direst pang that he had yet experienced. His neck ached horribly; his brain was on fire; his heart, which had been fluttering faintly, gave a great leap, trying to force itself out at his mouth. His whole body was racked and wrenched with an insupportable anguish! But his disobedient hands gave no heed to the command. They beat the water vigorously with quick, downward strokes, forcing him to the surface. He felt his head emerge; his eyes were blinded by the sunlight; his chest expanded convulsively, and with a supreme and crowning agony his lungs engulfed a great draught of air, which instantly he expelled in a shriek!

20 He was now in full possession of his physical senses. They were indeed, preternaturally keen and alert. Something in the awful disturbance of his organic system had so exalted and refined them that they made record of things never before perceived. He felt the ripples upon his face and heard their separate sounds as they struck. He looked at the forest on the bank of the stream, saw the individual trees, the leaves and the veining of each leaf—saw the very insects upon them: the locusts, the brilliant-bodied flies, the gray spiders stretching their webs from twig to twig. He noted the prismatic colors in all the dewdrops upon a million blades of grass. The humming of the gnats that danced above the eddies of the stream, the beating of the dragon flies' wings, the strokes of the water-spiders' legs, like oars which had lifted their boat—all these made audible music. A fish slid along beneath his eyes and he heard the rush of its body parting the water.

He had come to the surface facing down the stream; in a moment the visible world seemed to wheel slowly round, himself the pivotal point, and he saw the bridge, the fort, the soldiers upon the bridge, the captain, the sergeant, the two privates, his executioners. They were in silhouette against the blue sky. They shouted and gesticulated, pointing at

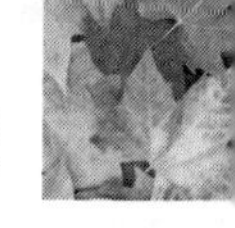

him. The captain had drawn his pistol, but did not fire; the others were unarmed. Their movements were grotesque and horrible, their forms gigantic.

Suddenly he heard a sharp report and something struck the water smartly within a few inches of his head, spattering his face with spray. He heard a second report, and saw one of the sentinels with his rifle at his shoulder, a light cloud of blue smoke rising from the muzzle. The man in the water saw the eye of the man on the bridge gazing into his own through the sights of the rifle. He observed that it was a gray eye and remembered having read that gray eyes were keenest, and that all famous marksmen had them. Nevertheless, this one had missed.

A counter-swirl had caught Farquhar and turned him half round; he was again looking into the forest on the bank opposite the fort. The sound of a clear, high voice in a monotonous singsong now rang out behind him and came across the water with a distinctness that pierced and subdued all other sounds, even the beating of the ripples in his ears. Although no soldier, he had frequented camps enough to know the dread significance of that deliberate, drawling, aspirated chant; the lieutenant on shore was taking a part in the morning's work. How coldly and pitilessly—with what an even, calm intonation, presaging, and enforcing tranquility in the men—with what accurately measured intervals fell those cruel words:

"Attention, company! . . . Shoulder arms! . . . Ready! . . . Aim! . . . Fire!"

Farquhar dived—dived as deeply as he could. The water roared in his ears like the voice of Niagara, yet he heard the dulled thunder of the volley and, rising again toward the surface, met shining bits of metal, singularly flattened, oscillating slowly downward. Some of them touched him on the face and hands, then fell away, continuing their descent. One lodged between his collar and neck; it was uncomfortably warm and he snatched it out. 25

As he rose to the surface, gasping for breath, he saw that he had been a long time under water; he was perceptibly farther down stream—nearer to safety. The soldiers had almost finished reloading; the metal ramrods flashed all at once in the sunshine as they were drawn from the barrels, turned in the air, and thrust into their sockets. The two sentinels fired again, independently and ineffectually.

The hunted man saw all this over his shoulder; he was now swimming vigorously with the current. His brain was as energetic as his arms and legs; he thought with the rapidity of lightning.

"The officer," he reasoned, "will not make that martinet's error a second time. It is as easy to dodge a volley as a single shot. He has probably already given the command to fire at will. God help me, I cannot dodge them all!"

An appalling plash within two yards of him was followed by a loud, rushing sound, *diminuendo,* which seemed to travel back through the air to the fort and died in an explosion which stirred the very river to its deeps! A rising sheet of water curved over him, fell down upon him, blinded him, strangled him! The cannon had taken a hand in the game. As he shook his head free from the commotion of the smitten water he heard the deflected shot humming through the air ahead, and in an instant it was cracking and smashing the branches in the forest beyond.

"They will not do that again," he thought; "the next time they will use a charge of grape. I must keep my eye upon the gun; the smoke will apprise me—the report arrives too late; it lags behind the missile. That is a good gun." 30

Suddenly he felt himself whirled round and round—spinning like a top. The water, the banks, the forests, the now distant bridge, fort and men—all were commingled and blurred. Objects were represented by their colors only; circular horizontal streaks of color—that was all he saw. He had been caught in a vortex and was being whirled on with a velocity of advance and gyration that made him giddy and sick. In a few moments he was flung upon the gravel at the foot of the left bank of the stream—the southern bank—and behind a projecting point which concealed him from his enemies. The sudden arrest of his motion,

the abrasion of one of his hands on the gravel, restored him, and he wept with delight. He dug his fingers into the sand, threw it over himself in handfuls and audibly blessed it. It looked like diamonds, rubies, emeralds; he could think of nothing beautiful which it did not resemble. The trees upon the bank were giant garden plants; he noted a definite order in their arrangement, inhaled the fragrance of their blooms. A strange, roseate light shone through the spaces among their trunks and the wind made in their branches the music of æolian harps. He had no wish to perfect his escape—was content to remain in that enchanting spot until retaken.

A whiz and rattle of grapeshot among the branches high above his head roused him from his dream. The baffled cannoneer had fired him a random farewell. He sprang to his feet, rushed up the sloping bank, and plunged into the forest.

All that day he traveled, laying his course by the rounding sun. The forest seemed interminable; nowhere did he discover a break in it, not even a woodman's road. He had not known that he lived in so wild a region. There was something uncanny in the revelation.

By nightfall he was fatigued, footsore, famishing. The thought of his wife and children urged him on. At last he found a road which led him in what he knew to be the right direction. It was as wide and straight as a city street, yet it seem untraveled. No fields bordered it, no dwelling anywhere. Not so much as the barking of a dog suggested human habitation. The black bodies of the trees formed a straight wall on both sides, terminating on the horizon in a point, like a diagram in a lesson in perspective. Overhead, as he looked up through this rift in the wood, shone great golden stars looking unfamiliar and grouped in strange constellations. He was sure they were arranged in some order which had a secret and malign significance. The wood on either side was full of singular noises, among which—once, twice, and again—he distinctly heard whispers in an unknown tongue.

35 His neck was in pain and lifting his hand to it found it horribly swollen. He knew that it had a circle of black where the rope had bruised it. His eyes felt congested; he could no longer close them. His tongue was swollen with thirst; he relieved its fever by thrusting it forward from between his teeth into the cold air. How softly the turf had carpeted the untraveled avenue—he could no longer feel the roadway beneath his feet!

Doubtless, despite his suffering, he had fallen asleep while walking, for now he sees another scene—perhaps he has merely recovered from a delirium. He stands at the gate of his own home. All is as he left it, and all bright and beautiful in the morning sunshine. He must have traveled the entire night. As he pushes open the gate and passes up the wide white walk, he sees a flutter of female garments; his wife, looking fresh and cool and sweet, steps down from the veranda to meet him. At the bottom of the steps she stands waiting, with a smile of ineffable joy, an attitude of matchless grace and dignity. Ah, how beautiful she is! He springs forward with extended arms. As he is about to clasp her he feels a stunning blow upon the back of the neck; a blinding white light blazes all about him with a sound like the shock of a cannon—then all is darkness and silence!

Peyton Farquhar was dead; his body, with a broken neck, swung gently from side to side beneath the timbers of the Owl Creek bridge.

QUESTIONS

1. What is the situation in the story? What did Farquhar do to deserve his execution?
2. Describe the various shifts in the story's point of view, particularly as indicated in paragraphs 5 and 37. How does Bierce make you aware of Farquhar's heightened consciousness?
3. According to Farquhar's perception of time, how long does it take him to get home after his escape (see paragraphs 33 and 36)?

4. What evidence can you find to indicate that Farquhar is experiencing great pain, despite his feelings that he is escaping?
5. What is the effect of the shift into the present tense in paragraph 36?

EDWIDGE DANTICAT (b. 1969)

Danticat is a native of Haiti and came to this country in 1981, when she was twelve, to live with her parents in Brooklyn. It was then that she started learning English even though at home she and her parents continued to speak the Creole of their native Haiti. She was educated at Barnard College and Brown University. Her first novel, Breath, Eyes, Memory *(1994), was selected for the Oprah Winfrey Book Club and was therefore assured wide circulation and recognition. Her collection of stories* Krik? Krak! *appeared in 1995, and* The Farming of Bones *was published in 1998. Most recently she has published* Behind the Mountains *(2002) and* The Dew Breaker *(2004).*

 Night Talkers (2002)

He thought that the mountain would kill him, that he would never see the other side. He had been walking for two hours when suddenly he felt a sharp pain in his side. He tried some breathing exercises he remembered from medical shows on television, but it was hard to concentrate. All he could think of, besides the pain, was his roommate Michel, who'd had an emergency appendectomy a few weeks before in New York. What if he was suddenly stricken with appendicitis, here on top of a mountain, deep in the Haitian countryside, where the closest village seemed like a grain of sand in the valley below?

Hugging his midsection, he took cover from the scorching midday sun under a tall, arched, wind-deformed tree. He slid down onto his back, over the grainy pebbled soil, and closed his eyes, shutting out, along with the indigo sky, the sloping hills and craggy mountains that made up the rest of his journey.

He was on his way to visit his aunt Estina, his father's older sister, whom he'd not seen since he'd moved to New York six years before. He had lost his parents to the dictatorship when he was a boy, and his aunt Estina had raised him in the capital. After he'd moved to New York, she had returned to her home in the mountains, where she had always taken him during school holidays. This was the first time he was going to her village, as he had come to think of it, without her. If she were with him, she would have made him start his journey earlier in the day. They would have boarded a camion at the bus depot in Port-au-Prince before dawn and started climbing the mountain at sunrise to avoid sunstroke at high noon. If she knew he was coming, she would have hired him a mule and sent a child to accompany him, a child who would have known all the shortcuts to her village. She also would have advised him to wear a sun hat and bring more than the two bottles of water he'd consumed hours ago.

But no, he wanted to surprise her. However, the only person he was surprising was himself, by getting lost and nearly passing out and possibly lying there long enough to draw a few mountain vultures to come pick his skeleton clean.

When he finally opened his eyes, the sun was beating down on his face in pretty, symmetrical designs. Filtered through the long upturned branches of what he recognized as a giant saguaro cactus, the sunrays had patterned themselves into hearts, starfishes, and circles looped around one another. 5

He reached over and touched the cactus's thick trunk, which felt like a needle-filled pincushion or a field of dry grass. The roots were close to the soil, which his aunt Estina had once told him were designed to collect as much rainwater as possible. Further up along the spine, on the stem, was a tiny cobalt flower. He wanted to pluck it and carry it with him the rest of the way, but his aunt would scold him if she knew what he had done. Cactus flowers bloomed only for a few short days, then withered and died. He should let the cactus enjoy its flower for this brief time, his aunt would say.

The pain in his midsection had subsided, so he decided to get up and continue his walk until he reached his destination. There were many paths to his aunt's house, and seeing the lone saguaro had convinced him that he was on one of them.

He soon found himself in a village where a girl was pounding a pestle into a mortar, forming a small crater in the ground beneath the mortar as a group of younger children watched.

The girl stopped her pounding as soon as she saw him, causing the other children to turn their almost identical brown faces toward him.

10 "Bonjou, cousins," he said, remembering the childhood greeting his aunt had taught him. When he was a boy, in spite of the loss of his parents, he had thought himself part of a massive family, every child his cousin and every adult his aunt or uncle.

"Bonjou," the children replied.

"Ki jan ou ye?" How are you? the oldest girl added, distinguishing herself.

"Could I have some water, please?" he said to the oldest girl, determining that she was indeed the one in charge.

The girl turned her pestle over to the next oldest child and ran into the limestone house as he dropped his backpack on the ground and collapsed on the front gallery. The ground felt chilly against his bare legs, as though he had stumbled into a cold stream.

15 As one of the younger boys ran off behind the house, the other children settled down on the ground next to him, some of them reaching over and stroking his backpack.

The oldest girl came back with a glass in one hand and an earthen jar in the other. He watched as she poured the water, wondering if it, like her, was a mirage fabricated by his intense thirst. When she handed him the water, he drank it faster than it took her to pour him another glass, then another and another, until the earthen jar was clearly empty.

She asked if he wanted more.

"No," he replied. "Mèsi anpil."° Thank you.

The girl went back into the house to put the earthen jar and glass away. The children were staring up at him, too coy to question him and too curious not to stare. When the girl returned, she went back to her spot behind the mortar and pestle and just stood there as though she no longer knew what to do.

20 An old man carrying a machete and a sisal knapsack walked up to the bamboo gate that separated the road from the house. The boy who had run off earlier was at his side.

"How are you, konpê?"° the old man asked.

"Uncle," he said, "I was dying of thirst until your granddaughter here gave me some water to drink."

"My granddaughter?" the old man laughed. "She's my daughter. Do you think I look that old?"

He looked old, with a grizzly salt-and-pepper beard and a face full of folds and creases that seemed to map out every road he had traveled in his life.

25 The old man reached over and grabbed one of three wooden poles that held up the front of the house. He stood there for a while, saying nothing, catching his breath. After the children

---

° *Mèsi anpil:* I am full. I've had enough.
° *konpê:* i.e., French "copain," companion, friend, chum.

had brought him a calabash filled with water—the glass was obviously reserved for strangers—and two chairs for him and the stranger, he lit his pipe and exhaled a fragrant cloud of fresh tobacco and asked, "Where are you going, my son?"

"I am going to see my aunt, Estina Estème," he replied. "She lives in Beau Jour."

The old man removed the pipe from his mouth and reached up to scratch his beard.

"Estina Estème? The same Estina Estème from Beau Jour?"

"The same," he said, growing hopeful that he was not too far from his aunt's house.

"You say she is your aunt?" 30

"She is," he replied. "You know her?"

"Know her?" the old man retorted. "There are no strangers in these mountains. My grandfather Nozial and her grandfather Osnac were cousins. Who was your father?"

"My father was Maxo Jean Osnac," he said.

"The one who was killed in that explosion?" the old man asked. "He only had one boy. The mother died too, didn't she? Estina nearly died in that explosion too. Only the boy came out whole."

"I am the boy," he said, an egg-sized lump growing in his throat. 35

He didn't expect to be talking about these things so soon. He had prepared himself for only one conversation about his parents' death, the one he would inevitably have with his aunt.

The children moved a few inches closer to him, their eyes beaming as though they were being treated to a frightening folktale in the middle of the day.

"Even after all these years," the old man said, "I am sad for you. So you are that young man who used to come here with Estina, the one who left for New York some years back?"

The old man looked him up and down, as if searching for burn marks on his body, then ordered the children to retreat.

"Shoo," he commanded. "This is no talk for young ears." 40

The children quickly vanished, the oldest girl resuming her work with the mortar and pestle.

Rising from his chair, the old man said, "Come, I will take you to Estina Estème." Estina Estème lived in a valley between two lime-green mountains and a giant waterfall, which was constantly spraying a fine mist over the banana grove that surrounded her one-room house and the teal mausoleum that harbored the bones of her forebears. Her nephew recognized the house as soon as he saw it. It had not changed much, the sloped tin roof and the wooden frame intact. His aunt's banana grove seemed to have flourished, however. It was greener and denser than he remembered; her garden was packed with orange and avocado trees, a miracle given the barren mountain range he had just traveled through.

When he entered his aunt's yard, he was greeted by a flock of hens and roosters, which scattered quickly, seeking shelter on top of the family mausoleum.

He rushed to the front porch, where an old faded skirt and blouse were drying on the wooden railing. The door was open, so he ran into the house, leaving behind the old man and a small group of neighbors whom the old man had enticed into following them by announcing as he passed their houses that he had with him Estina Estème's only nephew.

In the small room was his aunt's cot, covered with a pale blue sheet. Nearby was a calabash filled with water, within easy reach so she could drink from it at night without leaving her bed. Under the cot was her porcelain chamber pot and baskets filled with her better dresses and a few Sunday hats and shoes. 45

The old man peeked in to ask, "She's not here?"

"No," he replied. "She is not."

He was growing annoyed with the old man, even though he was now certain that he would have never found his aunt's house so quickly without his help.

When he walked out of the house, he found himself facing a dozen or so more people gathered in his aunt's yard. He scanned the faces and recognized some, but could not recall their names. Many in the group were nudging each other, whispering while pointing at him. Others called out, "Dany, don't you know me anymore?"

50 He walked over and kissed the women, shook hands with the men, and patted the children's heads.

"Please, where is my aunt?" he asked of the entire crowd.

"She will soon be here," a woman replied. "We sent for her."

Once he knew his aunt was on her way, he did his best to appear interested in catching up. Many in the crowd complained that once he got to New York, he forgot about them, never sending the watch or necklace or radio he had promised. Surprised that they had taken his youthful pledges so seriously, he made feeble excuses: "It's not so easy to earn money in New York . . . I thought you had moved to the capital . . . I didn't know your address."

"Where would we have gone?" one of the men rebutted. "We were not so lucky as you."

55 He was glad when he heard his aunt's voice, calling his name from the back of the crowd. The crowd parted and she appeared, pudgy yet graceful in a drop-waist dress. Her face was round and full, her few wrinkles more like tribal marks than signs of old age. Two people were guiding her by the elbows. As they were leading her to him, she pulled herself away and raised her hands in front of her, searching for him in the breeze. He had to remind himself once more that she was blind, had been since the day of the fire that had taken his parents' life.

The crowd moved back a few feet as he ran into her arms. She held him tightly, angling her head to kiss the side of his face.

"Dany, is it you?" She patted his back and shoulders to make sure.

"I brought him here for you," the old man said.

"Old Zo, why is it that you're always mixed up in everything?" she asked, joking.

60 "True to my name," the old man replied, "I am a bone that fits every stew."

The crowd laughed.

"Let's go in the house, Da," his aunt said. "It's hot out here."

As they started for her front door, he took her hand and tried to guide her, but found himself an obstacle in her path and let go. Once they were inside, she felt her way to her cot and sat down on the edge.

"Sit with me, Da," she said. "You have made your old aunt a young woman again."

65 "How are you?" He sat down next to her. "Truly?"

"Truly fine," she said. "Did Popo tell you different?"

For many years now, he had been paying a boyhood friend in Port-au-Prince, Popo, to come and check on her once a month. He would send Popo money to buy her whatever she needed, and Popo would in turn call him in New York to brief him on how she was doing.

"No," he said, "Popo didn't tell me anything."

"Then why did you come?" she asked. "I am not unhappy to see you, but you just dropped out of the sky, there must be a reason."

70 She felt for his face, found it, and kissed it for what seemed like a hundredth time since he'd seen her. "Were you sent back?" she asked. "We have a few boys here in the village who have been sent back. Many don't even speak Creole° anymore. They come here because this is the only place they have any family. There's one boy not far from here. I'll take you to visit him. You can speak to him, one American to another."

"You still go on your visits?" he asked.

° *Creole:* a local Haitian dialect.

"When they came to fetch me, I was with a girl in labor," she said.

"Still a midwife?"

"Helping the midwife," she replied. "You know I know every corner of these mountains. If a new tree grows, I learn where it is. Same with children. A baby's still born the same way it was when I had sight."

"I meant to come sooner," he said, watching her join and separate her fingers randomly, effortlessly, like tree branches brushing against each other in a gentle breeze. 75

"I know," she said. "But why didn't you send word that you were on your way?"

"You're right," he said. "I didn't just drop out of the sky. I came because I wanted to tell you something."

"What is it, Da?" she asked, weaving and unweaving her fingers. "Are you finally getting married?"

"No," he said. "That's not it. I found him. I found him in New York, the man who killed Papa and Manman° and took your sight."

Why the old man chose that exact moment to come through the door he will never know. 80 Perhaps it was chance, serendipity, or maybe simply because the old man was a nosy pain in the ass. But just then Old Zo appeared in the doorway, pushing the mortar-and-pestle girl ahead of him with a covered plate of food in her hand.

"We brought you something to refresh you," he told Dany.

His aunt seemed neither distressed nor irritated by the interruption. She could have sent Old Zo and the girl away, but she didn't. Instead she told them to put their offering down on an old table in the corner. The girl quietly put the plate down and backed out of the room, avoiding Dany's eyes.

"I hope you're both hungry," the old man said, not moving from his spot. "Everyone is going to bring you something."

Clusters of food-bearing people streamed in and out of the house all afternoon. He and his aunt would sample each plate, then share the rest with the next visitor, until everyone in the valley had tasted at least one of their neighbor's dishes.

By the time all the visitors had left and he and his aunt were alone together, it was dark 85 and his aunt showed no interest in hearing what he had to say. Instead she offered him her cot, and he talked her into letting him have the sisal mat that she had laid out on the floor for herself.

She fell asleep much more quickly than he did. Mid-dream, she laughed, paid compliments, made promises, or gave warnings. "Listen, don't go too far. Come back soon. What a strong baby! I'll make you a dress. I'll make you coffee." Then she sat up in her cot to scold herself—"Estina, you are waking the boy"—before drifting once again into the movie in her head.

In the dark, listening to his aunt conduct entire conversations in her sleep, he realized that aside from blood, she and he shared nocturnal habits. They were both night talkers. He too spoke his dreams aloud in the night, in his sleep, to the point of sometimes jolting himself awake with the sound of his own voice. Usually he could only remember the very last words he spoke, but a lingering sensation remained that he had been talking, laughing, and at times crying all night long.

His aunt was already awake by the time he got up the next morning. With help from Old Zo's daughter, who seemed to have been rented out to his aunt for the duration of his visit, she had already set up breakfast on the small table brought out to the front gallery from inside the house. His aunt seemed fidgety, almost anxious, as if she had been waiting for him to rise for hours.

° *Manman:* Mama.

"Go wash yourself, Da," she said, handing him a towel. "I'll be waiting for you here."

90 Low shrubs covered in dew brushed against his ankles as he made his way down a trail toward the stream at the bottom of the fall. The water was freezing cold when he slipped in, but he welcomed the sensation of having almost every muscle in his body contract, as if to salute the dawn.

Had his father ever bathed in this stream? Had his parents bathed here together when they'd come to stay with his aunt? Had they enjoyed it, or had they wished for warmer waters and more privacy?

A group of women were coming down the path with calabashes and plastic jugs balanced on top of their heads. They would bathe, then fill their containers farther up, closer to the fall. He remembered spending hours as a boy watching the women bathe topless, their breasts flapping against their chests as they soaped and scrubbed themselves with mint and parsley sprigs, as if to eradicate every speck of night dust from their skin.

When he got back to his aunt's house, he had a visitor. It was a boy named Claude, a deportee. Claude was sitting next to his aunt, on the top step in front of the house; he was dipping his bread in the coffee that Old Zo's daughter had just made.

"I sent for Claude," his aunt announced. "Claude understands Creole and is learning to speak bit by bit, but he has no one to speak English to. I would like you to talk with him."

95 It was awkward at first, especially with the giant, overly muscular Claude looking so absolutely thrilled to see him, yet trying to hide it with a restrained smile and an overly firm handshake. Both of Claude's brawny arms were covered with tattoos from his shoulders down to his wrists, his skin a collaged canvas of Chinese characters plus kings and queens from a card deck: One-Eyed Jack, Hector, Lancelot, Judith, Rachel, Argine and Palas, they were all there, carved into his coal-black skin in blue ink. His hands were large too, his fingers long, thick, callused, perhaps the hands of a killer.

"What's up?" Claude stood up only to sit down again. "How you doing?"

Claude was probably in his late teens—too young, it seemed, to have been expatriated twice, from both his native country and his adopted land. Dany sat down on the step next to Claude as Old Zo's daughter handed him a cup of coffee and a piece of bread.

"How long you been here?" he asked Claude.

"Too long, man," Claude replied, "but I guess it could be worse. I could be down in the city, in Port, eating crap and sleeping on the street. Everyone here's been really cool to me, especially your aunt. She's kind of taken me under her wing. When I first got here, I thought I would get stoned. I mean I thought people would throw rocks at me, man, not the other kind of stoned. I mean, coming out of New York, then being in prison in Port for like three months because no one knew what to do with me, then finally my moms, who didn't speak to me for like the whole time I was locked up, came to Port and hooked me up with some family up here."

100 His aunt was leaning forward with both hands holding up her face, her white hair braided like a crown of gardenias around her head. She was listening to them speak, like someone trying to capture the indefinable essence of a great piece of music. Watching her face, the pleasure she was taking in the unfamiliar words, made him want to talk even more, find something drawn-out to say, tell a story of some kind, even recite some poetry, if only he knew any.

"So you're getting by all right?" he asked Claude.

"It took a lot of getting used to, but I'm settling in," Claude replied. "I got a roof over my head and it's quiet as hell here. No trouble worth a damn to get into. It's cool that you've come back to see your aunt, man. Some of the folks around here told me she had someone back in New York. I had a feeling when she'd ask me to speak English for her, it was because she really wanted to hear somebody else's voice, maybe yours. It's real cool that you didn't forget her, that you didn't forget your folks. I really wish I had stayed in touch more with my people, you know, then it wouldn't be so weird showing up here like I did. These people don't even know me, man. They've never seen my face before, not even in pictures. They still took me in, after everything I did, because my moms told them I was their blood. I look at them and I see nothing of me, man, blank, nada, but they look at me and they say he has so-and-so's nose and his grandmother's forehead, or some shit like that. It's like a puzzle, man, a weird-ass kind of puzzle. I am the puzzle and these people are putting me back together, telling me things about myself and my family that I never knew or gave a fuck about. Man, if I had run into these people back in Brooklyn, I would have laughed my ass off at them. I would have called them backward-ass peasants. But here I am, man, one of those backwardass peasants myself."

His aunt was engrossed, enthralled by Claude's speech, smiling at times while the morning sunrays danced across her eyes, never penetrating her pupils. He was starting to think of his aunt's eyes as a strange kind of prism, one that consumed light rather than reflected it.

"I can't honestly say I love it here, man"—Claude seemed to be wrapping up—"but it's worked out all right for me. It saved my life. I am at peace here and my family seems to have made peace with me. I came around, man. I can honestly say I was reformed in prison. I would have been a better citizen than most if they hadn't deported me."

"You still have a chance," Dany said, not believing it himself. "You can do something with your life. Maybe you're back here for a reason, to make things better."

He was growing tired of Claude, tired of what he considered his lame excuses and an apparent lack of remorse for whatever it was he had done.

"How long will you be staying?" Claude asked.

"A while," Dany said.

"Is there anything you want to do?" Claude asked. "I know the area pretty well now. I take lots of walks to clear my head. I could show you around."

"I know where things are," Dany said. "And if I don't remember, my aunt can—"

"It's just with her not being able to see—"

"She can see, in her own way—"

"All right, cool, my man. I was just trying to be helpful."

Even with the brusque way their conversation ended, Claude seemed happy as he left. He had gotten his chance to speak English and tell his entire life story in the process.

After Claude's departure, Old Zo's daughter came up and took the empty coffee cup from Dany's hand. She lingered in front of him for a minute, her palm accidentally brushing against his fingertips. At times she seemed older than she looked. Maybe she was twenty, twenty-five, but she looked twelve. He wondered what her story was. Were those children he had seen in Old Zo's yard hers? Did she have a husband? Was he in the city? Dead?

She hesitated before stepping away, as though she gave too much thought to every move she made. When she finally walked away, Dany's aunt asked him, "Do you know why Claude was in prison?"

"He didn't say."

"Do you know what his people say?"

"What do his people say?"

"They say he killed his father."

That night, Dany dreamed that he was having the conversation he'd come to have with his aunt. They were sitting on the step where he and Claude had spoken. He began the conversation by recalling with his aunt the day his parents died.

He was six years old and his father was working as a driver for a family in Port-au-Prince. The morning of the fire, his father had rushed home to tell his mother and aunt, who was visiting from Beau Jour, that his father's employer's family home had been burned down, but not before the family had escaped and gone into hiding. His father

thought they should leave for Beau Jour, for the people who were looking for his employer might think his workers were hiding him. His parents and Estina were throwing a few things in a knapsack when his father told him to go out in the yard and watch out for any strangers. He was watching the street carefully, for even then he felt that he had never been given such an important job. That's when a very large man came up and threw two grenades in quick succession at his house. Before he could even turn his head, the house was on fire, pieces of wood and cement chunks flying everywhere. The man got back in his car, a black German DKW—he remembered it very well because it was the same type of car many of the military men drove and his father had pointed out to him that he should avoid those cars as much as possible—and drove away, but not before Dany got a good look at the man's large round face, a widow's peak dipping into the middle of his forehead.

A few moments later, his aunt came crawling out of the house, unable to see. His parents never came out.

He dreamed his aunt saying, "Yes this is how it happened," then urging him to elaborate on what he had begun to tell her before Old Zo had walked into the room. "You said you saw that same man in New York? Are you sure it was him?"

125 "Yes," he replied. "He is a barber now."

The man who had killed his parents was calling himself Albert Bienaimé:° these days. He had a wife and a grown daughter, both of whom seemed unaware of his past. Some men he had met at work told him that Albert Bienaimé was renting a room in the basement of his house, where they also lived. When he went to Albert Bienaimé's barbershop to ask about the room, he recognized Albert Bienaimé as the same man who had thrown the grenades at his parents' house. When he asked Albert Bienaimé where he was from, Albert Bienaimé said that he was from the mountains somewhere above Jacmel and had never lived in a city before moving to New York.

"You see," the dream aunt said, "he may not be the one."

He took the empty room in Albert Bienaimé's basement. He couldn't sleep for months, spending his weekends in nightclubs to pass the time. He visited Albert Bienaimé's barbershop regularly for haircuts, in order to observe him and reassure himself that he was indeed the same man who had thrown the explosives at his house. Finally, two nights ago, when Albert Bienaimé's wife was away at a religious retreat—he looked for such opportunities all the time and hadn't found one until then—he climbed the splintered steps to the first floor, then made his way with a flashlight to Albert Bienaimé's bedroom.

"What did you do?" the dream aunt asked.

130 He stood there and listened to Albert Bienaimé breathing. Albert Bienaimé was snoring, each round of snores beginning in a low groan and ending in a high-pitched shrill. He lowered his face toward Albert Bienaimé's widow's peak, hoping Albert Bienaimé would wake up and be startled to death. Even when he was a boy, he had heard about how some of the military people, like Albert Bienaimé, would choke their prisoners in their sleep, watching their faces swell and their eyes bulge out of their heads. He was certain when he'd come up the stairs that he was going to kill Albert Bienaimé. He thought of pressing a pillow down on Albert Bienaimé's face, but something stopped him. It wasn't fear, because he was feeling bold, fearless. It wasn't pity; he was too angry to feel pity. It was something else, something less measurable. Perhaps it was the dread of being wrong, of harming the wrong man, of making the wrong woman a widow and the wrong child an orphan. At that moment, all he wanted to do was run as far away from Albert Bienaimé as possible, leave and never come back. He left Albert Bienaimé's room and went down to the basement, booking himself on the next available flight to Port-au-Prince and knowing he would never be coming back. Even though he knew he

° *Bienaimé:* "well loved."

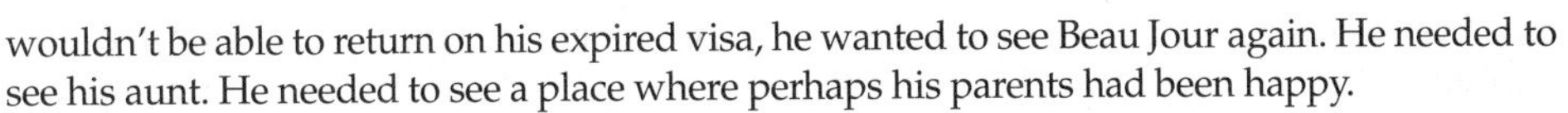

wouldn't be able to return on his expired visa, he wanted to see Beau Jour again. He needed to see his aunt. He needed to see a place where perhaps his parents had been happy.

Dany woke himself with the sound of his own voice reciting his story. His aunt was awake too, sitting up on her cot.

"Da, were you dreaming your parents?" she asked. "You were calling their names."

"Was I?" He would have thought he was calling Albert Bienaimé's name.

"You were calling your parents," she said, "just this instant."

He was still back there, in the yard, waiting for his parents to come out of that burning house, in the room with Albert Bienaimé, wishing he could watch Albert Bienaimé die. His aunt's voice was just an echo of things he could no longer hear, his mother's voice praying, his father's voice laughing.

"I am sorry I woke you," he said, wiping the sweat off his forehead with the backs of his hands.

"I should have let you continue telling me what you came here to say. It's like walking up these mountains and losing something precious halfway. For you it would be no problem walking back, because you are still young and strong, but for me it would take a lot more time and effort."

He heard the cot squeak as she lay back down.

"I understand," he said.

She went back to sleep, whispering something under her breath, then growing completely silent. When he woke up the next morning, she was dead.

It was Old Zo's daughter who let out the first cry, announcing the death to the entire valley. Sitting near the body, on the edge of his aunt's cot, Dany was doubled over with an intense bellyache. Old Zo's daughter took over immediately, brewing him some tea while waiting for their neighbors to arrive.

The tea did nothing for him. He was not expecting it to. Part of him was grateful for the pain, for the physically agonizing diversion it was providing him.

Soon after Old Zo's daughter's cry, a few of the village women began to arrive. It was only then that he learned Old Zo's daughter's name, at least her nickname, Ti Fanm (Little Woman),° which the others kept shouting as they badgered her with questions.

"What happened, Ti Fanm?"

"Ti Fanm, did she die in her sleep?"

"Did she fall, Ti Fanm?"

"Ti Fanm, did she suffer?"

"Ti Fanm, she wasn't even sick."

"She was old," Ti Fanm said in a firm and mature voice. "It can happen like that."

They did not bother asking him anything. He wouldn't have known how to answer anyway. After he and his aunt had spoken in the middle of the night, he thought she had fallen asleep. When he woke up in the morning, even later than he had the day before, she was still lying there, her eyes shut, her hands resting on her belly, her fingers intertwined. He tried to find her pulse, but she had none. He lowered his face to her nose and felt no breath. Then he walked out of the house and found Ti Fanm, sitting on the steps, waiting to cook his breakfast. The pain was already starting in his stomach. Ti Fanm came in and performed her own investigation, then let out that cry, a cry as loud as any siren he had heard on the streets of New York or the foghorns that blew occasionally from the harbor near the house where he had lived with his parents as a boy.

His aunt's house was filled with people now, each of them taking turns examining his aunt's body for signs of life, and when finding none immediately assigning themselves,

° *Ti Fanm:* a shortened form of "petite femme," or "little woman."

and each other, tasks related to her burial. One group ran off to get purple curtains, to hang shroudlike over the front door to show that this was a household in mourning. Another group went off to fetch an unused washbasin to bathe the corpse. Others were searching through the baskets beneath his aunt's cot for an appropriate dress to change her into after her bath. Another went looking for a carpenter to build her coffin.

The men assigned themselves to him and his pain.

"He is in shock," they said.

"Can't you see he's not able to speak?"

155 "He's not even looking at her. He's looking at the floor."

"He has a stomachache," Ti Fanm intercepted.

She brought him some warm salted coffee, which he drank in one gulp.

"He should lie down," one of the men said.

"But where?" Another rebutted. "Not next to her."

160 "He must have known she was going to die." He heard Old Zo's voice rising above the others. "He came just in time. Blood calls blood. She made him come so he could see her before she died. It would have been sad if she had died behind his back, especially since he never buried his parents."

They were speaking about him as though he couldn't understand, as if he were solely an English-speaker, like Claude. Perhaps this was the only way they could think of to console him right then, to offer him solace.

He wished that his stomach would stop hurting, that he could rise from the edge of the cot and take control of the situation, or at least participate in the preparations, but all he wanted to do was lie down next to his aunt, rest his head on her chest, and wrap his arms around her, the way he had done when he was a little boy. He wanted to close his eyes until he could wake up from this unusual dream where everyone was able to speak except the two of them. By midday he felt well enough to join Old Zo and some of the men, who were opening up a slot in the family mausoleum. He was in less pain now, but was still uncomfortable and moved slower than the others.

The women were inside the house, bathing his aunt's body and changing her into a blue dress he had sent her through Popo. He had seen it in a store window in Brooklyn and had chosen it for her, remembering that blue was her favorite color. The wrapping was still intact; she had never worn it.

Once the slot was opened, Old Zo announced that a Protestant minister would be coming by the next morning to say a prayer during the burial. Old Zo had wanted to transport the body to a church in the next village for a full service, but he didn't want his aunt to travel so far, only to return to her own yard to be buried.

165 "The coffin is almost ready," Old Zo said. "She will be able to rest in it during the wake."

He had always been perplexed by the mixture of jubilation and sorrow that was part of Beau Jour's wakes, by the fact that some of the participants played cards and dominoes while others served tea and wept. But what he had always enjoyed was the time carved out for the mourners to tell stories about the deceased, singular tales of first or last encounters, which could either make him holler with laughter or have his stomach spasms return as his grief grew.

The people of his aunt's village were telling such stories about her now. They told of how she once tried to make coffee and filtered dirt through her coffee pouch even though she was able to deliver twins without any trouble. They told of how as a young woman she had embroidered a trousseau that she carried everywhere with her, thinking it would attract a husband. They spoke of her ambition, of her wanting to be a baby seamstress, so she could make clothes for the very same children she was ushering into the world. If he could have managed it, he would have spoken of her sacrifices, of the fact that she had spent most of her life trying to keep him safe. He would have told of how he hadn't wanted to leave

her, to go to New York, but she had insisted that he go so he would be as far away as possible from the people who had murdered his parents.

Claude arrived at the wake just as it was winding down, at a time when everyone was too tired to do anything but sit, stare, and moan, when through sleepy eyes the reason for the all-night gathering had become all too clear, when the purple shroud blowing from the doorway into the night breeze could no longer be ignored.

"I am so sorry, man," Claude said. "I was in Port today and when I came back my people told me. I am truly sorry, man. Your aunt was such good people. One of a kind, really. I am so sorry."

Claude moved forward, as if to hug him, Claude's broad shoulders towering over his head. Dany stepped back, moving away, cringing. Perhaps it was what his aunt had told him, about Claude's having killed his father, but he did not want Claude to touch him. 170

Claude got the message and walked away, drifting toward a group of men who were nodding off at a table near the porch railing.

When he walked back inside the house, he found a small group of women sitting near the open coffin, keeping watch over his aunt. He was still unable to look at her in the coffin for too long. He envied these women the six years they had spent with her while he was gone. He dragged his sisal mat, the one he had been sleeping on these last two nights, to a corner as far away from the coffin as he could get, coiled himself into a ball, and tried to fall asleep.

It could happen like that, Ti Fanm had said. A person his aunt's age could fall asleep talking and wake up dead. He wouldn't have believed it if he hadn't seen it for himself. Death was supposed to be either quick and furious or drawn-out and dull, after a long illness. His aunt had chosen a middle ground. Perhaps Old Zo was right.

Blood calls blood. Perhaps she had summoned him here so he could at last witness a peaceful death and see how it was meant to be mourned. Perhaps Albert Bienaimé was not his parents' murderer after all, but just a phantom who'd shown up to escort him back here. He didn't know what to believe anymore.

He could not fall asleep, not with the women keeping watch over his aunt's body being so close by. Not with Ti Fanm coming over every hour with a cup of tea, which was supposed to cure his bellyaches forever. 175

He didn't like her nickname, was uncomfortable using it. It was too generic, as though she was one of many from a single mold, with no distinctive traits of her own.

"What is your name?" he asked when she brought him her latest brew.

She seemed baffled, as though she were thinking he might need a stronger infusion, something to calm his nerves and a memory aid, too.

"Ti Fanm," she replied.

"Non," he said, "your true name, your full name." 180

"Alice Denise Auguste," she said.

The women who were keeping watch over his aunt were listening to their conversation, cocking their heads ever so slightly in their direction.

"How old are you?" he asked.

"Thirty," she said.

"Thank you," he said.

"You're deserving," she said, using an old-fashioned way of acknowledging his gratitude. 185

She was no longer avoiding his eyes, as though his grief and stomach ailment and the fact that he had asked her real name had rendered them equals.

He got up and walked outside, where many of his aunt's neighbors were sleeping on mats on the porch. There was a full moon overhead and a calm in the air that he was not expecting. In the distance he could hear the waterfall, a sound that, once you got used to it,

you never paid much attention to. He walked over to the mausoleum, removed his shirt, and began to wipe the mausoleum with it, starting at the base and working his way up toward the headstone. It was clean already. The men had done a good job removing the leaves, pebbles, and dust that had accumulated on it while they were opening his aunt's slot, but he wanted to make sure it was spotless, that every piece of debris that had fallen on it since was gone.

"Need help?" Claude asked from a few feet away.

190 He must have been sleeping somewhere on the porch with the others before he saw Dany.

Dany threw his dusty shirt on the ground, climbed up on one of the mausoleum ledges, and sat down. He had wanted to do something, anything, to keep himself occupied until dawn.

"I'm sorry," Dany said, "for earlier."

"I understand," Claude said. "I'd be a real asshole if I got pissed off at you for anything you did or said to me at a time like this. You're in pain, man. I get that."

"I don't know if I'd call it pain," Dany said. "There's no word yet for it. No one has thought of a word yet."

195 "I know, man," Claude said. "It's a real bitch."

In spite of his huge muscles and oversized tattoos, Claude seemed oddly defenseless, like a refugee lost at sea, or a child looking for his parents in a supermarket aisle. Or maybe that's just how Dany wanted to see him, to make him seem more normal, less frightening.

"I hear you killed your father," Dany said.

The words sounded less severe coming out of his mouth than they did rolling around in his head.

"Can I sit?" Claude asked, pointing to a platform on the other side of the headstone.

200 Dany nodded.

"Yes, I killed my old man," Claude said. "Everyone here knows that shit by now. I wish I could say it was an accident. I wish I could say he was a bastard who beat the crap out of me and forced me to defend myself. I wish I could tell you I hated him, never loved him, didn't give a fuck about him at all. I was fourteen and strung out on shit. He came into my room and took the shit. It wasn't just my shit. It was shit I was hustling for someone else. I was really fucked up and wanted the shit back. I had a gun I was using to protect myself out on the street. I threatened him with it. He wouldn't give my shit back, so I shot him."

There was even less sorrow in Claude's voice than Dany had been able to muster over these past twenty-four hours. Dany was still numb, even as tears rolled down Claude's face; he had never known how to grieve or help others grieve. It was as though his parents' death had paralyzed that instinct in him.

"I am sorry," he said, feeling that someone should also think of a better word for this type of commiseration.

"Sorry?" Claude wiped the tears from his face with a quick swipe of his hand. "I am the luckiest fucker alive. I have done something really bad that now makes me want to live my life like a fucking angel. If I hadn't been a minor, I would have been locked up for the rest of my life. And if the prisons in Port had had more room, or if the police down there was worth a damn, I'd be in a small cell with a thousand people right now, not sitting here talking to you. Even with everything I've done, with everything that's happened to me, I am the luckiest fucker on this goddamned planet. Someone, somewhere, must be looking out for my ass."

205 It would be an hour or so before dawn. The moon was already fading, slipping away, on its way someplace else.

The only thing he could think to do for his aunt now was to get Claude to speak and speak and speak, which wouldn't be so hard, since Claude was already one of them, a member of their tribe. Claude was a night talker, one of those who spoke their nightmares

out loud, to themselves, except Claude was also able to speak his nightmares to others, in the daytime, even when the moon had completely vanished and the sun had come out.

QUESTIONS

1. What is meant by "night talkers"? Who are the night talkers in the story? Why is the story titled "Night Talkers"?
2. Why has Dany returned to Haiti? Whom has he come to see? What has happened earlier, before Dany went to live in New York? How does Albert Bienaimé figure into Dany's life?
3. What is the significance of Estina's skepticism about Albert Bienaimé's involvement in the death of Dany's parents and in her loss of sight? What is the significance of Estina's death in the middle of the night?
4. Who is Claude? What crime has he committed, and under what circumstances? Describe the attitudes he expresses in his speech in paragraph 204. In what way is Claude's crime parallel with that of Albert Bienaimé?

WILLIAM FAULKNER (1897–1962)

Faulkner spent his childhood in Mississippi and became one of the foremost American novelists of the twentieth century. He twice received the Pulitzer Prize for Fiction (in 1955 and 1963), and he also received the Nobel Prize in Literature (in 1949). Throughout his extensive fiction about the special world that he named "Yoknapatawpha County," which is modeled on his own home area in Oxford, Mississippi, he treats life in the Southern United States as a symbol of humankind generally, emphasizing the decline of civilization and culture in the wake of the Civil War. Emily Grierson in "A Rose for Emily" is representative of this decline, for she maintains the appearances of status long after the substance is past. It is not unusual to find degraded, sullen, disturbed, and degenerate characters in Faulkner's fiction.

A Rose for Emily (1931)

I

When Miss Emily Grierson died, our whole town went to her funeral; the men through a sort of respectful affection for a fallen monument, the women mostly out of curiosity to see the inside of her house, which no one save an old manservant—a combined gardener and cook—had seen in at least ten years.

It was a big, squarish frame house that had once been white, decorated with cupolas and spires and scrolled balconies in the heavily lightsome style of the seventies, set on what had once been our most select street. But garages and cotton gins had encroached and obliterated even the august names of that neighborhood; only Miss Emily's house was left, lifting its stubborn and coquettish decay above the cotton wagons and the gasoline pumps—an eyesore among eyesores. And now Miss Emily had gone to join the representatives of those august names where they lay in the cedar-bemused cemetery among the ranked and anonymous graves of Union and Confederate soldiers who fell at the battle of Jefferson.

Alive, Miss Emily had been a tradition, a duty, and a care; a sort of hereditary obligation upon the town, dating from that day in 1894 when Colonel Sartoris, the mayor—he who fathered the edict that no Negro woman should appear on the streets without an apron—remitted her taxes, the dispensation dating from the death of her father on into perpetuity. Not that Miss Emily would have accepted charity. Colonel Sartoris invented an involved tale to the effect that Miss Emily's father had loaned money to the town, which the town, as a matter of business, preferred this way of repaying. Only a man of Colonel Sartoris' generation and thought could have invented it, and only a woman could have believed it.

When the next generation, with its more modern ideas, became mayors and aldermen, this arrangement created some little dissatisfaction. On the first of the year they mailed her a tax notice. February came, and there was no reply. They wrote her a formal letter, asking her to call at the sheriff's office at her convenience. A week later the mayor wrote her himself, offering to call or to send his car for her, and received in reply a note on paper of an archaic shape, in a thin, flowing calligraphy in faded ink, to the effect that she no longer went out at all. The tax notice was also enclosed, without comment.

5 They called a special meeting of the Board of Aldermen. A deputation waited upon her, knocked at the door through which no visitor had passed since she ceased giving china-painting lessons eight or ten years earlier. They were admitted by the old Negro into a dim hall from which a stairway mounted into still more shadow. It smelled of dust and disuse—a close, dank smell. The Negro led them into the parlor. It was furnished in heavy, leather-covered furniture. When the Negro opened the blinds of one window, they could see that the leather was cracked; and when they sat down, a faint dust rose sluggishly about their thighs, spinning with slow motes in the single sun-ray. On a tarnished gilt easel before the fireplace stood a crayon portrait of Miss Emily's father.

They rose when she entered—a small, fat woman in black, with a thin gold chain descending to her waist and vanishing into her belt, leaning on an ebony cane with a tarnished gold head. Her skeleton was small and spare; perhaps that was why what would have been merely plumpness in another was obesity in her. She looked bloated, like a body long submerged in motionless water, and of that pallid hue. Her eyes, lost in the fatty ridges of her face, looked like two small pieces of coal pressed into a lump of dough as they moved from one face to another while the visitors stated their errand.

She did not ask them to sit. She just stood in the door and listened quietly until the spokesman came to a stumbling halt. Then they could hear the invisible watch ticking at the end of the gold chain.

Her voice was dry and cold. "I have no taxes in Jefferson. Colonel Sartoris explained it to me. Perhaps one of you can gain access to the city records and satisfy yourselves."

"But we have. We are the city authorities, Miss Emily. Didn't you get a notice from the sheriff, signed by him?"

10 "I received a paper, yes," Miss Emily said. "Perhaps he considers himself the sheriff . . . I have no taxes in Jefferson."

"But there is nothing on the books to show that, you see. We must go by the—"

"See Colonel Sartoris. I have no taxes in Jefferson."

"But, Miss Emily—"

"See Colonel Sartoris." (Colonel Sartoris had been dead almost ten years.) "I have no taxes in Jefferson. Tobe!" The Negro appeared. "Show these gentlemen out."

II

15 So she vanquished them, horse and foot, just as she had vanquished their fathers thirty years before about the smell. That was two years after her father's death and a short time after her sweetheart—the one we believed would marry her—had deserted her. After her father's death she went out very little; after her sweetheart went away, people hardly saw her at all. A few of

the ladies had the temerity to call, but were not received, and the only sign of life about the place was the Negro man—a young man then—going in and out with a market basket.

"Just as if a man—any man—could keep a kitchen properly," the ladies said; so they were not surprised when the smell developed. It was another link between the gross, teeming world and the high and mighty Griersons.

A neighbor, a woman, complained to the mayor, Judge Stevens, eighty years old.

"But what will you have me do about it, madam?" he said.

"Why, send her word to stop it," the woman said. "Isn't there a law?"

"I'm sure that won't be necessary," Judge Stevens said. "It's probably just a snake or a rat that nigger of hers killed in the yard. I'll speak to him about it." 20

The next day he received two more complaints, one from a man who came in diffident deprecation. "We really must do something about it, Judge. I'd be the last one in the world to bother Miss Emily, but we've got to do something." That night the Board of Aldermen met—three graybeards and one younger man, a member of the rising generation.

"It's simple enough," he said. "Send her word to have her place cleaned up. Give her a certain time to do it in, and if she don't . . ."

"Dammit, sir," Judge Stevens said, "will you accuse a lady to her face of smelling bad?"

So the next night, after midnight, four men crossed Miss Emily's lawn and slunk about the house like burglars, sniffing along the base of the brickwork and at the cellar openings while one of them performed a regular sowing motion with his hand out of a sack slung from his shoulder. They broke open the cellar door and sprinkled lime there, and in all the outbuildings. As they recrossed the lawn, a window that had been dark was lighted and Miss Emily sat in it, the light behind her, and her upright torso motionlesss as that of an idol. They crept quietly across the lawn and into the shadow of the locusts that lined the street. After a week or two the smell went away.

That was when people had begun to feel really sorry for her. People in our town, remembering how old lady Wyatt, her great-aunt, had gone completely crazy at last, believed that the Griersons held themselves a little too high for what they really were. None of the young men were quite good enough for Miss Emily and such. We had long thought of them as a tableau, Miss Emily a slender figure in white in the background, her father a spraddled silhouette in the foreground, his back to her and clutching a horsewhip, the two of them framed by the back flung front door. So when she got to be thirty and was still single, we were not pleased exactly, but vindicated; even with insanity in the family she wouldn't have turned down all of her chances if they had really materialized. 25

When her father died, it got about that the house was all that was left to her; and in a way, people were glad. At last they could pity Miss Emily. Being left alone, and a pauper, she had become humanized. Now she too would know the old thrill and the old despair of a penny more or less.

The day after his death all the ladies prepared to call at the house and offer condolence and aid, as is our custom. Miss Emily met them at the door, dressed as usual and with no trace of grief on her face. She told them that her father was not dead. She did that for three days, with the ministers calling on her, and the doctors, trying to persuade her to let them dispose of the body. Just as they were about to resort to law and force, she broke down, and they buried her father quickly.

We did not say she was crazy then. We believed she had to do that. We remembered all the young men her father had driven away, and we knew that with nothing left, she would have to cling to that which had robbed her, as people will.

III

She was sick for a long time. When we saw her again, her hair was cut short, making her look like a girl, with a vague resemblance to those angels in colored church windows—sort of tragic and serene.

30 The town had just let the contracts for paving the sidewalks, and in the summer after her father's death they began the work. The construction company came with niggers and mules and machinery, and a foreman named Homer Barron, a Yankee—a big, dark, ready man, with a big voice and eyes lighter than his face. The little boys would follow in groups to hear him cuss the niggers, and the niggers singing in time to the rise and fall of picks. Pretty soon he knew everybody in town. Whenever you heard a lot of laughing anywhere about the square, Homer Barron would be in the center of the group. Presently we began to see him and Miss Emily on Sunday afternoons driving in the yellow-wheeled buggy and the matched team of bays from the livery stable.

At first we were glad that Miss Emily would have an interest, because the ladies all said, "Of course a Grierson would not think seriously of a Northerner, a day laborer." But there were still others, older people, who said that even grief could not cause a real lady to forget *noblesse oblige* without calling it *noblesse oblige*. They just said, "Poor Emily. Her kinsfolk should come to her." She had some kin in Alabama; but years ago her father had fallen out with them over the estate of old lady Wyatt, the crazy woman, and there was no communication between the two families. They had not even been represented at the funeral.

And as soon as the old people said, "Poor Emily," the whispering began. "Do you suppose it's really so?" they said to one another. "Of course it is. What else could. . . ." This behind their hands; rustling of craned silk and satin behind jalousies closed upon the sun of Sunday afternoon as the thin, swift clop-clop-clop of the matched team passed: "Poor Emily."

She carried her head high enough—even when we believed that she was fallen. It was as if she demanded more than ever the recognition of her dignity as the last Grierson; as if it had wanted that touch of earthiness to reaffirm her imperviousness. Like when she bought the rat poison, the arsenic. That was over a year after they had begun to say "Poor Emily," and while the two female cousins were visiting her.

"I want some poison," she said to the druggist. She was over thirty then, still a slight woman, though thinner than usual, with cold, haughty black eyes in a face the flesh of which was strained across the temples and about the eyesockets as you imagine a lighthouse-keeper's face ought to look. "I want some poison," she said.

35 "Yes, Miss Emily. What kind? For rats and such? I'd recom—"

"I want the best you have. I don't care what kind."

The druggist named several. "They'll kill anything up to an elephant. But what you want is—"

"Arsenic," Miss Emily said. "Is that a good one?"

"Is . . . arsenic? Yes, ma'am. But what you want—"

40 "I want arsenic."

The druggist looked down at her. She looked back at him, erect, her face like a strained flag. "Why, of course," the druggist said. "If that's what you want. But the law requires you to tell what you are going to use it for."

Miss Emily just stared at him, her head tilted back in order to look him eye for eye, until he looked away and went and got the arsenic and wrapped it up. The Negro delivery boy brought her the package; the druggist didn't come back. When she opened the package at home there was written on the box, under the skull and bones: "For rats."

IV

So the next day we all said, "She will kill herself"; and we said it would be the best thing. When she had first begun to be seen with Homer Barron, we had said, "She will marry him." Then we said, "She will persuade him yet," because Homer himself had remarked—he liked men, and it was known that he drank with the younger men in the Elks' Club—that he was not a marrying man. Later we said, "Poor Emily" behind the jalousies as they

passed on Sunday afternoon in the glittering buggy, Miss Emily with her head high and Homer Barron with his hat cocked and a cigar in his teeth, reins and whip in a yellow glove.

Then some of the ladies began to say that it was a disgrace to the town and a bad example to the young people. The men did not want to interfere, but at last the ladies forced the Baptist minister—Miss Emily's people were Episcopal—to call upon her. He would never divulge what happened during that interview, but he refused to go back again. The next Sunday they again drove about the streets, and the following day the minister's wife wrote to Miss Emily's relations in Alabama.

45 So she had blood-kin under her roof again and we sat back to watch developments. At first nothing happened. Then we were sure that they were to be married. We learned that Miss Emily had been to the jeweler's and ordered a man's toilet set in silver, with the letters H. B. on each piece. Two days later we learned that she had bought a complete outfit of men's clothing, including a nightshirt, and we said, "They are married." We were really glad. We were glad because the two female cousins were even more Grierson than Miss Emily had ever been.

So we were not surprised when Homer Barron—the streets had been finished some time since—was gone. We were a little disappointed that there was not a public blowing-off, but we believed that he had gone on to prepare for Miss Emily's coming, or to give her a chance to get rid of the cousins. (By that time it was a cabal, and we were all Miss Emily's allies to help circumvent the cousins.) Sure enough, after another week they departed. And, as we had expected all along, within three days Homer Barron was back in town. A neighbor saw the Negro man admit him at the kitchen door at dusk one evening.

And that was the last we saw of Homer Barron. And of Miss Emily for some time. The Negro man went in and out with the market basket, but the front door remained closed. Now and then we would see her at a window for a moment, as the men did that night when they sprinkled the lime, but for almost six months she did not appear on the streets. Then we knew that this was to be expected too; as if that quality of her father which had thwarted her woman's life so many times had been too virulent and too furious to die.

When we next saw Miss Emily, she had grown fat and her hair was turning gray. During the next few years it grew grayer and grayer until it attained an even pepper-and-salt iron gray, when it ceased turning. Up to the day of her death at seventy-four it was still that vigorous iron-gray, like the hair of an active man.

From that time on her front door remained closed, save for a period of six or seven years, when she was about forty, during which she gave lessons in china-painting. She fitted up a studio in one of the downstairs rooms, where the daughters and granddaughters of Colonel Sartoris' contemporaries were sent to her with the same regularity and in the same spirit that they were sent to church on Sundays with a twenty-five-cent piece for the collection plate. Meanwhile her taxes had been remitted.

50 Then the newer generation became the backbone and the spirit of the town, and the painting pupils grew up and fell away and did not send their children to her with boxes of color and tedious brushes and pictures cut from the ladies' magazines. The front door closed upon the last one and remained closed for good. When the town got free postal delivery, Miss Emily alone refused to let them fasten the metal numbers above her door and attach a mailbox to it. She would not listen to them.

Daily, monthly, yearly we watched the Negro grow grayer and more stooped, going in and out with the market basket. Each December we sent her a tax notice, which would be returned by the post office a week later, unclaimed. Now and then we would see her in one of the downstairs windows—she had evidently shut up the top floor of the house—like the carven torso of an idol in a niche, looking or not looking at us, we could never tell which. Thus she passed from generation to generation—dear, inescapable, impervious, tranquil, and perverse.

And so she died. Fell ill in the house filled with dust and shadows, with only a doddering Negro man to wait on her. We did not even know she was sick; we had long since given up trying to get any information from the Negro. He talked to no one, probably not even to her, for his voice had grown harsh and rusty, as if from disuse.

She died in one of the downstairs rooms, in a heavy walnut bed with a curtain, her gray head propped on a pillow yellow and moldy with age and lack of sunlight.

V

The Negro met the first of the ladies at the front door and let them in, with their hushed, sibilant voices and their quick, curious glances, and then he disappeared. He walked right through the house and out the back and was not seen again.

55 The two female cousins came at once. They held the funeral on the second day, with the town coming to look at Miss Emily beneath a mass of bought flowers, with the crayon face of her father musing profoundly above the bier and the ladies sibilant and macabre; and the very old men—some in their brushed Confederate uniforms—on the porch and the lawn, talking of Miss Emily as if she had been a contemporary of theirs, believing that they had danced with her and courted her perhaps, confusing time with its mathematical progression, as the old do, to whom all the past is not a diminishing road but, instead, a huge meadow which no winter ever quite touches, divided from them now by the narrow bottleneck of the most recent decade of years.

Already we knew that there was one room in that region above stairs which no one had seen in forty years, and which would have to be forced. They waited until Miss Emily was decently in the ground before they opened it.

The violence of breaking down the door seemed to fill this room with pervading dust. A thin, acrid pall as of the tomb seemed to lie everywhere upon this room decked and furnished as for a bridal: upon the valance curtains of faded rose color, upon the rose-shaded lights, upon the dressing table, upon the delicate array of crystal and the man's toilet things backed with tarnished silver, silver so tarnished that the monogram was obscured. Among them lay a collar and tie, as if they had just been removed, which, lifted, left upon the surface a pale crescent in the dust. Upon a chair hung the suit, carefully folded; beneath it the two mute shoes and the discarded socks.

The man himself lay in the bed.

For a long while we just stood there, looking down at the profound and fleshless grin. The body had apparently once lain in the attitude of an embrace, but now the long sleep that outlasts love, that conquers even the grimace of love, had cuckolded him. What was left of him, rotted beneath what was left of the nightshirt, had become inextricable from the bed in which he lay; and upon him and upon the pillow beside him lay that even coating of the patient and biding dust.

60 Then we noticed that in the second pillow was the indentation of a head. One of us lifted something from it, and leaning forward, that faint and invisible dust dry and acrid in the nostrils, we saw a long strand of iron-gray hair.

QUESTIONS

1. Who is Emily Grierson? What was the former position of her family in the town? What has happened to Emily after her father died? What are her economic circumstances? How does the deputation of alderman from the town of Jefferson treat her?
2. How do we learn about Emily? How do reports and rumors about her create the narrative of her life?
3. What has happened between Emily and Homer Barron? What is the significance, if any, of the fact that Homer is from the North?

4. Describe the plot of "A Rose for Emily." What contrasts and oppositions are developed in the story?
5. How does Faulkner shape the story's events to make Emily mysterious or enigmatic? In what ways does the ending come as a surprise?

TIM O'BRIEN (B. 1946)

William Timothy O'Brien was born in Minnesota and attended Macalester College in St. Paul. He saw duty in Vietnam during some of the more controversial times of that conflict, and after returning home he did graduate study, worked as a reporter, and became a writer. Among the works he has regularly published since the 1970s are If I Die in a Combat Zone, Box Me Up and Ship Me Home *(1973);* Northern Lights *(1974);* Going After Cacciato *(1978);* The Things They Carried *(1990), and* July, July *(2002). In his stories, which interweave fiction and autobiography, he realistically treats both the horrors of the Vietnam War and the ways in which returning veterans and their loved ones adjust to life after returning home. Because he portrays the lives and feelings of combat soldiers so well, he has been called one of the best American writers about war.*

 The Things They Carried (1990)

First Lieutenant Jimmy Cross carried letters from a girl named Martha, a junior at Mount Sebastian College in New Jersey. They were not love letters, but Lieutenant Cross was hoping, so he kept them folded in plastic at the bottom of his rucksack. In the late afternoon, after a day's march, he would dig his foxhole, wash his hands under a canteen, unwrap the letters, hold them with the tips of his fingers, and spend the last hour of light pretending. He would imagine romantic camping trips into the White Mountains in New Hampshire. He would sometimes taste the envelope flaps, knowing her tongue had been there. More than anything, he wanted Martha to love him as he loved her, but the letters were mostly chatty, elusive on the matter of love. She was a virgin, he was almost sure. She was an English major at Mount Sebastian, and she wrote beautifully about her professors and roommates and midterm exams, about her respect for Chaucer and her great affection for Virginia Woolf. She often quoted lines of poetry; she never mentioned the war, except to say, Jimmy, take care of yourself. The letters weighed 10 ounces. They were signed Love, Martha, but Lieutenant Cross understood that Love was only a way of signing and did not mean what he sometimes pretended it meant. At dusk, he would carefully return the letters to his rucksack. Slowly, a bit distracted, he would get up and move among his men, checking the perimeter, then at full dark he would return to his hole and watch the night and wonder if Martha was a virgin.

The things they carried were largely determined by necessity. Among the necessities or near-necessities were P-38 can openers, pocket knives, heat tabs, wristwatches, dog tags, mosquito repellent, chewing gum, candy, cigarettes, salt tablets, packets of Kool-Aid, lighters, matches, sewing kits, Military Payment Certificates, C rations, and two or three canteens of water. Together, these items weighed between 15 and 20 pounds, depending upon a man's habits or rate of metabolism. Henry Dobbins, who was a big man, carried extra rations; he was especially fond of canned peaches in heavy syrup over pound cake. Dave Jensen, who practiced field hygiene, carried a toothbrush, dental floss, and several

hotel-sized bars of soap he'd stolen on R&R in Sydney, Australia. Ted Lavender, who was scared, carried tranquilizers until he was shot in the head outside the village of Than Khe in mid-April. By necessity, and because it was SOP, they all carried steel helmets that weighed 5 pounds including the liner and camouflage cover. They carried the standard fatigue jackets and trousers. Very few carried underwear. On their feet they carried jungle boots—2.1 pounds—and Dave Jensen carried three pairs of socks and a can of Dr. Scholl's foot powder as a precaution against trench foot. Until he was shot, Ted Lavender carried six or seven ounces of premium dope, which for him was a necessity. Mitchell Sanders, the RTO, carried condoms. Norman Bowker carried a diary. Rat Kiley carried comic books. Kiowa, a devout Baptist, carried an illustrated New Testament that had been presented to him by his father, who taught Sunday school in Oklahoma City, Oklahoma. As a hedge against bad times, however, Kiowa also carried his grandmother's distrust of the white man, his grandfather's old hunting hatchet. Necessity dictated. Because the land was mined and booby-trapped, it was SOP for each man to carry a steel-centered, nylon-covered flak jacket, which weighed 6.7 pounds, but which on hot days seemed much heavier. Because you could die so quickly, each man carried at least one large compress bandage, usually in the helmet band for easy access. Because the nights were cold, and because the monsoons were wet, each carried a green plastic poncho that could be used as a raincoat or groundsheet or makeshift tent. With its quilted liner, the poncho weighed almost two pounds, but it was worth every ounce. In April, for instance, when Ted Lavender was shot, they used his poncho to wrap him up, then to carry him across the paddy, then to lift him into the chopper that took him away.

They were called legs or grunts.

To carry something was to hump it, as when Lieutenant Jimmy Cross humped his love for Martha up the hills and through the swamps. In its intransitive form, to hump meant to walk, or to march, but it implied burdens far beyond the intransitive.

5 Almost everyone humped photographs. In his wallet, Lieutenant Cross carried two photographs of Martha. The first was a Kodacolor snapshot signed Love, though he knew better. She stood against a brick wall. Her eyes were gray and neutral, her lips slightly open as she stared straight-on at the camera. At night, sometimes, Lieutenant Cross wondered who had taken the picture, because he knew she had boyfriends, because he loved her so much, and because he could see the shadow of the picture-taker spreading out against the brick wall. The second photograph had been clipped from the 1968 Mount Sebastian yearbook. It was an action shot—women's volleyball—and Martha was bent horizontal to the floor, reaching, the palms of her hands in sharp focus, the tongue taut, the expression frank and competitive. There was no visible sweat. She wore white gym shorts. Her legs, he thought, were almost certainly the legs of a virgin, dry and without hair, the left knee cocked and carrying her entire weight, which was just over one hundred pounds. Lieutenant Cross remembered touching that left knee. A dark theater, he remembered, and the movie was *Bonnie and Clyde*, and Martha wore a tweed skirt, and during the final scene, when he touched her knee, she turned and looked at him in a sad, sober way that made him pull his hand back, but he would always remember the feel of the tweed skirt and the knee beneath it and the sound of the gunfire that killed Bonnie and Clyde, how embarrassing it was, how slow and oppressive. He remembered kissing her good night at the dorm door. Right then, he thought, he should've done something brave. He should've carried her up the stairs to her room and tied her to the bed and touched that left knee all night long. He should've risked it. Whenever he looked at the photographs, he thought of new things he should've done.

What they carried was partly a function of rank, partly of field specialty.

As a first lieutenant and platoon leader, Jimmy Cross carried a compass, maps, code books, binoculars, and a .45-caliber pistol that weighed 2.9 pounds fully loaded. He carried a strobe light and the responsibility for the lives of his men.

As an RTO, Mitchell Sanders carried the PRC-25 radio, a killer, 26 pounds with its battery.

As a medic, Rat Kiley carried a canvas satchel filled with morphine and plasma and malaria tablets and surgical tape and comic books and all the things a medic must carry, including M&M's for especially bad wounds, for a total weight of nearly 20 pounds.

As a big man, therefore a machine gunner, Henry Dobbins carried the M-60, which weighed 23 pounds unloaded, but which was almost always loaded. In addition, Dobbins carried between 10 and 15 pounds of ammunition draped in belts across his chest and shoulders. 10

As PFCs or Spec 4s, most of them were common grunts and carried the standard M-16 gas-operated assault rifle. The weapon weighed 7.5 pounds unloaded, 8.2 pounds with its full 20-round magazine. Depending on numerous factors, such as topography and psychology, the riflemen carried anywhere from 12 to 20 magazines, usually in cloth bandoliers, adding on another 8.4 pounds at minimum, 14 pounds at maximum. When it was available, they also carried M-16 maintenance gear—rods and steel brushes and swabs and tubes of LSA oil—all of which weighed about a pound. Among the grunts, some carried the M-79 grenade launcher, 5.9 pounds unloaded, a reasonably light weapon except for the ammunition, which was heavy. A single round weighed 10 ounces. The typical load was 25 rounds. But Ted Lavender, who was scared, carried 34 rounds when he was shot and killed outside Than Khe, and he went down under an exceptional burden, more than 20 pounds of ammunition, plus the flak jacket and helmet and rations and water and toilet paper and tranquilizers and all the rest, plus the unweighed fear. He was dead weight. There was no twitching or flopping. Kiowa, who saw it happen, said it was like watching a rock fall, or a big sandbag or something—just boom, then down—not like the movies where the dead guy rolls around and does fancy spins and goes ass over teakettle—not like that, Kiowa said, the poor bastard just flat-fuck fell. Boom. Down. Nothing else. It was a bright morning in mid-April. Lieutenant Cross felt the pain. He blamed himself. They stripped off Lavender's canteens and ammo, all the heavy things, and Rat Kiley said the obvious, the guy's dead, and Mitchell Sanders used his radio to report one U.S. KIA and to request a chopper. Then they wrapped Lavender in his poncho. They carried him out to a dry paddy, established security, and sat smoking the dead man's dope until the chopper came. Lieutenant Cross kept to himself. He pictured Martha's smooth young face, thinking he loved her more than anything, more than his men, and now Ted Lavender was dead because he loved her so much and could not stop thinking about her. When the dustoff arrived, they carried Lavender aboard. Afterward they burned Than Khe. They marched until dusk, then dug their holes, and that night Kiowa kept explaining how you had to be there, how fast it was, how the poor guy just dropped like so much concrete. Boom-down, he said. Like cement.

In addition to the three standard weapons—the M-60, M-16, and M-79—they carried whatever presented itself, or whatever seemed appropriate as a means of killing or staying alive. They carried catch-as-catch-can. At various times, in various situations, they carried M-14s and CAR-15s and Swedish Ks and grease guns and captured AK-47s and Chi-Coms and RPGs and Simonov carbines and black market Uzis and .38-caliber Smith & Wesson handguns and 66 mm LAWs and shotguns and silencers and blackjacks and bayonets and C-4 plastic explosives. Lee Strunk carried a slingshot; a weapon of last resort, he called it. Mitchell Sanders carried brass knuckles. Kiowa carried his grandfather's feathered hatchet. Every third or fourth man carried a Claymore antipersonnel mine—3.5 pounds with its firing device. They all carried fragmentation grenades—14 ounces each. They all carried at least one M-18 colored smoke grenade—24 ounces. Some carried CS or tear gas grenades. Some carried white phosphorus grenades. They carried all they could bear, and then some, including a silent awe for the terrible power of the things they carried.

• • •

In the first week of April, before Lavender died, Lieutenant Jimmy Cross received a good-luck charm from Martha. It was a simple pebble, an ounce at most. Smooth to the touch, it was a milky white color with flecks of orange and violet, oval-shaped, like a miniature egg. In the accompanying letter, Martha wrote that she had found the pebble on the Jersey shoreline, precisely where the land touched water at high tide, where things came together but also separated. It was this separate-but-together quality, she wrote, that had inspired her to pick up the pebble and to carry it in her breast pocket for several days, where it seemed weightless, and then to send it through the mail, by air, as a token of her truest feelings for him. Lieutenant Cross found this romantic. But he wondered what her truest feelings were, exactly, and what she meant by separate-but-together. He wondered how the tides and waves had come into play on that afternoon along the Jersey shoreline when Martha saw the pebble and bent down to rescue it from geology. He imagined bare feet. Martha was a poet, with the poet's sensibilities, and her feet would be brown and bare, the toenails unpainted, the eyes chilly and somber like the ocean in March, and though it was painful, he wondered who had been with her that afternoon. He imagined a pair of shadows moving along the strip of sand where things came together but also separated. It was phantom jealousy, he knew, but he couldn't help himself. He loved her so much. On the march, through the hot days of early April, he carried the pebble in his mouth, turning it with his tongue, tasting sea salt and moisture. His mind wandered. He had difficulty keeping his attention on the war. On occasion he would yell at his men to spread out the column, to keep their eyes open, but then he would slip away into daydreams, just pretending, walking barefoot along the Jersey shore, with Martha, carrying nothing. He would feel himself rising. Sun and waves and gentle winds, all love and lightness.

What they carried varied by mission.

15 When a mission took them to the mountains, they carried mosquito netting, machetes, canvas tarps, and extra bug juice.

If a mission seemed especially hazardous, or if it involved a place they knew to be bad, they carried everything they could. In certain heavily mined AOs, where the land was dense with Toe Poppers and Bouncing Betties, they took turns humping a 28-pound mine detector. With its headphones and big sensing plate, the equipment was a stress on the lower back and shoulders, awkward to handle, often useless because of the shrapnel in the earth, but they carried it anyway, partly for safety, partly for the illusion of safety.

On ambush, or other night missions, they carried peculiar little odds and ends. Kiowa always took along his New Testament and a pair of moccasins for silence. Dave Jensen carried night-sight vitamins high in carotene. Lee Strunk carried his slingshot; ammo, he claimed, would never be a problem. Rat Kiley carried brandy and M&M's candy. Until he was shot, Ted Lavender carried the starlight scope, which weighed 6.3 pounds with its aluminum carrying case. Henry Dobbins carried his girlfriend's panty-hose wrapped around his neck as a comforter. They all carried ghosts. When dark came, they would move out single file across the meadows and paddies to their ambush coordinates, where they would quietly set up the Claymores and lie down and spend the night waiting.

Other missions were more complicated and required special equipment. In mid-April, it was their mission to search out and destroy the elaborate tunnel complexes in the Than Khe area south of Chu Lai. To blow the tunnels, they carried one-pound blocks of pentrite high explosives, four blocks to a man, 68 pounds in all. They carried wiring, detonators, and battery-powered clackers. Dave Jensen carried earplugs. Most often, before blowing the tunnels, they were ordered by higher command to search them, which was considered bad news, but by and large they just shrugged and carried out orders. Because he was a big man, Henry Dobbins was excused from tunnel duty. The others would draw numbers. Before Lavender died there were 17 men in the platoon, and whoever drew the number 17 would

strip off his gear and crawl in headfirst with a flashlight and Lieutenant Cross's .45-caliber pistol. The rest of them would fan out as security. They would sit down or kneel, not facing the hole, listening to the ground beneath them, imagining cobwebs and ghosts, whatever was down there—the tunnel walls squeezing in—how the flashlight seemed impossibly heavy in the hand and how it was tunnel vision in the very strictest sense, compression in all ways, even time, and how you had to wiggle in—ass and elbows—a swallowed-up feeling—and how you found yourself worrying about odd things: Will your flashlight go dead? Do rats carry rabies? If you screamed, how far would the sound carry? Would your buddies hear it? Would they have the courage to drag you out? In some respects, though not many, the waiting was worse than the tunnel itself. Imagination was a killer.

On April 16, when Lee Strunk drew the number 17, he laughed and muttered something and went down quickly. The morning was hot and very still. Not good, Kiowa said. He looked at the tunnel opening, then out across a dry paddy toward the village of Than Khe. Nothing moved. No clouds or birds or people. As they waited, the men smoked and drank Kool-Aid, not talking much, feeling sympathy for Lee Strunk but also feeling the luck of the draw. You win some, you lose some, said Mitchell Sanders, and sometimes you settle for a rain check. It was a tired line and no one laughed.

Henry Dobbins ate a tropical chocolate bar. Ted Lavender popped a tranquilizer and went off to pee. 20

After five minutes, Lieutenant Jimmy Cross moved to the tunnel, leaned down, and examined the darkness. Trouble, he thought—a cave-in maybe. And then suddenly, without willing it, he was thinking about Martha. The stresses and fractures, the quick collapse, the two of them buried alive under all that weight. Dense, crushing love. Kneeling, watching the hole, he tried to concentrate on Lee Strunk and the war, all the dangers, but his love was too much for him, he felt paralyzed, he wanted to sleep inside her lungs and breathe her blood and be smothered. He wanted her to be a virgin and not a virgin, all at once. He wanted to know her. Intimate secrets: Why poetry? Why so sad? Why that grayness in her eyes? Why so alone? Not lonely, just alone—riding her bike across campus or sitting off by herself in the cafeteria—even dancing, she danced alone—and it was the aloneness that filled him with love. He remembered telling her that one evening. How she nodded and looked away. And how, later, when he kissed her, she received the kiss without returning it, her eyes wide open, not afraid, not a virgin's eyes, just flat and uninvolved.

Lieutenant Cross gazed at the tunnel. But he was not there. He was buried with Martha under the white sand at the Jersey shore. They were pressed together, and the pebble in his mouth was her tongue. He was smiling. Vaguely, he was aware of how quiet the day was, the sullen paddies, yet he could not bring himself to worry about matters of security. He was beyond that. He was just a kid at war, in love. He was twenty-four years old. He couldn't help it.

A few moments later Lee Strunk crawled out of the tunnel. He came up grinning, filthy but alive. Lieutenant Cross nodded and closed his eyes while the others clapped Strunk on the back and made jokes about rising from the dead.

Worms, Rat Kiley said. Right out of the grave. Fuckin' zombie.

The men laughed. They all felt great relief. 25

Spook city, said Mitchell Sanders.

Lee Strunk made a funny ghost sound, a kind of moaning, yet very happy, and right then, when Strunk made that high happy moaning sound, when he went *Ahhooooo,* right then Ted Lavender was shot in the head on his way back from peeing. He lay with his mouth open. The teeth were broken. There was a swollen black bruise under his left eye. The cheekbone was gone. Oh shit, Rat Kiley said, the guy's dead. The guy's dead, he kept saying, which seemed profound—the guy's dead. I mean really.

• • •

The things they carried were determined to some extent by superstition. Lieutenant Cross carried his good-luck pebble. Dave Jensen carried a rabbit's foot. Norman Bowker, otherwise a very gentle person, carried a thumb that had been presented to him as a gift by Mitchell Sanders. The thumb was dark brown, rubbery to the touch, and weighed four ounces at most. It had been cut from a VC corpse, a boy of fifteen or sixteen. They'd found him at the bottom of an irrigation ditch, badly burned, flies in his mouth and eyes. The boy wore black shorts and sandals. At the time of his death he had been carrying a pouch of rice, a rifle and three magazines of ammunition.

You want my opinion, Mitchell Sanders said, there's a definite moral here.

30 He put his hand on the dead boy's wrist. He was quiet for a time, as if counting a pulse, then he patted the stomach, almost affectionately, and used Kiowa's hunting hatchet to remove the thumb.

Henry Dobbins asked what the moral was.

Moral?

You know. *Moral.*

Sanders wrapped the thumb in toilet paper and handed it across to Norman Bowker. There was no blood. Smiling, he kicked the boy's head, watched the flies scatter, and said, It's like with that old TV show—Paladin. Have gun, will travel.

35 Henry Dobbins thought about it.

Yeah, well, he finally said. I don't see no moral.

There it *is,* man.

Fuck off.

They carried USO stationery and pencils and pens. They carried Sterno, safety pins, trip flares, signal flares, spools of wire, razor blades, chewing tobacco, liberated joss sticks and statuettes of the smiling Buddha, candles, grease pencils, *The Stars and Stripes,* fingernail clippers, Psy Ops leaflets, bush hats, bolos, and much more. Twice a week, when the resupply choppers came in, they carried hot chow in green mermite cans and large canvas bags filled with iced beer and soda pop. They carried plastic water containers, each with a two-gallon capacity. Mitchell Sanders carried a set of starched tiger fatigues for special occasions. Henry Dobbins carried Black Flag insecticide. Dave Jensen carried empty sandbags that could be filled at night for added protection. Lee Strunk carried tanning lotion. Some things they carried in common. Taking turns, they carried the big PRC-77 scrambler radio, which weighed 30 pounds with its battery. They shared the weight of memory. They took up what others could no longer bear. Often, they carried each other, the wounded or weak. They carried infections. They carried chess sets, basketballs, Vietnamese-English dictionaries, insignia of rank, Bronze Stars and Purple Hearts, plastic cards imprinted with the Code of Conduct. They carried diseases, among them malaria and dysentery. They carried lice and ringworm and leeches and paddy algae and various rots and molds. They carried the land itself—Vietnam, the place, the soil—a powdery orange-red dust that covered their boots and fatigues and faces. They carried the sky. The whole atmosphere, they carried it, the humidity, the monsoons, the stink of fungus and decay, all of it, they carried gravity. They moved like mules. By daylight they took sniper fire, at night they were mortared, but it was not battle, it was just the endless march, village to village, without purpose, nothing won or lost. They marched for the sake of the march. They plodded along slowly, dumbly, leaning forward against the heat, unthinking, all blood and bone, simple grunts, soldiering with their legs, toiling up the hills and down into the paddies and across the rivers and up again and down, just humping, one step and then the next and then another, but no volition, no will, because it was automatic, it was anatomy, and the war was entirely a matter of posture and carriage, the hump was everything, a kind of inertia, a kind of emptiness, a dullness of desire and intellect and conscience and hope and human sensibility. Their principles were in their feet. Their calculations were biological. They had no sense of strategy or mission.

They searched the villages without knowing what to look for, not caring, kicking over jars of rice, frisking children and old men, blowing tunnels, sometimes setting fires and sometimes not, then forming up and moving on to the next village, then other villages, where it would always be the same. They carried their own lives. The pressures were enormous. In the heat of early afternoon, they would remove their helmets and flak jackets, walking bare, which was dangerous but which helped ease the strain. They would often discard things along the route of march. Purely for comfort, they would throw away rations, blow their Claymores and grenades, no matter, because by nightfall the resupply choppers would arrive with more of the same, then a day or two later still more, fresh watermelons and crates of ammunition and sunglasses and woolen sweaters—the resources were stunning—sparklers for the Fourth of July, colored eggs for Easter—it was the great American war chest—the fruits of science, the smokestacks, the canneries, the arsenals at Hartford, the Minnesota forests, the machine shops, the vast fields of corn and wheat—they carried like freight trains; they carried it on their backs and shoulders—and for all the ambiguities of Vietnam, all the mysteries and unknowns, there was at least the single abiding certainty that they would never be at a loss for things to carry.

After the chopper took Lavender away, Lieutenant Jimmy Cross led his men into the village of Than Khe. They burned everything. They shot chickens and dogs, they trashed the village well, they called in artillery and watched the wreckage, then they marched for several hours through the hot afternoon, and then at dusk, while Kiowa explained how Lavender died, Lieutenant Cross found himself trembling. 40

He tried not to cry. With his entrenching tool, which weighed five pounds, he began digging a hole in the earth.

He felt shame. He hated himself. He had loved Martha more than his men, and as a consequence Lavender was now dead, and this was something he would have to carry like a stone in his stomach for the rest of the war.

All he could do was dig. He used his entrenching tool like an ax, slashing, feeling both love and hate, and then later, when it was full dark, he sat at the bottom of his foxhole and wept. It went on for a long while. In part, he was grieving for Ted Lavender, but mostly it was for Martha, and for himself, because she belonged to another world, which was not quite real, and because she was a junior at Mount Sebastian College in New Jersey, a poet and a virgin and uninvolved, and because he realized she did not love him and never would.

Like cement, Kiowa whispered in the dark. I swear to God—boom, down. Not a word.

I've heard this, said Norman Bowker. 45

A pisser, you know? Still zipping himself up. Zapped while zipping.

All right, fine. That's enough.

Yeah, but you had to see it, the guy just—

I *heard*, man. Cement. So why not shut the fuck *up*?

Kiowa shook his head sadly and glanced over at the hole where Lieutenant Jimmy Cross sat watching the night. The air was thick and wet. A warm dense fog had settled over the paddies and there was the stillness that precedes rain. 50

After a time Kiowa sighed.

One thing for sure, he said. The lieutenant's in some deep hurt. I mean that crying jag—the way he was carrying on—it wasn't fake or anything, it was real heavy-duty hurt. The man cares.

Sure, Norman Bowker said.

Say what you want, the man does care.

We all got problems. 55

Not Lavender.

No, I guess not, Bowker said. Do me a favor, though.

Shut up?

That's a smart Indian. Shut up.

60 Shrugging, Kiowa pulled off his boots. He wanted to say more, just to lighten up his sleep, but instead he opened his New Testament and arranged it beneath his head as a pillow. The fog made things seem hollow and unattached. He tried not to think about Ted Lavender, but then he was thinking how fast it was, no drama, down and dead, and how it was hard to feel anything except surprise. It seemed unchristian. He wished he could find some great sadness, or even anger, but the emotion wasn't there and he couldn't make it happen. Mostly he felt pleased to be alive. He liked the smell of the New Testament under his cheek, the leather and ink and paper and glue, whatever the chemicals were. He liked hearing the sounds of night. Even his fatigue, it felt fine, the stiff muscles and the prickly awareness of his own body, a floating feeling. He enjoyed not being dead. Lying there, Kiowa admired Lieutenant Jimmy Cross's capacity for grief. He wanted to share the man's pain, he wanted to care as Jimmy Cross cared. And yet when he closed his eyes, all he could think was Boom-down, and all he could feel was the pleasure of having his boots off and the fog curling in around him and the damp soil and the Bible smells and the plush comfort of night.

After a moment Norman Bowker sat up in the dark.

What the hell, he said. You want to talk, *talk*. Tell it to me.

Forget it.

No, man, go on. One thing I hate, it's a silent Indian.

65 For the most part they carried themselves with poise, a kind of dignity. Now and then, however, there were times of panic, when they squealed or wanted to squeal but couldn't, when they twitched and made moaning sounds and covered their heads and said Dear Jesus and flopped around on the earth and fired their weapons blindly and cringed and sobbed and begged for the noise to stop and went wild and made stupid promises to themselves and to God and to their mothers and fathers, hoping not to die. In different ways, it happened to all of them. Afterward, when the firing ended, they would blink and peek up. They would touch their bodies, feeling shame, then quickly hiding it. They would force themselves to stand. As if in slow motion, frame by frame, the world would take on the old logic—absolute silence, then the wind, then sunlight, then voices. It was the burden of being alive. Awkwardly, the men would reassemble themselves, first in private, then in groups, becoming soldiers again. They would repair the leaks in their eyes. They would check for casualties, call in dust-offs, light cigarettes, try to smile, clear their throats and spit and begin cleaning their weapons. After a time someone would shake his head and say, No lie. I almost shit my pants, and someone else would laugh, which meant it was bad, yes, but the guy had obviously not shit his pants, it wasn't that bad, and in any case nobody would ever do such a thing and then go ahead and talk about it. They would squint into the dense, oppressive sunlight. For a few moments, perhaps, they would fall silent, lighting a joint and tracking its passage from man to man, inhaling, holding in the humiliation. Scary stuff, one of them might say. But then someone else would grin or flick his eyebrows and say, Roger-dodger, almost cut me a new asshole, *almost*.

There were numerous such poses. Some carried themselves with a sort of wistful resignation, others with pride or stiff soldierly discipline or good humor or macho zeal. They were afraid of dying but they were even more afraid to show it.

They found jokes to tell.

They used a hard vocabulary to contain the terrible softness. *Greased* they'd say. *Offed, lit up, zapped while zipping*. It wasn't cruelty, just stage presence. They were actors. When someone died, it wasn't quite dying, because in a curious way it seemed scripted, and because

they had their lines mostly memorized, irony mixed with tragedy, and because they called it by other names, as if to encyst and destroy the reality of death itself. They kicked corpses. They cut off thumbs. They talked grunt lingo. They told stories about Ted Lavender's supply of tranquilizers, how the poor guy didn't feel a thing, how incredibly tranquil he was.

There's a moral here, said Mitchell Sanders.

They were waiting for Lavender's chopper, smoking the dead man's dope. 70

The moral's pretty obvious, Sanders said, and winked. Stay away from drugs. No joke, they'll ruin your day every time.

Cute, said Henry Dobbins.

Mind blower, get it? Talk about wiggy. Nothing left, just blood and brains.

They made themselves laugh.

There it is, they'd say. Over and over—there it is, my friend, there it is—as if the repetition 75 itself were an act of poise, a balance between crazy and almost crazy, knowing without going, there it is, which meant be cool, let it ride, because Oh yeah, man, you can't change what can't be changed, there it is, there it absolutely and positively and fucking well *is*.

They were tough.

They carried all the emotional baggage of men who might die. Grief, terror, love, longing—these were intangibles, but the intangibles had their own mass and specific gravity, they had tangible weight. They carried shameful memories. They carried the common secret of cowardice barely restrained, the instinct to run or freeze or hide, and in many respects this was the heaviest burden of all, for it could never be put down, it required perfect balance and perfect posture. They carried their reputations. They carried the soldier's greatest fear, which was the fear of blushing. Men killed, and died, because they were embarrassed not to. It was what had brought them to the war in the first place, nothing positive, no dreams of glory or honor, just to avoid the blush of dishonor. They died so as not to die of embarrassment. They crawled into tunnels and walked point and advanced under fire. Each morning, despite the unknowns, they made their legs move. They endured. They kept humping. They did not submit to the obvious alternative, which was simply to close the eyes and fall. So easy, really. Go limp and tumble to the ground and let the muscles unwind and not speak and not budge until your buddies picked you up and lifted you into the chopper that would roar and dip its nose and carry you off to the world. A mere matter of falling, yet no one ever fell. It was not courage, exactly; the object was not valor. Rather, they were too frightened to be cowards.

By and large they carried these things inside, maintaining the masks of composure. They sneered at sick call. They spoke bitterly about guys who had found release by shooting off their own toes or fingers. Pussies, they'd say. Candy-asses. It was fierce, mocking talk, with only a trace of envy or awe, but even so the image played itself out behind their eyes.

They imagined the muzzle against flesh. So easy: squeeze the trigger and blow away a toe. They imagined it. They imagined the quick, sweet pain, then the evacuation to Japan, then a hospital with warm beds and cute geisha nurses.

And they dreamed of freedom birds. 80

At night, on guard, staring into the dark, they were carried away by jumbo jets. They felt the rush of takeoff. *Gone!* they yelled. And then velocity—wings and engines—a smiling stewardess—but it was more than a plane, it was a real bird, a big sleek silver bird with feathers and talons and high screeching. They were flying. The weights fell off; there was nothing to bear. They laughed and held on tight, feeling the cold slap of wind and altitude, soaring, thinking *It's over, I'm gone!*—they were naked, they were light and free—it was all lightness, bright and fast and buoyant, light as light, a helium buzz in the brain, a giddy bubbling in the lungs as they were taken up over the clouds and the war, beyond duty, beyond gravity and mortification and global entanglements—*Sin loi!* they yelled. *I'm sorry, motherfuckers, but I'm out of it, I'm goofed, I'm on a space cruise, I'm gone!*—and it was a restful,

unencumbered sensation, just riding the light waves, sailing that big silver freedom bird over the mountains and oceans, over America, over the farms and great sleeping cities and cemeteries and highways and the golden arches of McDonald's, it was flight, a kind of fleeing, a kind of falling, falling higher and higher, spinning off the edge of the earth and beyond the sun and through the vast, silent vacuum where there were no burdens and where everything weighed exactly nothing—*Gone!* they screamed. *I'm sorry but I'm gone!*—and so at night, not quite dreaming, they gave themselves over to lightness, they were carried, they were purely borne.

On the morning after Ted Lavender died, First Lieutenant Jimmy Cross crouched at the bottom of his foxhole and burned Martha's letters. Then he burned the two photographs. There was a steady rain falling, which made it difficult, but he used heat tabs and Sterno to build a small fire, screening it with his body, holding the photographs over the tight blue flame with the tips of his fingers.

He realized it was only a gesture. Stupid, he thought. Sentimental, too, but mostly just stupid.

Lavender was dead. You couldn't burn the blame.

85 Besides, the letters were in his head. And even now, without photographs, Lieutenant Cross could see Martha playing volleyball in her white gym shorts and yellow T-shirt. He could see her moving in the rain.

When the fire died out, Lieutenant Cross pulled his poncho over his shoulders and ate breakfast from a can.

There was no great mystery, he decided.

In those burned letters Martha had never mentioned the war, except to say, Jimmy, take care of yourself. She wasn't involved. She signed the letters Love, but it wasn't love, and all the fine lines and technicalities did not matter. Virginity was no longer an issue. He hated her. Yes, he did. He hated her. Love, too, but it was a hard, hating kind of love.

The morning came up wet and blurry. Everything seemed part of everything else, the fog and Martha and the deepening rain.

90 He was a soldier, after all.

Half smiling, Lieutenant Jimmy Cross took out his maps. He shook his head hard, as if to clear it, then bent forward and began planning the day's march. In ten minutes, or maybe twenty, he would rouse the men and they would pack up and head west, where the maps showed the country to be green and inviting. They would do what they had always done. The rain might add some weight, but otherwise it would be one more day layered upon all the other days.

He was realistic about it. There was that new hardness in his stomach. He loved her but he hated her.

No more fantasies, he told himself.

Henceforth, when he thought about Martha, it would be only to think that she belonged elsewhere. He would shut down the daydreams. This was not Mount Sebastian, it was another world, where there were no pretty poems or midterm exams, a place where men died because of carelessness and gross stupidity. Kiowa was right. Boom-down, and you were dead, never partly dead.

95 Briefly, in the rain, Lieutenant Cross saw Martha's gray eyes gazing back at him.

He understood.

It was very sad, he thought. The things men carried inside. The things men did or felt they had to do.

He almost nodded at her, but didn't.

Instead he went back to his maps. He was now determined to perform his duties firmly and without negligence. It wouldn't help Lavender, he knew that, but from this point on he

would comport himself as an officer. He would dispose of his good-luck pebble. Swallow it, maybe, or use Lee Strunk's slingshot, or just drop it along the trail. On the march he would impose strict field discipline. He would be careful to send out flank security, to prevent straggling or bunching up, to keep his troops moving at the proper pace and at the proper interval. He would insist on clean weapons. He would confiscate the remainder of Lavender's dope. Later in the day, perhaps, he would call the men together and speak to them plainly. He would accept the blame for what had happened to Ted Lavender. He would be a man about it. He would look them in the eyes, keeping his chin level, and he would issue the new SOPs in a calm, impersonal tone of voice, a lieutenant's voice, leaving no room for argument or discussion. Commencing immediately, he'd tell them, they would no longer abandon equipment along the route of march. They would police up their acts. They would get their shit together, and keep it together, and maintain it neatly and in good working order.

He would not tolerate laxity. He would show strength, distancing himself. 100

Among the men there would be grumbling, of course, and maybe worse, because their days would seem longer and their loads heavier, but Lieutenant Jimmy Cross reminded himself that his obligation was not to be loved but to lead. He would dispense with love; it was not now a factor. And if anyone quarreled or complained, he would simply tighten his lips and arrange his shoulders in the correct command posture. He might give a curt little nod. Or he might not. He might just shrug and say, Carry on, then they would saddle up and form into a column and move out toward the villages west of Than Khe.

QUESTIONS

1. What do we learn about Lieutenant Jimmy Cross? How do we learn about him? Why does he blame himself for Lavender's death? How does Kiowa misinterpret his emotions? How do his concerns unify the story? What other unifying elements does the story contain?
2. What is the effect of the repetitions in the story (the constant descriptions of how much things weigh, the regular need to carry things, the way in which Lavender died)?
3. Why is Mitchell Sanders unable to put into words the moral of the dead man's thumb? How would you describe the moral?
4. Analyze paragraph 39. Discuss the various burdens the men of the platoon must carry. What bearing does this paragraph have upon other parts of the story?

LUIGI PIRANDELLO (1867–1936)

Pirandello was born in southern Sicily into a wealthy family. At first he was home schooled, but eventually went to high school in Palermo, the capital of Sicily. Later he attended the University of Palermo and the University of Rome, but then he went to Bonn, Germany (the birth city of Beethoven), where he gained a doctorate in humanities in 1891. His resources failed because of a disastrous flood in the family's Sicilian sulfur mine, and he was left mainly to his own resources as a teacher and writer. His marriage, which produced three children, proved disastrous as his wife eventually was declared insane and had to be institutionalized. Pirandello's early years were taken up mainly with the writing of stories and dramas. One of his three sons fought in World War I, and survived, unlike the son in the story "War." Eventually Pirandello developed a masterly career as a dramatist, his best known and highly original play being Six Characters in Search of an Author *in*

1921. *With the support of Benito Mussolini, the Prime Minister and Dictator of Italy—support that many claimed was highly controversial because of Mussolini's later alliance with Adolf Hitler—Pirandello became well known internationally. In 1934, he was awarded the Nobel Prize in Literature.*

NEW War (1919)

The passengers who had left Rome by the night express had had to stop until dawn at the small station of Fabriano in order to continue their journey by the small old-fashioned local joining the main line with Sulmona.

At dawn, in a stuffy and smoky second-class carriage in which five people had already spent the night, a bulky woman in deep mourning was hoisted in—almost like a shapeless bundle. Behind her, puffing and moaning, followed her husband—a tiny man, thin and weakly, his face death-white, his eyes small and bright and looking shy and uneasy.

Having at last taken a seat he politely thanked the passengers who had helped his wife and who had made room for her; then he turned round to the woman trying to pull down the collar of her coat, and politely inquired:

"Are you all right, dear?"

5 The wife, instead of answering, pulled up her collar again to her eyes, so as to hide her face.

"Nasty world," muttered the husband with a sad smile.

And he felt it his duty to explain to his traveling companions that the poor woman was to be pitied, for the war was taking away from her her only son, a boy of twenty to whom both had devoted their entire life, even breaking up their home at Sulmona to follow him to Rome, where he had to go as a student, then allowing him to volunteer for war with an assurance, however, that at least for six months he would not be sent to the front and now, all of a sudden, receiving a wire saying that he was due to leave in three days' time and asking them to go and see him off.

The woman under the big coat was twisting and wriggling, at times growling like a wild animal, feeling certain that all those explanations would not have aroused even a shadow of sympathy from those people who—most likely—were in the same plight as herself. One of them, who had been listening with particular attention, said:

"You should thank God that your son is only leaving now for the front. Mine has been sent there the first day of the war. He has already come back twice wounded and been sent back again to the front."

10 "What about me? I have two sons and three nephews at the front," said another passenger.

"Maybe, but in our case it is our only son," ventured the husband.

"What difference can it make? You may spoil your only son with excessive attentions, but you cannot love him more than you would all your other children if you had any. Paternal love is not like bread that can be broken into pieces and split amongst the children in equal shares. A father gives all his love to each one of his children without discrimination, whether it be one or ten, and if I am suffering now for my two sons, I am not suffering half for each of them but double.

"True . . . true . . . " sighed the embarrassed husband, "but suppose (of course we all hope it will never be your case) a father has two sons at the front and he loses one of them, there is still one left to console him . . . while . . ."

"Yes," answered the other, getting cross, "a son left to console him but also a son left for whom he must survive, while in the case of the father of an only son if the son dies the father can die too and put an end to his distress. Which of the two positions is the worse? Don't you see how my case would be worse than yours?"

15 "Nonsense," interrupted another traveler, a fat, red-faced man with bloodshot eyes of the palest gray.

He was panting. From his bulging eyes seemed to spurt inner violence of an uncontrolled vitality which his weakened body could hardly contain.

"Nonsense," he repeated, trying to cover his mouth with his hand so as to hide the two missing front teeth. "Nonsense. Do we give life to our children for our own benefit?"

The other travelers stared at him in distress. The one who had had his son at the front since the first day of the war sighed: "You are right. Our children do not belong to us, they belong to the Country. . . ."

"Bosh," retorted the fat traveler. "Do we think of the Country when we give life to our children? Our sons are born because . . . well, because they must be born and when they come to life they take our own life with them. This is the truth. We belong to them but they never belong to us. And when they reach twenty they are exactly what we were at their age. We too had a father and mother, but there were so many other things as well . . . girls, cigarettes, illusions, new ties . . . and the Country, of course, whose call we would have answered—when we were twenty—even if father and mother had said no. Now at our age, the love of our Country is still great, of course, but stronger than it is the love for our children. Is there any one of us here who wouldn't gladly take his son's place at the front if he could?"

20 There was a silence all round, everybody nodding as to approve.

"Why then," continued the fat man, "shouldn't we consider the feelings of our children when they are twenty? Isn't it natural that at their age they should consider the love for their Country (I am speaking of decent boys, of course) even greater than the love for us? Isn't it natural that it should be so, as after all they must look upon us as upon old boys who cannot move any more and must stay at home? If Country exists, if Country is a natural necessity, like bread, of which each of us must eat in order not to die of hunger, somebody must go to defend it. And our sons go, when they are twenty, and they don't want tears, because if they die, they die inflamed and happy (I am speaking, of course, of decent boys). Now, if one dies young and happy, without having the ugly sides of life, the boredom of it, the pettiness, the bitterness of disillusion . . . what more can we ask for him? Everyone should stop crying; everyone should laugh, as I do . . . or at least thank God—as I do—because my son, before dying, sent me a message saying that he was dying satisfied at having ended his life in the best way he could have wished. That is why, as you see, I do not even wear mourning. . . ."

He shook his light fawn coat as to show it; his livid lip over his missing teeth was trembling, his eyes were watery and motionless, and soon after he ended with a shrill laugh which might well have been a sob.

"Quite so . . . quite so . . ." agreed the others.

The woman who, bundled in a corner under her coat, had been sitting and listening had—for the last three months—tried to find in the words of her husband and her friends something to console her in her deep sorrow, something that might show her how a mother should resign herself to send her son not even to death but to a probably dangerous life. Yet not a word had she found amongst the many which had been said . . . and her grief had been greater in seeing that nobody—as she thought—could share her feelings.

25 But now the words of the traveler amazed and almost stunned her. She suddenly realized that it wasn't the others who were wrong and could not understand her, but herself who could not rise up to the same height of those fathers and mothers willing to resign themselves, without crying, not only to the departure of their sons but even to their death.

She lifted her head, she bent over from her corner trying to listen with great attention to the details which the fat man was giving to his companions about the way his son had fallen as a hero, for his King and his Country, happy and without regrets. It seemed to her that she

had stumbled into a world she had never dreamt of, a world so far unknown to her and she was so pleased to hear everyone joining in congratulating that brave father who could so stoically speak of his child's death.

Then suddenly, just as if she had heard nothing of what had been said and almost as if waking up from a dream, she turned to the old man, asking him:

"Then . . . is your son really dead?"

Everybody stared at her. The old man, too, turned to look at her, fixing his great, bulging, horribly watery light gray eyes, deep in her face. For some little time he tried to answer, but words failed him. He looked and looked at her, almost as if only then—at that silly, incongruous question—he had suddenly realized at last that his son was really dead—gone forever—forever. His face contracted, became horribly distorted, then he snatched in haste a handkerchief from his pocket and, to the amazement of everyone, broke into harrowing, heart-rending, uncontrollable sobs.

QUESTIONS

1. Explain the means by which Pirandello develops the narrative structure of the story. Why does he include so much conversation? What might the story be like if it had been carried out exclusively through description?
2. Describe the thoughts about death expressed by the "fat, red-faced man with bloodshot eyes." How does this man seem to be defending the need for battlefield deaths? How do his true thoughts emerge in the story? How does he seem to be contradictory?
3. What do you think is the story's major idea, as it develops in the discussion by the passengers? Why does Pirandello choose the man who seems least appealing as the one to whom the ultimate sacrifice has happened?
4. In paragraph 28, why does the woman who is "bundled in a corner under her coat" ask the simple question of the fat man? Why is it she who asks the question, and not one of the other passengers?

ALICE WALKER (b. 1944)

Walker was born in Georgia and attended Sarah Lawrence College, graduating in 1965. In addition to teaching at Yale, Wellesley, and other schools, she has edited and published fiction, poetry, and biography, and she received a Guggenheim Fellowship in 1977. Her main hobby is gardening. For her collection of poems Revolutionary Petunias *(1973), she received a Wall Book Award nomination. Her best-known novel,* The Color Purple *(1982), was made into a movie that won an Academy Award in 1985. Her most recent novel is* By the Light of My Father's Smile *(1998).*

 Everyday Use (1973)

for your grandmama

I will wait for her in the yard that Maggie and I made so clean and wavy yesterday afternoon. A yard like this is more comfortable than most people know. It is not just a yard. It is like an extended living room. When the hard clay is swept clean as a floor and the fine sand

around the edges lined with tiny, irregular grooves, anyone can come and sit and look up into the elm tree and wait for the breezes that never come inside the house.

Maggie will be nervous until after her sister goes: she will stand hopelessly in corners, homely and ashamed of the burn scars down her arms and legs, eying her sister with a mixture of envy and awe. She thinks her sister has held life always in the palm of one hand, that "no" is a word the world never learned to say to her.

You've no doubt seen those TV shows° where the child who has "made it" is confronted, as a surprise, by her own mother and father, tottering in weakly from backstage. (A pleasant surprise, of course: What would they do if parent and child came on the show only to curse out and insult each other?) On TV mother and child embrace and smile into each other's faces. Sometimes the mother and father weep, the child wraps them in her arms and leans across the table to tell how she would not have made it without their help. I have seen these programs.

Sometimes I dream a dream in which Dee and I are suddenly brought together on a TV program of this sort. Out of a dark and soft-seated limousine I am ushered into a bright room filled with many people. There I meet a smiling, gray, sporty man like Johnny Carson who shakes my hand and tells me what a fine girl I have. Then we are on the stage and Dee is embracing me with tears in her eyes. She pins on my dress a large orchid, even though she has told me once that she thinks orchids are tacky flowers.

5 In real life I am a large, big-boned woman with rough, man-working hands. In the winter I wear flannel nightgowns to bed and overalls during the day. I can kill and clean a hog as mercilessly as a man. My fat keeps me hot in zero weather. I can work outside all day, breaking ice to get water for washing; I can eat pork liver cooked over the open fire minutes after it comes steaming from the hog. One winter I knocked a bull calf straight in the brain between the eyes with a sledge hammer and had the meat hung up to chill before nightfall. But of course all this does not show on television. I am the way my daughter would want me to be: a hundred pounds lighter, my skin like an uncooked barley pancake. My hair glistens in the hot bright lights. Johnny Carson has much to do to keep up with my quick and witty tongue.

But that is a mistake, I know even before I wake up. Who ever knew a Johnson with a quick tongue? Who can even imagine me looking a strange white man in the eye? It seems to me I have talked to them always with one foot raised in flight, with my head turned in whichever way is farthest from them. Dee, though. She would always look anyone in the eye. Hesitation was no part of her nature.

"How do I look, Mama?" Maggie says, showing just enough of her thin body enveloped in pink skirt and red blouse for me to know she's there, hidden by the door.

"Come out into the yard," I say.

Have you ever seen a lame animal, perhaps a dog run over by some careless person rich enough to own a car, sidle up to someone who is ignorant enough to be kind to him? That is the way my Maggie walks. She has been like this, chin on chest, eyes on ground, feet in shuffle, ever since the fire that burned the other house to the ground.

10 Dee is lighter than Maggie, with nicer hair and a fuller figure. She's a woman now, though sometimes I forget. How long ago was it that the other house burned? Ten, twelve years? Sometimes I can still hear the flames and feel Maggie's arms sticking to me, her hair smoking and her dress falling off her in little black papery flakes. Her eyes seemed stretched open, blazed open by the flames reflected in them. And Dee, I see her standing off

° *TV shows:* In the early days of television, a popular show was *This Is Your Life*, which the narrator describes exactly here.

under the sweet gum tree she used to dig gum out of; a look of concentration on her face as she watched the last dingy gray board of the house fall in toward the red-hot brick chimney. Why don't you do a dance around the ashes? I'd wanted to ask her. She had hated the house that much.

I used to think she hated Maggie, too. But that was before we raised the money, the church and me, to send her to Augusta° to school. She used to read to us without pity; forcing words, lies, other folks' habits, whole lives upon us two, sitting trapped and ignorant underneath her voice. She washed us in a river of make-believe, burned us with a lot of knowledge we didn't necessarily need to know. Pressed us to her with the serious way she read, to shove us away at just the moment, like dimwits, we seemed about to understand.

Dee wanted nice things. A yellow organdy dress to wear to her graduation from high school; black pumps to match a green suit she'd made from an old suit somebody gave me. She was determined to stare down any disaster in her efforts. Her eyelids would not flicker for minutes at a time. Often I fought off the temptation to shake her. At sixteen she had a style of her own: and knew what style was.

I never had an education myself. After second grade the school was closed down. Don't ask me why: in 1927 colored asked fewer questions than they do now. Sometimes Maggie reads to me. She stumbles along good-naturedly, but can't see well. She knows she is not bright. Like good looks and money, quickness passed her by. She will marry John Thomas (who has mossy teeth in an earnest face) and then I'll be free to sit here and I guess just sing church songs to myself. Although I never was a good singer. Never could carry a tune. I was always better at a man's job. I used to love to milk till I was hooked in the side° in '49. Cows are soothing and slow and don't bother you, unless you try to milk them the wrong way.

I have deliberately turned my back on the house. It is three rooms, just like the one that burned, except the roof is tin; they don't make shingle roofs any more. There are no real windows, just some holes cut in the sides, like the portholes on a ship, but not round and not square, with rawhide holding the shutters up on the outside. This house is in a pasture, too, like the other one. No doubt when Dee sees it she will want to tear it down. She wrote me once that no matter where we "choose" to live, she will manage to come see us. But she will never bring her friends. Maggie and I thought about this and Maggie asked me, "Mama, when did Dee ever *have* any friends?"

15 She has a few. Furtive boys in pink shirts hanging about on washday after school. Nervous girls who never laughed. Impressed with her they worshiped the well-turned phrase, the cute shape, the scalding humor that erupted like bubbles in lye. She read to them.

When she was courting Jimmy T she didn't have much time to pay to us, but turned all her faultfinding power on him. He *flew* to marry a cheap city girl from a family of ignorant flashy people. She hardly had time to recompose herself.

When she comes I will meet—but there they are!

Maggie attempts to make a dash for the house, in her shuffling way, but I stay her with my hand. "Come back here," I say. And she stops and tries to dig a well in the sand with her toe.

It is hard to see them clearly through the strong sun. But even the first glimpse of leg out of the car tells me it is Dee. Her feet were always neat-looking, as if God himself had shaped them with a certain style. From the other side of the car comes a short, stocky man. Hair is all over his head a foot long and hanging from his chin like a kinky mule tail. I hear Maggie suck in her breath. "Uhnnnh," is what it sounds like. Like when you see the wriggling end of a snake just in front of your foot on the road. "Uhnnnh."

° *Augusta:* city in eastern Georgia, the location of Paine College.
° *hooked in the side:* kicked by a cow.

Dee next. A dress down to the ground, in this hot weather. A dress so loud it hurts my eyes. There are yellows and oranges enough to throw back the light of the sun. I feel my whole face warming from the heat waves it throws out. Earrings gold, too, and hanging down to her shoulders. Bracelets dangling and making noises when she moves her arm up to shake the folds of the dress out of her armpits. The dress is loose and flows, and as she walks closer, I like it. I hear Maggie go "Uhnnnh" again. It is her sister's hair. It stands straight up like the wool on a sheep. It is black as night and around the edges are two long pigtails that rope about like small lizards disappearing behind her ears. 20

"Wa-su-zo-Tean-o!"° she says, coming on in that gliding way the dress makes her move. The short stocky yellow with the hair to his navel is all grinning and he follows up with "Asalamalakim,° my mother and my sister!" He moves to hug Maggie but she falls back, tight up against the back of my chair. I feel her trembling there and when I look up I see the perspiration falling off her chin.

"Don't get up," says Dee. Since I am stout it takes something of a push. You can see me trying to move a second or two before I make it. She turns, showing white heels through her sandals, and goes back to the car. Out she peeks next with a Polaroid. She stoops down quickly and lines up picture after picture of me sitting there in front of the house with Maggie cowering behind me. She never takes a shot without making sure the house is included. When a cow comes nibbling around the edge of the yard she snaps it and me and Maggie *and* the house. Then she puts the Polaroid in the back seat of the car, and comes up and kisses me on the forehead.

Meanwhile Asalamalakim is going through motions with Maggie's hand. Maggie's hand is as limp as a fish, and probably as cold, despite the sweat, and she keeps trying to pull it back. It looks like Asalamalakim wants to shake hands but wants to do it fancy. Or maybe he don't know how people shake hands. Anyhow, he soon gives up on Maggie.

"Well," I say, "Dee."

"No, Mama," she says. "Not 'Dee,' Wangero Leewanika Kemanjo!" 25

"What happened to 'Dee'?" I wanted to know.

"She's dead," Wangero said. "I couldn't bear it any longer, being named after the people who oppress me."

"You know as well as me you was named after your aunt Dicie," I said. Dicie is my sister. She named Dee. We called her "Big Dee" after Dee was born.

"But who was *she* named after?" asked Wangero.

"I guess after Grandma Dee," I said. 30

"And who was she named after?" asked Wangero.

"Her mother," I said, and saw Wangero was getting tired. "That's about as far back as I can trace it," I said. Though, in fact, I probably could have carried it back beyond the Civil War through the branches.

"Well," said Asalamalakim, "there you are."

"Uhnnnh," I heard Maggie say.

"There I was not," I said, "before 'Dicie' cropped up in our family, so why should I try to trace it that far back?" 35

He just stood there grinning, looking down on me like somebody inspecting a Model A° car. Every once in a while he and Wangero sent eye signals over my head.

"How do you pronounce this name?" I asked.

"You don't have to call me by it if you don't want to," said Wangero.

° *Wa-su-zo-Tean-o:* greeting used by black Muslims.

° *Asalamalakim:* Muslim salutation meaning "Peace be with you."

° *Model A car:* the Ford car that replaced the Model T in the late 1920s. The Model A was proverbial for its quality and durability.

"Why shouldn't I?" I asked. "If that's what you want us to call you, we'll call you."

40 "I know it might sound awkward at first," said Wangero.

"I'll get used to it," I said. "Ream it out again."

Well, soon we got the name out of the way. Asalamalakim had a name twice as long and three times as hard. After I tripped over it two or three times he told me to just call him Hakim-a-barber. I wanted to ask him was he a barber, but I didn't really think he was, so I didn't ask.

"You must belong to those beef-cattle peoples down the road," I said. They said "Asalamalakim" when they met you, too, but they didn't shake hands. Always too busy: feeding the cattle, fixing the fences, putting up salt-lick shelters,° throwing down hay. When the white folks poisoned some of the herd the men stayed up all night with rifles in their hands. I walked a mile and a half just to see the sight.

Hakim-a-barber said, "I accept some of their doctrines, but farming and raising cattle is not my style." (They didn't tell me, and I didn't ask, whether Wangero (Dee) had really gone and married him.)

45 We sat down to eat and right away he said he didn't eat collards and pork was unclean. Wangero, though, went on through the chitlins and corn bread, the greens and everything else. She talked a blue streak over the sweet potatoes. Everything delighted her. Even the fact that we still used the benches her daddy made for the table when we couldn't afford to buy chairs.

"Oh, Mama!" she cried. Then turned to Hakim-a-barber. "I never knew how lovely these benches are. You can feel the rump prints," she said, running her hands underneath her and along the bench. Then she gave a sigh and her hand closed over Grandma Dee's butter dish. "That's it!" she said. "I knew there was something I wanted to ask you if I could have." She jumped up from the table and went over in the corner where the churn stood, the milk in it clabber° by now. She looked at the churn and looked at it.

"This churn top is what I need," she said. "Didn't Uncle Buddy whittle it out of a tree you all used to have?"

"Yes," I said.

"Uh huh," she said happily. "And I want the dasher, too."

50 "Uncle Buddy whittle that, too?" asked the barber.

Dee (Wangero) looked up at me.

"Aunt Dee's first husband whittled the dash," said Maggie so low you almost couldn't hear her. "His name was Henry, but they called him Stash."

"Maggie's brain is like an elephant's," Wangero said, laughing. "I can use the churn top as a centerpiece for the alcove table," she said, sliding a plate over the churn, "and I'll think of something artistic to do with the dasher."

When she finished wrapping the dasher the handle stuck out. I took it for a moment in my hands. You didn't even have to look close to see where hands pushing the dasher up and down to make butter had left a kind of sink in the wood. In fact, there were a lot of small sinks; you could see where thumbs and fingers had sunk into the wood. It was beautiful light yellow wood, from a tree that grew in the yard where Big Dee and Stash had lived.

55 After dinner Dee (Wangero) went to the trunk at the foot of my bed and started rifling through it. Maggie hung back in the kitchen over the dishpan. Out came Wangero with two quilts. They had been pieced by Grandma Dee and then Big Dee and me had hung them on the quilt frames on the front porch and quilted them. One was in the Lone Star pattern. The

---

° *salt-lick shelters:* shelters built to prevent rain from dissolving the large blocks of rock salt set up on poles for cattle.

° *clabber:* curdled, turned sour.

other was Walk Around the Mountain. In both of them were scraps of dresses Grandma Dee had worn fifty and more years ago. Bits and pieces of Grandpa Jarrell's Paisley shirts. And one teeny faded blue piece, about the size of a penny matchbox, that was from Great Grandpa Ezra's uniform that he wore in the Civil War.

"Mama," Wangero said sweet as a bird. "Can I have these old quilts?"

I heard something fall in the kitchen, and a minute later the kitchen door slammed.

"Why don't you take one or two of the others?" I asked, "These old things was just done by me and Big Dee from some tops your grandma pieced before she died."

"No," said Wangero. "I don't want those. They are stitched around the borders by machine."

"That'll make them last better," I said. 60

"That's not the point," said Wangero. "These are all pieces of dresses Grandma used to wear. She did all this stitching by hand. Imagine!" She held the quilts securely in her arms, stroking them.

"Some of the pieces, like those lavender ones, come from old clothes her mother handed down to her," I said, moving up to touch the quilts. Dee (Wangero) moved back just enough so that I couldn't reach the quilts. They already belonged to her.

"Imagine!" she breathed again, clutching them closely to her bosom.

"The truth is," I said, "I promised to give them quilts to Maggie, for when she marries John Thomas."

She gasped like a bee had stung her. 65

"Maggie can't appreciate these quilts!" she said. "She'd probably be backward enough to put them to everyday use."

"I reckon she would," I said. "God knows I been saving 'em for long enough with nobody using 'em. I hope she will!" I didn't want to bring up how I had offered Dee (Wangero) a quilt when she went away to college. Then she had told me they were old-fashioned, out of style.

"But they're *priceless!*" she was saying now, furiously; for she has a temper. "Maggie would put them on the bed and in five years they'd be in rags. Less than that!"

"She can always make some more," I said. "Maggie knows how to quilt."

Dee (Wangero) looked at me with hatred. "You just will not understand. The point is these quilts, *these* quilts!" 70

"Well," I said, stumped. "What would *you* do with them?"

"Hang them," she said. As if that was the only thing you *could* do with quilts.

Maggie by now was standing in the door. I could almost hear the sound her feet made as they scraped over each other.

"She can have them, Mama," she said, like somebody used to never winning anything, or having anything reserved for her. "I can 'member Grandma Dee without the quilts."

I looked at her hard. She had filled her bottom lip with checkerberry snuff and it gave her face a kind of dopey, hangdog look. It was Grandma Dee and Big Dee who taught her how to quilt herself. She stood there with her scarred hands hidden in the folds of her skirt. She looked at her sister with something like fear but she wasn't mad at her. This was Maggie's portion. This was the way she knew God to work. 75

When I looked at her like that something hit me in the top of my head and ran down to the soles of my feet. Just like when I'm in church and the spirit of God touches me and I get happy and shout. I did something I never had done before: hugged Maggie to me, then dragged her on into the room, snatched the quilts out of Miss Wangero's hands and dumped them into Maggie's lap. Maggie just sat there on my bed with her mouth open.

"Take one or two of the others," I said to Dee.

But she turned without a word and went out to Hakim-a-barber.

"You just don't understand," she said, as Maggie and I came out to the car.

80 "What don't I understand?" I wanted to know.

"Your heritage," she said. And then she turned to Maggie, kissed her, and said, "You ought to try to make something of yourself, too, Maggie. It's really a new day for us. But from the way you and Mama still live you'd never know it."

She put on some sunglasses that hid everything above the tip of her nose and her chin.

Maggie smiled; maybe at the sunglasses. But a real smile, not scared. After we watched the car dust settle I asked Maggie to bring me a dip of snuff. And then the two of us sat there just enjoying, until it was time to go in the house and go to bed.

QUESTIONS

1. Describe the narrator. Who is she? What is she like? Where and how does she live? What kind of life has she had? How does the story bring out her judgments about her two daughters?
2. Describe the narrator's daughters. How are they different physically and mentally? How have their lives been different?
3. Why did Dee change her name to "Wangero"? How is this change important, and how is it reflected in her attitude toward the family artifacts?
4. Describe the importance of the phrase "everyday use" (paragraph 66). How does this phrase highlight the conflicting values in the story?

EUDORA WELTY (1909–2001)

One of the major Southern writers, Welty was born in Jackson, Mississippi. She attended the Mississippi State College for Women and the University of Wisconsin, and she began her writing career during the Great Depression. By 1943 she had published two major story collections, Curtain of Green *(1941, including "A Worn Path") and* The Wide Net *(1943). She is the author of many stories and was awarded the Pulitzer Prize in 1973 for her short novel* The Optimist's Daughter *(1972). "A Worn Path" received an O. Henry Award in 1941.*

A Worn Path° (1941)

It was December—a bright frozen day in the early morning. Far out in the country there was an old Negro woman with her head tied in a red rag, coming along a path through the pinewoods. Her name was Phoenix Jackson. She was very old and small and she walked slowly in the dark pine shadows, moving a little from side to side in her steps, with the balanced heaviness and lightness of a pendulum in a grandfather clock. She carried a thin, small cane made from an umbrella, and with this she kept tapping the frozen earth in front of her. This made a grave and persistent noise in the still air, that seemed meditative like the chirping of a solitary little bird.

° "A Worn Path," from *A Curtain of Green and Other Stories*, Copyright 1941 and renewed 1969 by Eudora Welty, reprinted by permission of Harcourt, Inc.

She wore a dark striped dress reaching down to her shoe tops, and an equally long apron of bleached sugar sacks, with a full pocket: all neat and tidy, but every time she took a step she might have fallen over her shoelaces, which dragged from her unlaced shoes. She looked straight ahead. Her eyes were blue with age. Her skin had a pattern all its own of numberless branching wrinkles and as though a whole little tree stood in the middle of her forehead, but a golden color ran underneath, and the two knobs of her cheeks were illuminated by a yellow burning under the dark. Under the rag her hair came down on her neck in the frailest of ringlets, still black, and with an odor like copper.

Now and then there was a quivering in the thicket. Old Phoenix said, "Out of my way, all you foxes, owls, beetles, jack rabbits, coons and wild animals! . . . Keep out from under these feet, little bob-whites. . . . Keep the big wild hogs out of my path. Don't let none of those come running my direction. I got a long way." Under her small black-freckled hand her cane, limber as a buggy whip, would switch at the brush as if to rouse up any hiding things.

On she went. The woods were deep and still. The sun made the pine needles almost too bright to look at, up where the wind rocked. The cones dropped as light as feathers. Down in the hollow was the mourning dove—it was not too late for him.

5 The path ran up a hill. "Seem like there is chains about my feet, time I get this far," she said, in the voice of argument old people keep to use with themselves. "Something always take a hold of me on this hill—pleads I should stay."

After she got to the top she turned and gave a full, severe look behind her where she had come. "Up through pines," she said at length. "Now down through oaks."

Her eyes opened their widest, and she started down gently. But before she got to the bottom of the hill a bush caught her dress.

Her fingers were busy and intent, but her skirts were full and long, so that before she could pull them free in one place they were caught in another. It was not possible to allow the dress to tear. "I in the thorny bush," she said. "Thorns, you doing your appointed work. Never want to let folks pass, no sir. Old eyes thought you was a pretty little *green* bush."

Finally, trembling all over, she stood free, and after a moment dared to stoop for her cane.

10 "Sun so high!" she cried, leaning back and looking, while the thick tears went over her eyes. "The time getting all gone here."

At the foot of this hill was a place where a log was laid across the creek.

"Now comes the trial," said Phoenix.

Putting her right foot out, she mounted the log and shut her eyes. Lifting her skirt, leveling her cane fiercely before her, like a festival figure in some parade, she began to march across. Then she opened her eyes and she was safe on the other side.

"I wasn't as old as I thought," she said.

15 But she sat down to rest. She spread her skirts on the bank around her and folded her hands over her knees. Up above her was a tree in a pearly cloud of mistletoe. She did not dare to close her eyes, and when a little boy brought her a plate with a slice of marble-cake on it she spoke to him. "That would be acceptable," she said. But when she went to take it there was just her own hand in the air.

So she left that tree, and had to go through a barbed-wire fence. There she had to creep and crawl, spreading her knees and stretching her fingers like a baby trying to climb the steps. But she talked loudly to herself: she could not let her dress be torn now, so late in the day, and she could not pay for having her arm or leg sawed off if she got caught fast where she was.

At last she was safe through the fence and risen up out in the clearing. Big dead trees, like black men with one arm, were standing in the purple stalks of the withered cotton field. There sat a buzzard.

"Who you watching?"

In the furrow she made her way along.

20 "Glad this is not the season for bulls," she said, looking sideways, "and the good Lord made his snakes to curl up and sleep in the winter. A pleasure I don't see no two-headed snake coming around that tree, where it come once. It took a while to get by him, back in the summer."

She passed through the old cotton and went into a field of dead corn. It whispered and shook and was taller than her head. "Through the maze now," she said, for there was no path.

Then there was something tall, black, and skinny there, moving before her.

At first she took it for a man. It could have been a man dancing in the field. But she stood still and listened, and it did not make a sound. It was as silent as a ghost.

"Ghost," she said sharply, "who be you the ghost of? For I have heard of nary death close by."

25 But there was no answer—only the ragged dancing in the wind.

She shut her eyes, reached out her hand, and touched a sleeve. She found a coat and inside that an emptiness, cold as ice.

"You scarecrow," she said. Her face lighted. "I ought to be shut up for good," she said with laughter. "My senses is gone. I too old, I the oldest people I ever know. Dance, old scarecrow," she said, "while I dancing with you."

She kicked her foot over the furrow, and with mouth drawn down, shook her head once or twice in a little strutting way. Some husks blew down and whirled in steamers about her skirts.

Then she went on, parting her way from side to side with the cane, through the whispering field. At last she came to the end, to a wagon track where the silver grass blew between the red ruts. The quail were walking around like pullets, seeming all dainty and unseen.

30 "Walk pretty," she said. "This is the easy place. This the easy going."

She followed the track, swaying through the quiet bare fields, through the little strings of trees silver in their dead leaves, past cabins silver from weather, with the doors and windows boarded shut, all like old women under a spell sitting there. "I walking in their sleep," she said, nodding her head vigorously.

In a ravine she went where a spring was silently flowing through a hollow log. Old Phoenix bent and drank. "Sweet-gum makes the water sweet," she said, and drank more. "Nobody know who made this well, for it was here when I was born."

The track crossed a swampy part where the moss hung as white as lace from every limb. "Sleep on, alligators, and blow your bubbles." Then the track went into the road.

Deep, deep the road went down between the high green-colored banks. Overhead the live-oaks met, and it was as dark as a cave.

35 A black dog with a lolling tongue came up out of the weeds by the ditch. She was meditating, and not ready, and when he came at her she only hit him a little with her cane. Over she went in the ditch, like a little puff of milkweed.

Down there, her sense drifted away. A dream visited her, and she reached her hand up, but nothing reached down and gave her a pull. So she lay there and presently went to talking. "Old woman," she said to herself, "that black dog come up out of the weeds to stall you off, and now there he sitting on his fine tail smiling at you."

A white man finally came along and found her—a hunter, a young man, with his dog on a chain.

"Well, Granny!" he laughed. "What are you doing there?"

"Lying on my back like a June-bug waiting to be turned over, mister," she said, reaching up her hand.

40 He lifted her up, gave her a swing in the air, and set her down. "Anything broken, Granny?"

"No sir, them old dead weeds is springy enough," said Phoenix, when she had got her breath. "I thank you for your trouble."

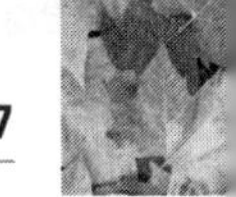

"Where do you live, Granny?" he asked, while the two dogs were growling at each other.

"Away back yonder, sir, behind the ridge. You can't even see it from here."

"On your way home?"

"No sir, I goin to town." 45

"Why, that's too far! That's as far as I walk when I come out myself, and I get something for my trouble." He patted the stuffed bag he carried, and there hung down a little closed claw. It was one of the bob-whites, with its beak hooked bitterly to show it was dead. "Now you go on home, Granny!"

"I bound to go to town, mister," said Phoenix. "The time come around."

He gave another laugh, filling the whole landscape. "I know you old colored people! Wouldn't miss going to town to see Santa Claus!"

But something held old Phoenix very still. The deep lines in her face went into a fierce and different radiation. Without warning, she had seen with her own eyes a flashing nickel fall out of the man's pocket onto the ground.

"How old are you, Granny?" he was saying. 50

"There is no telling, mister," she said, "no telling."

Then she gave a little cry and clapped her hands and said, "Git on away from here, dog! Look! Look at that dog!" She laughed as if in admiration. "He ain't scared of nobody. He a big black dog." She whispered, "Sic him!"

"Watch me get rid of that cur," said the man. "Sic him, Pete! Sic him!"

Phoenix heard the dogs fighting, and heard the man running and throwing sticks. She even heard a gunshot. But she was slowly bending forward by that time, further and further forward, the lids stretched down over her eyes, as if she were doing this in her sleep. Her chin was lowered almost to her knees. The yellow palm of her hand came out from the fold of her apron. Her fingers slid down and along the ground under the piece of money with the grace and care they would have in lifting an egg from under a setting hen. Then she slowly straightened up, she stood erect, and the nickel was in her apron pocket. A bird flew by. Her lips moved. "God watching me the whole time. I come to stealing."

The man came back, and his own dog panted about them. "Well, I scared him off that time," he said, and then he laughed and lifted his gun and pointed it at Phoenix. 55

She stood straight and faced him.

"Doesn't the gun scare you?" he said, still pointing it.

"No sir. I seen plenty go off closer by, in my day, and for less than what I done," she said, holding utterly still.

He smiled, and shouldered the gun. "Well, Granny," he said, "you must be a hundred years old, and scared of nothing. I'd give you a dime if I had any money with me. But you take my advice and stay home, and nothing will happen to you."

"I bound to go on my way, mister," said Phoenix. She inclined her head in the red rag. Then they went in different directions, but she could hear the gun shooting again and again over the hill. 60

She walked on. The shadows hung from the oak trees to the road like curtains. Then she smelled wood-smoke, and smelled the river, and she saw a steeple and the cabins on their steep steps. Dozens of little black children whirled around her. There ahead was Natchez shining. Bells were ringing. She walked on.

In the paved city it was Christmas time. There were red and green electric lights strung and crisscrossed everywhere, and all turned on in the daytime. Old Phoenix would have been lost if she had not distrusted her eyesight and depended on her feet to know where to take her.

She paused quietly on the sidewalk where people were passing by. A lady came along in the crowd, carrying an armful of red-, green-, and silver-wrapped presents; she gave off perfume like the red roses in hot summer, and Phoenix stopped her.

"Please, missy, will you lace up my shoe?" She held up her foot.

65 "What do you want, Grandma?"

"See my shoe," said Phoenix. "Do all right for out in the country, but wouldn't look right to go in a big building."

"Stand still then, Grandma," said the lady. She put her packages down on the sidewalk beside her and laced and tied both shoes tightly.

"Can't lace 'em with a cane," said Phoenix. "Thank you, missy. I doesn't mind asking a nice lady to tie up my shoe, when I gets out on the street."

Moving slowly and from side to side, she went into the big building, and into a tower of steps, where she walked up and around and around until her feet knew to stop.

70 She entered a door, and there she saw nailed up on the wall the document that had been stamped with the gold seal and framed in the gold frame, which matched the dream that was hung up in her head.

"Here I be," she said. There was a fixed and ceremonial stiffness over her body.

"A charity case, I suppose," said an attendant who sat at the desk before her.

But Phoenix only looked above her head. There was sweat on her face, the wrinkles in her skin shone like a bright net.

"Speak up, Grandma," the woman said, "What's your name? We must have your history, you know. Have you been here before? What seems to be the trouble with you?"

75 Old Phoenix only gave a twitch to her face as if a fly were bothering her.

"Are you deaf?" cried the attendant.

But then the nurse came in.

"Oh, that's just old Aunt Phoenix," she said. "She doesn't come for herself—she has a little grandson. She makes these trips just as regular as clockwork. She lives away back off the Old Natchez Trace." She bent down. "Well, Aunt Phoenix, why don't you just take a seat? We won't keep you standing after your long trip." She pointed.

The old woman sat down, bolt upright in the chair.

80 "Now, how is the boy?" asked the nurse.

Old Phoenix did not speak.

"I said, how is the boy?"

But Phoenix only waited and stared straight ahead, her face very solemn and withdrawn into rigidity.

"Is his throat any better?" asked the nurse. "Aunt Phoenix, don't you hear me? Is your grandson's throat any better since the last time you came for the medicine?"

85 With her hands on her knees, the old woman waited, silent, erect, and motionless, just as if she were in armor.

"You mustn't take up our time this way, Aunt Phoenix," the nurse said. "Tell us quickly about your grandson, and get it over. He isn't dead, is he?"

At last there came a flicker and then a flame of comprehension across her face, and she spoke.

"My grandson. It was my memory had left me. There I sat and forgot why I made my long trip."

"Forgot?" the nurse frowned. "After you came so far?"

90 Then Phoenix was like an old woman begging a dignified forgiveness for waking up frightened in the night. "I never did go to school, I was too old at the Surrender," she said in a soft voice. "I'm an old woman without an education. It was my memory fail me. My little grandson, he is just the same, and I forgot it in the coming."

"Throat never heals, does it?" said the nurse, speaking in a loud, sure voice to old Phoenix. By now she had a card with something written on it, a little list. "Yes. Swallowed lye. When was it—January—two, three years ago—"

Phoenix spoke unasked now. "No missy, he not dead, he just the same. Every little while his throat begin to close up again, and he not able to swallow. He not get his breath. He not able to help himself. So the time come around, and I go on another trip for the soothing medicine."

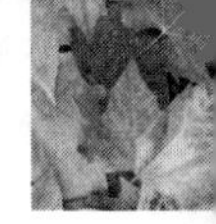

"All right. The doctor said as long as you came to get it, you could have it," said the nurse. "But it's an obstinate case."

"My little grandson, he sit up there in the house all wrapped up, waiting by himself," Phoenix went on. "We is the only two left in the world. He suffer and it don't seem to put him back at all. He got a sweet look. He going to last. He wear a little patch quilt and peep out holding his mouth open like a little bird. I remembers so plain now. I not going to forget him again, no, the whole enduring time. I could tell him from all the others in creation."

"All right." The nurse was trying to hush her now. She brought her a bottle of medicine. "Charity," she said, making a check mark in a book. 95

Old Phoenix held the bottle close to her eyes, and then carefully put it into her pocket.

"I thank you," she said.

"It's Christmas time, Grandma," said the attendant. "Could I give you a few pennies out of my purse?"

"Five pennies is a nickel," said Phoenix stiffly. 100

"Here's a nickel," said the attendant.

Phoenix rose carefully and held out her hand. She received the nickel and then fished the other nickel out of her pocket and laid it beside the new one. She stared at her palm closely, with her head on one side.

Then she gave a tap with her cane on the floor.

"This is what come to me to do," she said, "I going to the store and buy my child a little windmill they sells, made out of paper. He going to find it hard to believe there such a thing in the world. I'll march myself back where he waiting, holding it straight up in this hand."

She lifted her free hand, gave a little nod, turned around, and walked out of the doctor's office. Then her slow step began on the stairs, going down. 105

QUESTIONS

1. From the description of Phoenix, what do you conclude about her economic condition? How do you know that she has taken the path through the woods before? Is she accustomed to being alone? What do you make of her speaking to animals, and of her imagining a boy offering her a piece of cake? What does her speech show about her education and background?
2. Describe the plot of the story. With Phoenix as the protagonist, what are the obstacles ranged against her? How might Phoenix be considered to be in the grip of large and indifferent social and political forces?
3. Comment on the meaning of this dialogue between Phoenix and the hunter:

   > "Doesn't the gun scare you?" he said, still pointing it.
   > "No, sir. I seen plenty go off closer by, in my day, and for less than what I done," she said, holding utterly still.

4. A number of responses might be made to this story, among them admiration for Phoenix, pity for her and her grandson and for the downtrodden generally, anger at her impoverished condition, and apprehension about her approaching senility. Do you share in any of these responses? Do you have any others?

Plot: The Motivation and Causality of Fiction

Stories are made up mostly of actions or incidents that follow one another in chronological order. The same is also true of life, but there is a major difference. Fiction must make sense even though life itself does not always seem to make sense at all. Finding a sequential or narrative order is therefore only a first step in

our consideration of fiction. What we depend on for the sense or meaning of fiction is **plot**—the elements governing the unfolding of the actions.

The English novelist E. M. Forster, in *Aspects of the Novel*, presents a memorable illustration of plot. To illustrate a bare set of actions, he proposes the following: "The king died, and then the queen died." Forster points out, however, that this sequence does not form a plot because it lacks *motivation* and *causation;* it is too much like life itself to be fictional. Thus he introduces motivation and causation in his next example: "The king died, and then the queen died of grief." The phrase "of grief" shows that one thing (grief) controls or overcomes another (the normal desire to live), and motivation and causation enter the sequence to form a plot. In a well-plotted story or play, one thing precedes or follows another not simply because time ticks away, but more importantly because *effects* follow *causes.* In a good work of fiction, nothing is irrelevant or accidental; everything is related and causative.

Determining the Conflicts in a Story

The controlling impulse in a connected pattern of causes and effects is **conflict,** which refers to people or circumstances that a character must face and try to overcome. Conflicts bring out extremes of human energy, causing characters to engage in the decisions, actions, responses, and interactions that make up fictional literature.

In its most elemental form, a conflict is the opposition of two people. Their conflict may take the shape of anger, hatred, envy, argument, avoidance, political or moral opposition, gossip, lies, fighting, and many other actions and attitudes. Conflicts may also exist between groups, although conflicts between individuals are more identifiable and therefore more suitable for stories. Conflicts may also be abstract—for example, when an individual opposes larger forces such as natural objects, ideas, modes of behavior, or public opinion. A difficult or even impossible *choice*—a dilemma—is a natural conflict for an individual person. A conflict may also be brought out in ideas and opinions that clash. In short, conflict shows itself in many ways.

DIRECTLY RELATING CONFLICT TO DOUBT, TENSION, AND INTEREST. Conflict is the major element of plot because opposing forces arouse *curiosity*, cause *doubt*, create *tension*, and produce *interest*. The same responses are the lifeblood of athletic competition. Consider which kind of athletic event is more interesting: (1) One team gets so far ahead that the outcome is no longer in doubt, or (2) both teams are so evenly matched that the outcome is uncertain until the final seconds. Obviously, games are uninteresting—as games—unless they develop as contests between teams of comparable strength. The same principle applies to conflicts in stories and dramas. There should be uncertainty about a protagonist's success or failure. Unless there is doubt, there is no tension, and without tension there is no interest.

FINDING THE CONFLICTS TO DETERMINE THE PLOT. To see a plot in operation, let us build on Forster's description. Here is a simple plot for a story of our own: "John and Jane meet, fall in love, and get married." This sentence contains a plot

because it shows cause and effect (they get married *because* they fall in love), but with no conflict, the plot is not interesting. However, let us introduce conflicting elements into this common "boy meets girl" story:

> John and Jane meet in college and fall in love. They go together for a number of years and plan to marry, but a problem arises. Jane first wants to establish herself in a career, and after marriage she wants to be an equal contributor to the family. John understands Jane's wishes for equality, but he wants to get married first and let her finish her studies and have her career after they have children. Jane believes that John's plan is unacceptable because she thinks of it as a trap from which she might not escape. As they discuss their options they find themselves increasingly more irritated and unhappy with each other. Finally they bring their plans to an end, and they part in both anger and sorrow. Their love is not dead, however, but both go on to marry someone else and build separate lives and careers. In their new lives, neither is totally happy even though they like and respect their spouses. The years pass, and, after children and grandchildren, Jane and John meet again. He is now divorced and she is a widow. Because their earlier conflict is no longer a barrier, they rekindle their love, marry, and try to make up for the past. Even their new happiness, however, is tinged with regret and reproach because of their earlier conflicts, their unhappy decision to part, their lost years, and their increasing age.

Here we find a true plot because our original "boy meets girl" topic now contains a major conflict from which a number of related complications develop. These complications embody disagreements, choices, arguments, and ill feelings that produce tension, uncertainty, rupture, and regret. When we learn that John and Jane finally join together at the end we might still find the story painful to contemplate because it does not give us a "happily ever after" ending. Nevertheless, the story makes sense—as a story—because its plot brings out the plausible consequences of the understandable aims and hopes of John and Jane during their long relationship. It is the imposition of necessary causes and effects upon a series of events in time that creates the story's plot.

WRITING ABOUT THE PLOT OF A STORY

An essay about plot is an analysis of the story's conflict and its developments. The organization of your essay should not be modeled on sequential sections and principal events, however, because these invite only a retelling of the story. Instead, the organization is to be developed from the important elements of conflict. As you look for ideas about plot, try to answer the following questions.

Questions for Discovering Ideas

- Who are the major and minor characters, and how do their characteristics put them in conflict? How can you describe the conflict or conflicts?
- How does the story's action grow out of the major conflict?

- If the conflict stems from contrasting ideas or values, what are these, and how are they brought out?
- What problems do the major characters face? How do the characters deal with these problems?
- How do the major characters achieve (or not achieve) their major goal(s)? What obstacles do they overcome? What obstacles overcome them or alter them?
- At the end, are the characters successful or unsuccessful, happy or unhappy, satisfied or dissatisfied, changed or unchanged, enlightened or ignorant? How has the resolution of the major conflict produced these results?

Strategies for Organizing Ideas

To keep your essay brief, you need to be selective. Rather than detailing everything a character does, for example, stress the major elements in his or her conflict. Such an essay on Eudora Welty's "A Worn Path" might emphasize Phoenix as she encounters the various obstacles both in the woods and in town. When there is a conflict between two major characters, the obvious approach is to focus equally on both. For brevity, however, emphasis might be placed on just one. Thus, an essay on the plot of "A Rose for Emily" might stress the details about Emily's life that make her the central participant in the story's conflict.

In addition, the plot may be analyzed more broadly in terms of impulses, goals, values, issues, and historical perspectives. Thus, you might emphasize the elements of chance working against Mathilde in Maupassant's "The Necklace" (Part I p. 6) as a contrast to her dreams about wealth. A discussion of the plot of Poe's "The Masque of the Red Death" (Chapter 9) might stress the haughtiness of Prospero, the major character, because the plot could not develop without his egotism.

The conclusion may contain a brief summary of the points you have made. It is also a fitting location for a brief consideration of the effect or *impact* produced by the conflict. Additional ideas might focus on whether the author has arranged actions and dialogue to direct your favor toward one side or the other, or whether the plot is possible or impossible, serious or comic, fair or unfair, powerful or indifferent, and so on.

Illustrative Student Essay

Underlined sentences in this paper *do not* conform to MLA style and are used solely as teaching tools to emphasize the central idea, thesis sentence, and topic sentences throughout the paper.

Getty 1

Beth Getty

Professor Farmer

English 214

12 March 2008

The Plot of Eudora Welty's "A Worn Path"°

[1] At first, the complexity of Eudora Welty's plot in "A Worn Path" is not clear. The main character is Phoenix Jackson, an old, poor, and frail woman; the story seems to be no more than a record of her walk to Natchez through the woods from her rural home. By the story's end, however, the plot is clear: It consists of the brave attempts of a courageous, valiant woman to carry on against overwhelming forces.* Her determination despite the great odds against her gives the story its impact. The powers ranged against her are old age, poverty, environment, and illness.†

[2] Old age as a silent but overpowering antagonist is shown in signs of Phoenix's increasing senility. Not her mind but her feet tell her where to find the medical office in Natchez. Despite her inner strength, she is unable to explain her errand when the nursing attendant asks her. Instead she sits dumbly and unknowingly for a time, until "a flame of comprehension" comes across her face (paragraph 87, p. 118). Against the power of advancing age, Phoenix is slowly losing. The implication is that soon she will lose entirely.

[3] An equally crushing opponent is her poverty. She cannot afford to ride to town, but must walk. She has no money, and acquires her ten cents for the paper windmill by stealing and begging. The "soothing medicine" she gets for her grandson (paragraph 92, p. 118) is given to her out of charity. Despite the

°This story appears on page 114.
***Central idea.**
†Thesis sentence.

Getty 2

boy's need for advanced medical care, she has no money to provide it, and the story therefore shows that her guardianship is doomed.

[4] Closely connected to her poverty is the way through the woods, which during her walk seems to be an almost active opponent. The long hill tires her, the thorn bush catches her clothes, the log endangers her balance as she crosses the creek, and the barbed-wire fence threatens to puncture her skin. Another danger on her way is the stray dog, which topples her over. Apparently not afraid, however, Phoenix carries on a cheerful monologue:

> Out of my way, all you foxes, owls, beetles, jack rabbits, coons and wild animals! . . . Keep out from under these feet, little bobwhites. . . . Keep the big wild hogs out of my path. Don't let none of these come running my direction. I got a long way. (115; paragraph 3)

She prevails for the moment as she enters Natchez, but all the hazards of her walk are still there, waiting for her to return.

[5] The force against Phoenix which shows her plight most clearly and pathetically is her grandson's incurable illness. His condition highlights her helplessness, for she is his only support. Her difficulties would be enough for one person alone, but with the grandson the odds against her are doubled. Despite her care, there is nothing anyone can do for the grandson but take the long worn path to get something to help him endure his pain.

[6] This brief description of the conflicts in "A Worn Path" only hints at the story's power. Welty layers the details to bring out the full range of the conditions against Phoenix, who cannot win despite her determination and devotion. The most hopeless fact, the condition of the invalid grandson, is not revealed until she reaches the medical office, and this delayed final revelation makes one's heart go out to her. The plot is strong because it is so real, and Phoenix is a pathetic but memorable protagonist struggling against overwhelming odds.

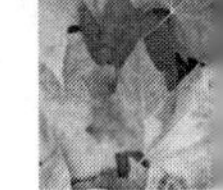

Getty 3

Work Cited

Welty, Eudora. "A Worn Path." Literature: An Introduction to Reading and Writing. Ed. Edgar V. Roberts. 9th ed. New York: Pearson Longman, 2009. 114–19.

Commentary on the Essay

The strategy of this essay is to explain the elements of plot in "A Worn Path" selectively, without duplicating the story's narrative order. Thus the third aspect of conflict, the woods, might be introduced first if the story's narrative order were to be followed, but it is deferred while the more personal elements of old age and poverty are considered. It is important to note that the essay does not deal with the story's other characters as part of Phoenix's conflict. Rather Phoenix's antagonist takes the shape of impersonal and unconquerable forces, like her grandson's illness.

Paragraph 1 briefly describes how one's first impressions are changed because of what happens at the end of the story. The thesis statement anticipates the body by listing the four topics about to be treated. Paragraph 2 concerns Phoenix's old age; paragraph 3 her poverty; paragraph 4 the woods; and paragraph 5 her grandson's illness. The concluding paragraph (6) points out that in this set of conflicts the protagonist cannot win, except as she lives out her duty and her devotion to help her grandson. Continuing the theme of the introduction, the last paragraph also accounts for the power of the plot: By building up to Phoenix's personal strength against unbeatable forces, the story evokes sympathy and admiration.

Writing Topics About Plot in Fiction

1. Suppose that someone has told you that "The Things They Carried" is too detailed and realistic to be considered a story. Explain to this person why the assertion should be considered wrong. What elements of narrative, character, plot, point of view, idea, and description justify calling "The Things They Carried" a story?
2. Consider the illustrative essay on the plot of Welty's "A Worn Path." How well does the essay organize the details about the story's plot? Do you accept the arguments in the essay? What other details and arguments can you think of that might explain Welty's plot more fully?
3. In "War," by Pirandello, why is the father whose son is dead made so initially unappealing? What effect on the plot of the story is made plain by the apparent nature of his character?

4. How do the separate sections of "An Occurrence at Owl Creek Bridge" affect the story's plot? Why is the second section a "flashback" of events that occurred before the actual story is taking place? Why is this flashback necessary to your understanding of the plot?
5. Write contrasting paragraphs about a character (whom you know or about whom you have read). In the first, try to make your reader like the character. In the second, try to create a hostile response to the character. Write an additional paragraph explaining the ways in which you tried to create these opposite responses. How fair would it be for a reader to dislike your negative paragraph even though your hostile portrait is successful?
6. Write a brief episode or story that takes place in a historical period you believe you know well, being as factually accurate as you can. Introduce your own fictional characters as important "movers and shakers," and deal with their public or personal affairs or both. You may model your characters and episodes on historical persons, but you are free to exercise your imagination completely and construct your own characters.

Chapter 10A

Writing Research Essays On Fiction

The enclosed sample chapter includes the book's comprehensive research coverage as well as information specific to doing research on fiction. Key topics include:

- Selecting a Topic
- Setting up a Bibliography
- Consulting Bibliographical Guides
- Using Online Resources
- Taking Notes and Paraphrasing Material
- Documenting Your Work
- Works Cited (Bibliography)
- Footnotes and Endnotes
- Strategies for Organizing Ideas
- Plagiarism
- Illustrative Student Research Essay—Fiction
- Writing Topics: How to Undertake Research Essays

Two additional chapters cover research for poetry and drama. Each chapter features genre-specific pointers and annotated research papers that provide MLA information specific to writing in the genre.

22A Writing Essays on Poetry

- Topics to Discover in Research
- Illustrative Student Essay—Poetry

28A Writing Research Essays on Drama

- Topics to Discover in Research
- Illustrative Student Research Essay—Drama

Chapter 10A

Writing Research Essays on Fiction

Broadly, **research** is systematic investigation, examination, and experimentation. It is the basic tool of intellectual inquiry for anyone working in any discipline—physics, chemistry, biology, psychology, anthropology, history, and literature, to name just a few disciplines. With research, and with the breakthroughs of knowledge that research brings, our understanding and our civilization grow; without research, they languish.

The major assumption of doing research is that the researcher is reaching out to find and master new areas of knowledge. With each assignment the researcher acquires not only the knowledge gained from the particular task but also the skills needed to undertake further research and thereby to gain further knowledge. Some research tasks are elementary, such as using a dictionary to discover the meaning of a word and thereby aiding the understanding of an important passage. Many people would not even call that research. More detailed research uses an array of resources: critical studies, biographies, introductions, bibliographies, and histories. When you begin a research task you usually have little or no knowledge about your topic, but with such resources you can acquire expert knowledge in a relatively short time.

Although research is the animating spark of all disciplines, our topic here is **literary research**—the systematic use of primary and secondary sources in studying a literary problem. In doing literary research, you consult not only individual works themselves (primary sources) but many other works that shed light on them and interpret them (secondary sources). Typical research tasks are to learn important facts about a work and about the period in which it was written; to learn about the lives, careers, and other works of authors; to discover and apply the comments and judgments of modern or earlier critics; to learn details that help explain the meaning of works; and to learn about critical and artistic taste.

Selecting a Topic

In most instances, your instructor assigns a research essay on a specific topic. Sometimes, however, the choice of a topic will be left in your hands. For such assignments, it is helpful to know the types of research essays you might find most congenial. Here are some possibilities:

1. **A particular work.** At first, this type of research essay is probably the most common one, as shown in the illustrative essay (p. 614). You might treat character (for example, "The Character of Louise in Chopin's 'The Story of an Hour'" or "The Question of Whether Young Goodman Brown Is a Hero or a dupe in

Hawthorne's 'Young Goodman Brown'") or tone and style, ideas, structure, form, and the like. A research paper on a single work is similar to an essay on the same work, except that the research paper takes into account more views and facts than those you are likely to have without the research.

2. **A particular author.** A project might focus on an idea or some facet of style, imagery, setting, or tone of the author, tracing the origins and development of the topic through a number of different stories, poems, or plays. Examples are "Hardy's Treatment of Local Country Folkways in His Short Stories" and "Faulkner's Use of the Yoknapatawpha Environment in His Stories." This type of essay is suitable for a number of shorter works, although it is also applicable for a single major work, such as a longer story, novel, or play.
3. **Comparison and contrast** (see Chapter 30). There are two types.
   a. *An idea or quality common to two or more authors.* Here you show points of similarity or contrast, or else you show how one author's work can be taken to criticize another's. A possible subject is "Contrasting Uses of Dialogue in Ellison's 'Battle Royal' and Tan's 'Two Kinds,'" or "The Theme of Love and Sexuality in Faulkner's 'A Rose for Emily,' Munro's 'The Found Boat,' and Joyce's 'Araby.'"
   b. *Different critical views of a particular work or body of works.* Sometimes much is to be gained from an examination of differing critical opinions on topics like "The Meaning of Poe's 'The Masque of the Red Death'" or "Various Views of Hawthorne's 'Young Goodman Brown.'" Such a study would attempt to determine the critical opinion and taste to which a work did or did not appeal, and it might also aim at conclusions about whether the work was in the advance or rear guard of its time.
4. **The influence of an idea, author, philosophy, political situation, or artistic movement on specific works of an author or authors.** An essay on influences can be specific and to the point, as in "Details of Twentieth-Century Native American Life as Reflected in Whitecloud's 'Blue Winds Dancing,'" or else it can be more abstract and critical, as in "The Influence of Traditional Religion on Hawthorne's 'Young Goodman Brown.'"
5. **The origin of a particular work or type of work.** Such an essay might examine an author's biography to discover the germination and development of a work—for example, "Poe's 'The Masque of the Red Death' or his Theory of the Short Story" or "Shaw's 'Act of Faith' and Its Relationship to Post–World War II Literature."

If you consider these types, an idea of what to write may come to you. Perhaps you have particularly liked one author or several authors. If so, you might start to think along the lines of types 1, 2, or 3. If you are interested in influences or origins, then type 4 or 5 may suit you better.

If you still cannot decide on a topic after rereading the works you have liked, then you should carry your search for a topic into your school library. Look up your author or authors in the library's retrieval system. Your first goal should be to find a relatively recent book-length critical study published by a university press. Look for a title indicating that the book is a general one dealing with the author's major works rather than just one work. Study those chapters relevant to the work or works you have chosen. Most writers of critical studies describe their purpose and plan in their introductions or first chapters, so begin with the first part of the book. If there is no separate chapter on your primary text, use the index as your guide to the relevant pages. Reading in this way will give you enough knowledge about the issues and ideas raised by the work to enable you to select a promising topic. Once you make your decision, you are ready to develop a working bibliography.

Setting Up a Bibliography

The best way to develop a working bibliography of books and articles is to begin by finding major critical studies of the writer or writers. Again, use a book or books published by university presses—maybe the books you used to determine your topic. Such books will contain comprehensive bibliographies. Be careful to read the chapters on your primary work or works and to look for the footnotes or endnotes, for often you can save time if you record the names of books and articles listed in these notes. Then refer to the bibliographies included at the ends of the books, and select likely looking titles. Now, look at the dates of publication of the scholarly books. Let us suppose that you have found three books, published in 2001, 2006, and 2007. Unless you are planning an extensive research assignment, you can safely assume that the writers of critical works will have done the selecting for you of important works published before the date of publication. These bibliographies will be reliable, and you can use them with confidence. Thus, the bibliography in a book published in 2007 will be complete up through about 2006, for the writer will have finished the manuscript a year or so before the book was published. But such bibliographies will not go up to the present. For that, you will need to search for works published after the most recent of the books.

Consult Bibliographical Guides

Fortunately for students doing literary research, the Modern Language Association (MLA) of America has been providing a complete bibliography of literary studies for years, not only in English and American literatures but also in the literatures of many foreign languages. This is the *MLA International Bibliography of Books and Articles on the Modern Languages and Literatures* ("*MLA Bibliography*"). The *MLA Bibliography* started achieving completeness in the late 1950s. By 1969 the project had grown so huge that it was published in many parts, which are bound together in library editions. In the latest volume, dated 2006, this comprehensive bibliography lists 20,213 books and articles that were published in the year 2006. In addition, following these numbered listings there is a second half of the bibliography, 970 pages long, containing a detailed subject index. University and college libraries have sets of the *MLA Bibliography* on open shelves or tables. The bibliography is also published on CD-ROM and on the Internet—formats accessible to you through your college library services. You will need to consult a librarian about Internet access.

In the traditional book format, the *MLA Bibliography* is conveniently organized by period and author. Should you be doing research about James Joyce, look him up in *Volume I* under the category "Irish literature/1900–1999," where there are 190 entries of works about him. In this same volume you will also find references to most other authors of works in English, such as Shakespeare (drama, poetry), Wordsworth (poetry), and Arnold (poetry). You will find most books and articles listed under the author's last name. Journal references are abbreviated, but a lengthy list explaining abbreviations appears at the beginning of the volume. Using the *MLA Bibliography* in the book format, begin with the most recent one and then go backward to your stopping point. If your library has computers dedicated to electronic versions of the bibliography, you can search by typing in the name of your author or subject. By whatever means you gain access to the bibliography, be sure to get the complete information—especially volume numbers and years of publication—for each article and book.

There are many other bibliographies useful for students doing literary research, such as the *Essay and General Literature Index,* the *Readers' Guide to Periodical Literature,* and various specific indexes. The *MLA Bibliography* contains far in excess of abundance, however, for your present research purposes. Remember that as you progress in your reading, the notes and bibliographies in the works you consult will also constitute an unfolding selective bibliography. For the illustrative research essay in this chapter, a number of entries were discovered not from bibliographies like those just listed but from the reference lists in critical books.

Your list will make up a fairly comprehensive search bibliography, which you can use when you physically enter the library to begin collecting and using materials. An additional convenience is that many associated libraries, such as state colleges and urban public libraries, have pooled their resources. Thus, if you use the services of a network of nearby county libraries, you can go to another library to use materials that are not accessible at your own college or branch. If distances are great, however, and your own library does not have a book that you think is important to your project, you can ask a librarian to get the book for you through the Interlibrary Loan Service. Usually, given time, the libraries will accommodate as many of your needs as they can.

You are now ready to find your sources and take notes. Make the maximum use of your college library. Call out the books themselves, the kind you can hold in your hands, and the relevant journals containing the articles in which you are interested. Read them, and make the best use you can of them.

Online Library Services

Through computer access, many college and university libraries are constantly connected to a vast array of local, national, and even international libraries, so that by using various online services, you can extend your research far beyond the capacities of your own library. You can use one of the computers in your library, or your own personal computer, to gain access to the catalogs of large research libraries, provided that you enter the correct information, are able and willing to follow the program codes, and are patient and persistent.

GAINING ACCESS TO BOOKS AND ARTICLES THROUGH THE INTERNET. At one time, many smaller schools did not have copies of all the books and scholarly periodicals containing the results and reports of research. Many students were therefore frustrated in their attempts to find all the works that they had listed on their working bibliographies. Times, however, have changed. You may now gain access to many sources that are not in your library, for many of the works you want to read, which are not in your school's library, are now directly available to you through computer, page by page. A major source is *Questia,* an electronic depository of books and articles which is likely available to you through your college library. In total, *Questia* contains 67,000 "full text" books, and more than 1.5 million articles. For students doing research on Hawthorne's short stories, for example, *Questia* claims to have more than 6,000 books and more than 1,300 scholarly articles. *EBSCOhost* is a multidisciplinary database that includes "MagillOnLiteraturePlus" which has plot summaries and analysis of fictional works; *EBSCOhost* also has "Book Index with Reviews" that includes excerpts of book reviews along with book summaries. *WilsonWeb* has databases in many disciplines and includes "Book Review Digest Plus," which has summaries of books as well as complete book reviews. *WilsonWeb* also has "Short Story Index" which indexes stories appearing in collections and periodicals since 1984. *Columbia Grangers World of Poetry* has references to many types of poetry.

Another major electronic source is *JSTOR* (i.e., *Journal Storage*), a scholarly journal archive. Most college and university libraries, and many high schools, subscribe to this service, and it is available to you as a registered student. It includes computerized copies of complete sets of more than 600 scholarly journals in the arts and sciences. By gaining the proper credentials available to you as a student, you will have access to virtually any item you have entered in your bibliography.

Still another vital research source is Google Scholar, which is in the process of duplicating the pages of many thousands of scholarly works. The service is available, like Questia and JSTOR, through your college library. In other words, these electronic book and article services are available right now to provide you with abundant materials that previously were not readily available to most students at American colleges and universities.

IMPORTANT CONSIDERATIONS ABOUT COMPUTER-AIDED RESEARCH

You must always remind yourself that online catalogs, such as those you might select from other colleges and universities, and from private organizations, can give you only what has been entered into them. If one university library classifies a work under "criticism and interpretation" and another classifies it under "characters," a search of "criticism and interpretation" at the first library will find the work but the same search at the second will not. Sometimes the inclusion of an author's life dates immediately following the name might throw off your search. Typographic errors in the system will cause additional search problems, although many programs try to forestall such difficulties by providing "nearby" entries to enable you to determine whether incorrectly entered topics may in fact be helpful to you.

Also, if you use online services, be careful to determine the year when the computerization began. Many libraries have a recent commencement date—1978, for example, or 1985. For completeness, therefore, you would need assistance in finding catalog entries for items published before these years.

It is particularly important *to avoid the many and varied so-called "free essays" on literary topics that fill a number of today's extremely popular search engines.* These essays are written largely by people who are themselves just beginning, not by scholars who have studied particular topics for many years and who have become experts in their analyses. The reason for using books and articles approved by scholarly publishers is that the works have been *refereed* by authorities in the particular field. If these authorities, or referees, have recommended publication, you are entitled to expect that the breadth and depth of the critical analyses will be well considered and reliable. That is not the case with the innumerable "free essays" that you might find in more general and unrefereed entries in the search engine.

Just a few years ago, the broadness of scope that electronic searches provide for most undergraduate students doing research assignments was not possible; today, it is commonplace. Even with the astounding possibilities of electronic resources, however, it is still necessary to take out actual books and articles—and read them and take notes on them—before you can begin and complete a research essay. These days, electronic services can supply you with actual copies of many of the materials you are seeking, but they cannot do your reading, note taking, and writing. All that is still up to you, as it always has been for all students doing research.

Taking Notes and Paraphrasing Material

There are many ways of taking notes, but a few things are clear. Because your notes should facilitate, not hinder, your writing of the final research essay, you will need a systematic way of handling your notes. Notes should not be taken helter-skelter. Nor should they be written on the front and back of a notebook, with only one side showing and the other side being out of your sight. The best way is to develop a method whereby you will be able to see all your notes together, laid out on a table in front of you. You might type your notes into your computer—leaving space between them, printing them out, and then, after cutting the separate items on your printout, laying these notes side by side and group by group. If you are taking handwritten notes, you can achieve simultaneous viewability by using note cards. If you have never used cards before, you might profit from consulting any one of a number of handbooks and special workbooks on research.[1] The principal advantage of cards is the ease with which you can see them at a

[1]See Muriel Harris, *Prentice Hall Reference Guide to Grammar and Usage*, 5th ed. (Upper Saddle River: Prentice Hall, 2003) 283–301.

glance when you lay them out on a desk or other large surface. Cards are also sturdy and will easily maintain their physical integrity as you handle them and assign them to their relevant piles. As a result, cards—or notes taken from printouts from your computer—may be easily classified; they may be numbered and renumbered; shuffled; tried out in one place, rejected, and then used in another place (or thrown away); and arranged in order when you start to write.

Taking Complete and Accurate Notes

WRITE THE SOURCE OF EACH NOTE YOU TAKE. Be especially diligent about writing the source of your information on each card or computer note. This may seem bothersome, but it is easier than going back to the library to locate the correct source after you have begun your essay. You can save time if you take the complete data on one card or computer file—a "master card" for that source—and then create an abbreviation for the separate notes you take from the source. Here is an example, which also includes the location where the reference was originally found (e.g., card or computer catalog, computer search, bibliography in a book, the *MLA Bibliography,* etc.). Observe that the author's last name goes first.

DONOVAN, JOSEPHINE, ED. FEMINIST — PN
Literary Criticism: Explorations — 98
in Theory. 2nd ed. Lexington: — W64
UP of Kentucky. 1989 — F4
DONOVAN
CARD CATALOG, "WOMEN"

If you take many notes from this book, the name "Donovan" will serve as identification. Be sure not to lose your master group of references because you will need them when you prepare your list of works cited. If you are working with a computer, record the complete bibliographical data in a computer file.

RECORD THE PAGE NUMBER FOR EACH NOTE. It would be hard to guess how much exasperation has been caused by the failure to record page numbers in notes. Be sure to write the page number down first, before you begin to take your note, and, to be doubly sure, write the page number again at the end of your note. If the detail goes from one page to the next in your source, record the exact spot where the page changes, as in this example.

HEILBRUN AND STIMSON, IN DONOVAN, PP. 63–64

[63]After the raising of the feminist consciousness it is necessary to develop/ [64]"the growth of moral perception" through anger and the "amelioration of social inequities."

The reason for such care is that you may wish to use only a part of a note you have taken, and when there are two pages you will need to be accurate in locating what goes where.

RECORD ONLY ONE FACT OR OPINION ON A CARD OR COMPUTER ENTRY. Record only one major detail for each of your notes—one quotation, one paraphrase, one observation—never two or more. You might be tempted to fill up the entire notes with many separate but unrelated details, but such a try at economy often gets you in trouble because you might want to use some of the details in other places. If you have only one entry per note, you will avoid such problems and also retain the freedom you need.

USE QUOTATION MARKS FOR ALL QUOTED MATERIAL. In taking notes it is extremely important—vitally important, urgently important—to distinguish copied material from your own words. Always put quotation marks around every direct quotation you copy verbatim from a source. Make the quotation marks immediately, before you forget, so that you will always know that the words of your notes within quotation marks are the words of another writer.

Often, as you write your notes, you may use some of your own words and some of the words from your source. In cases like this you should be even more cautious. ***Put quotation marks around every word that you take directly from the source, even if your note looks like a picket fence.*** Later, when you begin writing your essay, your memory of what is yours and not yours will be dim, and if you use another's words in your own essay without proper acknowledgment, you are risking the charge of plagiarism. Much of the time, plagiarism is caused not by deliberate deception but rather by sloppy note taking.[2]

IF YOUR SOURCE IS LONG, MAKE A BRIEF AND ACCURATE PARAPHRASE. When you take notes, it is best to paraphrase the sources. A paraphrase is a restatement in your own words, and because of this it is actually a first step in the writing of your essay. A big problem in paraphrasing is to capture the idea in the source without copying the words in the source. The best way is to read and reread the passage you are noting. Turn over the book or journal—or turn away from your computer screen—and write out the idea in your own words as accurately as you can. Once you have completed this note, compare it with the original and make corrections to improve your thought and emphasis. Add a short quotation if you believe it is needed, but be sure to use quotation marks. If your paraphrase is too close to the original, throw out the note and write another one. This effort may have its own reward because often you may be able to transfer some or even all of your note, word for word, directly to the appropriate place in your research essay.

To see the problems of paraphrasing, let us look at a paragraph of criticism and then see how a student doing research might take notes on it. The paragraph

[2]See page 612 for a further discussion of plagiarism.

is by Richard F. Peterson, from an essay entitled "The Circle of Truth: The Stories of Katherine Mansfield and Mary Lavin," published in *Modern Fiction Studies* 24 (1978): 383–94. In the passage to be quoted, Peterson is considering the structures of two Mansfield stories, "Bliss" and "Miss Brill":

> "Bliss" and "Miss Brill" are flawed stories, but not because the truth they reveal about their protagonists is too brutal or painful for the tastes of the common reader. In each story, the climax of the narrative suggests an arranged reality that leaves a lasting impression, not of life, but of the author's cleverness. This strategy of arrangement for dramatic effect or revelation, unfortunately, is common in Katherine Mansfield's fiction. Too often in her stories a dropped remark at the right or wrong moment, a chance meeting or discovery, an intrusive figure in the shape of a fat man at a ball or in the Café de Madrid, a convenient death of a hired man or a stranger dying aboard a ship, or a *deus ex machina* in the form of two doves, a dill pickle, or a fly plays too much of a role in / 386 creating a character's dilemma or deciding the outcome of the narrative. 385–386

Because taking notes forces a shortening of this or any criticism, it also requires you to discriminate, judge, interpret, and select; good note taking is not easy. There are some things to guide you, however, when you go through the many sources you uncover.

THINK ABOUT THE PURPOSE OF YOUR RESEARCH. You may not know exactly what you are "fishing for" when you start to take notes, for you cannot prejudge what your essay will contain. Research is a form of discovery. But soon you will notice subjects and issues that your sources constantly explore. If you can accept one of these as your major topic, or focus of interest, you can use that as your guide in all further note taking.

For example, suppose you start to take notes on criticism about Katherine Mansfield's "Miss Brill," and after a certain amount of reading, you decide to focus on the story's structure. This decision guides your further research and note taking. Thus, for example, Richard Peterson criticizes Mansfield's technique of arranging climaxes in her stories. With your topic being "structure," it would therefore be appropriate to write a note about Peterson's judgment. The following note is adequate as a brief reminder of the content in the passage:

> Peterson 385 structure: negative
>
> Peterson claims that Mansfield creates climaxes that are too artificial, too unlifelike, giving the impression not of reality but of Mansfield's own "cleverness." 385

Let us now suppose that you want a fuller note, in the expectation that you need not just Peterson's general idea but also some of his supporting detail. Such a note might look like this :

> Peterson 385 structure: negative
>
> Peterson thinks that "Bliss" and "Miss Brill" are "flawed" because they have contrived endings that give the impression "not of life but of" Mansfield's "cleverness." She arranges things artificially, according to Peterson, to cause the endings in many other stories. Some of these things are chance remarks, discoveries, or meetings, together with other unexpected or chance incidents and objects. These contrivances make their stories imperfect. 385

In an actual research essay, any part of this note would be useful. The words are almost all the note taker's own, and the few quotations are within quotation marks. Note that Peterson, the critic, is properly recognized as the source of the criticism, so you could adapt the note easily when you are doing your writing. The key here is that your note taking should be guided by your developing plan for your essay.

Note taking is part of your thinking and composing process. You may not always know whether you will be able to use each note that you take, and you will always exclude many notes when you write your essay. You will always find, however, that taking notes is easier once you have determined your purpose.

GIVE YOUR NOTES TITLES. To help plan and develop the various parts of your essay, write a title for each of your notes, as in the examples in this chapter. This practice is a form of outlining. Let us continue discussing the structure of Mansfield's "Miss Brill," the actual subject of the illustrative research essay (p. 614–20). As you do your research, you discover that there is a divergence of critical thought about how the ending of the story should be understood. Here is a note about one of the diverging interpretations:

> Daly 90 Last sentence of the story
>
> Miss Brill's "complete" "identification" with the shabby fur piece at the very end may cause readers to conclude that she is the one in tears but bravely does not recognize this fact, and also to conclude that she may never use the fur in public again because of her complete defeat. Everything may be for "perhaps the very last time." 90

Notice that the title classifies the topic of the note. If you use such classifications, a number of like-titled cards or computer notes could form the basis for a section in your essay about how to understand the conclusion of "Miss Brill." Whether you use this note or not—and very often you may not, for it may not fit into your final plan for your essay—the topic itself will guide you in further study and note taking.

WRITE DOWN YOUR OWN ORIGINAL THOUGHTS, AND BE SURE TO MARK THEM AS YOUR OWN. As you take notes, you will be acquiring your own observations and thoughts. Do not push these aside in your mind, on the chance of remembering them later, *but write them down immediately*. Often you may notice a detail that your source does not mention, or you may get a hint for an idea that the critic does not develop. Often, too, you may get thoughts that can serve as "bridges" between details in your notes or as introductions or concluding observations. Be sure to title your comments and also to mark them as your own thought. Here is such a note, which is about Katherine Mansfield's emphasis on the impoverished existence of her heroine, Miss Brill, and the many people inhabiting the park where the action of the story takes place:

> My Own — About Miss Brill's "cupboard"
>
> Mansfield's speaker avoids taking us to the homes of the other people in the park, as she does when we follow Miss Brill into her living quarters. Instead, she lets us know that the silent couple, the complaining wife and suffering husband, the unseen man rejected by the young woman dumping the flowers, the "ermine toque," and the funny gentleman, not to mention the many people resembling statues in the park, all return to loneliness and personal pain.

Observe that the substance of this note (also most of the language) is used as the basis for much of paragraph 10 in the illustrative essay. The point here is that as you make your own observations while doing your research, you are also free to develop materials that can go directly into your final essay.

CLASSIFY YOUR CARDS OR COMPUTER NOTES, AND GROUP THEM. If you do a careful and thorough job of taking notes, your essay will already have been forming in your mind. The titles of your notes and cards will suggest areas to be developed as you do your planning and initial drafting. Once you have assembled a stack of materials derived from a reasonable number of sources (your instructor may have assigned an approximate number or a minimum number), you can sort them into groups according to the topics and titles. For the illustrative research essay, after some shuffling and retitling, the cards were assembled in the following groups:

General structure

Specific structures: season, time of day, levels of cruelty, Miss Brill's own "hierarchies" of unreality

The concluding paragraphs, especially the last sentence

If you look at the major sections of the illustrative essay, you will see that the topics are closely adapted from these groups of cards. In other words, the arrangement of the cards is an effective means of outlining and organizing a research essay. Be smart; do it this way.

MAKE LOGICAL ARRANGEMENTS OF THE NOTES AND CARDS IN EACH GROUP. There is still much to do with each group of cards or printed notes. You cannot use the details as they happen to fall randomly in your stack. You need to decide which notes are relevant. You might also need to retitle some cards and use them elsewhere. Those that remain will have to be arranged in a logical order for you to find use for them in your essay.

Once you have your notes or cards in order, you can write whatever comments or transitions are needed to move from detail to detail. Write this material directly on the cards and be sure to use a different color ink so that you can distinguish later between the original note and what you add. Here is an example of such a "developed" note, with quotation and commentary distinguished by different kinds of type:

> Magalaner 39 — Structure, general
>
> **Magalaner, using "Miss Brill" as an example, speaks of Mansfield's weaving "a myriad of threads into a rigidly patterned whole" in her stories. (39).** *Some of these "threads" are the fall season, the time of day, examples of unkindness, the park bench sitters from the cupboards, and Miss Brill's stages of unreality. Each of these is separate, but all work together structurally to unify the story.*

By adding such commentary to your notes, you are also simplifying the writing of your first draft. In many instances, the note and whatever comments you make may be moved directly into the paper with minor adjustments (some of the content of this note appears in paragraph 6 of the illustrative essay, and almost all the topics introduced here are developed in paragraphs 9 to 14).

Being Creative and Original While Doing Research

You will not always transfer your notes directly into your essay. The major trap to avoid in a research paper is that your use of sources can become an end in itself and therefore a shortcut for your own thinking and writing. Often, students make the mistake of introducing details the way a master of ceremonies introduces performers in a variety show. This is unfortunate because it is the student whose essay will be judged, even though the sources, like the performers, do all the work. Thus, it is important to be creative and original in a research essay and to do your own thinking and writing, even though you are relying heavily on your sources. Here are five ways in which research essays may be original.

1. Your selection of material is original with you. In each major part of your essay you will include many details from your sources. To be creative you should select different but related details and avoid overlapping or repetition. Your completed essay will be judged on the basis of the thoroughness with which you make your points with different details (which in turn will represent the completeness of your research). Even though you are relying on published materials and cannot be original on that score, your selection can be original because you bring these materials together for the first time, and because you emphasize some details and minimize others. Inevitably, your assemblage of details from your sources will be unique and therefore original.

2. The development of your essay is yours alone. Your arrangement of various points is an obvious area of originality: One detail seems naturally to precede another, and certain conclusions stem from certain details. As you present the details, conclusions, and arguments from your sources, you can also add an original stamp by introducing supporting details different from those in the source material. You can also add your own emphasis to particular points—an emphasis that you do not find in your sources.

3. The words are yours and yours alone. Naturally, the words that you use will be original because they are yours. Your topic sentences, for example, will all be your own. As you introduce details and conclusions, you will need to write "bridges" to get yourself from point to point. These can be introductory remarks or transitions. In other words, as you write, you are not just stringing your notes together, but rather you are actively assembling and arranging your thoughts, based on your notes, in creative and unique ways.

4. Explaining and contrasting controversial views is an original presentation of material. Closely related to your selection is that in your research you may have found conflicting or differing views on a topic. If you make a point to describe and distinguish these views, and explain the reasons for the differences, you are presenting material originally.

5. Your own insights and positions are uniquely your own. There are three possibilities here, all related to how well you have learned the primary texts on which your research in secondary sources is based.

a. *Weave your own interpretations and ideas into your essay.* An important part of taking notes is to make your own points precisely when they occur to you. Often you can expand these as truly original parts of your essay. Your originality does not need to be extensive; it may consist of no more than a single insight. Here is such a card, which was written during research on the structure of "Miss Brill."

My Own	Miss Brill's unreality
In light of this hierarchical structure of unrealities, it is ironic that the boy and girl sit down next to her just when she is at the height of her fancy about her own importance. When she hears the girl's insults, the couple introduces objective reality to her with a vengeance, and she is plunged from rapture to pain.	

The originality here is built around the contrast between Miss Brill's exhilaration and her rapid and cruel deflation. This observation is not unusual or startling, but it nevertheless represents original thought about the story. When modified and adapted (and put into full sentences with proper punctuation), the material of the card supplies much of paragraph 13 of the illustrative essay. You can see that your development of a "My Own" note card is an important part of the prewriting stage of a research essay.

b. *Filling gaps in the sources enables you to present original thoughts and insights.* As you read your secondary sources, you may realize that an obvious conclusion is not being made or that an important detail is not being stressed. Here is an area that you can develop on your own. Your conclusions may involve a particular interpretation or major point of comparison, or they may rest on a particularly important but understressed word or fact. For example, paragraphs 10 to 13 in the illustrative essay form an argument based on observations that critics have overlooked, or have not stressed, about the attitudes of the heroine of "Miss Brill." In your research, whenever you find such a critical "vacuum" (assuming that you cannot read all the articles about some of your topics, where your discovery may already have been made a number of times), it is right to include whatever is necessary to fill it.

c. *By disputing your sources with your own arguments, you are being original.* The originality of your disagreement is that you will be using details in a different way from that of the critic or critics whom you are disputing, and your conclusions will be your own. This area of originality is similar to the laying out of controversial critical views, except that you furnish one of the opposing views yourself. The approach is limited because it is difficult to find many substantive points of interpretation on which there are not already clearly delineated opposing views. Paragraph 13 of the illustrative research essay shows how a disagreement can lead to a different, if not original, interpretation.

Documenting Your Work

It is necessary and essential to acknowledge—to *document*—all sources from which you have quoted or paraphrased factual and interpretive information. Because of the need to avoid being challenged for plagiarism, this point cannot be overemphasized. As the means of documentation, various reference systems use parenthetical references, footnotes, or endnotes. Whatever system is used, documentation almost always includes a carefully prepared bibliography, or list of works cited.

We will first discuss the list of works cited and then review the two major reference systems for use in a research paper. Parenthetical references, preferred by the Modern Language Association (MLA) since 1984, are described in Joseph Gibaldi, *MLA Handbook for Writers of Research Papers*, 6th ed., 2003. Footnotes or endnotes, recommended by the MLA before 1984, are still required by many instructors.

Include All the Works You Have Used in a List of Works Cited (Bibliography)

The key to any reference system is a carefully prepared list of works cited that is included at the end of the essay. "Works cited" means exactly that; the list should include just those books and articles you have actually used in your essay. If, however, your instructor requires that you use footnotes or endnotes, you can extend your concluding list to be a complete bibliography both of works cited and also of works consulted but not actually used. Always, always, always, follow your instructor's directions.

The list of works cited should include the following information, in each entry, in the form indicated.

FOR A BOOK

- The author's name: last name first, followed by first name and middle name or initial. Period.
- The title, underlined. Period.
- The city of publication (not state or nation), colon; publisher (easily recognized abbreviations or key words can be used unless they seem awkward or strange; see the *MLA Handbook,* pp. 272–74), comma; year of publication. Period.

FOR AN ARTICLE

- The author's name: last name first, followed by first name and middle name or initial. Period.
- The title of the article in quotation marks. Period.
- The title of the journal or periodical, underlined, followed by the volume number in Arabic (not Roman) numbers with no punctuation, then the year of publication within parentheses. Colon. For a daily paper or weekly magazine, omit the parentheses and cite the date in the British style followed by a colon (day, month, year, as in 2 Feb. 2007). Inclusive page numbers (without any preceding p. or pp.). Period.

The works you are citing should be listed alphabetically according to the last names of authors, with unsigned articles included in the list alphabetically by titles. Bibliographical lists are begun at the left margin, with subsequent lines in a five-space hanging indentation, so that the key locating word—the author's last name or the first title word of an unsigned article—can be easily seen. Many unpredictable and complex combinations, including ways to describe works of art, musical or other performances, and films, are detailed extensively in the *MLA Handbook* (142–235). Here are two model entries:

BOOK:

Alpers, Antony. The Life of Katherine Mansfield. New York: Viking, 1980.

ARTICLE:

Hankin, Cheryl. "Fantasy and the Sense of an Ending in the Work of Katherine Mansfield." Modern Fiction Studies 24 (1978): 465–74.

Refer to Works Parenthetically as You Draw Details from Them

Within the text of your research essay, use parentheses in referring to works from which you are using facts and conclusions. This parenthetical citation system is recommended in the *MLA Handbook* (238–60), and its guiding principle is to provide documentation without asking readers to interrupt their reading to find footnotes or endnotes. Readers wanting to see the complete reference can easily find it in your list of works cited. With this system, you incorporate the author's last name and the relevant page number or numbers directly, whenever possible, into the body of your essay. If the author's name is mentioned in your discussion, you need to give only the page number or numbers in parentheses. Here are two examples, from a critical study of another author, the eighteenth-century poet Alexander Pope:

> Alexander Pope believed in the idea that the universe is a whole, a totally unified body, which provides a "viable benevolent system for the salvation of everyone who does good" (Kallich 24).

> Martin Kallich draws attention to Alexander Pope's belief in the idea that the universe is a whole, a totally unified body, which provides a "viable benevolent system for the salvation of everyone who does good" (24).

Use Footnotes and Endnotes—Formal and Traditional Reference Formats

The most formal system of documentation still widely used is that of footnotes (references at the bottom of each page) or endnotes (references listed numerically at the end of the essay). If your instructor wants you to use one of these formats, do the following: Make a note the first time you quote or refer to a source, with the details ordered as outlined below.

FOR A BOOK

- The author's name: first name or initials first, followed by middle name or initial, then last name. Comma.
- The title, underlined for a book, no punctuation. If you are referring to a work in a collection (article, story, poem) use quotation marks for that, but underline the title of the book. No punctuation, but use a comma after the title if an editor, translator, or edition number follows.
- The name of the editor or translator, if relevant. Abbreviate "editor" or "edited by" as "ed.," "editors" as "eds." Use "trans." for "translator" or "translated by." No punctuation, but use a comma if an edition number follows.
- The edition (if indicated), abbreviated thus: 2nd ed., 3rd ed., and so on. No additional punctuation.
- The publication facts, within parentheses, without any preceding or following punctuation, in the following order:

  City (but not the state or nation) of publication, colon.

  Publisher (clear abbreviations are acceptable and desirable), comma.

  Year of publication.

- The page number(s) with no "p." or "pp.," for example, 5, 6–10, 15–19, 295–307, 311–16. Period. If you are referring to longer works, such as novels or longer stories with division or chapter numbers, include these numbers for readers who may be using an edition different from yours.

FOR A JOURNAL OR MAGAZINE ARTICLE

- The author: first name or initials first, followed by middle name or initial, then last name. Comma.
- The title of the article, in quotation marks. Comma.
- The name of the journal, underlined. No punctuation.
- The volume number, in Arabic letters. No punctuation.
- The year of publication within parentheses. Colon. For newspaper and journal articles, omit the parentheses, and include day, month, and year (in the British style: 21 May 2005). Colon.
- The page number(s) with no "p." or "pp.": 5, 6–10, 34–36, 98–102, 345–47. Period.

For later notes to the same work, use the last name of the author as the reference unless you are referring to two or more works by the same author. Thus, if you refer to only one work by, say, Thomas Hardy, the name Hardy will be enough for all later references. Should you be referring to other works by Hardy, however, you will also need to make a short reference to the specific works to distinguish them, such as Hardy, "The Three Strangers," and Hardy, "The Man He Killed."

Footnotes are placed at the bottom of each page, and endnotes are included on separate page(s) at the end of the essay. The first lines of both footnotes and endnotes should be paragraph indented, and continuing lines should be flush with the left margin. Both endnote and footnote numbers are set in a smaller font and positioned slightly above the line (as superior numbers) like this:[12]. You can single-space footnotes and endnotes and leave a line of space between them. *Most computer programs have specially designed and consecutively numbered footnote formats. These are generally acceptable, but be sure to consult your instructor.* (For more detailed coverage of footnoting practices, see *MLA Handbook*, 298–313.)

Sample Footnotes

In the examples below, book titles and periodicals are underlined.

[3] Blanche H. Gelfant, Women Writing in America: Voices in Collage (Hanover: UP of New England, for Dartmouth College, 1984) 110.

[1] Günter Grass, "Losses," Granta 42 (Winter 1992): 99.

[5] John O'Meara, "Hamlet and the Fortunes of Sorrowful Imagination: A Re-examination of the Genesis and Fate of the Ghost," Cahiers Elisabéthains 35 (1989): 21.

[8] Grass 104.

[15] Gelfant 141.

[21] O'Meara 17.

In principle, you do not need to repeat in a footnote or endnote any material you have already mentioned in your own discourse. For example, if you recognize the author and title of your source, then the footnote or endnote should give no more than the data about publication. Here is an example:

> In The Fiction of Katherine Mansfield,[9] Marvin Magalaner points out that Mansfield was as skillful in the development of epiphanies (that is, the use of highly significant though perhaps unobtrusive actions or statements to reveal the depths of a particular character) as James Joyce himself, the "inventor" of the technique.
>
> ---
>
> [9](Carbondale: Southern Illinois UP, 1971) 130.

Follow the Requirements for Documentation Set by Other Academic Disciplines

A variety of reference systems and style manuals have been adopted by certain disciplines (e.g., mathematics, medicine, psychology) to serve their own special needs. If you receive no instructions from your instructors in other courses, you can adapt the systems described here. If you need to use the documentation methods of other fields, however, use the *MLA Handbook* (316–17) for guidance about which style manual to select.

When in Doubt, Consult Your Instructor

As long as all you want from a reference is the page number of a quotation or paraphrase, the parenthetical system described briefly here—and detailed fully in the *MLA Handbook*—is the most suitable and convenient one you can use. However, you may wish to use footnotes or endnotes if you need to add more details, provide additional explanations, or refer your readers to other materials that you are not using. Whatever method you follow, you must always acknowledge sources properly. Remember that whenever you begin to write and cite references, you might forget a number of specific details about documentation, and you will certainly discover that you have many questions. Be sure, then, to ask your instructor, who is your final authority.

Strategies for Organizing Ideas in Your Research Essay

INTRODUCTION In your research essay you may wish to expand your introduction more than usual because of the need to relate the problem of research to your topic. You may wish to bring in relevant historical or biographical information. You may also wish to summarize critical opinion or describe critical problems about your topic. The idea is to lead your reader into your topic by providing interesting and significant materials that you have found.

Because of the length of many research essays, some instructors require a topic outline, which is in effect a brief table of contents. Because the inclusion of an outline is a matter of the instructor's choice, be sure to learn whether your instructor requires it.

BODY AND CONCLUSION As you write the body and conclusion of your research essay, its development will be governed by your choice of topic. Consult the relevant chapters in this book about what to include for whatever approach or approaches you select (setting, ideas, point of view, character, tone, etc.).

In length, the research essay can be anywhere from as few as two or three or as many as fifteen or thirty or more pages, depending on your instructor's assignment. Obviously, an essay on a single work will be shorter than one based on several. If you narrow the scope of your topic, as suggested in the approaches described at the beginning of this chapter, you can readily keep your essay within the assigned length. The following illustrative research essay, for example, illustrates approach 1 (page 594) by being limited to only one character in one story. Were you to write on characters in a number of other stories by Mansfield or any other writer (approach 2), you could limit your total number of pages by stressing comparative treatments and by avoiding excessive detail about problems pertaining to only one work.

Although you limit your topic yourself in consultation with your instructor, you may encounter problems because you will deal not with one source alone but with many. Naturally the sources will provide you with details and also trigger many of your ideas. The problem is to handle the many strands without piling on too many details, and also without being led into digressions. It is important therefore to keep your central idea foremost; the constant stressing of your central idea will help you both to select relevant materials and to reject irrelevant ones.

PLAGIARISM: AN EMBARRASSING BUT VITAL SUBJECT—AND A DANGER TO BE OVERCOME

When you are using sources as the substance of many of the details in your essay, you run the risk of *plagiarism*—using the words and ideas of other writers without their consent and without acknowledgment. Recognizing the source means being clear about the identity of other authors, together with the name or names of the works from which one gets details and ideas. When there is no recognition, readers, and the intellectual world generally, are deceived. They assume that the material they are reading is the original work and the intellectual possession of the writer. When there is no recognition, the plagiarizing author is committing intellectual theft.

This is no small matter. In the world of publications, many people who have committed plagiarism have suffered irreparable damage to their credibility and reputations as writers and authorities. Some well-known writers have found it hard if not impossible to continue their careers, and all because of the wide knowledge of their plagiarism. It does not end there. A plagiarist might be open to legal actions, and might, if the situation is grave enough, be required to supply financial restitution to the author or authors whose work has been illegally appropriated. In schools and colleges, students who plagiarize may face academic discipline. Often the discipline is a failure for the course, but it might also include suspension and expulsion. It is not possible to predict all the ill consequences of committing an act of plagiarism.

It therefore bears constant awareness and emphasis that you need to distinguish between the sources you are using and your own work. Your readers will assume that everything you write is your own unless you indicate otherwise. Therefore, when blending your words with the ideas from sources, ***be clear about proper acknowledgments.*** Most commonly, if you are simply presenting details and facts, you can write straightforwardly and let parenthetical references suffice as your authority, as in the following sentence from the illustrative research essay:

> Marvin Magalaner, using "Miss Brill" as an example, speaks of Mansfield's weaving of "a myriad of threads into a rigidly patterned whole" (39). Also noting Mansfield's control over form, Cheryl Hankin suggests that Mansfield's structuring is perhaps more "instinctive" than deliberate (474).

Here there can be no question about plagiarism, for the names of the authors of the critical sources are fully acknowledged, the page numbers are specific, and the quotation marks clearly distinguish the words of the critics from the words of the essay writer. If you grant recognition as recommended here, no confusion can result about the authority underlying your essay. The linking words obviously belong to the writer of the essay, but the parenthetical references clearly indicate that the sentence is based on two sources.

If you use an interpretation unique to a particular writer, or if you rely on a significant quotation from your source, you should make your acknowledgment an essential part of your discussion, as in this sentence.

> Saralyn Daly, referring to Miss Brill as one of Mansfield's "isolatoes"—that is, solitary persons cut off from normal human contacts—fears that the couple's callous insults have caused Miss Brill to face the outside world with her fur piece "perhaps for the very last time" (88, 90).

Here the idea of the critic is singled out for special acknowledgment. If you recognize your sources in this way, no confusion can arise about how you have used them.

Please, always keep foremost in your mind that ***the purpose of research is to acquire knowledge and details from which to advance your own thoughts and interpretations.*** You should consider your research discoveries as a kind of springboard from which you can launch yourself into your own written work. In this way, research should be creative. A test of how you use research is to determine how well you move from the details you are using to the development of your own ideas. Once you have gone forth in this way, you are using research correctly and creatively. Plagiarism will then no more be even a remote issue for you.

Illustrative Student Essay Using Research

Underlined sentences in this paper *do not* conform to MLA style and are used solely as teaching tools to emphasize the central idea, thesis sentence, and topic sentences throughout the paper.

Use 1/2 inch top margin, 1 inch bottom and side margin; double-space throughout.

Outline

I. Introduction. The parallel structures of "Miss Brill"

II. Season and time as structure

III. Insensitive or cruel actions as structure

IV. Miss Brill's "hierarchy of unrealities" as structure

V. The story's conclusion

VI. Conclusion

Use 1/2 inch top margin, 1 inch bottom and side margin; double-space throughout.

Delgado 1

In MLA style, the header has the student's last name and page number.

Put identifying information in upper-left corner, double-space.

Simone Delgado

Professor Leeshock

Composition 102

30 January 2008

Center title one double-space below identifying information.

The Structure of Katherine Mansfield's "Miss Brill"°

[1] In the story "Miss Brill," Mansfield creates an aging and emotionally vulnerable character, Miss Brill, whose good feelings are dashed when she overhears some cruel and shattering personal insults. In accord with Miss Brill's emotional deflation, the story is developed through a parallel number of structures.* This parallelling demonstrates Mansfield's power generally over tight narrative control. Marvin Magalaner, using "Miss Brill" as an example, speaks of Mansfield's weaving "a myriad of threads into a rigidly patterned

°This story appears on pages 202–05.
***Central idea**

Delgado 2

whole" (39). Also noting Mansfield's control over form, Cheryl Hankin suggests that Mansfield's structuring is perhaps more "instinctive" than deliberate (474). Either of these observations is great praise for Mansfield. The complementary parallels, threads, stages, or "levels" of "unequal length" (Harmat uses the terms "niveaux" and "longueur inégale," 49, 51) are the fall season, the time of day, insensitive or cruel actions, Miss Brill's own unreal perceptions, and the final section or dénouement.†

In MLA style, put only the page number in parentheses when the author is named in the text.

[2] An important aspect of structure in "Miss Brill" is Mansfield's use of the season of the year. Autumn, with its propulsion toward winter, is integral to the deteriorating life of the heroine. In the first paragraph, we learn that there is a "faint chill" in the air (is the word "chill" chosen to rhyme with "Brill"?), and this phrase is repeated in paragraph 10 (204). Thus the author establishes autumn and the approaching year's end as the beginning of the downward movement toward dashed hopes. This seasonal reference is also carried out when we read that "yellow leaves" are "down drooping" in the local Jardins Publiques (203, paragraph 6) and that leaves are drifting "now and again" from almost "nowhere, from the sky" (204, paragraph 1). It is the autumn cold that has caused Miss Brill to wear her shabby fur piece, which later the young girl considers the object of contempt. The chill, together with the fur, forms a structural setting for both the action and the mood of the story. Sewell notes that "Miss Brill" both begins and ends with the fur, which is the direct cause of the heroine's deep hurt at the conclusion (25).

[3] Like the seasonal structuring, the times of day parallel Miss Brill's darkening existence. At the beginning, the speaker points out that the day is "brilliantly fine--the blue sky powdered with gold," and that the light is "like white wine." This figurative language suggests the brightness and crispness of full sunlight. In paragraph 6 (203), where we also learn of the yellow leaves, "the blue sky with gold-veined clouds" indicates that time has been passing as clouds accumulate during late afternoon. By the story's end, Miss Brill has returned in sadness to her "little dark room" (205, paragraph 18).

†Thesis sentence

Delgado 3

In other words, the time moves from day to evening, from light to darkness, as a virtual accompaniment to Miss Brill's emotional pain.

[4] Mansfield's most significant structural device, which is not emphasized by critics, is the introduction of insensitive or cruel actions. It is as though the hurt felt by Miss Brill on the bright Sunday afternoon is also being felt by many others. Because she is the spectator who is closely related to Mansfield's narrative voice, Miss Brill is the filter through whom these negative examples reach the reader. Considering the patterns that emerge, one may conclude that Mansfield intends that the beauty of the day and the joyousness of the band be taken as an ironic contrast to the pettiness and insensitivity of the people in the park.

[5] The first of these people are the silent couple on Miss Brill's bench (203, paragraph 3) and the incompatible couple of the week before (203, paragraph 4). Because these seem no more than ordinary, they do not at first appear to be part of the story's pattern of cruelty and rejection. But their incompatibility, suggested by their silence and one-way complaining, establishes a structural parallel with the young and insensitive couple who later insult Miss Brill. Thus the first two couples prepare the way for the third, and all show increasing insensitivity and cruelty.

[6] Almost unnoticed as a second level of negation is the vast group of "odd, silent, nearly all old" people filling "the benches and green chairs" (203, paragraph 5). They seem to be no more than a normal part of the Sunday afternoon landscape. But these people are significant structurally because the "dark little rooms--or even cupboards" that Miss Brill associates with them also, ironically, describe the place where she lives (203, 205, paragraphs 5, 18). The reader may conclude from Miss Brill's quiet eavesdropping that she herself is one of these nameless and faceless ones who lead similarly dreary lives.

[7] After Mansfield sets these levels for her heroine, she introduces characters experiencing additional rejection and cruelty. The beautiful woman who throws down the bunch of violets is the first of these (203, paragraph 8). The story does not explain the causes of this woman's scorn,

Delgado 4

and Miss Brill does not know what to make of the incident; but the woman's actions suggest that she has been involved in a relationship that has ended in anger and bitterness.

[8] The major figure involved in rejection, who is important enough to be considered a structural double of Miss Brill, is the woman wearing the ermine toque (203, paragraph 8). It is clear that she, like Miss Brill, is one of "the lonely and isolated women in a hostile world" that Mansfield is so skillful in portraying (Gordon 6). This woman tries to please the "gentleman in grey," but this man insults her by blowing smoke in her face. It could be, as Peter Thorpe observes, that she is "obviously a prostitute" (661). But it is more likely that the "ermine toque" has had a broken relationship with the gentleman, or perhaps even no relationship. Being familiar with his Sunday habits, she comes to the park to meet him, as though by accident, to attempt to renew contact. After her rejection, her hurrying off to meet someone "much nicer" (there is no such person, for Mansfield uses the phrase "as though" to introduce "ermine toque's" departure) is her way of masking her hurt. Regardless of the exact situation, however, Mansfield makes it plain that the encounter demonstrates vulnerability, unkindness, and pathos, but also a certain amount of self defense.

In MLA style, put author and page number in parentheses when the author is not named in the sentence.

[9] Once Mansfield establishes this major incident, she introduces two additional examples of insensitivity. At the end of paragraph 8 (203), the hobbling old man "with long whiskers" is nearly knocked over by the group of four girls, who show arrogance if not contempt toward him. The final examples involve Miss Brill herself. These are her recollections of the apparent indifference of her students and of the old invalid "who habitually sleeps" when she reads to him.

[10] Although "Miss Brill" is a brief story, Mansfield creates a large number of structural parallels to the sudden climax brought about by the boorishly insensitive young couple. The boy and girl do not appear until the very end, in other words (204, paragraph 11), but extreme insults like theirs have been fully anticipated in the story's earlier parts. Mansfield's speaker does not take us to the homes of the other people in the park, as she does when we

Delgado 5

follow Miss Brill to her wretched room. Instead, the narrative invites us to conclude that the silent couple, the complaining wife and long-suffering husband, the unseen man rejected by the young woman, the "ermine toque," and the funny gentleman, not to mention the many silent and withdrawn people sitting like statues in the park, all return to loneliness and personal pain that are comparable to the feelings of Miss Brill.

[11] The intricacy of the structure of "Miss Brill" does not end here. Of great importance is the structural development of the protagonist herself. Peter Thorpe notes a "hierarchy of unrealities" that govern the reader's increasing awareness of Miss Brill's plight (661). By this measure, the story's actions progressively bring out Miss Brill's failures of perception and understanding--failures that in this respect make her like her namesake fish, the lowly brill (Gargano).

[12] These unrealities begin with Miss Brill's fanciful but harmless imaginings about her shabby fur piece. This beginning sets up the pattern of her pathetic inner life. When she imagines that the park band is a "single, responsive, and very sensitive creature" (Thorpe 661), we realize that she is unrealistically making too much out of a mediocre band of ordinary musicians. Although she cannot interpret the actions of the beautiful young woman with the violets, she does see the encounter between the "ermine toque" and the gentleman in grey as a vision of rejection. Her response is correct, but then her belief that the band's drumbeats are sounding out "The Brute! The Brute!" indicates her vivid overdramatization of the incident. The "top of the hierarchy of unrealities" (Thorpe 661) is her fancy that Miss Brill is an actor with a vital part in a gigantic drama played by all the people in the park. The most poignant aspect of this daydream is her unreal thought that someone would miss her if she were to be absent.

Quotation marks around phrases show that they appeared separately in the source.

[13] In light of this hierarchical structure of unrealities, it is ironic that the boy and girl sit down next to her just when she is at the height of her fancy about her own importance. When she hears the girl's insults, the couple has introduced objective reality to her with a vengeance, and she is plunged from rapture to pain.

Delgado 6

The concluding two paragraphs of "Miss Brill" hence form a rapid dénouement to reflect her loneliness and solitude.

[14] Of unique importance in the structure of "Miss Brill" are these final two paragraphs, in which Miss Brill, all alone, returns to her wretched little room. Saralyn Daly, referring to Miss Brill as one of Mansfield's "isolatoes"--that is, solitary persons cut off from normal human contacts--fears that the couple's callous insults have caused Miss Brill to face the outside world with her fur piece "perhaps for the very last time" (88, 90). Sydney Kaplan adds a political dimension to Miss Brill's defeat, asserting that here and in other stories Mansfield is expressing "outrage" against "a society in which privilege is . . . marked by indifference" to situations like those of Miss Brill (192).

[15] It is clear that Mansfield is asking readers to consider not only Miss Brill alone, but also her similarity to the many park inhabitants who are like her. Miss Brill's grim existence exemplifies a common personal pattern in which the old are destroyed "by loneliness and sickness, by fear of death, by the thoughtless energy of the younger world around them" (Zinman 457). More generally, Mansfield herself considered such negative situations as "the snail under the leaf," which implies that a gnawing fate is waiting for everyone, not just those who are old (Meyers 213). With such a crushing experience for the major character, "Miss Brill" may be fitted to the structuring of Mansfield's stories described by André Maurois: "moments of beauty suddenly broken by contact with ugliness, cruelty, or death" (342–43).

Delgado 7

Works Cited

Daly, Saralyn R. Katherine Mansfield. New York: Twayne, 1965.

Gargano, James W. "Mansfield's Miss Brill." Explicator 19. 2 (1960): item 10 (one page, unnumbered).

In MLA style, the list of sources, called the "Works Cited," begins a new page. Double-space throughout.

Delgado 8

List sources in alphabetical order.

Gordon, Ian A. “Katherine Mansfield: Overview.” Reference Guide to English Literature, 2nd ed. Ed. D. L. Kirkpatrick. London: St. James Press, 1991 (found at <www.galenet.com>).

Hankin, Cheryl. “Fantasy and the Sense of an Ending in the Work of Katherine Mansfield.” Modern Fiction Studies 24 (1978): 465–74.

Harmat, Andrée-Marie. “Essai D’Analyse Structurale d’une Nouvelle Lyrique Anglaise: ‘Miss Brill’ de Katherine Mansfield.” Les Cahiers de la Nouvelle 1 (1983): 49–74.

Kaplan, Sydney Janet. Katherine Mansfield and the Origins of Modernist Fiction. Ithaca and London: Cornell UP, 1991.

McLaughlin, Ann L. “The Same Job: The Shared Writing Aims of Katherine Mansfield and Virginia Woolf.” Modern Fiction Studies 24 (1978): 369–82.

Magalaner, Marvin. The Fiction of Katherine Mansfield. Carbondale: Southern Illinois UP, 1971.

---. The Short Stories of Katherine Mansfield. New York: Knopf, 1967.

Mansfield, Katherine. “Miss Brill.” Literature: An Introduction to Reading and Writing. Ed. Edgar V. Roberts. 9th ed. New York: Pearson Longman, 2009. 202–05. Parenthetical page numbers to “Miss Brill” refer to pages in this book.

Maurois, André. Points of View from Kipling to Graham Greene. 1935. New York: Ungar, 1968.

Meyers, Jeffrey. Katherine Mansfield: A Darker View. 1978. New York: Cooper Square Press, 2002.

Sewell, Arthur. Katherine Mansfield: A Critical Essay. Auckland: Unicorn, 1936.

Thorpe, Peter. “Teaching ‘Miss Brill.’” College English 23 (1962): 661–63.

Zinman, Toby Silverman. “The Snail Under the Leaf: Katherine Mansfield’s Imagery.” Modern Fiction Studies 24 (1978): 457–64.

Commentary on the Essay

This essay fulfills an assignment of 1500–2000 words, with ten to fifteen sources. (There are actually fifteen.) The bibliography was developed from a college library computer catalog, references in books of criticism (Magalaner, Daly); the *MLA International Bibliography*; the *Essay and General Literature Index*, and the Literature Resource Center available through Netscape and a county library system (www.wls.lib.ny.us). The sources themselves were found in a college library with selective holdings, in a local public library, and in online resources. There is only one rare source, an article (Harmat) obtained in photocopy through interlibrary loan from one of only two U.S. libraries holding the journal in which it appears. The location was made through the national Online Computer Library Center (OCLC). For most semester-long or quarter-long courses, you will probably not have time to add to your sources by such a method, but the article in question refers specifically to "Miss Brill," and it was therefore desirable to examine it.

The sources consist of books, articles, and chapters or portions of books. One article (Sewell) has been published as a separate short monograph. Also, one of the sources is the story "Miss Brill" itself (with locations made by paragraph and page numbers), together with a collection of her stories. The sources are used for facts, interpretations, reinforcement of conclusions, and general guidance and authority.

All necessary thematic devices, including overall organization and transitions, are unique to the illustrative essay. The essay also contains passages taking issue with certain conclusions in a few of the sources. Additional particulars about the handling of sources and developing a research essay are included in the discussion of note taking and related matters in this chapter.

The central idea of the essay (paragraph 1) is built out of this idea, explaining that the movement of emotions in the story is accompanied by an intricate and complementary set of structures. Paragraphs 2 through 13 examine various elements of the story for their structural relationship to Miss Brill's emotions.

Paragraphs 2 and 3 detail the structural uses of the settings of autumn and times of day, pointing out how they parallel her experiences.

The longest part, paragraphs 4 through 10, is based on an idea not found in the sources—that a number of characters are experiencing difficulties and cruelties such as those that befall Miss Brill. Paragraph 5 cites the three couples of the story, paragraph 6 the silent old people, and paragraph 7 the scornful woman with violets. Paragraph 8 is developed in disagreement with one of the sources, showing how an essay involving research may be original even though the sources form the basis of discussion. Paragraph 9 contains additional examples of insensitivity—two of them involving Miss Brill herself. Paragraph 10 summarizes the story's instances of insensitivity and cruelty, once again emphasizing parallels to Miss Brill's situation.

Paragraphs 11 through 13 of the essay are based on ideas about the story's structure found in one of the sources (Thorpe). It is hence more derivative than paragraphs 4 through 10. Paragraphs 14 and 15, the concluding paragraphs of the essay, are devoted to the story's dénouement and to the broader application of the story: Miss Brill is to be considered an example of the anonymous "isolatoes" who inhabit the park. Because they are comparable to Miss Brill, their lives are unlikely just as sad and anguishing as hers is.

The list of works cited is the basis of all references in the essay, in accord with the *MLA Handbook*. By locating these references, a reader might readily examine, verify, and study any of the ideas and details drawn from the sources and developed in the essay.

Writing Topics About How to Undertake Research Essays

In beginning research on any of the following topics, follow the steps in research described in this chapter.

1. Common themes in a number of stories by Hawthorne, Poe, Hardy, or Mansfield (just one, not all).
2. Various critical views of a Hemingway story.
3. Hawthorne's use of religious and moral topic material.
4. Porter's exemplification of Granny Weatherall's strength of character.
5. Views about women in Chopin, Welty, Mansfield, or Steinbeck.
6. Poe's view of the short story as represented in "The Masque of the Red Death."

Color Insert

This four-color insert features classic works of art and connects them to various pieces of literature throughout the book. These images help reinforce the themes found in the literature. One example is found in Moreau's painting *Thracian Girl Carrying the Head of Orpheus on His Lyre.*

Gustave Moreau (1826–1898), *Thracian Girl Carrying the Head of Orpheus on His Lyre,* 1865. Oil on wood, 60 5/8 x 39 1/8 in. (154 x 99.5 cm). Musée d'Orsay, Paris, France. Image courtesy of The Art Renewal Center.

The story of Orpheus is briefly summarized in Chapter 20 (p. 1003). Compare the *Thracian Girl* with Hirsch's "The Swimmers" (p. 1004) and Strand's "Orpheus Alone" (p. 1005).

The following additional artworks appear in the insert:

- **Martin Johnson Heade,** *Approaching Storm: Beach Near Newport*
- **Claude Lorrain,** *Harbour at Sunset*
- **Thomas Cole,** *View from Mount Holyoke, Northampton, Massachusetts, after a Thunderstorm—The Oxbow*
- **Albert Bierstadt,** *Among the Sierra Nevada Mountains, California*
- **François Boucher,** *Madame de Pompadour*
- **Edward Hopper,** *Automat*
- **Sir Hubert von Herkomer,** *Hard Times*
- **Pieter Brueghel the Elder,** *Landscape with the Fall of Icarus*
- **Pieter Brueghel the Elder,** *Peasants' Dance*
- **Ferdinand Léger** *The City*
- **Pablo Picasso,** *Guernica*
- **Jacques-Louis David,** *The Death of Socrates*
- **James Abbott McNeill Whistler,** *The Little White Girl, Symphony in White, No. 2*
- **Auguste Renoir,** *The Umbrellas*
- **Francisco de Goya y Lucientes** *The Colossus*
- *Hercules and the Infant Telephus* (A Roman fresco from Herculaneum)
- *Photograph of Theater of Dionysus*
- Three photographs of the reconstructed *Globe Theater*—stage, interior, and exterior

Chapter 29

Critical Approaches Important in the Study of Literature (Literary Criticism Chapter)

All the literary criticism coverage has been updated to reflect new scholarship. Additionally, criticism in the manner of each school is applied to "Young Goodman Brown" as well as a different selection for each school, to provide students with both a consistent selection throughout as well as to help students understand the distinct characteristics of each form of criticism. Finally, a list of suggested readings is provided for additional information on each school. Each of the following areas of criticism is represented in the chapter:

- Moral/Intellectual
- Topical/Historical
- New Critical/Formalist
- Structuralist
- Feminist Criticism/Gender Studies/Queer Theory
- Economic Determinist/Marxist
- Psychological/Psychoanalytic
- Archetypal/Symbolic/Mythic
- Deconstructionist
- Reader-Response

Part V

Special Writing Topics About Literature

Chapter 29

Critical Approaches Important in the Study of Literature

A number of critical theories or approaches for understanding and interpreting literature are available to critics and students alike.[1] Many of these were developed during the twentieth century to create a discipline of literary studies comparable with disciplines in the natural and social sciences. Literary critics have often borrowed liberally from other disciplines (e.g., history, psychology, politics, anthropology) but have primarily aimed at developing literature as a study in its own right.

At the heart of the various critical approaches are many fundamental questions: What is literature? What does it do? Is its concern primarily to tell stories, to divert attention, to entertain, to communicate ideas, to persuade, and to teach, or is it to describe and interpret reality, or to explore and explain emotions—or is it all of these? To what degree is literature an art, as opposed to a medium for imparting knowledge? What more does it do than express ideas? How does it get its ideas across? What can it contribute to intellectual, artistic, political, and social thought and history? How is literature used, and how and why is it misused? Is it private? Public? What theoretical and technical expertise may be invoked to enhance literary studies? How valuable was literature in the past, and how valuable is it now? To what degree should literature be in the vanguard of social and political change?

Questions such as these indicate that criticism is concerned not only with reading and interpreting stories, poems, and plays but also with establishing theoretical understanding. Because of such extensive aims, a full explanation and illustration of the approaches would fill the pages of a long book. The following descriptions are therefore intended as no more than brief introductions. Bear in mind that in the hands of skilled critics, the approaches are so subtle, sophisticated, and complex that they are not only critical stances but also philosophies.

Although the various approaches provide widely divergent ways to study literature and literary problems, they reflect major tendencies rather than absolute straitjacketing. Not every approach is appropriate for every work, nor are the approaches always mutually exclusive. Even the most devoted practitioners of the methods do not pursue them rigidly. In addition, some of the approaches are more "user friendly" than others for certain types of discovery. To a degree at least, most critics therefore take a particular approach but utilize methods that technically belong to one or more of the other approaches. A critic stressing the topical/historical approach, for example, might introduce the close study of a work that is associated with the method of the New Criticism.

[1]Some of the approaches described in this chapter are presented more simply in Part I as basic study techniques for writing about literary works.

Similarly, a psychoanalytical critic might include details about archetypes. In short, a great deal of criticism is *pragmatic* or *eclectic* rather than rigid.

Ten approaches will be considered here: (1) *moral/intellectual;* (2) *topical/historical;* (3) *New Critical/formalist;* (4) *structuralist*; (5) *feminist/gender studies/queer theory;* (6) *economic determinist/Marxist;* (7) *psychological/psychoanalytic;* (8) *archetypal/symbolic/mythic;* (9) *deconstructionist;* and (10) *reader-response.*

The object of learning about these approaches, like everything else in this book, is to help you develop your own capacities as a reader and writer. Accordingly, following each of the descriptions is a brief paragraph showing how Hawthorne's story "Young Goodman Brown" (Chapter 8) might be considered in the light of the particular approach. The illustrative paragraphs following the discussion of structuralism, for example, shows an application of the structuralist approach to Goodman Brown and his story, and so also with the feminist approach, the economic determinist approach, and the others. These paragraphs are followed by additional commentary illustrating the same approaches based on other literary works. Whenever you are doing your own writing about literature, you are free to use the various approaches as part or all of your assignment, if you believe the approach may help you.

Moral/Intellectual

The **moral/intellectual critical approach** is concerned with content, ideas, and values (see also Chapter 8). The approach is as old as literature itself, for literature is a traditional mode of inculcating thought, morality, philosophy, and religion. The concern in moral/intellectual criticism is not only to discover meaning but also to determine whether works of literature are both *true* and *significant*.

To study literature from the moral/intellectual perspective is therefore to determine whether a work conveys a lesson or a message and whether it can help readers lead better lives and improve their understanding of the world. What ideas does the work contain? How strongly does the work bring forth its ideas? What application do the ideas have to the work's characters and situations? How may the ideas be evaluated intellectually? Morally? Discussions based on such questions do not imply that literature is primarily a medium of moral and intellectual exhortation. Ideally, moral/intellectual criticism should differ from sermonizing to the degree that readers should always be left with their own decisions about whether to assimilate the ideas of a work and about whether the ideas—and values—are personally or morally acceptable.

Sophisticated critics have sometimes demeaned the moral/intellectual approach on the grounds that "message hunting" reduces a work's artistic value by treating it like a sermon or political speech; but the approach will be valuable as long as readers expect literature to be applicable to their own lives.

Example: Hawthorne's "Young Goodman Brown"

"Young Goodman Brown" raises the issue of how an institution designed for human elevation, such as the religious system of colonial Salem, can be so ruinous. Does the failure result from the system itself or from the people who misunderstand it? Is what is true of religion as practiced by Brown also true of social and political institutions? Should any religious or political philosophy

be given greater significance than goodwill and mutual trust? One of the major virtues of "Young Goodman Brown" is that it provokes questions like these but at the same time provides a number of satisfying answers. A particularly important one is that religious and moral beliefs should not be used to justify the condemnation of others. Another important answer is that attacks made from the refuge of a religion or group, such as Brown's Puritanism, are dangerous because the judge may condemn without thought and without personal responsibility.

Second Example: Stafford's "Traveling Through the Dark," page 1179

William Stafford's "Traveling Through the Dark" presents a moral quandary. While the speaker is driving along a narrow road at night, he comes upon the carcass of a doe. Upon investigation, he finds that the doe is pregnant with a live fawn. It is customary to throw dead animals off the side of the road in order to remove the danger of having a swerving car veer off the road. But in the present situation, the speaker "hesitates." The living fawn complicates the moral option, for now life must be taken. As the speaker hesitates, he "could hear the wilderness listen" because moral decisions are not only an individual's domain but affect all of us. "I thought hard for us all " the speaker says, but then adds "my only swerving" as if uncertain if it is presumptuous for one person to think for all people. Sometimes, however, it is a human being's responsibility to make a decision, and one may argue whether the right one was made in this instance. As if to highlight the human quandary that moral situations put us in, Stafford refers to the car as aiming its headlights, as if the car were conscious. Despite that, it is only human beings who are responsible for moral action. Nature merely "listens," and objects merely "light" the path toward decision. In "Traveling Through the Dark" Stafford, through a simple situation that might confront almost anyone, probes many of the issues raised by moral action.

READINGS

Buckley, Vincent. *Poetry and Morality: Studies in the Criticism of Matthew Arnold, T. S. Eliot, and F. R. Leavis*. London: Chato and Windus, 1959.

Else, Gerald F. *Plato and Aristotle on Poetry*. Chapel Hill: U of North Carolina P, 1986.

Farrell, James T. *Literature and Morality*. New York: Vanguard, 1947.

Foerster, Norman. *American Criticism: A Study in Literary Theory from Poe to the Present*. 1928. New York: Russell and Russell, 1962.

Gardner, John. *On Moral Fiction*. New York: Basic Books, 1978.

McCloskey, Mary A. *Kant's Aesthetic*. Basingstoke: Macmillan, 1987.

Olson, Elder. *Aristotle's Poetics and English Literature*. Chicago: U of Chicago P, 1965.

Sartre, Jean Paul. *What is Literature?* New York: Philosophical Library, 1966.

Wallis, R. T. *Neoplatonism*. London: Duckworth, 1995.

Topical/Historical

The **topical/historical critical approach** stresses the relationship of literature to its historical period, and for this reason it has had a long life. Although much literature may be applicable to many places and times, much of it also directly reflects

the intellectual and social worlds of the authors. When was the work written? What were the circumstances that produced it? What major issues does it deal with? How does it fit into the author's career? Keats's poem "On First Looking into Chapman's Homer" (page 762), for example, is his excited response to his reading of one of the major literary works of Western civilization. Hardy's "Channel Firing" (page 738) is an ironically acerbic response to continued armament and preparation for war in the past, in the present, and in the future.

The topical/historical approach investigates relationships of this sort, including the elucidation of words and concepts that today's readers may not immediately understand. It may also include biographical information about the author or be informed by a sociological study. For instance, knowing that William Butler Yeats spent his summers at Coole, in County Galway, Ireland, gives resonance to his poem, "The Wild Swans at Coole" (page 1193). Obviously, the approach requires the assistance of footnotes, dictionaries, library catalogs, histories, and handbooks.

A common criticism of the topical/historical approach is that in the extreme, it deals with background knowledge rather than with literature itself. It is possible, for example, for a topical/historical critic to describe a writer's life, the period of the writer's work, and the social and intellectual ideas of the time—all without ever considering the meaning, importance, and value of any of that writer's works themselves.

A reaction against such an unconnected use of historical details is the so-called **New Historicism.** This approach justifies the parallel reading of both literary and nonliterary works in order to bring an informed understanding of the context of a literary work. The new historicist assumes that history is not a "fixed" essence but a literary construction. As such, history is a prism through which a society views itself; a work of literature is given resonance by seeing the nonobjective context in which it was produced. This approach justifies the introduction of historical knowledge by integrating it with the understanding of particular texts. Readers of Arnold's "Dover Beach" (page 694), for example, sometimes find it difficult to follow the meaning of Arnold's statement "The Sea of Faith / Was once, too, at the full." Historical background has a definite role to play here. In Arnold's time there developed a method of treating the Bible as a historical document rather than a divinely inspired revelation. This approach has been called the "Higher Criticism" of the Bible, and to many thoughtful people the Higher Criticism undermined the concept that the Bible was divine, infallible, and inerrant. Therefore Arnold's idea is that the "Sea of Faith" is no longer at full tide but is now rather at an ebb. Because the introduction of such historical material is designed to facilitate the reading of the poem—and also the reading of other literature of the period—the New Historicism represents an integration of knowledge and interpretation. As a principle, New Historicism entails the acquisition of as much historical information as possible because our knowledge of the relationship of literature to its historical period can never be complete. The practitioner of historical criticism must always seek new information on the grounds that it may prove relevant to the understanding of various literary works.

Cultural Study is a more recent approach that justifies the analyses of nonliterary materials such as television and radio shows, movies, brochures, and advertisements.

By not privileging literature over mass culture, Cultural Studies critics are able to open up new areas of interest. Langston Hughes' poem "Harlem," for example, was written in 1951 about possible resentment of African Americans when faced with constant discrimination. In 1985, August Wilson created his drama *Fences*, in which baseball has been a vital element in the life of the major character, Troy Maxson. Both works—the poem and the play—are made vital because they reflect the treatment of African Americans by the dominant white races in American society. It therefore becomes relevant that in 1947 Jackie Robinson became the first African American ball player to play baseball for a major league team, and that soon after, increasing numbers of black ballplayers were joining major league clubs. Reading newspaper accounts of the problems they faced provides insights into both "Harlem" and *Fences*.

Example: Hawthorne's "Young Goodman Brown"

"Young Goodman Brown" is an allegorical story by Nathaniel Hawthorne (1804–1864), the major New England writer who probed deeply into the relationship between religion and guilt. His ancestors had been involved in religious persecutions, including the Salem witch trials, and he, living 150 years afterward, wanted to analyze the weaknesses and uncertainties of the sin-dominated religion of the earlier period, a tradition of which he was a resentful heir. Not surprisingly, therefore, the story about "Young Goodman Brown" takes place in Salem during Puritan times, and Hawthorne's implied judgments are those of a severe critic of how the harsh old religion destroyed personal and family relationships. Although the immediate concerns of the story belong to a vanished age, Hawthorne's treatment remains valuable because it remains timely.

Second Example: Jarrell's "The Death of the Ball Turret Gunner," page 639

Juxtaposing World War II propaganda posters with Randall Jarrell's 1945 poem "The Death of the Ball Turret Gunner," gives special meaning to both. In an American poster of 1943 the words BATTLE OF GERMANY at the top and JOIN THE AIR CREW at the bottom are boldly visible. In the middle is a group of bombers flying in neat formation high above a bombed German city. All that is rising from below is smoke emanating from the site of the bombing. One gets the impression that a bombing run is an orderly operation and that the bombers are high above any danger, and immune from it. A British poster of the same year, with the words BACK THEM UP at the bottom, shows a fighter plane in close-up as it drops bombs on a German city. In the background other fighters can be seen in formation, apparently leaving the city after a successful bombing raid. While these posters imply a heroic struggle against an enemy, they only point obliquely to any danger. Jarrell's poem confronts the darker realities of war. The gunner of this poem is not consumed by his heroic duty. He seems to be born into his nightmarish situation, for he says "From my mother's sleep I fell into the State." His height above the action does not suggest safety but rather a remote detachment from the "dream of life." Describing his own death and how he was "washed . . . out of the turret with a hose," the speaker manifests the horrifying impersonality of war. This "dialogue" between World War II posters and Randell Jarell's poem gives the reader a richer understanding of the many motives and outcomes of an event so dangerous and complex as war.

READINGS

During, Simon, ed. *The Cultural Studies Reader.* New York: Routledge, 1993.

Greenblatt, Stephen. *Renaissance Self-Fashioning: From More to Shakespeare.* Chicago: U of Chicago P, 1980.

———, ed. *Repressing the English Renaissance.* Berkeley: U of California P, 1988.

Hoggart, Richard. *The Uses of Literacy: Changing Patterns in English Mass Culture.* Harmondsworth: Penguin, 1957.

LaCapra, Dominick. *History and Criticism.* Ithaca: Cornell UP, 1985.

Lindenberger, Herbert, ed. *History in Literature: On Value, Genre, Institutions.* New York: Columbia UP, 1990.

McGann, Jerome. *The Beauty of Inflections: Literary Investigations in Historical Method and Theory.* Oxford: Clarendon P, 1985.

———, ed. *Historical Studies and Literary Criticism.* Madison: U of Wisconsin P, 1985.

Said, Edward W. *Orientalism.* New York: Random House, 1978.

———. *Culture and Imperialism.* New York: Knopf, 1993.

Thomas, Brook. *The New Historicism and Other Old-Fashioned Topics.* Princeton: Princeton UP, 1991.

New Critical/Formalist

The **New Critical / formalist approach** (the **New Criticism**) has been a dominant force in modern literary studies. It focuses on literary texts as formal works of art, and for this reason it can be seen as a reaction against the topical/historical approach. The objection raised by New Critics is that as topical/historical critics consider literary history, they evade direct contact with actual texts.

The inspiration for the New Critical/formalist approach was the French practice of *explication de texte,* a method that emphasizes detailed examination and explanation. (See "Writing an Explication of a Poem," Chapter 11.) The New Criticism is at its most brilliant in the formal analysis of smaller units such as entire poems and short passages. For the analysis of larger structures, the New Criticism also utilizes a number of techniques that have been selected as the basis of chapters in this book. Discussions of point of view, tone, plot, character, and structure, for example, are formal ways of looking at literature that are derived from the New Criticism.

The aim of the new critical study of literature is to provide readers not only with the means of explaining the content of works (what, specifically, does a work say?) but also with the insights needed for evaluating the artistic quality of individual works and writers (how well is it said?). A major aspect of New Critical thought is that content and form—including all ideas, ambiguities, subtleties, and even apparent contradictions—were originally within the conscious or subconscious control of the author. There are no accidents. It does not necessarily follow, however, that today's critic is able to define the author's intentions exactly, for such intentions require knowledge of biographical details that are irretrievably lost. Each literary work therefore takes on its own existence and identity, and the

critic's work is to discover a reading or readings that explain the facts of the text. It should be noted that the New Critic does not claim infallible interpretations and does not exclude the validity of multiple readings of the same work.

Dissenters from the New Criticism have noted a tendency by New Critics to ignore relevant knowledge that history and biography can bring to literary studies. In addition, the approach has been subject to the charge that stressing the explication of texts alone fails to deal with literary value and appreciation. In other words, the New Critics, in explaining the meaning of literature, sometimes neglect the reasons for which readers find literature stimulating and valuable.

Example: Hawthorne's "Young Goodman Brown"

A major aspect of Hawthorne's "Young Goodman Brown" is that the details are so vague and dreamlike that many readers are uncertain about what is happening. The action is a nighttime walk by the protagonist, Young Goodman Brown, into a deep forest where he encounters a mysterious satanic ritual that leaves him bitter and misanthropic. This much seems clear, but the precise nature of Brown's experience is not clear, nor is the identity of the stranger (father, village elder, devil) who accompanies Brown as he begins his walk. At the story's end Hawthorne's narrator states that the whole episode may have been no more than a dream or nightmare. Yet when morning comes, Brown walks back into town as though returning from an overnight trip, and he recoils in horror from his fellow villagers, including his wife Faith (paragraph 70). Could his attitude result from nothing more than a nightmare? Even at the story's end these uncertainties remain. For this reason one may conclude that Hawthorne deliberately creates the uncertainties to reveal how people like Brown build defensive walls of judgment around themselves. The story thus implies that the real source of Brown's anger is as vague as his nocturnal walk, but he doesn't understand it in this way. Because Brown's vision and judgment are absolute, he rejects everyone around him, even if the cost is a life of bitter suspicion and spiritual isolation.

Example: Robinson's "Richard Cory," page 675

Edwin Arlington Robinson's *Richard Cory* is a tightly structured poem in which all the traditional elements of verse are orchestrated to form a unified and clear meaning. The four quatrains, in iambic pentameter lines, rhyme *abab cdcd efef ghgh*, forming a predictable pattern that boldly frames the ironic ending: "And Richard Cory, one calm summer night, / Went home and put a bullet through his head." The "regal" diction describing Richard Cory, contrasted with the bland circumstances of the townspeople, lets the reader know why Cory was so envied, and the diction also carries the poem forward to its shocking conclusion. The people of the town are walking on the "pavement" and "flutter" at the sight of the neighbor they envy: Richard Cory is "a gentleman from sole to crown, /. . . and imperially slim." Each stanza is modulated by images of Cory himself, or at least as he is perceived by those around him, along with the images of the townspeople themselves. The townspeople, including the speaker who is one of them, are so envious of Cory that they "curse" their own predicament and would rather be in his place. Yet, upon close scrutiny, the reader can see how the images describing Cory are superficial, as if only the "surface" of his personality were enough to judge him. He was "slim" and "rich" and "admirably schooled," but no reference is made to his thoughts, feelings, or aspirations. By the common and unimaginative standards of the speaker, the final irony is surprising, yet by the standards of the reader it is not surprising. As in many works of art, the title of the poem is significant. Did anyone know the "heart" of Richard Cory, the "core" of his existence?

READINGS

Brooks, Cleanth, and Robert Penn Warren. *Understanding Poetry.* 4th ed. New York: Holt, 1938.

Brooks, Cleanth. *The Well Wrought Urn: Studies in the Structure of Poetry.* New York: Reynal and Hitchcock, 1947.

Empson, William. *Seven Types of Ambiguity.* London: Chatto and Windus, 1930.

Krieger, Murray. *The New Apologists for Poetry.* Minneapolis: U of Minnesota P, 1986.

Ransom, John Crowe. *The New Criticism.* Norfolk: New Directions, 1941.

Richards, I. A. *Principles of Literary Criticism.* New York: Harcourt Brace, 1924.

Wellek, Rene, and Austin Warren. *Theory of Literature.* New York: Harcourt, Brace, 1949.

Wimsatt, William K. *The Verbal Icon: Studies in the Meaning of Poetry.* Lexington: UP of Kentucky, 1954.

Structuralist

The principle of the **stucturalist critical approach** stems from the attempt to find relationships and connections among elements that appear to be separate and unique. Just as physical science reveals unifying universal principles of matter such as gravity and the forces of electromagnetism (and is constantly searching for a "unified field theory"), the structuralist critic attempts to discover the forms unifying all literature. Thus a structuralist description of Maupassant's "The Necklace" (page 6) stresses that the main character, Mathilde, is an *active* protagonist who undergoes a *test* (or series of tests) and emerges with a victory, though not the kind she had originally hoped for. The same might be said of Mrs. Popov and Smirnov in Chekhov's *The Bear* (page 1582). If this same kind of structural view is applied to Bierce's "An Occurrence at Owl Creek Bridge" (page 71), the protagonist is defeated in the test. Generally, the structuralist approach applies such patterns to other works of literature to determine that certain protagonists are active or submissive, that they pass or fail their tests, or that they succeed or fail at other encounters. The key is that many apparently unrelated works reveal many common patterns or contain similar structures with important variations.

The structuralist approach is important because it enables critics to discuss works from widely separate cultures and historical periods. In this respect, critics have followed the leads of modern anthropologists, most notably Claude Lévi-Strauss (1908–1990). Along such lines, critics have undertaken the serious examination of folk and fairy tales. Some of the groundbreaking structuralist criticism, for example, was devoted to the structural analysis of themes, actions, and characters to be found in Russian folktales. The method also bridges popular and serious literature, making little distinction between the two insofar as the description of the structures is concerned. Indeed, structuralism furnishes an ideal approach for comparative literature, and the method also enables critics to consolidate genres such as modern romances, detective tales, soap operas, sitcoms, and film.

Like New Criticism, structuralism aims at comprehensiveness of description, and many critics would insist that the two are complementary and not separate. A distinction is that New Criticism is at its best in dealing with smaller units of

literature, whereas structuralist criticism is best in the analysis of narratives and therefore larger units such as novels, myths, stories, plays, and films. Because structuralism shows how fiction is organized into various typical situations, the approach merges with the *archetypal* approach (see below, page 1869), and at times it is difficult to find any distinctions between structuralist and archetypal criticism.

Structuralism, however, deals not just with narrative structures but also with structures of any type, wherever they occur. For example, structuralism makes considerable use of linguistics. Modern linguistic scholars have determined that there is a difference between "deep structures" and "surface structures" in language. A structuralist analysis of style, therefore, emphasizes how writers utilize such structures. The structuralist interpretation of language also perceives distinguishing types or "grammars" of language that are recurrent in various types of literature. Suppose, for example, that you encounter opening passages like the following:

1. Once upon a time a young prince fell in love with a young princess. He was in love so deeply that he wanted to declare his love for her, and early one morning he left his castle on his white charger, along with his retainers and servants, riding toward her castle home high in the distant and cloud-topped mountains.
2. Early that morning, Alan found himself thinking about Anne. He had thought that she was being ambiguous when she said she loved him, and his feelings about her were not certain. His further thought left him still unsure.

The words of these two passages create different and distinct frames of reference. One is a fairy tale of the past, the other a modern internalized reflection of feeling. The passages therefore demonstrate how language itself fits into predetermined patterns or structures. Similar uses of language structures can be associated with other types of literature.

Example: Hawthorne's "Young Goodman Brown"

Young Goodman Brown is a hero who is passive, not active. He is a *witness*, a *receiver* rather than a *doer*. His only action—taking his trip in the forest—occurs at the story's beginning. After that point, he no longer acts but instead is acted upon, and his reactions to what he sees around him put his life's beliefs to a test. Of course, many protagonists undergo similar testing (such as rescuing victims and overcoming particularly terrible dragons), and they emerge as heroes or conquerors. Not so with Goodman Brown. He is a responder who allows himself to be victimized by his own perceptions—or misperceptions. Despite all his previous experiences with his wife and with the good people of his village, he generalizes too hastily. He lets the single disillusioning experience of his nightmare govern his entire outlook on others, and thus he fails his test and turns his entire life into darkness.

Second Example: Jackson's "The Lottery," page 141

Shirley Jackson's story "The Lottery" is a powerful indictment of tradition for its own sake. The narrator/resident of a small town explains how a yearly lottery is held to determine who among its citizens is to be stoned. Apparently the purpose of this ritual has generally been forgotten, but the rules governing its execution are known in great detail. The

plot is given resonance and predictability by following two structurally determined elements—the basic outline of a tragedy and the outlines of a contest. Like a traditional tragedy the story begins in apparent innocence and happiness and ends in definite calamity. It is a "sunny" day when the lottery is about to begin, "the flowers . . . [are] blossoming profusely," and the town folk are in a jovial mood. The tension builds with the "drawing" from the black box, and the story ends with the stoning and presumed death of the victim. The horror of the story is not to be found in an individual but rather in the collective, slavish acquiescence to a shockingly anachronistic ritual. As in tragedy, the end is the inevitable outcome, for once we know that the people accept the rules of the town lottery, the end is predictable. The townspeople do not know why they must stone someone, but they know that when they partake in the lottery and follow its rules, someone will "win" the contest and meet his or her doom. Understanding the basic elements of tragedy and reading "The Lottery" as a contest or game gives the story a comprehensible and predictable form.

READINGS

Barthes, Roland. *Writing Degree Zero.* 1953. New York: Beacon, 1970.

———*Critical Essays.* 1964. Evanston: Northwestern UP, 1970.

———*Mythologies.* 1957. New York: Hill and Wang, 1972.

Cassirer, Ernst. *Symbol, Myth, and Culture.* New Haven: Yale UP, 1979.

Caws, Peter. *Structuralism: The Art of the Intelligible.* Atlantic Highlands: Humanities, 1988.

Culler, Jonathan. *Structuralist Poetics.* Ithaca: Cornell UP, 1975.

Genette, Gerard. *Narrative Discourse: An Essay in Method.* Ithaca: Cornell UP, 1980.

Greimas, A. J. *Structural Semantics: An Attempt at a Method.* Lincoln: U of Nebraska P, 1984.

Lane, Michael, ed. *Structuralism: A Reader.* London: Cape, 1970.

Macksey, Richard, and Eugenio Donato, eds. *The Structuralism Controversy: The Languages of Criticism and the Sciences of Man.* Baltimore: Johns Hopkins UP, 1970.

Feminist Criticism/Gender Studies/Queer Theory

Feminism/Gender Studies/Queer Theory displays divergent interests drawing insights from many disciplines. It is a still evolving and rich field of inquiry. *Feminist Criticism* had its genesis in the women's movement of the 1960s, shares many of its concerns, and has applied them to the study of literature. One of the early aims of feminist critics was to question the traditional canon and claim a place in it for neglected women writers. Writers such as Mary Shelley, Elizabeth Gaskell, Christina Rossetti, Kate Chopin, and Charlotte Perkins Gillman—three of whom are represented in this book—have been given great critical attention as a result. Feminist critics also delineate the ways both male and female characters are portrayed in literature, looking at how societal norms about sexual difference are either enforced or subverted, and focusing partly on patriarchal structures and institutions such as marriage. As early as the beginning of the twentieth century, Virginia Woolf questioned whether there was a feminine/masculine divide in writing styles, a contentious subject among feminist critics to this day. Feminist critics are

also interested in how interpreting texts differs between the sexes. For instance, in *A Map for Rereading* (1980), the critic Annette Kolodny analyzes how men and women read the same stories differently.

Gender Studies, a more recent critical approach, brings attention to gender rather than to sexual differences. Gender Studies critics see the masculine/feminine divide as socially constructed and not innate. Drawing partly on the works of the French philosopher Michel Foucault (1926–1984) such as *The History of Sexuality* and *Madness and Civilization*, which explore the way powerful institutions organize our society and way of thinking. Such critics apply Foucault's ideas to understanding patriarchal structures and their representations in literature. Many studies have also built on the insights of psychoanalysis and deconstruction (see below), questioning Freud's male-oriented categories and seeking insights into the way language is constructed and the way it affects our thinking. In the essay, *Laugh of the Medusa* (1975), Hélène Cixous applies deconstructionist insights about binary oppositions to a study of discourse about women, showing how it disparages women. Thus, while men's discourse in relation to women's may highlight such separate ways of thinking as logic/inconsistency, it is the traditional patriarchal way of thinking that values male over female experience.

A more recent critical orientation, which came to prominence in the early 1990s is *Queer Theory*, which also appropriates many of the insights of deconstruction, particularly its understanding that binary oppositions are relative and that thinking about matters such as sexual orientation is partly ideological and partly social. Many Queer theorists see the heterosexual/homosexual divide as less distinct than has commonly been believed. Queer theorists are interested in how homosexuals are portrayed in literature and whether they write or read literature differently than heterosexuals. Queer Theory has brought attention to recent literary works, dealing explicitly with lesbian and gay themes, along with attention to sometimes "veiled" references to the same themes in writers whose works make up the standard canon. Much of Queer Theory is theoretical; one example, applied to reading a particular work, is Jonathan Crewe's essay, "Queering 'The Yellow Wallpaper'? Charlotte Perkins Gilman and the Politics of Form" (*Tulsa Studies in Women's Literature* 14.2 [1995]: 273–93).

Example: Hawthorne's "Young Goodman Brown"

At the beginning of "Young Goodman Brown," Brown's wife, Faith, is seen only peripherally. In the traditional patriarchal spirit of wife-as-adjunct, she tells her new husband of her fears, and then asks him to stay at home and take his journey at some other time. Hawthorne does not give her the intelligence or dignity, however, to let her explain her concern (or might he not have been interested in what she had to say?) and she therefore remains in the background with her pink hair ribbon as her distinguishing symbol of submissive inferiority. During the mid-forest satanic ritual, she appears again and is given power, but only the power to cause her husband to go astray. Once she is led in as a novice in the practice of demonism, her husband falls right in step. Unfortunately, by following her, Brown can conveniently excuse himself from guilt by claiming that "she" had made him do it, just as Eve, in some traditional views of the fall of humankind, compelled Adam to eat the apple (Genesis 3:16–17). Hawthorne's attention to the male

protagonist, in other words, permits him to neglect the independence and integrity of a female protagonist.

Second Example: Chopin's "The Story of an Hour," page 331

"The Story of an Hour" by Kate Chopin is about a woman who is told that her husband has died in a train accident. Rather than feeling devastated by this news as her family and friends expect, she feels strangely free and happy to pursue a life for herself. While the story's plot suggests obvious themes of interest for feminist critics, a closer look at many details reveals how language, institutions, and expected demeanor suppress the natural desires and aspirations of women. The protagonist of the story is referred to as "Mrs. Mallard" while her husband is called by his name, Brently Mallard, which has nothing to do with his marital status. Assuming that because of a heart condition Louise Mallard might not survive the bad news, she is told by her sister indirectly "in broken sentences:" of her husband's fate. At first she reacts predictably by weeping "with sudden, wild abandonment." Soon, however, Louise finds herself resisting a feeling that is finally identified as "freedom." In her last few moments of solitude, she imagines a life devoted only to herself, and not to being molded by the will of another. Her resistance indicates the pull of societal norms, while her anticipation of possible liberation is a sign of her true inner self. When, at the end of the story, Louise sees her husband appear, perfectly safe and unharmed, she dies of a heart attack, which is diagnosed by attending doctors as a result "of joy that kills." Since there is no indication that Brently Mallard was anything but a good husband, we may assume that it was freedom from the bonds of marriage itself and the overpowering will of a man that turned a supposedly tragic event into a liberating one. "The Story of an Hour" is a powerful commentary on the institution of marriage as it suppresses the natural desires and pursuits of women.

READINGS

Brownstein, Rachel. *Becoming a Heroine: Reading about Women in Novels.* New York: Viking, 1982.

Cameron, Deborah. *Feminism in Linguistic Theory.* London: Macmillan, 1992.

Delany, Sheila. *Writing Women: Women Writers and Women in Literature, Medieval to Modern.* New York: Schocken, 1984.

Gilbert, Sandra M., and Susan Gubar. *The Madwoman in the Attic: The Woman Writer and the Nineteenth-Century Literary Imagination.* New Haven: Yale UP, 1979.

Jacobus, Mary. *Women's Writing and Writing about Women.* New York: Barnes and Noble, 1979.

Kauffman, Linda, ed. *Gender and Theory: Dialogues on Feminist Criticism.* New York: Blackwell, 1985.

Kolodny, Annette. "Some Notes on Defining a 'Feminist Literary Criticism.'" *Critical Inquiry 2* (1975): 75–92.

Lilly, Mark, ed. *Lesbian and Gay Writing.* London: Macmillian, 1990.

Sedgwick, Eve Kosovsky. *Between Men: English Literature and Male Homosocial Desire.* New York: Columbia UP, 1985.

Showalter, Elaine. *A Literature of Their Own: British Women Novelists from Bronte to Lessing.* Princeton: Princeton UP, 1977.

Woods, Greg, *A History of Gay Literature.* New Haven: Yale UP, 1999.

Economic Determinist/Marxist

The concept of cultural and economic determinism—and its corollary, the **economic determinist/Marxist critical approach**—is one of the major political ideas of the nineteenth century. Karl Marx (1818–1883) emphasized that the primary influence on life was economic, and he saw society enmeshed in a continuous conflict between capitalist oppressors and oppressed working people. The literature that emerged from this kind of analysis often features individuals who are coping with the ill effects of economic disadvantage. Sometimes called "proletarian" literature, it focuses on persons of the lower class—the poor and oppressed who spend their lives in endless drudgery and misery, and whose attempts to rise to the top usually result in renewed oppression.

Marx's political ideas were never widely accepted in the United States and have faded still more after the political breakup of the Soviet Union, but the idea of economic determinism (and the related term *Social Darwinism*) is still credible. As a result, much literature can be judged from an economic perspective even though the economic critics may not be Marxian: What is the economic status of the characters? What happens to them as a result of this status? How do they fare against economic and political odds? What other conditions stemming from their class does the writer emphasize (e.g., poor education, poor nutrition, poor health care, inadequate opportunity)? To what extent does the work fail by overlooking the economic, social, and political implications of its material? In what other ways does economic determinism affect the work? How should readers consider the story in today's developed or underdeveloped world? Seemingly, Hawthorne's story "Young Goodman Brown," which we have used for analysis in these discussions, has no major economic implications, but an economic determinist/Marxist critical approach might take the following turns. (See also page 1835.)

Example: Hawthorne's "Young Goodman Brown"

"Young Goodman Brown" is a fine story just as it is. It deals with the false values instilled by the skewed acceptance of sin-dominated religion, but it overlooks the economic implications of this situation. One might suspect that the real story in the little world of Goodman Brown's Salem should be about the disruption that an alienated member of society can produce. After Brown's condemnation and distrust of others forces him into his own shell of sick imagination, Hawthorne does not consider how such a disaffected character would injure the economic and public life of the town. Consider this, just for a moment: Why would the people from whom Brown recoils in disgust want to deal with him in business or personal matters? In town meetings, would they want to follow his opinions on crucial issues of public concern and investment? Would his preoccupation with sin and damnation make him anything more than a horror in his domestic life? Would his wife, Faith, be able to discuss household management with him, or to ask him about methods of caring for the children? All these questions of course are pointed toward another story—a story that Hawthorne did not write. They also indicate the shortcomings of Hawthorne's approach, because it is clear that the major result of Young Goodman Brown's selfish preoccupation with evil would be a serious disruption of the economic and political affairs of his small community.

 Second Example: Miller's "Death of a Salesman," page 1424

Arthur Miller's *Death of a Salesman* is a devastating indictment of capitalism. Willy Loman is an aging salesman who is struggling to live his later life in dignity. Although his desire to live the American dream of economic security is partly shattered by his own personal inadequacies and increasing age, much of his deterioration and death can be traced to the cruel system that he accepts and in which he believes. As a salesman, Willy represents the purist form of capitalism. He is worth only what he sells, and he is selling less and less. The cost of fixing his car and home appliances weighs heavily on him. When he confronts his boss about a better job close to home, he is ignored and rejected, and he faces indigence and humiliation. His descent into irrationality stems from his confusion about the grimness of his economic reality. On the one hand he professes the importance to his adult children of being well-liked, as if personality were a substitute for the harsh realities of capitalistic economic necessity. On the other hand, referring to his own "vital" role as a salesman indicates an acceptance of the values inherent in capitalism. The problem is that he is no longer productive and is therefore of no value to his employer. At the play's end, Willy kills himself for the insurance money his wife will gain, and when the last payment on his mortgage has been made, the irony only underscores how capitalism degrades life by equating human worth with economic productivity. In *Death of a Salesman* Arthur Miller has written a powerful critique of the American economic system.

READINGS

Adorno, Theodor. *Prisms: Cultural Criticism and Society.* 1955. London: Neville Spearman, 1967.

Althusser, Louis. *For Marx.* New York: Pantheon, 1969.

Bakhtin, Mikhail. *Between Phenomenology and Marxism.* New York: Cambridge UP, 1995.

Demetz, Peter. *Marx, Engels, and the Poets: Origins of Marxist Literary Criticism.* Chicago, U of Chicago P, 1967.

Dowling, William. *Jameson, Althusser, Marx: An Introduction to the Political Unconscious.* Ithaca: Cornell UP, 1984.

Eagleton, Terry. *Criticism and Ideology: A Study in Marxist Literary Theory.* London: New Left, 1976.

Frow, John. *Marxism and Literary History.* Ithaca: Cornell UP, 1986.

Jameson, Frederic. *Marxism and Form: Twentieth Century Dialectical Theories of Literature.* Princeton: Princeton UP, 1971.

Lukacs, Georg. *Realism in Our Time: Literature and the Class Struggle.* 1957. New York: Harper and Row, 1964.

Marcuse, Herbert. *The Aesthetic Dimension: Toward a Critique of Marxist Aesthetics.* Boston: Beacon, 1978.

Psychological/Psychoanalytic

The scientific study of the mind is a product of psychodynamic theory as established by Sigmund Freud (1856–1939) and of the psychoanalytic method practiced by his followers. Psychoanalysis provided a new key to the understanding of

character by claiming that behavior is caused by hidden and unconscious motives. It was greeted as a revelation with far-reaching implications for all intellectual pursuits. Not surprisingly it has had a profound and continuing effect on post-Freudian literature.

In addition, its popularity produced the **psychological/psychoanalytic approach** to criticism.[2] Some critics use the approach to explain fictional characters, as in the landmark interpretation by Freud and Ernest Jones that Shakespeare's Hamlet suffers from an Oedipus complex. Still other critics use it as a way of analyzing authors and the artistic process. For example, John Livingston Lowes's study *The Road to Xanadu* presents a detailed examination of the mind, reading, and neuroses of Coleridge, the author of "Kubla Khan" (p. 734).

Critics using the psychoanalytic approach treat literature somewhat like information about patients in therapy. In the work itself, what are the obvious and hidden motives that cause a character's behavior and speech? How much background (e.g., repressed childhood trauma, adolescent memories) does the author reveal about a character? How purposeful is this information with regard to the character's psychological condition? How much is important in the analysis and understanding of the character?

In the consideration of authors, critics utilizing the psychoanalytic model consider questions like these: What particular life experiences explain characteristic subjects or preoccupations? Was the author's life happy? Miserable? Upsetting? Solitary? Social? Can the death of someone in the author's family be associated with melancholy situations in that author's work? All eleven brothers and sisters of the English poet Thomas Gray, for example, died before reaching adulthood. Gray was the only one of the twelve to survive. In his poetry, Gray often deals with death, and he is therefore considered one of the "Graveyard School" of eighteenth-century poets. A psychoanalytical critic might make much of this connection.

 Example: Hawthorne's "Young Goodman Brown"

At the end of "Young Goodman Brown," Hawthorne's major character is no longer capable of normal existence. His nightmare should be read as a symbol of what in reality would have been lifelong mental subjection to the type of puritanical religion that emphasizes sin and guilt. Such preoccupation with sin is no hindrance to psychological health if the preoccupied people are convinced that God forgives them and grants them mercy. In their dealings with others, they remain healthy as long as they believe that other people have the same sincere trust in divine forgiveness. If their own faith is weak and uncertain, however, and if they cannot believe in forgiveness, then they are likely to transfer their own guilt—really a form of personal terror—to others. They remain conscious of their own sins, but they find it easy to claim that others are sinful—even those who are spiritually spotless, and even their own family, who should be dearest to them. When this process of projection or transference occurs, such people have created the rationale of condemning others because of their own guilt. The price that they pay is a life of gloom, a fate that Hawthorne designates for Goodman Brown after his nightmare about demons in human form.

---

[2] See also Chapter 3, "Characters: The People in Fiction."

 Example: Browning's "My Last Duchess," page 697

"My Last Duchess" by Robert Browning is a dramatic monologue based loosely on the real-life Duke of Ferrara, Alfonso II (1533–1597). In presumably discussing a marriage proposal with an envoy, the duke reveals his jealousy, egocentrism, and greed. The duke points to a painting of his former duchess and notices her happy "countenance," which was easily aroused by strangers. From what we gather from Browning's poem about the malevolent duke, it is plausible that he had his apparently cheerful wife killed. Getting back to the business at hand, the duke escorts the envoy down the stairs, but not before pointing out a painting of Neptune "taming a seahorse." Besides indicating a love of possessions, his reference to the painting and its subject of taming also suggests a consciousness of subjugation and the desire to bend others to his will—certainly a sign of how he will treat the future duchess. While some psychological studies may point to the poet's frame of mind, "My Last Duchess " is a study of how a poem may imply a personality through a speaker's unsuspecting words.

READINGS

Bloom, Harold. *The Anxiety of Influence*. New York: Oxford UP, 1975.

Bowie, Malcolm. *Freud, Proust, and Lacan: Theory as Fiction*. New York: Cambridge UP, 1987.

Gilbert, Sandra, and Susan Gubar. *The Madwoman in the Attic*. New Haven: Yale UP, 1979.

Gilman, Sander L. ed. *Introducing Psychoanalytic Theory.* New York: Brunner/Mazel, 1982.

Holland, Norman N. *The Dynamics of Literary Response.* New York: Oxford UP, 1968.

Lacan, Jacques. *Ecrits: A Selection.* New York: Norton, 2004.

Shamdsani, Sonu, and Michael Munchow, eds. *Speculations After Freud: Psychoanalysis, Philosophy, and Culture.* New York: Routledge, 1994.

Skura, Meredith Anne. *The Literary Use of the Psychoanalytic Process.* New Haven: Yale UP, 1981.

Wright, Elizabeth. *Psychoanalytic Criticism: Theory in Practice.* New York and London: Methuen, 1984.

Archetypal/Symbolic/Mythic

The **archetypal/symbolic/mythic critical approach,** derived from the work of the Swiss psychoanalyst Carl Jung (1875–1961), presupposes that human life is built up out of patterns, or *archetypes* ("first molds" or "first patterns") that are similar throughout various cultures and historical times.[3] The approach is similar to the structuralist analysis of literature, for both approaches stress the connections that may be discovered in literature written in different times and in vastly different locations in the world.

In literary evaluation, the archetypal approach is used to support the claim that the very best literature is grounded in archetypal patterns. The archetypal critic therefore looks for archetypes such as God's creation of human beings, the

---

[3]Symbolism is also considered in Chapters 7 and 19.

sacrifice of a hero, or the search for paradise. How does an individual story, poem, or play fit into any of the archetypal patterns? What truths does this correlation provide (particularly truths that cross historical, national, and cultural lines)? How closely does the work fit the archetype? What variations can be seen? What meaning or meanings do the connections have?

The most tenuous aspect of archetypal criticism is Jung's assertion that the recurring patterns provide evidence for a "universal human consciousness" that all of us, by virtue of our humanity, still retain in our minds and in our very blood.

Not all critics accept the hypothesis of a universal human consciousness, but they nevertheless consider the approach important for comparisons and contrasts (see Chapter 30). Many human situations, such as adolescence, dawning love, the search for success, the reconciliation with one's mother and father, and the encroachment of age and death, are similar in structure and can be analyzed as archetypes. For example, the following situations can be seen as a pattern or archetype of initiation: A young man discovers the power of literature and understanding (Keats's "On First Looking into Chapman's Homer"); a man determines the importance of truth and fidelity amidst uncertainty (Arnold's "Dover Beach"); a man and woman fall in love despite their wishes to remain independent (Chekhov's *The Bear*); a woman gains strength and integrity because of previously unrealized inner resources (Maupassant's "The Necklace"). The archetypal approach encourages the analysis of variations on the same theme, as in Glaspell's "A Jury of Her Peers" (page 189) and Faulkner's "A Rose for Emily" (page 89) when characters choose to ignore the existence of a crime (one sort of initiation) and also, as a result, assert their own individuality and freedom (another sort of initiation).

Example: Hawthorne's "Young Goodman Brown"

In the sense that Young Goodman Brown undergoes a change from psychological normality to rigidity, the story is a reverse archetype of the initiation ritual. According to the archetype of successful initiation, initiates seek to demonstrate their worthiness to become full-fledged members of society. Telemachus in Homer's *Odyssey*, for example, is a young man who in the course of the epic goes through the initiation rituals of travel, discussion, and battle. But in "Young Goodman Brown" we see initiation in reverse, for just as there is an archetype of successful initiation, Brown's initiation leads him into failure. In the private areas of life on which happiness depends, he falls short. He sees evil in his fellow villagers, condemns his minister, and shrinks even from his own family. His life therefore becomes filled with despair and gloom. His suspicions are those of a Puritan of long ago, but the timeliness of Hawthorne's story is that the archetype of misunderstanding and condemnation has not changed. Today's headlines of misery and war are produced by the same kind of intolerance that is exhibited by Goodman Brown.

Second Example: Frost's "Birches," page 1066

Interpreting Frost's poem "Birches" symbolically gives the poem a special depth that it otherwise might not have. On the literal level the poem is about a man who describes birch trees in winter and who states his belief that a lonely boy has perhaps been swinging on them. The poem moves from the third person to the first and we come to realize that the speaker is reminiscing about his own childhood: "So I was once myself a swinger of birches."

Many of the rich images of the poem are sexually suggestive. The trunks of the trees are "trailing their leaves on the ground / Like girls on hands and knees that throw their hair / Before them over their heads to dry in the sun." The speaker also describes a boy "riding" the trees "Until he took the stiffness out of them." And While hanging on the tree branches he learned "about not launching out too soon." While these images have clear suggestions about sexuality, the poem ends with the alternate yearning to ride the trees toward heaven and to return back to earth. Reading the poem symbolically thus opens up resonant avenues of interpretation. Expression is given to the dual nature of humankind—physical and spiritual release. By describing the boy swinging on birch trees Frost is expressing the desire for sexual fulfillment and spiritual release from earthly constraints. A rich, evocative poem emerges when "Birches" is read symbolically.

READINGS

Barber, C. L. *Shakespeare's Festive Comedy: A Study of Dramatic Form and Its Relation to Social Custom*. Princeton, Princeton UP, 1972.

Bloom, Harold. *Shelley's Mythmaking*. New Haven: Yale UP, 1959.

Bodkin, Maud. *Archetypal Patterns in Poetry*. London: Oxford UP, 1934.

Bush, Douglas. *Mythology and the Renaissance Tradition in English Poetry*. New York: W. W. Norton, 1963.

Chase, Richard. *Quest for Myth*. Baton Rouge: Louisiana State UP, 1949.

Frye, Northrop *Anatomy of Criticism: Four Essays*. Princeton: Princeton UP, 1957.

Hyman, Stanley Edgar. *The Tangled Bank*. New York: Atheneum, 1962.

Deconstructionist

The **deconstructionist critical approach**—which deconstructionists explain not as an approach but rather as a performance or as a strategy of reading—was developed by the French philosopher Jacques Derrida (1930–2004). In the 1970s and 1980s it became a major mode of criticism by critiquing a Western philosophical tradition known as logocentrism—the belief that speech is a direct expression of a speaker's intention, that it has a direct correspondence to reality, and that it is therefore the privileged arbiter of interpretation. By exposing what he saw as the fallacious assumptions of logocentrism, Derrida sought to undermine the basis of stable meanings derivable from language. The implications for reading and therefore for literary studies were far-reaching.

Deconstructionist critics begin literary analysis by assuming the instability of language and the impossibility of arriving at a fixed standard to anchor interpretation. The dictum, in Derrida's *Of Grammatology*, that "There is nothing outside the text" indicates the denial of any authoritative referent outside of words. Texts are always self-contradictory because they can always be reread to undermine an apparently stable interpretation. In part, this is due to how meaning is derived from binary oppositions such as speech/writing, male/female, good/evil. Each word of the pair obtains its significance by contrast with the other, so that its meaning is relative, not absolute. A female may therefore be defined as lacking male features or a male as lacking female traits. In addition, each set of opposites

has been arranged hierarchically; speech, for instance, is considered more immediate and therefore closer to reality than writing and therefore speech is the privileged member of the set speech/writing. These pairings are social constructs and form part of our way of thinking, even if they do not necessarily reflect reality.

Other strategies for undermining the stability of texts are to see how they have "gaps," or missing pieces of information, or words with several meanings and connotations, that therefore "de-center" the meaning of the texts. While a poem may seem to mean one thing when our habitual, formalistic reading strategies are applied to it, it can be shown to have a completely different meaning as well. Additional readings will yield still other meanings. The text is therefore said to "deconstruct" itself as the reading strategies applied to it are merely pointing out contradictory elements that inhere in the nature of language itself.

While formalist critics aim at resolving contradictions and ambiguities to form a unified literary work, deconstructionists aim to find disunity and disruptions in the language of a text. The typical deconstructionist strategy is to start with a standard formalistic reading of a text and then undermine that interpretation in order to yield a new one. The deconstructionist does not deny that interpretations are possible, only that there is no basis for appealing to final, absolute ones. Deconstruction has yielded some new, imaginative readings of canonical literature. Some critics of deconstruction argue that the "initial" formalistic readings of the deconstructionist strategy are the most rewarding and that often deconstructionist interpretations are incoherent.

 Example: Hawthorne's "Young Goodman Brown"

There are many uncertainties in the details of "Young Goodman Brown." If one starts with the stranger on the path, one might conclude that he could be Brown's father, because he recognizes Brown immediately and speaks to him jovially. On the other hand, the stranger could be the devil (he is recognized as such by Goody Cloyse) because of his wriggling walking stick. After disappearing, the stranger also takes on the characteristics of an omniscient cult leader and seer, because at the satanic celebration he knows all the secret sins committed by Brown's neighbors and the community of greater New England. Additionally, he might represent a perverted conscience whose aim is to mislead and befuddle people by steering them into the holier-than-thou judgmental attitude that Brown adopts. This method would be truly diabolical—to use religion in order to bring people to their own damnation. That the stranger is an evil force is therefore clear, but the pathways of his evil are not as clear. He seems to work his mission of damnation by reaching the souls of persons like Goodman Brown through means ordinarily attributed to conscience. If the stranger represents a satanic conscience, what are we to suppose that Hawthorne is asserting about what is considered real conscience?

 Second Example: Auden's "Musée des Beaux Arts," page 998

"Musée des Beaux Arts" may be read as a poem about an indifferent universe in the face of human suffering. Auden posits the "old master" painters of the Renaissance as depicting this situation correctly: "About suffering they were never wrong." Suffering apparently takes place in the midst of the dull happenings of everyday life, the speaker asserts. The poem ends by focusing on a specific example—Breughel's depiction of the mythic Icarus,

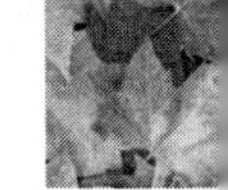

who fell into the sea because he flew too close to the sun. No notice is apparently taken by the characters in the painting of the splash made by the falling body as it enters the water. While the poem may be read as being unified around the theme of indifference to suffering, alternate interpretations arise when the poem is deconstructed. The title of the poem indicates the museum where Breughel's painting may be seen. Museums are, in part, repositories of historical events. By referring to a painting in a specific place, Auden lets the reader know that he or she may see a depiction of Icarus's suffering. While the figures in the painting turn away from the fallen Icarus, the observer of the painting—like the reader of the poem—is made conscious of Icarus' story and his suffering. While the dichotomy-event (Icarus falling)/depiction of event (painting and poem of Icarus falling) may suggest a priority to the event itself, it is ironically Auden's poem that encourages us to think of the anguish Icarus must have felt as he fell. In describing the "white legs [of Icarus] disappearing into the green / Water," Auden focuses our attention to suffering and death. "Turns" is a key word in the poem. Auden describes how everyone in the scene "turns away / Quite leisurely from the disaster." Just as something may turn away from an event, the same motion of turning may return us to the same event, in this instance, a contemplation of suffering. While indifference to suffering may be one theme of "Musée des Beaux Arts," deconstructing the poem also shows how it "pulls" in other directions. The language of the poem itself tugs the reader in different directions.

READINGS

Abrams, M. H. "The Deconstructive Angel." in *Doing Things with Texts*. New York and London: Norton, 1989.

Arac, Jonathan, Wlad Godzich, and Wallace Martin, eds. *The Yale Critics: Deconstruction in America*. Minneapolis: U of Minnesota P, 1983.

De Man, Paul. *Blindness and Insight*. New York: Oxford UP, 1971.

Derrida, Jacques. *Of Grammatology*. 1967. Baltimore: Johns Hopkins UP, 1976.

———. *Writing and Difference*. 1967. Chicago: U of Chicago P, 1978.

Hartman, Geoffrey. *Saving the Text: Literature/Derrida/Philosophy*. Baltimore: Johns Hopkins UP, 1981.

Miller, J. Hillis. *Fiction and Repetition: Seven English Novels*. Cambridge: Harvard UP, 1982.

———. *The Linguistic Moment: From Wordsworth to Stevens*. Princeton: Princeton UP, 1985.

———. *The Ethics of Reading: Kant, de Man, Eliot, Trollope, James, and Benjamin*. New York: Columbia UP, 1987.

Silverman, Hugh J., and Gary E. Aylesworth, eds. *The Textual Sublime: Deconstruction and Its Differences*. Albany: State U of New York P, 1990.

Reader-Response

The **reader-response critical approach** is rooted in *phenomenology*, a branch of philosophy that deals with the understanding of how things appear. The phenomenological idea of knowledge is based on the separation of the reality of our thoughts from the reality of the world. Our quest for truth is to be found not in the external world itself but rather in our mental *perception* and interpretation of externals. All that we human beings can know—actual *knowledge*—is our collective and personal understanding of the world and our conclusions about it.

As a consequence of the phenomenological concept, reader-response theory holds that the reader is a necessary third party in the author-text-reader relationship that constitutes the literary work. The work, in other words, is not fully created until readers make a *transaction* with it by assimilating it and *actualizing* it in the light of their own knowledge and experience. The representative questions of the theory are these: What does this work mean to me, in my present intellectual and moral makeup? How can the work improve my understanding and widen my insights? How can my increasing understanding help me understand the work more deeply? The theory is that the free interchange or transaction that such questions bring about leads toward interest and growth, so that readers can assimilate literary works and accept them as parts of their lives and as parts of the civilization in which they live.

As an initial way of reading, the reader-response method may be personal and anecdotal. In addition, by stressing response rather than interpretation, one of the leading exponents of the method (Stanley Fish) has raised the extreme question about whether texts, by themselves, have objective identity. These aspects have been cited as both a shortcoming and an inconsequentiality of the method.

It is therefore important to stress that the reader-response theory is *open*. It permits beginning readers to bring their own personal reactions to literature, but it also aims to increase their discipline and skill. The more that readers bring to literature through their interests and disciplined studies, the more "competent" and comprehensive their "transactions" will be. It is possible, for example, to explain the structure of a work not according to commonly recognized categories such as exposition and climax, but rather according to the personal reactions of representative readers. The contention is that structure, like other avenues of literary study such as tone or the comprehension of figurative language, refers to clearly definable responses that readers experience when reading and transacting with works. By such means, literature is subject not only to outward and objective analysis, but also to inward and psychological response.

The reader-response approach thus lends an additional dimension to the critical awareness of literature. If literary works imply that readers should possess special knowledge in fields such as art, politics, science, philosophy, religion, or morality, then competent readers will seek out such knowledge and utilize it in developing their responses. Also, because students experience many similar intellectual and cultural disciplines, it is logical to conclude that responses will tend not to diverge but rather to coalesce; agreements result not from personal but from cultural similarities. The reader-response theory, then, can and should be an avenue toward informed and detailed understanding of literature, but the initial emphasis is the *transaction* that readers make with literary works.

 Example: Hawthorne's "Young Goodman Brown"

"Young Goodman Brown" is worrisome because it shows so disturbingly that good intentions may cause harmful results. I think that a person with too high a set of expectations is ripe for disillusionment, just as Goodman Brown is. When people don't measure up to this person's standard of perfection, they can be thrown aside as though they are worthless. They may be good people, but whatever past mistakes they have made make it impossible for the person with high expectations to endure them. Goodman Brown makes the same

kind of misjudgment, expecting perfection and turning sour when he learns about flaws. It is not that he is not a good man, because he is shown at the start as a person of belief and stability. He uncritically accepts his nightmare revelation that everyone else is evil, however (including his parents), and he finally distrusts everyone because of this baseless suspicion. He cannot look at his neighbors without avoiding them like an "anathema," and he turns away from his own wife "without a greeting" (paragraph 70). Brown's problem is that he equates being human with being unworthy. By such a distorted standard of judgment, all of us fail, and that is what makes the story so disturbing.

Second Example: Roethke's "My Papa's Waltz," page 828

"My Papa's Waltz" by Theodore Roethke shows how complicated relationships between father and son may be. While it is the memory of a spirited "waltz" that the speaker, as a child, had with his father, the emotions it evokes are not so easy to pin down. On the one hand, the speaker recalls what might have seemed a happy time, with father and son romping "until the pans / slid from the kitchen shelf" and the boy danced off to bed "Still clinging to your [the father's] shirt." There is, however, a darker side to this memory as suggested by images that border on abuse. The whiskey on the father's breath "Could make a small boy dizzy." Also, the father "scraped a buckle" every time he missed a step of the dance and "beat time" on the boy's head; in addition, the speaker's memory is that his mother was an unhappy witness to this rough play. That her "countenance / Could not unfrown itself" suggests a disapproving uneasiness. The regular stanzas and short lines indicate the symmetry and balance of an orderly dance, but the more disturbing images imply violence. This double-edged emotion points to the complex nature of love and the ambivalent feelings we may have toward a parent. We might wish sometimes that our memories could be resolved into one overwhelming feeling, but "My Papa's Waltz," through its rich imagery, evokes the true nature of most relationships. They aren't easily categorized.

READINGS

Altick, Richard. *The English Common Reader: A Social History of the Mass Reading Public 1800–1900.* Chicago: U of Chicago P, 1957.

Bleich, David. *Readings and Feelings: An Introduction to Subjective Criticism.* Urbana: National Council of Teachers of English, 1975.

Booth, Wayne C. *The Rhetoric of Fiction.* 2nd ed. Chicago: U of Chicago P, 1983.

Fish, Stanley. *Is There a Text in This Class? The Authority of Interpretive Communities.* Cambridge: Harvard UP, 1980.

Holland, Norman N. *The Dynamics of Literary Response.* New York: Oxford UP, 1968.

Iser, Wolfgang. *The Implied Reader: Pattern of Communication in Prose Fiction From Bunyan to Beckett.* Baltimore: Johns Hopkins UP, 1974.

Leavis, Q. D. *Fiction and the Reading Public.* London: Chatto and Windus, 1932.

Mailloux, Steven J. *Interpretive Convections.* Ithaca: Cornell UP, 1982.

Richards, I. A. *Practical Criticism: A Study of Literary Judgment.* New York: Harcourt, Brace, 1935.

Sartre, Jean-Paul. *What Is Literature?* New York: Philosophical Library, 1966.

Suleiman, Susan, and Inge Crosman, eds. *The Reader in the Text: Essays on Audience and Interpretation.* Princeton: Princeton UP, 1980.

Appendixes and Additional Resources

This section provides key reference material for you and your students. The following sections include some important selections from the full book:

- **MLA Appendix:** Provides a list of frequently cited sources (over 40 examples) and five visual document maps of the most frequently cited sources. This section makes it easier for students to prepare their works cited lists. The five visual document maps highlight how to cite:
  - A work in an anthology
  - An article in a journal
  - A professional Web site
  - A newspaper
  - A book

- **Glossary:** Lists all the key terms in the book along with definitions and page references. This provides students with a convenient reference to look up key terms quickly.

- **Inside Back Cover and Facing Page:** Offers two lists of all the authors featured in the anthology—one arranged alphabetically and one arranged chronologically. These lists put the authors in historical context and offer a quick alphabetical reference to featured authors. (See also inside front cover and facing page for easy reference to writing topics, student essays, and research topics.)

Appendix I

MLA Recommendations for Documenting Sources

This appendix provides general guidelines for making source citations, and therefore it is intended to augment the section titled "Documenting Your Work" in Chapter 10A. For general information on citation recommendations by the Modern Language Association (MLA), see Joseph Gibaldi, *MLA Handbook for Writers of Reasearch Papers,* 6th ed. (New York: MLA, 2003).

The following examples show the formats you are likely to use most often, both for nonelectronic and electronic references.

(NonElectronic) Books, Articles, Poems, Letters, Reviews, Recordings, Programs

Book by One Author

Fitzgerald, F. Scott. The Great Gatsby. New York: Scribner, 1925.

Book with No Author Listed

The Pictorial History of the Guitar. New York: Random, 1992.

Book by Two (or Three) Authors

Clemens, Samuel L., and Charles Dudley Warner. The Gilded Age: A Tale of Today. Hartford: American, 1874.

For a Book by Four or More Authors

Guerin, Wilfred L., Earle Labor, Lee Morgan, Jeanne C. Reesman, and John R. Willingham. A Handbook of Critical Approaches to Literature. New York: Oxford UP, 2004.

or

Guerin, Wilfred L., et al. A Handbook of Critical Approaches to Literature. New York: Oxford UP, 2004.

Two Books by the Same Author

Reynolds, David S. Beneath the American Renaissance. Cambridge: Harvard UP, 1988.

———. Walt Whitman's America: A Cultural Biography. New York: Knopf, 1995.

Citing a Book

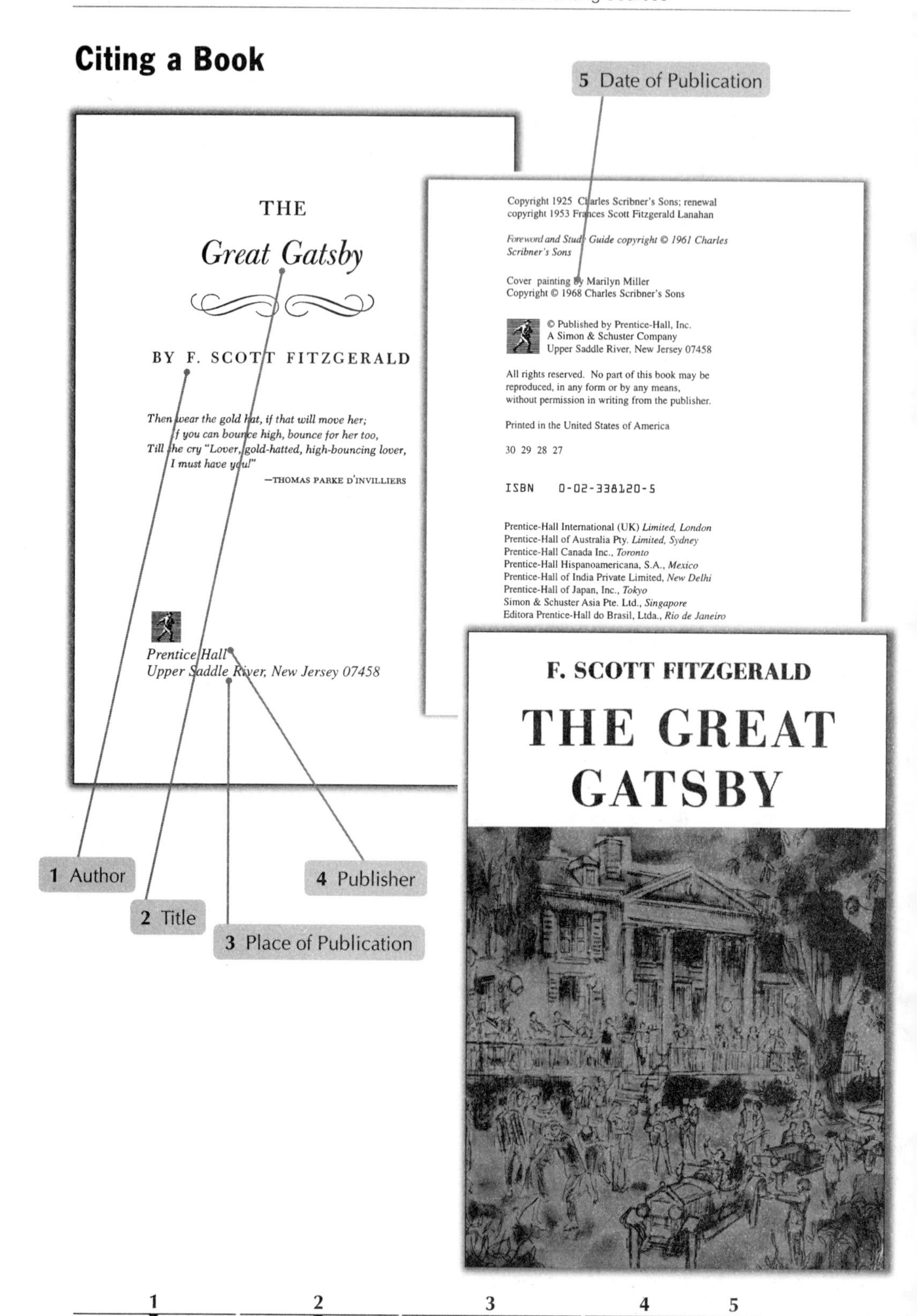

THE

Great Gatsby

BY F. SCOTT FITZGERALD

Then wear the gold hat, if that will move her;
If you can bounce high, bounce for her too,
Till she cry "Lover, gold-hatted, high-bouncing lover,
I must have you!"

—THOMAS PARKE D'INVILLIERS

Prentice Hall
Upper Saddle River, New Jersey 07458

Copyright 1925 Charles Scribner's Sons; renewal copyright 1953 Frances Scott Fitzgerald Lanahan

Foreword and Study Guide copyright © 1961 Charles Scribner's Sons

Cover painting by Marilyn Miller
Copyright © 1968 Charles Scribner's Sons

© Published by Prentice-Hall, Inc.
A Simon & Schuster Company
Upper Saddle River, New Jersey 07458

All rights reserved. No part of this book may be reproduced, in any form or by any means, without permission in writing from the publisher.

Printed in the United States of America

30 29 28 27

ISBN 0-02-338120-5

Prentice-Hall International (UK) *Limited, London*
Prentice-Hall of Australia Pty. *Limited, Sydney*
Prentice-Hall Canada Inc., *Toronto*
Prentice-Hall Hispanoamericana, S.A., *Mexico*
Prentice-Hall of India Private Limited, *New Delhi*
Prentice-Hall of Japan, Inc., *Tokyo*
Simon & Schuster Asia Pte. Ltd., *Singapore*
Editora Prentice-Hall do Brasil, Ltda., *Rio de Janeiro*

F. SCOTT FITZGERALD

THE GREAT GATSBY

1 2 3 4 5

Fitzgerald, F. Scott. The Great Gatsby. Upper Saddle River: Prentice Hall, 1968.

Book with an Editor

Scharnhorst, Gary, ed. Selected Letters of Bret Harte. Norman: U of Oklahoma P, 1997.

Book with Two Editors

Dionne, Craig, and Steve Mentz, eds. Rogues and Early Modern English Culture. Ann Arbor: U of Michigan P, 2004.

Book with an Author and an Editor

De Quille, Dan. The Fighting Horse of the Stanislaus. Ed. Lawrence I. Berkove. Iowa City: U of Iowa P, 1990.

Translated Book

Cervantes Saavedra, Miguel de. Don Quixote de la Mancha. Trans. Charles Jarvis. New York: Oxford UP, 1999.

Long Poem Published as a Book

Homer. The Odyssey. Trans. Robert Fitzgerald. New York: Vintage, 1990.

Collection of Poetry Published as a Book

Mueller, Lisel. Alive Together: New and Selected Poems. Baton Rouge: Louisiana State UP, 1996.

Literary Work in an Anthology

Chopin, Kate. "The Storm." Fiction 100: An Anthology of Short Fiction. Ed. James H. Pickering. 10th ed. Upper Saddle River: Pearson, 2004. 226–29.

Introduction, Preface, Foreword, or Afterword in a Book

Pryse, Marjorie. Introduction. The Country of the Pointed Firs and Other Stories. By Sarah Orne Jewett. New York: Norton, 1981. v–xix.

Article in a Reference Book

Gerber, Phillip. "Naturalism." The Encyclopedia of American Literature. Ed. Steven Serafin. New York: Continuum, 1999. 808–09.

Article in a Journal with Continuous Paging

Rhodes, Chip. "Satire in Romanian Literature." Humor 8 (1995): 275–86.

Article in a Journal That Pages Each Issue Separately

Kruse, Horst. "The Motif of the Flattened Corpse." Studies in American Humor 4 (Spring 1997): 47–53.

Signed Book Review

Bird, John. Rev. of The Singular Mark Twain, by Fred Kaplan. *Mark Twain Annual* 2 (2004): 57–61.

Unsigned Book Review

Rev. of Canons by Consensus: Critical Trends and American Literature Anthologies, by Joseph Csicsila. *Essays in Arts and Sciences* 24 (2000): 69–74.

Citing a Work in an Anthology

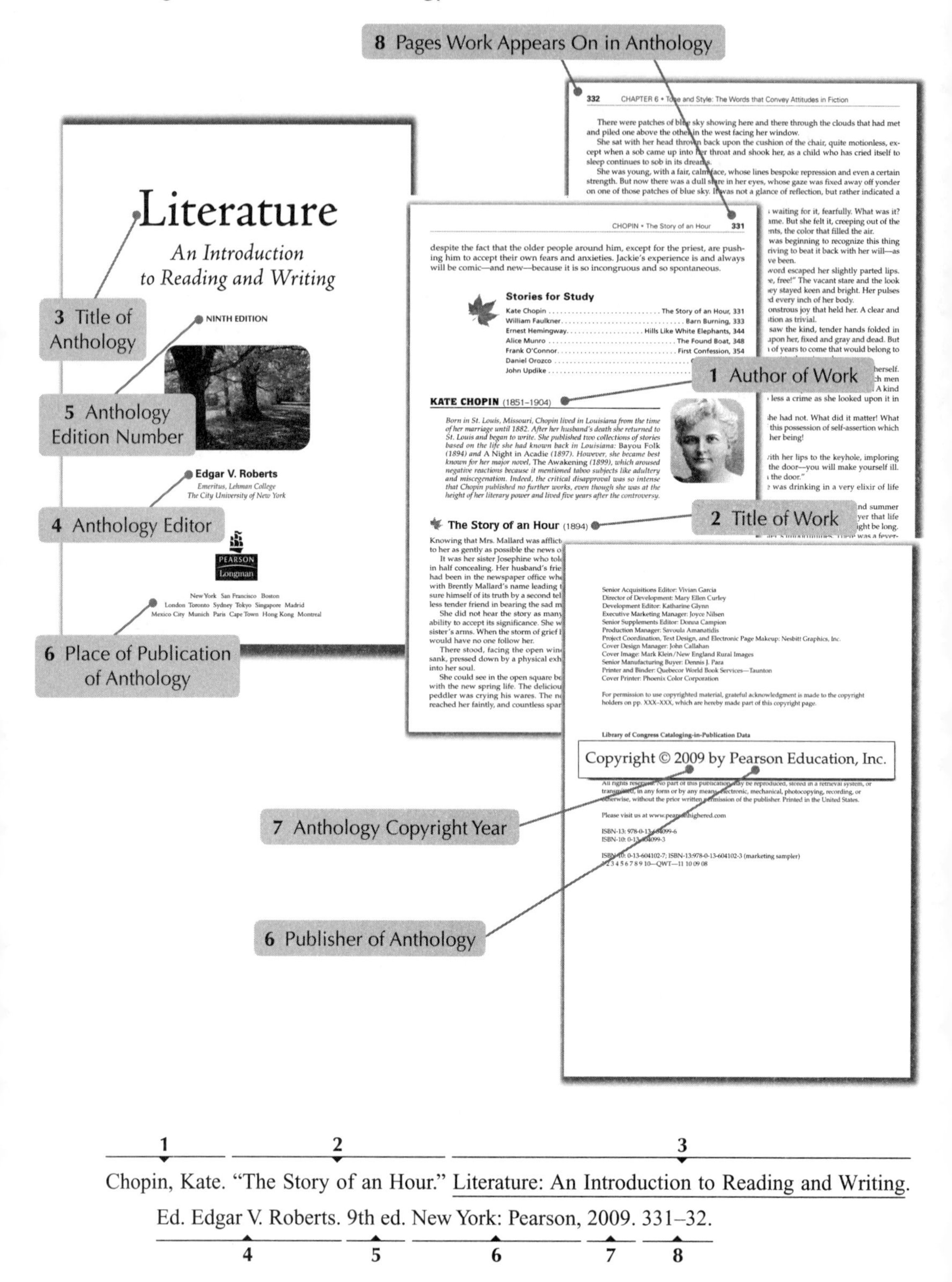

Chopin, Kate. "The Story of an Hour." Literature: An Introduction to Reading and Writing. Ed. Edgar V. Roberts. 9th ed. New York: Pearson, 2009. 331–32.

1 (Chopin, Kate.) 2 ("The Story of an Hour.") 3 (Literature: An Introduction to Reading and Writing.) 4 (Ed. Edgar V. Roberts.) 5 (9th ed.) 6 (New York: Pearson,) 7 (2009.) 8 (331–32.)

Citing an Article in a Journal

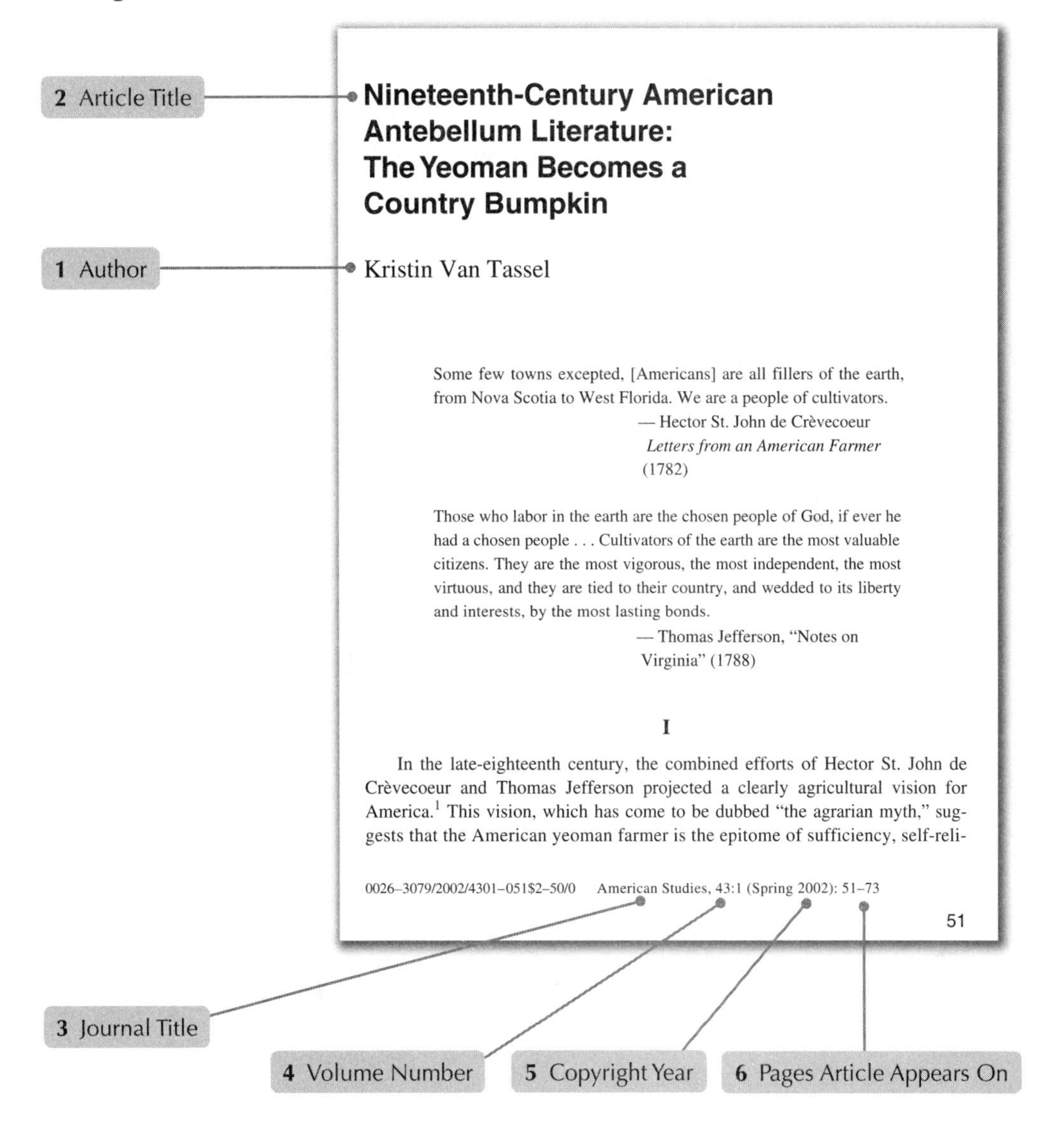

Note: A scholarly article in printed form ordinarily provides all necessary information on its first page.

Van Tassel, Kristin. "Nineteenth-Century American Antebellum Literature: The Yeoman Becomes a Country Bumpkin." American Studies 43:1 (2002): 51–73.

1 — Van Tassel, Kristin.
2 — "Nineteenth-Century American Antebellum Literature: The Yeoman
2 cont. — Becomes a Country Bumpkin."
3 — American Studies
4 — 43:1
5 — (2002):
6 — 51–73.

Article in a Newspaper

Album, Mitch. "Longing for Another Slice of Dorm Pizza." Detroit Free Press 3 April 2005: C1.

Editorial

"Death Penalty Debate Finally Produces Useful Result." Editorial. USA Today 22 June 2005: A15.

Letter to the Editor

Mulder, Sara. Letter. New York Times. 27 September 2005, late ed: 2:5.

Article in a Magazine

McDermott, John R. "The Famous Moustache That Was." Life 20 Dec. 1968: 53–56.

Article in an Encyclopedia

"Afghanistan." The New Encyclopedia Britanica: Micropaedia. 15th ed. 1985.

Dictionary Entry

"Serendipity." The American Heritage Dictionary of the English Language. 4th ed. 1977.

Government Publication

United States. Cong. Joint Committee on the Investigation of Land Use in the Midwest. Hearings. 105th Cong., 2nd sess. 4 vols. Washington: GPO, 1997.

For a Lecture

Kaston Tange, Andrea. "The Importance of American Literature." Literature 100 class lecture. Eastern Michigan University, 5 Nov. 2002.

Letter

Hosko, John. Letter to the author. 23 Sept. 2000.

Email

Henderson, Elisabeth. E-mail to the author. 25 Feb. 2005.

Interview for which you did the interviewing

Stipe, Michael. Personal interview. 10 Nov. 2004.

Film

Napoleon Dynamite. Dir. Jared Hess. Fox Searchlight, 2004.

Television Program

"The Parking Garage." Seinfeld. NBC. WDIV, Detroit. 23 July 1994.

Sound Recording

R.E.M. Fables of the Reconstruction. IRS Records, 1985.

Song on a Recording

R.E.M. "Life and How to Live It." Fables of the Reconstruction. IRS Records, 1985.

Citing a Newspaper

"All the News That's Fit to Print"

The New York Times

Late Edition
New York: **Today,** some sun, a few storms, high 83. **Tonight,** early shower, low 70. **Tomorrow,** partly sunny and a bit less humid, high 83. **Yesterday,** high 71, low 65. Details, Page C10.

VOL. CLVI . . . No. 53,996 Copyright © 2007 The New York Times *NEW YORK, THURSDAY, JULY 5, 2007* *ONE DOLLAR*

THE Arts N E1

THURSDAY, JULY 5, 2007

The New York Times

Lauren Ambrose, as Juliet in "Romeo and Juliet," and Joseph Parks, as Orpheus in "Eurydice," are among the actors in the swim of a wet New York theater season.

Photographs by Sara Krulwich/The New York Times

Indoors and Out, Theater Is Making a Splash

By MELENA RYZIK

The actors who perform in Shakespeare in the Park are used to the vagaries of outdoor theater: the inclement weather, the planes buzzing overhead, the bugs, the yowling of mating raccoons (really). But this year's production of "Romeo and Juliet" added a new difficulty: water. Lots of it, the centerpiece of this Verona is a 70-foot, 4,000-gallon pool.

The cast members do not shy away from diving in. They tromp and wade and paddle through the pool, which is an inch and a half to two inches deep and takes four and a half hours to fill every day, via seven hoses, with New York City tap water. Though some of it comes from a specially constructed boiler heated to 125 degrees, the pool itself isn't heated, said Michael McGoff, the production's stage manager. By the death scenes the water temperature can dip into the 60s.

So the star-crossed lovers have another obstacle: wet suits. On cold nights Juliet (Lauren Ambrose) wears one underneath her virginal white gown. So does Romeo (Oscar Isaac) for his many splashy — literally — fight scenes. Most of the other citizens of Verona make do with Wellies and rehearsal Crocs, footwear that was approved as spill-safe by the actors' union. Still, Mr. McGoff said, "every night, somebody will slip or really get hit with some water where they normally don't."

And "Romeo and Juliet" is not the only piece of theater that's all wet this summer. For reasons of artistry, script or shock value a few other productions use a water effect onstage. They include the playwright Sarah Ruhl's adaptation of "Eurydice," at the Second Stage Theater, and two programs of 10-minutes plays that take place in and around the rooftop pool at the Holiday Inn Midtown, at 57th Street and Ninth Avenue. Despite the technical and practical challenges of dealing with water — from safety issues like waterproofing electrical cables to stage cleanliness to the towel supply — it's apparently worth it for the wow factor.

"We can't afford pyrotechnics, we can't afford Broadway budgets, we can't even afford fly space," said Josh Sherman, the director of the Impetuous Theater Group, a two-year-old Off Off Broadway company, which is staging "Swim Shorts 3" at the

Continued on Page 5

A Touching Romance, If They Just Don't Touch

By BILL CARTER

LOS ANGELES — In a quirky fairy tale of a mystery show called "Pushing Daisies," ABC, the network of "Lost," "Desperate Housewives" and "Ugly Betty," has yet another series that is building strong enthusiasm in advance of the fall television season.

Marked by a candy-colored palette, characters as sweet as freshly baked pie and a story line based on a touching (or in this case, no-touching) unrequited romance, "Pushing Daisies" is a dish that networks always promise but seldom serve: something completely different.

Sitting in his still-unfurnished office on the Warner Brothers lot here, Bryan Fuller, the show's creator, is working on muting expectations, which are coming from advertisers

A new TV series rides a big wave of early enthusiasm.

and critics who have seen the pilot. "I love that it's getting this positive buzz," he said, "but I'm taking it all with a grain of salt."

Mr. Fuller, 37, has been here before. Four years ago he created another oddball early favorite, a Fox drama called "Wonderfalls." That one got a sudden cold shoulder from its own network — Mr. Fuller said he thought it was because of the show's two lesbian characters — and found itself all but abandoned after only four episodes had been filmed.

But "Pushing Daisies" is an unabashed favorite at both its studio, Warner Brothers, and its network. Peter Roth, the president of Warner Brothers Television, said, "If a show of this quality works, it will renew my faith in the taste of the American audience."

Steven McPherson, the president of ABC Entertainment, said: "We

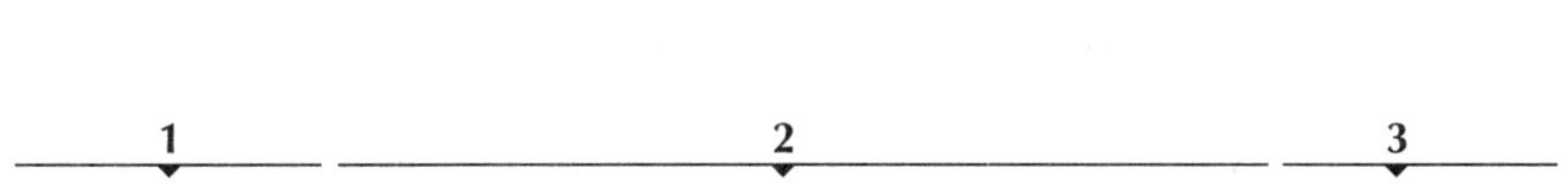

Ryzick, Melena "Indoors and Out, Theater Is Making a Splash." The New York Times 5 July 2007, late ed.: E1+.

For a Music Video

Outkast. "Hey Ya." Speakerboxx/The Love Below. La Face, 2003. Music video. Dir. Bryan Barber. MTV. 22 Aug. 2004.

The Citation of Electronic Sources

Both students and instructors routinely take advantage of the technology available to assist in research. While many libraries offer varied databases that enable researchers to locate information easily, the main thrust of research is now the exploration of the World Wide Web. Through the use of various search engines, such as Google and Yahoo, you simply need to enter the name of an author, a title, or a topic, upon which you will be linked to a host of resources from all over the world—home pages of specific authors, literary organizations, and works on various topics by contemporary writers. You'll find a good deal of what you're searching for in only a few seconds. An important caveat is that many sources still remain in printed journals and magazines that may be or, more probably, may not be on the Web. To make sure your searches are thorough, therefore, *you must never neglect to search for information provided by traditional printed sourcees.*

Because the available methods of obtaining electronic information are developing so rapidly, the printed style manuals have had difficulty keeping up with the changes. If you do a Web search looking for information on these styles, chances are that the information you discover will vary from site to site. Therefore, you need to know the basics that are required for the citation of your sources.

When recovering electronic sources, it is vital to type the letters, numbers, symbols, dots, underlines, and spaces in the uniform resource locator (URL) accurately. Recovery systems are unforgiving, and mistakes or omissions of any sort will make it impossible for you to retrieve your source. URLs are often transitory because someone, somewhere, must maintain them (through the updating of information and the paying of fees). If the URL you have used does not turn up the material for which you are searching, you may be able to locate it simply by typing in the name of the author or the name of the article on a search engine. You may often rely on search engines to turn up references for you, for the autofill feature will often complete the entire address automatically, with all the dots and other directions in the correct order.

By the same token, it is essential for you, when you are compiling your own list of works cited, to be absolutely accurate in reproducing the URLs of your sources. You must assume that someone reading your essay and using your list will want to check out the sources themselves, and any errors in your transcription may create confusion.

The style generally accepted in the cyber world, and the one recommended by the MLA, places angle brackets (< >) before and after Internet addresses and URLs. If you see brackets around an address you want to use, do not include them as part of the address when you are seeking retrieval. Also, since a number of word-processing programs now support the use of italics, you can use italics as a regular practice. Some researchers, however, still prefer underlines, and if your programs (or typewriter) cannot produce italics, of course use underlines. If in doubt about which to use, consult your instructor.

MLA Style Guidelines for Electronic Sources

Many of the guidelines the MLA has authorized for the citation of electronic sources overlap with the MLA recommendations for printed sources, but to avoid ambiguity a number of recommendations bear repetition. Electronic materials are to be documented in basically the same style as printed sources. According to the sixth edition of the *MLA Handbook,* which illustrates virtually all the situations you can ever encounter, the following items need to be included if they are available.

1. The name of the author, editor, compiler, or translator of the source (if available and relevant), last name first, followed by an abbreviation, such as *ed.*, if appropriate.
2. If there is no author listed in the source, you should list the title first: the title of a poem, short story, article, or similar short work within a scholarly project, database, or periodical (in quotation marks); or the title of a posting to a discussion list or forum (taken from the subject line and enclosed by quotation marks), concluded by the phrase "Online posting."
3. The title of a book, underlined or italicized.
4. The name of the editor, compiler, or translator of the text (if relevant and if not cited earlier), preceded by (not followed by) any necessary abbreviations, such as *Ed.*
5. Publication information for any printed version of the source.
6. The title of the scholarly project, database, periodical, or professional or personal site, underlined or italicized; or, for a professional or personal site with no title, a description such as "Home Page."
7. The name of the editor of the scholarly project or database (if available).
8. The version number of the source (if not part of the title), or, for a journal, the volume number, issue number, or other identifying number. All numbers should be in Arabic numerals, not Roman.
9. The date of publication or posting that you find in your source. Sometimes the original date is no longer available because it has been replaced with an update; if so, cite that. Dates should be arranged by (a) day of the month, (b) month (the names of longer months may be abbreviated), and (c) year.
10. For a work from a subscription service, the name of the service (and name, city, and state abbreviation if the subscriber is a library).
11. For a posting to a discussion list or forum, the name of the list or forum.
12. The number range or total number of pages, paragraphs, or other sections, if they are numbered. If you do your own numbering, include your numbers within square brackets [ ], and be sure to indicate what you have numbered.

13. The name of any institution or organization sponsoring or associated with the Web site.
14. The date when you consulted the source. If you have looked at the site a number of times, include the most recent date of use. The principle here is that the date immediately before the URL will mark the last time you used the source.
15. The electronic address or URL of the source in angle brackets < >. Many programs now automatically include the angle brackets. If the URL is too long to fit on one line, the line break should occur at a slash (/) if possible. (Do not introduce hyphenations into the URL as these may be mistaken for actual significant characters in that address.)

Book

Shaw, Bernard. Pygmalion. 1916, 1999. Bartleby Archive. 25 Mar. 2008 <http://www.bartleby.com/138/index.html>.

Poem

Carroll, Lewis. The Hunting of the Snark. 1876. 25 Mar. 2008 <http://www.everypoet.com/archive/poetry/Lewis_Carroll/lewis_carroll_the_hunting_of_the_snark.htm>.

Play

Shakespeare, William. Hamlet. c. 1601. Project Gutenberg. 25 Mar. 2008 <http://www.novelguide.com/hamlet/hamlet.txt>.

Journal Article

Hewlett, Beth L., and Christa Ehmann Powers. "How Do You Ground Your Training? Sharing the Principles and Processes of Preparing Educators for Online Writing Instruction." Kairos 10.1 (Fall 2005). Multiple Sections. 25 Mar. 2008 <http://english.ttu.edu/kairos/10.1/binder.html?praxis/hewett/index.htm>.

Magazine Article

Jones, Kenneth. "Bill Gates and Steve Jobs Sing and Dance in New Musical, Nerds, Already a Hit in NYMF." Playbill.com September 20, 2005. 25 March 2008 <http://www.playbill.com/news/article/95180.html>.

Posting to A Discussion List

McElhearn, Kirk. "J. S. Bach: Oxford Composer Companion [A review]." Online posting. 1 Dec. 2000. Google Groups. 24 March 2008 <http://groups.google.com/group/alt.music.j-s-bach/browse_thread/thread/30524010237bd51a/488691878789a15d?lnk=st&q=%22Kirk+Mcelhearn%22&rnum=5#488691878789a15d>.

Scholarly Project

Voice of the Shuttle: Web Site for Humanities Research. Ed. Alan Liu. 23 March 2008. U of California Santa Barbara. 23 Mar. 2008 <http://vos.ucsb.edu/>.

Professional Site

NobelMuseum. The Nobel Foundation. 25 March 2008. <http://nobelprize.org/index.html>

Personal Site

Barrett, Dan. The Gentle Giant Home Page. 19 February 2008. 25 March 2008. <http://www.blazemonger.com/GG/index.html>.

Citing a Professional Website

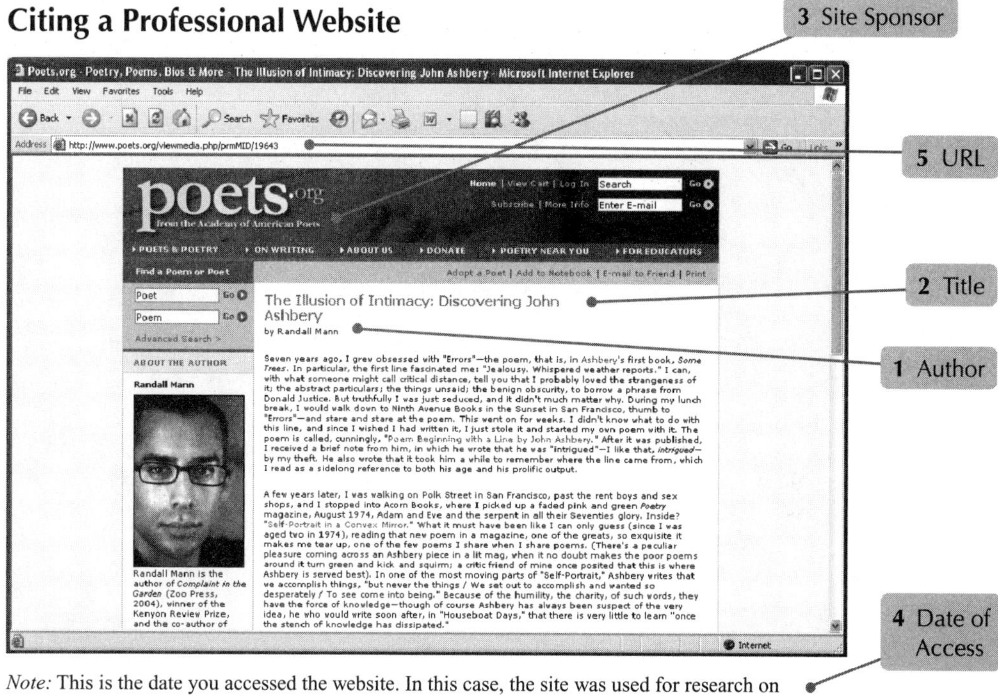

Note: This is the date you accessed the website. In this case, the site was used for research on June 20, 2007.

1 — 2 — 3

Mann, Randall. "The Illusion of Intimacy: Discovering John Asbherry." Academy of American Poets 20 June 2007 <http://www.poets.org/viewmedia.php/prmMID/19643>.

4 — 5

A Glossary of Important Literary Terms

This glossary presents brief definitions of terms and concepts that are boldfaced in the text. Page references indicate where readers may find additional detail and illustration, together with discussions about how the concepts can be utilized in studying and writing about literature. Generally, words italicized as parts of various definitions are also separately glossed in their own right.

abstract diction Language describing qualities that are rarefied and theoretical (e.g., "good," "interesting," "neat," and so on); distinguished from *concrete diction*. 000

absurd See *comedy of the absurd*.

accent or **beat** The heavy *stresses* or accents in lines of *poetry*. Because heavy stresses are paired with *light stresses* to compose metrical *feet*, the numbers of accents or beats in a *line* usually govern the meter of the line (five beats in a *pentameter* line, four in a *tetrameter* line, etc.). 000

accented syllable A syllable receiving a major, or heavy, *stress* or *accent*. 000

actions or incidents The events or occurrences in a work. 0, 00, 000, 000

actors Persons who perform as characters in a play. 000

allegory A complete *narrative* that may also be applied to a parallel set of moral, philosophical, political, religious, or social situations. 00, 000–000, 000, 000

alliteration The repetition of identical consonant sounds (most often the sounds beginning words) in close proximity (e.g., "*p*ensive *p*oets," "*s*omewhere *s*afe to *s*ea," "*g*racious, *g*olden, *gl*ittering *gl*eams," "And *d*eath once *d*ead, there's no more *d*ying then"). 000

allusion Unacknowledged references and quotations that authors make while assuming that readers will recognize the original sources and relate their meanings to the new context. Allusions are hence compliments that the author pays to readers for their perceptiveness, knowledge, and awareness. 000, 000–000, 000

amphibrach A three-syllable foot consisting of a light, heavy, and light stress, as in *I'm SING – ing*. 000

amphimacer or **cretic** A three-syllable foot consisting of a heavy, light, and heavy stress, as in *SING – ing SONGS*. 000

anagnorisis or **recognition** Aristotle's term describing that point in a play, usually the *climax*, when a character experiences understanding. 000

analysis See *commentary*.

analytical sentence outline A scheme or plan for an essay, arranged according to topics (A, B, C, etc.) and with the topics expressed in sentences. 00

anapest Sometimes spelled *anapaest*. A three-syllable *foot* consisting of two light *stresses* climaxed by a heavy stress, as in *ear-ly LIGHT*. 000

anaphora ("to carry again or repeat") The repetition of the same word or phrase throughout a work or section of a work. The effect is to lend weight and emphasis. 000, 000

ancillary characters *Characters* in a story or play who set off or highlight the protagonist and who provide insight into the action. The *foil*, *choric figure*, and *raisonneur* are all ancillary characters. 000

antagonist One who struggles against. The person, idea, force, or general set of circumstances opposing the *protagonist*; an essential element of *plot*. 00, 000

anticipation See *procatalepsis*.

antimetabole See *chiasmus*.

antithesis A rhetorical device of opposition in which one idea or word is established, and then the opposite idea or word is expressed, as in "I *burn* and *freeze*" and "I *love* and *hate*." 000, 000

apostrophe The addressing of a discourse to a real or imagined person who is not present; also a speech to an abstraction. 000

apron or **thrust stage** A stage that projects into the auditorium area, thus increasing the space for action; a characteristic feature of Elizabethan as well as contemporary theaters. 000

archetypal/symbolic/mythic critical approach The explanation of literature in terms of archetypal patterns (e.g., God's creation of human beings, the search for paradise, the sacrifice of a hero, the initiation or "test" of a young person). 0000

archetype A character, action, or situation that is a prototype or pattern of human life generally; a situation that occurs over and over again in literature, such as a quest, an initiation, or an attempt to overcome evil. Many *myths* are archetypes. 0000

archon, eponymous archon In ancient Athens, the Eponymous Archon, or Archon Eponymous, was a leading magistrate, after whom the year was named. He made arrangements for the tragedies and comedies to be performed at the yearly festivals in honor of the God Dionysus. 000

arena stage, or **theater-in-the-round** A theater arrangement, often outdoors, in which the audience totally surrounds a *platform stage*, with all actors entering and exiting along the same aisles used by the audience. 000

argument The development of a pattern of interpretation or thought with an intent to persuade. In most writing about literature, the persuasive situation is to show the validity of a particular idea or circumstance in a story, poem, or play. More broadly, the term *argument* applies to any situation about which there may be disagreement. Although sometimes argumentative discourse may become disputatious, one should never forget that true arguments should stem from the reasonable interpretation of correct and accurate data. 00

aside A speech, usually short and often witty or satirical, delivered by a character to the audience or to another character, the convention being that only the intended characters can hear it, along, of course, with the audience. A more extensive speech that is delivered only to the audience when the character is alone on stage is a *soliloquy*. 000

assertion A sentence putting an *idea* or *argument* (the subject) into operation (the predicate); necessary for both developing and understanding the idea. 000

assonance The repetition of identical vowel sounds in different words in close proximity, as in the d*ee*p gr*ee*n s*ea*. 000

atmosphere or **mood** The emotional aura invoked by a work. 00, 000

audience or **intended reader** or **listener** (1) The people attending a theatrical production. (2) The intended group of readers for whom a writer writes, such as a group of religious worshippers, or a group of rocket scientists. 000

auditory images References to sounds. 000

authorial symbol See *contextual symbol*.

authorial voice The *voice* or *persona* used by authors when seemingly speaking for themselves. The use of the term makes it possible to discuss a narration or presentation without assuming that the ideas are necessarily those of the author in his or her own person. See also *speaker*, *point of view*, and *third-person point of view*. 000

bacchius or **bacchic** A three-syllable foot consisting of a light stress followed by two heavy stresses, as in "*a NEW SONG*" or "*the OLD WAYS*." 000

ballad, ballad measure A narrative poem, originally a popular form, composed of quatrains in *ballad measure*; that is, a pattern of iambic tetrameter alternating with iambic trimeter and rhyming *x-a-x-a*. 0, 000

ballad opera An eighteenth-century comic drama, originated by John Gay (1685–1732) in *The Beggar's Opera* (1728), featuring lyrics written for existing and usually well-known tunes, such as "Greensleeves." See also *comic opera*. 0000

beast fable A narrative, usually short, attributing human characteristics to animals. 000

beat A *heavy stress* or *accent* in a line of poetry. The number of beats in a line dictates the *meter* of the line, such as five beats to a line of *iambic pentameter*, or three beats to a line of *trimeter*. See also *accent*. 000

blank verse Unrhymed *iambic pentameter*. Most of the poetry in Shakespeare's plays is blank verse, as is the poetry of Milton's *Paradise Lost*. 000

blocking In the performance of a play, the director's plan for the grouping and movement of characters on stage. 000

blocking agent A person, circumstance, or attitude that obstructs the plans of various characters, such as the parental denial of permission to marry, as in Shakespeare's *A Midsummer Night's Dream*. 0000

box set In the modern theater, the *realistic* setting of a single room from which the "fourth wall" is missing, so that the stage resembles a picture. 000

brainstorming The exploration, discovery, and development of details to be used in a composition. 00

breve In poetic *scansion*, a mark in the shape of a bowl-like half circle (˘) to indicate a light stress or unaccented syllable. 000

business or **stage business** The gestures, expressions, and general activity (beyond *blocking*) of *actors* onstage. Usually, business is designed to create laughter. It is often done spontaneously by actors. 000

buskins Elegantly laced boots (*kothorni* or *cothurni*) worn by actors in ancient Greek *tragedy*. Eventually the buskins became elevator shoes to stress the royal status of actors by making them seem especially tall. 000

cacophony Meaning "bad sound," but by no means bad, *cacophony* refers to words combining sharp or harsh sounds and rhythms, as in Pope's "When Ajax strives some rock's vast weight to throw." Cacophony is the opposite of *euphony*. 000

cadence group A coherent word group spoken as a single rhythmical unit, such as a prepositional phrase ("of human events") or noun phrase ("our sacred honor"). 000

caesura, (plural **caesurae**) The pause(s) or juncture(s) separating words and phrases within lines of poetry, as in Pope's line "Trees, where you sit, shall crowd into a shade" (*Second Pastoral*, "Summer," line 74), in which there is a caesura after "Trees" and also after "sit." In poetic *scansion* the caesura is marked by a double *virgule* (//). The control of caesurae is a vital aspect of poetic *rhythm*. 000

catastrophe The "overturning" of the dramatic *plot*, the fourth stage in the structure immediately following the *climax*; the *dénouement* of a play, in which things are explained and put into place. 000

catharsis (purgation) Aristotle's concept that *tragedy*, by arousing pity and fear (*eleos* and *phobos*), regularizes and shapes human emotions, and that therefore tragedy, like literature and art generally, is essential in civilized society. 000

central idea or **central argument** (1) The *thesis* or main idea of an essay. (2) The *theme* of a literary work. 00

character An extended verbal representation of a human being, the inner self that determines thought, speech, and behavior. 0, 00, 000–000, 000

character, comic Comic characters tend to be characters who are unrealistic and sometimes exaggerated, representing classes, types, and generations. 0000

chiasmus or **antimetabole** A rhetorical pattern in which words (and also ideas) are repeated in the sequence *a b b a*, as in "I lead the life I love; I love the life I lead," and "When the issue deteriorates to violence, violence becomes the issue." 000

choragos or **choregus** The sponsor or financial backer of a classical Athenian dramatic production. Often the Athenians honored the choragos by selecting him to serve as the leader (*koryphaios*) of the chorus. 000

choree See *trochee.*

choric figure A character who remains somewhat outside the dramatic *action* and who provides commentary when appropriate. See also *raisonneur*. 000

chorus In ancient Athenian drama, the chorus was composed of young men—fifteen in tragedies and twenty-four in comedies—who chanted or sang, probably in unison, and who performed dance movements to a flute accompaniment. The chorus was, in effect, a major (and also collective) character in the *drama*. 000

chronology (the **"logic of time"**) The sequence of events in a work, with emphasis on the complex intertwining of cause and effect. 00, 000

City Dionysia See *Dionysia.*

clerihew A comic and often satiric closed-form poem in four lines, rhyming *a b a b*, usually on the topic of a famous real or literary person. 000

cliché rhyme An overly used and particularly easy rhyme, such as *moon* and *June* or *trees* and *breeze*. 000

climax (from the Greek word for *ladder*) The high point of *conflict* and tension preceding the *resolution* or *dénoument* of a *story* or *play*; the point of decision, of inevitability and no return. The climax is sometimes equated with the *crisis* in the consideration of dramatic and narrative *structure*. 000, 000, 000

closed-form poetry Poetry written in specific and traditional patterns produced through control of *rhyme*, *meter*, line-length, and line groupings. 000

close reading The detailed study of a poem or passage, designed to explain characters, motivations, similarities and contrasts of sound, situations, ideas, style, organization, word selections, settings, etc. 000

close-up (film) A camera view of an actor's head and upper body, designed to emphasize the psychological makeup and reactions of the character being portrayed; contrasted with *long shot*. 000

comedy A literary genre which, like *tragedy*, originated in the *Dionysia* festivals of ancient Athens. Derived from the Greek *komos* songs or "songs of merrymakers," the first comedies were wildly boisterous. Later comedies became more subdued and realistic. In typical comedies today, confusions and doubts are resolved satisfactorily if not happily, and usually comedies are characterized by smiles, jokes, and laughter. 000, 0000–0000

comedy of the absurd A modern form of comedy dramatizing the apparent pointlessness, ambiguity, uncertainty, and absurdity of human existence. 0000, 0000

comedy of manners A form of comedy, usually a *regular play* (in five acts or three acts), in which attitudes and customs are examined and satirized in the light of high intellectual and moral standards. The *dialogue* is witty and sophisticated, and characters are often measured according to their linguistic and intellectual powers. 0000

comic action A pattern of action, including funny situations and language, that is solvable and correctible, and therefore satisfying. 0000

comic opera An outgrowth of eighteenth-century *ballad opera*, but different because the music in comic opera is composed for the lyrics. 0000

commedia dell'arte Broadly humorous farce that was developed in sixteenth-century Italy, featuring *stock characters*, stock situations, and much improvised *dialogue*. 0000

commentary, analysis, or **interpretation** Passages of explanation and reflection about the meaning of actions, thoughts, dialogue, historical movements, and so on. 00, 000

commentator See *raisonneur.*

common ground of assent Those interests, concerns, and assumptions that the writer assumes in common with readers so that an effective and persuasive *tone* may be maintained. 000

common measure A closed poetic quatrain, rhyming *a b a b*, in which lines of iambic tetrameter alternate with iambic trimeter. See also *ballad measure* and *hymnal measure.* 000

comparison-contrast A technique of analyzing two or more works in order to determine similarities and differences in topic, treatment, and quality. 0000–0000

complete, completeness The second element in Aristotle's definition of *tragedy*, emphasizing the logic and entirety of the play. 000

complication A stage of narrative and dramatic structure in which the major *conflicts* are brought out; the *rising action* of a *drama.* 000, 000, 000

compound-complex sentence A potentially complicated sentence built not only from two simple sentences but also, theoretically, from three or more. There may be a number of subordinate clauses, and possibly also one or more of the clauses may have a noun clause as subject of one or more of the basic compounded sentences. 000

concrete diction Words that describe exact and particular conditions or qualities, such as *cold*, *sweet*, and *creamy* in reference to an ice-cream sundae. These words are *concrete*, while the application of *good* or *neat* to the sundae is *abstract*. See also *abstract diction.* 000

concrete poetry See *visual poetry.*

conflict Opposition between two characters, between large groups of people, or between *protagonists* and larger forces such as natural objects, ideas, modes of behavior, public opinion, and the like. Conflict may also be internal and psychological, involving choices facing a *protagonist.* The resolution of conflict is the essence of *plot*. 00, 000

connotation The meanings that words suggest; the overtones of words beyond their bare dictionary definitions or denotations, as with "leave," "get away," "depart," "turn tail," and "vamoose," which have the same meaning, but differing connotations. 000, 000

consonant sounds or **consonant segments** Sounds that accompany ["con"] the (vowel) sound ["sonant"]). They are produced as a result of the touching or close proximity of the tongue or the lips in relation to the teeth or palate (e.g., *m, n, p, f, sh, ch*); to be compared and contrasted with *vowel sounds*. 000

contextual, private, or **authorial symbol** A symbol that is derived within the context of an individual work, not from common historical, cultural, or religious materials. See also *cultural symbol*. 00, 000, 000, 000

convention An accepted feature of a genre, such as the *point of view* in a story, the *form* of a *poem* (e.g., *sonnet, ode*), the competence or brilliance of the detective in detective fiction, the impenetrability of disguise and concealment in a Shakespearean play, or the *chorus* in Greek *drama.* 00

Corpus Christi play A type of medieval drama that enacts events from the Bible, such as the killing of Abel by Cain, the domestic problems of Noah, the jealous anger of Herod, and so on. The word is derived from the religious festival of Corpus Christi ("Christ's body"), held in the spring of each year, mainly during the fourteenth century. Also called *mystery plays* because they were performed by individual craft guilds, or *misteries.* See also *cycle.* 000

cosmic irony (irony of fate) *Situational irony* that is connected to a pessimistic or fatalistic view of life. 000

costumes The clothes worn by *actors,* designed to indicate historical periods, social status, economic levels, etc. 000, 000

cothurni See *buskins.*

couplet Two lines that may be unified by *rhyme* or, in biblical poetry, by content. 0, 000

creative nonfiction A type of literature that is technically nonfiction, such as diaries journals, and news features, but that nevertheless involves a high degree of imaginative and literary skill. 0

crisis The point of uncertainty and tension in a literary work—the turning point—that results from the *conflicts* and difficulties brought about through the *complications* of the plot. The crisis leads to the *climax*—that is, to the decision made by the protagonist to resolve the conflict. Sometimes the crisis and the climax are considered as two elements of the same stage of *plot* development. 000, 000

cultural (universal) context See *topical/historical context approach.*

cultural or **universal symbol** A symbol that is recognized and shared as a result of a common political, social, and cultural heritage. See also *contextual symbol.* 00, 000, 000

cycle (1) A group of closely related works. (2) In medieval religious drama, the complete set of plays performed during the *Corpus Christi* festival, from the creation of the world to the resurrection. As many as forty plays could make up the cycle. During those times when not many people were able to read, a complete cycle was one of the means by which stories of the Bible were brought to a wider audience. See also *Corpus Christi play.* 000

dactyl A three-syllable foot consisting of a heavy stress followed by two lights, as in the words *QUOT-a-ble* and *SYN-the-sis.* 000

dactylic rhyme Rhyming dactyls, such as *spillable* and *syllable* or *mortify* and *fortify.* 000–00

deconstructionist critical approach An interpretive literary approach that rejects absolutes, but that stresses ambiguities and contradictions. 0000

decorum The convention or expectation that words and subjects should be exactly appropriate—*high* or *formal* words for serious subjects (e.g., *epic poems, tragedy*), and *low* or *informal* words for low subjects (e.g., *limericks, farce*). 000

denotation The standard, minimal meaning of a word, without implications and connotations. See also *connotation.* 000, 000

dénouement (untying) or **resolution** The final stage of *plot development,* in which mysteries are explained, characters find their destinies, lovers are united, sanity is restored, and the work is completed. Usually the dénouement is done as speedily as possible, for it occurs after all *conflicts* are ended, and little that is new can then be introduced to hold the interest of readers. 000, 000, 000

description The exposition of scenes, actions, attitudes, and feelings. 00

developing character See *round character*.

device A *figure of speech*, such as a *metaphor* or a *simile*. 000

deus ex machina ("A god out of the machine"; *theos apo mechanes* in Greek, a phrase attributed to the ancient Greek playwright Menander). In ancient Athenian drama, the entrance of a god to unravel the problems in a *play*. Today, the phrase *deus ex machina* refers to the artificial and illogical solution of problems. 000

dialect Language characteristics—involving pronunciation, unique words, and vocal rhythms—particular to regions such as New England or the South, or to separate nations such as Britain and Australia. 000

dialogue The speeches of two or more characters in a *story*, *play*, or *poem*. 0, 000

diction Word choice, types of words, and the level of language. 000

diction, formal or **high** Proper, elevated, elaborate, and often polysyllabic language. 000, 000

diction, informal or **low** Relaxed, conversational, and familiar language, utilizing contractions and elisions, and sometimes employing *slang* and grammatical errors. 000, 000

diction, neutral or **middle** Correct language characterized by directness and simplicity. 000, 000

dilemma A situation, particularly in tragedy, presenting a character with two choices, either one of which is unacceptable, dangerous, or even lethal. 000

dimeter A *line* of two metrical feet. 000

Dionysia (also **City Dionysia)** The religious festivals of ancient Athens held to celebrate the god Dionysus. *Tragedy* developed as part of the Great, or City Dionysia in March-April, and *comedy* developed as part of a shorter festival, the Lenaea (in February). 000

diphthong A meaningful vowel segment (a phoneme) that begins with one sound and changes to another, with which it ends. Three examples in English are found in the words h*ou*se, c*oi*l, and f*i*ne. 000

dipody, dipodic foot, or **syzygy** A strong *beat* that creates a single *foot* out of two normal feet—usually *iambs* or *trochees*—so that a "galloping" or "rollicking" *rhythm* results. 000

director The person in charge of guiding and instructing all persons involved in a dramatic production. 000

discursive poetry Non-narrative *poetry* dealing primarily with ideas and personal, social, or political commentary. 0

discursive writing Distinguished from imaginative writing, discursive writing is concerned with factual presentation and the development of reasonable and logical conclusions. 0

dithyramb An ancient Athenian poetic form sung by choruses during the earliest *Dionysia*. The first *tragedies* originated as part of the dithyrambs. 000, 000

documentation Granting recognition to the ideas and words of others, either through textual, parenthetical, or footnote references. 000

donnée (French for "given") The given action or set of assumptions on which a work of literature is based, such as the unpredictability of love, the bleakness and danger of a postwar world, or the inescapability of guilt. See also *postulate* or *premise*. 00

double duple See *dipody*.

double entendre ("double meaning") Deliberate ambiguity, usually comic, and often sexual. 000

double rhyme See *trochaic rhyme*.

double take A structural device whereby a concluding event or "surprise" brings about a new and more complex understanding of the previous material. 000

drama An individual play; also plays considered as a group; one of the three major genres of *imaginative literature*. 0, 000–000

dramatic irony A special kind of *situational irony* in which a character perceives his or her plight in a limited way while the audience and one or more of the other characters understand it entirely. 00, 000, 000

dramatic monologue A type of *poem* in which a speaker addresses an internal listener or the reader. Often the speaker includes detail reflecting the listener's unrecorded responses. The form is related to the *soliloquy* and the *aside* in drama. 000

dramatic or **objective point of view** A *third-person narration* reporting speech and *action*, but excluding commentary on the actions and thoughts of the *characters*. 000, 000

dying rhyme See *falling rhyme*.

dynamic character A character who recognizes, changes with, and tries to adjust to circumstances. Such changes may be shown in (1) an action or actions, (2) the realization of new strength and therefore the affirmation of previous decisions, (3) the acceptance of new conditions and the need for making changes, (4) the discovery of unrecognized truths, or (5) the reconciliation of the character with adverse conditions. In a *short story*, there is usually only one dynamic character, whereas in a *novel* there may be many. 000, 000

echoic words Words echoing the actions they describe, such as *buzz*, *bump*, and *slap*; important in the device of *onomatopoeia*. 000

economic determinist/Marxist critical approach An interpretive literary approach based on the theories of Karl Marx (1818–1883), stressing that literature is to be judged from the perspective of economic and social inequality and oppression. 0000

editing (film) See *montage*.

elegy A *poem* of lamentation about a death. Often an elegy takes the form of a *pastoral*. 0, 000

enclosing setting See *framing* or *enclosing setting*.

end-stopped line A poetic line ending in a full pause, usually marked by a period or semicolon. 000

English (Shakespearean) sonnet A sonnet form developed by Shakespeare, in *iambic pentameter*, composed of three *quatrains* and a *couplet*, with seven rhymes in the pattern *a b a b, c d c d, e f e f, g g*. 000

epic A long *narrative poem* elevating *character*, *speech*, and *action*. 0, 00

epigram A short and witty *poem*, often in *couplets*, that makes a humorous or satiric point. 0, 000

episode or ***episodia*** (1) An acting *scene* or section of Greek tragedy. Divisions separating the episodes were called *stasima*, or sections for the chorus. (2) A self-enclosed portion of a work, such as a section, or a passage of particular narration, dialogue, or location. 00, 000

epitaph A short comment or description marking someone's death. Also, a short, witty, and often satiric poem about death. 000

essay A short and tightly organized written composition dealing with a topic such as a character, setting, or point of view. Essays also deal more broadly with any and all conceivable topics. 00

euphony ("good sound") Word groups containing consonants that permit an easy and pleasant flow of spoken sound. See also *cacophony*. 000

exact rhyme Also called *perfect rhyme*; the placement of rhyming words in which both the vowel and concluding consonant sounds, if any, are identical, as in "done" and "run," and "see" and "be." It is important to judge rhymes on the basis of *sound* rather than spelling, as in these examples. Words do not have to be spelled the same way to be exact rhymes. 000

exam, examination A written or oral test or inquiry designed to discover a person's understanding and capacity to deal with a particular topic or set of topics. 0000–00

exodos The final episode in a Greek tragedy, occurring after the last choral ode. 000

explication A detailed analysis of a work of literature, often word by word and line by line; a close reading. 000

exposition The stage of dramatic or narrative structure that introduces all things necessary for the development of the plot. 000, 000, 000

eye rhyme or **sight rhyme** Words that seem to rhyme because parts of them are spelled identically but pronounced differently (e.g., *bear, fear; fury, bury; stove, shove; wonder, yonder*). 000

fable A brief *story* illustrating a moral truth, most often associated with the ancient Greek writer Aesop. See also *beast fable*. 00, 000

falling action See *catastrophe.*

falling rhyme Trochaic rhymes, such as *often* and *soften,* and also multisyllabic rhymes, such as *flattery* and *battery, listening* and *glistening*. 000

fantasy The creation of events that are dreamlike or fantastic, departing from ordinary understanding of *reality* because of apparently illogical *setting*, movement, causality, and *chronology*. 00

farce (from the Latin word *farsus,* meaning "stuffed") An outlandish physical *comedy* overflowing with silly characters, improbable happenings, wild clowning, extravagant language, and bawdy jokes. 0000

feet See *foot.*

feminist critical approach A critical approach designed to raise consciousness about the importance and unique nature of women in literature. See also *gender studies* and *queer theory*. 0000

fiction *Narratives* based in the imagination of the author, not in literal, reportorial facts; one of the three major genres of imaginative literature. 0

figurative devices See *figures of speech.*

figurative language See *figures of speech.*

figure of speech A organized pattern of comparison that deepens, broadens, extends, illuminates, and emphasizes meaning, and also that conforms to particular patterns or forms such as *metaphor, simile,* and *parallelism*. 000–000

film Motion pictures, movies. 0000–00

film script The written dramatic text on which a film is based, including directions for movement and expression. 0000

first-person point of view The use of a first-person *speaker* or *narrator* who tells about things that he or she has seen, done, spoken, heard, thought, and also learned about in other ways. 000, 000

flashback Also called *selective recollection*. A method of *narration* in which past events are introduced into a present action. 000, 000

flat character A character, usually minor, who is not individual, but rather useful and structural, static and unchanging; distinguished from *round character*. 000, 000

foil A character, usually minor, designed to highlight qualities of a major character. 000

foot, feet A poetic foot consists of the measured combination of heavy and light *stresses*, such as the *iamb*, which contains a light stress followed by a heavy stress (e.g., "*of YEAR*"). In poetic scansion, one separates feet with a *virgule* or single slash mark (/), as in Shakespeare's "That TIME / of YEAR / thou MAY'ST / in ME / be - HOLD." 000

form, poetic The various shapes and organizational modes of poetry. 000–000

formal diction See *diction, formal* or *high.*

formalist critical approach See *New Critical/formalist critical approach.*

formal substitution See *substitution.*

framing or **enclosing setting** The same features of topic, technique, or setting used at both the beginning and ending of a work so as to "frame" or "enclose" the work. 000

free verse *Poetry* based on the natural *rhythms* of phrases and normal pauses, not *metrical feet.* See *open-form poetry.* 0, 000

freewriting See *brainstorming.*

Freytag pyramid A diagram graphically showing the stages of dramatic *structure. Complication* and emotional intensity go upward on the side of the pyramid rising to its peak or point. Once the high point is reached, intensity begins to decrease just as the other side of the pyramid descends to its base. 000

gallery The upper seats at the back and sides of a *theater.* 000

general language Words referring to broad classes of persons, objects, or phenomena; distinguished from *specific language.* 000, 000

gender studies A critical approach that brings attention to gender rather than to sexual differences, based on the concept that the masculine/feminine divide is socially constructed and not innate. See also *feminist critical approach* and *queer theory.* 0000

genre One of the major types of literature, such as *fiction* and *poetry.* Also, a type of work, such as detective fiction, epic poetry, tragedy, etc. 0

Globe Theatre The outdoor theater built at the end of the sixteenth century just south of the Thames, where many of Shakespeare's plays were originally performed. The Globe was rebuilt in the 1990s to its original appearance, and once again is a flourishing theater close to where it was at the time of Shakespeare. See Plate 00. 000

graph, graphics The writing of words on the page; the spelling of words as opposed to their actual sounds. For example, the *sh* sound may be spelled or graphed in many different ways, such as *sh*ip, na*ti*on, o*c*ean, fi*ss*ion, and fu*chs*ia. 000–00

graphic narrative, graphic novel A narrative composed of connected artistic or cartoon panels. The essential quality of graphic narrative is the combination of picture and dialogue to convey a story from beginning to end. 00

gustatory images References to impressions of taste. 000

haiku A verse form derived from Japanese poetry, traditionally containing three lines of 5, 7, and 5 syllables, in that order, and usually treating a topic derived from nature. 0, 000

half rhyme See *inexact rhyme.*

hamartia The Greek word for "error or frailty," indicating the tragic flaw that brings about the downfall or suffering of a protagonist. The same Greek word is translated as "sin" in the New Testament. 000

heavy-stress rhyme or **rising rhyme** A *rhyme,* such as rhyming *iambs* or *anapests,* ending with a *strong stress.* The rhymes may be produced with one syllable words, like *SKY* and *FLY,* or with multisyllabic words in which the accent falls on the last syllable, such as *de-CLINE* and *con-FINE.* 000

heptameter or **"the septenary"** A line consisting of seven metrical *feet.* 000

hero, heroine The major male and female *protagonists* in a *narrative* or *drama.* The terms are often used to describe leading characters in adventures and romances. 000

heroic couplet Also called the *neoclassic couplet.* Two successive rhyming lines of *iambic pentameter,* a characteristic of much *poetry* written between 1660 and 1800. Five-stress couplets are often called "heroic" regardless of their topic matter and the period in which they were written. 000

hexameter A line consisting of six metrical *feet*. 000

high comedy Elegant *comedies* characterized by wit and sophistication, in which the complications grow not out of *situation* but rather out of *character*. See also *comedy of manners*. 0000

historical critical approach See *topical/historical critical approach.*

hovering accent See *spondee.*

hubris or **hybris** ("Insolence, contemptuous violence") The pride and attitudes that lead tragic figures to commit their mistakes or offenses. 000

humor In literature, those features of a *situation* or expression that provoke laughter and amusement. 000

hymn A hymn is a religious *song*, consisting of one and usually many more replicating rhythmical *stanzas*. 000

hymnal measure The hymnal stanza, in iambics, consists of four lines of four stresses or else of four lines of alternating four and three stresses, rhyming *x a x a* or *a b a b*. See also *ballad measure* and *common measure*. 0, 000

hyperbole See *overstatement*.

hypocrites (pronounced hip-pock-rih-TAYSS, meaning "one who plays a part") The ancient Greek word for *actor*. Yes, our modern word "hypocrite" is derived from this word. 000

iamb A two-syllable *foot* consisting of a light *stress* followed by a heavy stress (e.g., *the WINDS, have FELT, of MAY*). The iamb is the most common metrical foot in English poetry because it closely resembles natural speech while it also follows measured poetic accents. 000

iambic pentameter A line consisting of five *iambic feet*, as in Shakespeare's "Shall I compare thee to a summer's day?" 000

iambic rhyme A *heavy-stress rhyme* that is built from rhyming *iambs* such as "the WEST" and "in REST," or from rhyming two-syllable words such as "ad-MIRE" and "de-SIRE." 000

idea or **theme** A concept, thought, opinion, or belief; in literature, a unifying, centralizing conception or *motif*. 000–000

idiom (private or personal language) Usage that produces unique words and phrases within regions, classes, or groups; e.g., standing *on* line or *in* line; carrying a *pail* or a *bucket*; drinking *pop* or *soda*. Also, the habits and structures of particular languages. 000

image, imagery References that trigger the mind to fuse together memories of sights (*visual*), sounds (*auditory*), tastes (*gustatory*), smells (*olfactory*), sensations of touch (*tactile*), and perceptions of motion (*kinetic, kinesthetic*). "Image" refers to a single mental creation, "imagery" to images throughout a work or works of a writer or group of writers. Images may be *literal* (descriptive and pictorial) and *metaphorical* (figurative and suggestive). 0, 000–000, 000

imaginative literature *Literature* based in the imagination of the writer; the genres of imaginative literature are *fiction, poetry,* and *drama*. 0, *passim*

imitation The theory that literature is derived from life and is an imaginative duplication of experience; closely connected to *realism* and *verisimilitude.* 00

imperfect foot A *metrical foot* consisting of a single syllable, either heavily or lightly stressed, as the *er* in "a joy forever." There is nothing imperfect about an imperfect foot. It is so named because, having only one syllable, it does not fit into the patterns of the other poetic feet. Some analysts of prosody explain the absence of a syllable within an established poetic foot as a *catalexis*. 000

incidents See *actions*.

incongruity A discrepancy between what is ordinarily or normally expected and what is actually experienced. The resulting gap is often, under the right circumstances, a cause of laughter. 000

inexact rhyme Rhymes that are created from words with similar but not identical sounds. In most of these instances, either the vowel segments are different while the consonants are the same, or vice versa. This type of rhyme is variously called *slant rhyme, near rhyme, half rhyme, off rhyme, analyzed rhyme*, or *suspended rhyme*. 000

informal diction See *diction, informal or low*.

intellectual critical approach See *moral/intellectual critical approach*.

internal rhyme The occurrence of rhyming words within a single line of verse, as Poe's "Can ever dissever" in "Annabel Lee." 000

interpretation See *commentary*.

intrigue plot The dramatic rendering of how a young woman and her lover, often aided by a maidservant or *soubrette*, usually foil a *blocking agent* (usually a parent or guardian). 0000

invention The process of discovering and determining materials to be included in a composition, whether an *essay* or an imaginative work; a vital phase of planning and developing a composition. 00

ironic comedy A form of comedy in which characters seem to be in the grips of uncontrollable, cosmic forces. The dominant tone is therefore ironic. 0000

irony Broadly, a means of indirection. *Verbal irony* is language that states the opposite of what is intended. *Dramatic irony* describes the condition of characters who do not know the nature, seriousness, and extent of their circumstances. See also *situational irony*. 00, 000, 000, 000, 000

irony of fate See *cosmic irony*.

irony of situation See *situational Irony*.

issue An assertion or idea to be debated, disputed, or discussed. Sometimes refers to a problematic or questionable circumstance. 000

Italian or **Petrarchan sonnet** An *iambic pentameter* poem of fourteen lines, divided between the first eight lines (the *octave*) and the last six (the *sestet*). An Italian sonnet uses five rhymes, unlike the *Shakespearean sonnet*, which has seven rhymes. 000

jargon Language exclusively used by particular groups, such as doctors, lawyers, astronauts, computer operators, and football players. 000

journal A notebook or word-processor file for recording responses and observations that, for purposes of writing, may be used in the development of *essays*. 00

kinesthetic images Words describing human or animal motion and activity. 000

kinetic images Words describing general motion. 000

kothorni See *buskins*.

Lenaia The ancient Athenian early spring festival for which comedy as a form was first created. 0000

lighting The general word describing the many types, positions, directions, and intensities of artificial lights used in the theater. 000

light stress In speech and in metrical scansion, the less emphasized syllables, as in Shakespeare's "That TIME of YEAR," in which *that* and *of* are pronounced less emphatically than *time* and *year*. 000

limerick A brief poem with preestablished line lengths and rhyming patterns, designed to be comic. More often than not, limericks are risqué. 0, 000

limited point of view or **limited third-person point of view** or **limited-omniscient point of view** A third-person narration in which the actions and thoughts of the protagonist are the primary focus of attention. 00, 000

line The basic unit of length of a poem, appearing as a row of words or sometimes, as a single word or even part of a word occupying the space of a line, and cohering grammatically through phrases and sentences. Lines in *closed-form poetry* are composed of determinable numbers of *metrical feet;* lines in *open-form poetry* are variable, depending on content and rhythmical speech patterns. 000

listener (internal audience) A character or characters imagined as the audience to whom a poem or story is spoken, and as a result one of the influences on the content of the work, as in Browning's "My Last Duchess." Although the listener is usually silent, the listener's imagined reactions may affect what the speaker says and the manner in which he or she says it. Using a listener therefore enables the author to make the narrative, or poem, both personal and dramatic. 000

literary research See *research.*

literature Written or oral compositions that tell stories, dramatize situations, express emotions, and analyze and advocate ideas. Literature is designed to engage readers emotionally as well as intellectually, with the major genres being *fiction, poetry, drama,* and *nonfiction prose,* and with many separate sub-forms. 0, *passim*

low comedy Crude, boisterous, and physical *comedies* and *farces,* characterized by sight gags, bawdy jokes, and outrageous situations. 0000

low diction See *diction, informal or low.*

lyric (1) A short *poem* or *song* written in a fixed stanzaic form. If the lyric is set to music for performance, each new stanza is usually sung to the original melody. (2) The Aristotelian term for the "several kinds of artistic ornament," such as strophes and antistrophes, that are to be used appropriately in a tragedy. 0, 000, 000

magnitude The third element in Aristotle's definition of *tragedy*, emphasizing that a *play* should be neither too long nor too short, so that artistic balance and proportion can be maintained. 000

main plot The central and major line of causality and action in a literary work. 000

major mover A major participant in a work's action who either causes things to happen or who is the subject of major events. If the first-person narrator is also a major mover, such as the *protagonist*, that fact gives first-hand authenticity to the narration. 000

makeup The materials, such as cosmetics, wigs, and padding, applied to an actor to change appearance for a specific role, such as a youth, an aged person, or a hunchback. 000

malapropism The comic use of an improperly pronounced word, so that what comes out is a real but also incorrect word. Examples are *odorous* for *odious* (Shakespeare) or *pineapple* for *pinnacle* (Sheridan). The new word must be close enough to the correct word so that the resemblance is immediately recognized, along with the error. See also *pun*. 0000, note to 1.2.2.

Marxist critical approach See *economic determinist/Marxist critical approach.*

masks Face coverings worn by ancient Athenian actors to illustrate and define dramatic characters such as youths, warriors, old men, and women. 000

meaning That which is to be understood in a work; the total combination of ideas, actions, descriptions, and effects. 000–000

mechanics of verse See *prosody*.

melodrama A sentimental dramatic form with an artificially happy ending. 000

melos See *lyric*.

metaphor ("carrying out a change") A *figure of speech* that describes something as though it actually were something else, thereby enhancing understanding and insight. One of the major qualities of poetic language. 0, 000

metaphorical language See *figure of speech.*

meter The number of *feet* within a line of traditional verse, such as *iambic pentameter* referring to a line containing five *iambs*. 0, 000

metonymy A *figure of speech* in which one thing is used as a substitute for another with which it is closely identified, such as when a speaker says "Dear Hearts" to refer to an audience. 000

metrical foot See *foot.*

metrics See *prosody.*

middle comedy The Athenian comedies written in the first two-thirds of the fourth century BCE Middle comedy lessened or eliminated the *chorus*, and did away with the exaggerated costumes of the *old comedy*. No complete middle comedies have survived from antiquity. 000, 0000

middle diction See *diction, neutral or middle.*

mimesis or **representation** Aristotle's idea that *drama* (*tragedy*) represents rather than duplicates history. 000

miracle play A late medieval play dramatizing a miracle or miracles performed by a saint. An outgrowth of the earlier medieval *Corpus Christi play*. 000

monologue A long speech spoken by a single character to himself or herself, to the audience, or to an off-stage character. See also *aside, soliloquy*. 000

monometer A line consisting of one metrical *foot.* 000

montage or **editing (film)** The editing or assembling of the various camera "takes," or separately filmed scenes, to make a continuous film. 0000

mood See *atmosphere.*

moral/intellectual critical approach An interpretive literary approach that is concerned primarily with content and values. 0000

morality play A type of medieval and early Renaissance play that dramatizes how to live a pious life. The best-known morality play is the anonymous *Everyman*. 000

motif ("something that moves") Sometimes used in reference to a main *idea* or *theme* in a single work or in many works, such as a *carpe diem* theme, or a comparison of lovers to little worlds. See also *archetype*. 000

motivation The ideas and impulses that propel characters to a particular act or course of action. Motivation is the hallmark quality of a *round character*. 000

multiple plot or **double plot** A development in which two or more stories are both contrasted and woven together, as in Shakespeare's *A Midsummer Night's Dream*. 0000

musical comedy A modern prose play integrated with lyrics—and also dances—set to specially composed music. Usually, musical comedies are elaborately and expensively produced. The form is in a line of development from *ballad opera* and *comic opera*. 0000

music of poetry See *prosody.*

muthos Aristotle's word for plot, from which our word *myth* is derived. 000

mystery play See *Corpus Christi play.*

myth, mythology, mythos A *myth* is a story that deals with the relationships of gods to humanity or with battles among heroes in time past. A myth may also be a set of beliefs or assumptions among societies. *Mythology* refers collectively to all the stories and beliefs, either of a single group or number of groups. A system of beliefs and religious or historical doctrines is a *mythos*. 0, 000, 000

mythical reader See *audience.*

mythic critical approach See *archetypal/symbolic/mythic critical approach.*

mythopoeic The propensity to create *myths* and to live in terms of them. 000

narration, narrative fiction The relating or recounting of a sequence of events or actions. Whereas a narration may be reportorial and historical, *narrative fiction* is primarily creative and imaginative. See also *prose fiction* and *creative nonfiction*. 0, 00, 00

narrative ballad A poem in *ballad measure* telling a story and also containing dramatic speeches. 000

narrator See *speaker.*

nasal A meaningful continuant consonant in which the sound is released through the nose. The nasals in English are *n*, *m*, and *ng*. 000

naturalistic setting A stage *setting* designed to imitate, as closely as possible, the everyday world, often to the point of emphasizing poverty and dreariness. 000

near rhyme See *inexact rhyme.*

neoclassic couplet See *heroic couplet.*

neutral diction See *diction, neutral* or *middle.*

new comedy Athenian comedy that developed at the end of the fourth century B.C.E., stressing wit, romanticism, and twists of plot. The most famous of the new comedy writers was Menander (342–292 BCE). His plays were long considered lost, but a small number have luckily come to light in the last hundred years. 000, 0000

New Critical/formalist critical approach An interpretive literary approach based on the French practice of *explication de texte*, stressing the form and details of literary works. 0000

new historicism A type of literary criticism that emphasizes the integration of literature with historical background and culture. 0000

nonfiction prose A *genre* consisting of essays, articles, and books about real as opposed to fictional occurrences and objects; one of the major *genres* of literature. 0

nonrealistic character An undeveloped and often *symbolic character* without full motivation or individual identity. 000

nonrealistic drama Dreamlike, fantastic, symbolic, and otherwise artificial plays that make no attempt to present an imitation of everyday reality. 000

novel A long work of prose fiction. 0

objective point of view See *dramatic point of view.*

octave The first eight *lines* of an *Italian sonnet*, unified by topic, rhythm, and *rhyme*. In practice, the first eight lines of any sonnet. 000

ode A variable stanzaic poetic *form* (usually long, to contrast it with the *song*) with varying line lengths and sometimes intricate *rhyme* schemes. 0, 000

Old Comedy or **Old Attic Comedy** The Athenian comedies of the fifth century BCE, featuring song, dance, ribaldry, satire, and invective. The most famous writer of the old comedy is Aristophanes, eleven of whose plays have survived from antiquity. 000, 0000

olfactory imagery *Images* referring to smell. 000

omniscient point of view A *third-person narrative* in which the *speaker* or *narrator*, with no apparent limitations, may describe intentions, actions, reactions, locations, and speeches of any or all of the characters, and may also describe their innermost thoughts (when necessary for the development of the *plot*). 00, 000

open-form poetry Poems that avoid traditional structural patterns, such as *rhyme* or *meter*, in favor of other methods of organization. 000–000

orchestra (a part of a **theater)** (1) In ancient Greek theaters, the *orchestra*, or "dancing place," was the circular area at the base of the amphitheater where the chorus performed. (2) In modern theaters, the word "orchestra" now refers to the ground floor or first floor where the audience sits. 000

organic unity The interdependence of all elements of a work, including character, actions, speeches, descriptions, thoughts, and observations. The concept of organic unity is attributed to Aristotle. 00

outline See *analytical sentence outline.*

overstatement or **hyperbole** or **overreacher.** A rhetorical *figure of speech* in which emphasis is achieved through exaggeration. 000, 000

parable A short *allegory* designed to illustrate a religious truth, often associated with Jesus as recorded in the Gospels, primarily Luke. 0, 00, 000

parados (1) A *parados* was either of the two front aisles leading from the sides to the *orchestra* in ancient Greek amphitheaters, along which the performers could enter or exit. (2) The entry and first lyrical ode of the *chorus* in Greek tragedy, after the *prologue*. 000, 000

paradox A *figure of speech* embodying a contradiction that is nevertheless true. 000

parallelism A *figure of speech* in which the same grammatical forms are repeated. 000, 000

paranomasia See *pun.*

paraphrase A brief restatement, in one's own words, of all or part of a literary work; a *précis*. 000

pastoral A traditional poetic form with topic material drawn from the usually idealized vocabulary of rural and shepherd life. Famous English pastorals are Milton's "Lycidas," Arnold's "Thyrsis," Pope's *Pastorals*, and Spenser's *The Shepherd's Calendar*. 000

pathos The "scene of suffering" in tragedy, which Aristotle defines as "a destructive or painful action, such as death on the stage, bodily agony, wounds, and the like." It is the scene of suffering that is intended to evoke the response of pity (*eleos*) from the audience. 000

pentameter A line of five metrical *feet*. 000

perfect rhyme See *exact rhyme.*

performance An individual production of a play, either for an evening or for an extended period, comprising acting, movement, lighting, sound effects, staging and scenery, ticket sales, and the accommodation of the audience. 000

peripeteia or **reversal** Aristotle's term for a sudden reversal, when the action of a work, particularly a play, veers around quickly to its opposite. 000

persona See *speaker.*

personification A *figure of speech* in which human characteristics are attributed to nonhuman things or abstractions. 000

perspective, dramatic The *point of view* in drama, the way in which the dramatist focuses on major characters and on particular problems. 000

Petrarchan sonnet See *Italian sonnet.*

phonetic, phonetics The actual pronunciation of sounds, as distinguished from spelling or *graphics*. 000–00

picture poetry See *visual poetry.*

plagiarism A writer's use of the language and ideas of another writer or writers without proper acknowledgment. Plagiarism is an exceedingly serious breach of academic honor; some call it intellectual theft, and others call it an academic crime. 000, 000, 000

platform stage A raised stage surrounded by seats for an *arena theater* or *theater-in-the-round*. 000

plausibility See *probability.*

play See *drama.*

plot The plan or groundwork for a *story* or a *play*, with the *actions* resulting from believable and authentic human responses to a *conflict*. It is causality, conflict, response, opposition, and interaction that make a plot out of a series of *actions*. Aristotle's word for plot is *muthos*, from which the word *myth* is derived. 00, 000, 000

plot of intrigue See *intrigue plot.*

poem, poet, poetry A variable literary genre that is, foremost, characterized by the rhythmical qualities of language. While poems may be short (including *epigrams* and *haiku* of just a few lines) or long (*epics* of thousands of lines), the essence of poetry is compression, economy, and force, in contrast with the expansiveness and logic of prose. There is no bar to the topics that poets may consider, and poems may range from the personal and lyric to the public and discursive. A *poem* is one poetic work.

A *poet* is a person who writes poems. *Poetry* may refer to the poems of one writer, to poems of a number of writers, to all poems generally, or to the aesthetics of poetry considered as an art. 0, 000, 000, *passim*.

point of view The *speaker, voice, narrator,* or *persona* of a work; the position from which details are perceived and related; a centralizing mind or intelligence; not to be confused with *opinion* or *belief*. 00, 000–000

point-of-view character The central figure or *protagonist* in a *limited-point-of-view narration*, the character about whom events turn, the focus of attention in the narration. 000

postulate or **premise** The assumption on which a work of literature is based, such as a level of absolute, literal *reality*, or as a dreamlike, fanciful set of events. See also *donnée*. 00

private or **contextual symbol** See *cultural symbol*.

probability or **plausibility** The standard that literature should be concerned with what is likely, common, normal, and usual. 000

problem A question or issue about the interpretation or understanding of a work. 0000

problem play A type of *play* dealing with a *problem*, whether personal, social, political, environmental, philosophical, or religious. 000, 0000, 0000

procatalepsis or **anticipation** A rhetorical strategy whereby the writer raises an objection and then answers it; the goal is to strengthen an argument by dealing with possible objections before a dissenter can raise them. Procatalepsis is thus a writer's way of taking the wind out of an objector's sails. 0000

producer The person in charge of practical matters connected with a stage production, such as securing finances, arranging for theater use, furnishing materials, renting or making costumes and properties, guaranteeing payments, and so on. 000

prologue In ancient Athenian *tragedy*, the introductory action and speeches before the *parados*, or first entry of the *chorus*. 000

props or **properties** The furniture, draperies, and the like used on stage during a play. 000

proscenium, proscenium stage An arch or frame that delineates a box set and holds the curtain, thus creating the invisible fourth wall through which the audience sees the action of the play. See also *proskenion*. 000

prose fiction *Imaginative* prose narratives (*short stories* and *novels*) that focus on one or a few *characters* who undergo a change or development as they interact with other characters and deal with their problems. 0, 00

prose poem A short work, laid out to look like prose, but employing the methods of verse, such as rhythm and imagery, for poetic ends. 000, 000

proskenion A raised stage built in front of the *skene* in ancient Greek theaters to separate the *actors* from the *chorus* and to make them more prominent. 000

prosody Metrics and versification; the *sounds*, *rhythms*, *rhymes*, and general physical qualities of *poetry*; the relationships between content and sound in poetry. 000

protagonist The central *character* and focus of interest in a *narrative* or *drama*. 000

psychological/psychoanalytic critical approach An interpretive literary approach stressing how psychology may be used in the explanation of both authors and literary works. 0000

public mythology See *universal mythology*.

pun, or ***paranomasia*** Witty wordplay based on the fact that certain words with different meanings have nearly identical or even identical sounds. See also *malapropism*. 000

purgation See *catharsis*.

pyrrhic A *substitute* metrical *foot* consisting of two unaccented *syllables*, as in the words "on their" in this line from Pope's *Pastorals*: "Now sleeping flocks on their soft fleeces lie." 000

quatrain (1) A four-line *stanza* or poetic unit. (2) In an *English* or *Shakespearean sonnet*, a group of four *lines* united by *rhyme*. 0, 000

queer theory An interpretive literary approach based on the idea that sexual orientation is partly ideological and partly social. Many queer theorists see the heterosexual/homosexual divide as less distinct than has traditionally been understood. 0000

raisonneur A character who remains somewhat detached from the dramatic action and who provides reasoned commentary; a *choric figure*. 000

reader-response critical approach An interpretive literary approach based on the proposition that literary works are not fully created until readers make *transactions* with them by *actualizing* them in the light of their particular knowledge and experience. 0000

realism or **verisimilitude** The use of true, lifelike, or probable situations and concerns. Also, the theory underlying the depiction of reality in literature. 00

realistic character The accurate *imitation* of individualized men and women. 000

realistic comedy See *ironic comedy*.

realistic drama The dramatic presentation of *action*, thoughts, and *character* that are designed to give the illusion of *reality*. 0000

realistic setting A *setting* designed to resemble places that actually exist or that might exist. The setting of Wilson's *Fences* is realistic. 000

recognition See *anagnorisis*.

regular play A play conforming to the traditional *rules* of drama, particularly the *three unities*. Usually a regular play contains five acts (as in the Renaissance up through much of the nineteenth century). More recent regular plays contain three acts, although there is nothing hard and fast about this number. See *rules of drama*. 000

reliable narrator A *speaker* who has nothing to hide by making misstatements and who is untainted by self-interest. This speaker's *narration* is therefore to be accepted at face value; contrasted with an *unreliable narrator*. 000

repetition See *anaphora*.

representation See *mimesis*.

representative character A *flat character* with the qualities of all other members of a group (i.e., clerks, cowboys, detectives, etc.); a *stereotype*. 000

research, literary The systematic use of primary and secondary sources for assistance in studying a literary *problem*. 000, 000, 0000

resolution See *dénouement*.

response A reader's intellectual and emotional reactions to a literary work. 0000

Restoration Comedy English *high comedies* written mainly between 1660 and 1700, dealing realistically with personal, social, and sexual issues. 0000

revenge tragedy A popular type of English Renaissance drama, developed by Thomas Kyd, in which a person is called upon (often by a ghost) to avenge the murder of a loved one. Shakespeare's *Hamlet* is in the tradition of revenge tragedy. 000

reversal See *peripeteia*.

rhetoric The art of persuasive writing; broadly, the art of all effective writing. 000

rhetorical figure See *figure of speech*.

rhetorical substitution See *substitution*.

rhyme The repetition of identical or closely related sounds in the syllables of different words, almost always in concluding syllables at the ends of lines, such as Shakespeare's *DAY* and *MAY* (Sonnet 18) and Swinburne's *forEVER, NEVER,* and *RIVER* "The Garden of Proserpine". 000

rhyme scheme A pattern of *rhyme*, usually indicated in prosodic analysis by the assignment of a letter of the alphabet to each rhyming sound, as in *a b b a a b b a* as the rhyming pattern of the octave of an *Italian* or *Petrarchan sonnet*. 000

rhythm The varying speed, intensity, elevation, pitch, loudness, and expressiveness of speech, especially *poetry*. 000

rising action The action in a *play* before the climax. See *Freytag pyramid*. 000

romance (1) Lengthy Spanish and French *stories* of the sixteenth and seventeenth centuries. (2) Modern formulaic *stories* describing the growth of an impulsive, passionate, and powerful love relationship. 0, 00

romantic comedy Sympathetic *comedy* that presents the adventures of young lovers trying to overcome opposition and achieve a successful union. 0000

round character A literary character, usually but not necessarily the *protagonist* of a story or play, who is three-dimensional, rounded, authentic, memorable, original, and true to life. A round character is the center of our attention, and is both individual and unpredictable. A round character profits from experience, and in the course of a story or play undergoes change or development. 000, 000

rules of drama An important concept of dramatic composition among Renaissance and eighteenth-century critics. The rules were based on ancient practice and theory, particularly the use of the five-act pyramidal (Freytag) structure and the embodiment of the *three unities* of action, place, and time. Sophocles followed the rules carefully; indeed, the rules were at least partially derived from his example. Shakespeare observed the *unity of action*, but in the interests of *probability* he apparently saw no reason to observe the others. See also *regular play*. 000

satire An attack on human follies or vices, as measured positively against a normative religious, moral, or social standard. 000

satiric comedy A form of *comedy* designed to correct social and individual behavior by ridiculing human vices and follies. 0000

satyr play A comic and burlesque *play* submitted by the ancient Athenian tragic dramatists along with their groups of three *tragedies*. On each day of tragic performances, the satyr play was performed after the three tragedies. See also *trilogy*. 000

scan, scansion The act of determining the prevailing *rhythm* and poetic characteristics of a *poem*. 000

scene In a *play*, a part or division (of an act, as in *Hamlet*, or of an entire play, as in *Fences*) in which there is a unity of subject, *setting*, and *actors*. 000

scenery The artificial environment created onstage to produce the illusion of a specific or generalized place and time. 000

schwa (from Hebrew) A middle, minimal vowel sound that in prosodic scansion occupies unstressed positions, even though the sound may be spelled as *a, e, i, o*, or *u*. The schwa is the most commonly pronounced vowel sound in English. 000

scrim A stage curtain that becomes transparent when illuminated from upstage, permitting action to take place under various lighting conditions. 000

second-person point of view A *narration* in which a second-person listener ("you") is the *protagonist* and the speaker is someone (e.g., doctor, parent, rejected lover) with knowledge that the protagonist does not possess or understand about his or her own actions. 000,000

segment The smallest meaningful unit of sound, such as the *l*, *uh*, and *v* sounds (phonemes) making up the word "love." Segments are to be distinguished from spellings. Thus, the *oo* segment may be spelled as *ui* in "fruit," *u* in "flute," *oo* in "foolish," *o* in "lose," *uu* in "vacuum," or *ou* in "troupe." 000

selective recollection See *flashback.*

sentimental comedy A type of comedy dramatizing how good nature and morality enable characters to overcome their character flaws, which otherwise seem problematic or even incorrigible. 0000

septenary See *heptameter.*

sequence The following of one thing upon another in time or chronology. It is the *realistic* or true-to-life basis of the cause-and-effect arrangement necessary in a *plot*. 00, 00

seriousness The first element in Aristotle's definition of *tragedy*, demonstrating the most elevated and significant aspects of human character. 000

sestet (1) A six-line stanza or unit of *poetry*. (2) The last six lines of an *Italian sonnet*. 000

sets The physical scenery and properties used in a theatrical production. 000

setting The natural, manufactured, and cultural environment in which characters live and move, including all their possessions, homes, ways of life, and assumptions. 000–000

Shakespearean sonnet *See English sonnet.*

shaped verse See *visual poetry.*

short story A compact, concentrated work of *narrative fiction* that may also contain description, dialogue, and commentary. Poe used the term "brief prose tale" before the term "short story" was created, and he emphasized that the form should create a powerful and unified impact. 0, 00

simile A *figure of speech*, using "like" with nouns and "as" with clauses, as in "the trees were bent by the wind *like actors bowing after a performance.*" 000

simple sentence A complete sentence containing only one subject and one verb, together with modifiers and complements. 000

sitcom A serial type of modern television comedy dramatizing the circumstances, assumptions, and actions of a fixed number of characters (hence "situation comedy" or "sitcom"). 0000

situation The given circumstances of a *story, poem*, or *play*; a *donnée*. 0

situational irony or **irony of situation** A type of *irony* emphasizing that human beings are enmeshed in forces beyond their comprehension and control. 00, 000, 000

skene ("tent," "hut") In ancient Greek theaters, a building in front of the *orchestra* that contained front and side doors from which actors could make entrances and exits. It served a variety of purposes, including the storage of *costumes* and *props*. The word has given us our modern word *scene*. 000

slang Informal diction and substandard vocabulary. Some slang is a permanent part of the language (e.g., phrases like "I'll be damned," "That sucks," and our many four-letter words). Other slang is spontaneous, rising within a group (*jargon*), and often then being replaced when new slang emerges. 000

slapstick comedy A type of low *farce* in which the humor depends almost entirely on physical actions and sight gags. 0000

social drama A type of *problem play* that deals with current social issues and the place of individuals in society. 000

soliloquy A speech made by a character, alone on stage, directly to the *audience*, the convention being that the character is revealing his or her inner thoughts, feelings, hopes, and plans. A soliloquy is to be distinguished from an *aside*, which is made to the audience (or confidentially to another character) when other characters are present. 000

song See *lyric.*

sonnet A poem of fourteen lines (originally designed to be spoken and not sung) in *iambic pentameter*. See *Italian sonnet* and *English sonnet*. 0, 000

sound The phonetics of language, separately and collectively considered. See also *prosody*. 000

speaker The *narrator* of a *story* or *poem*, the *point of view*, often an independent *character* who is completely imagined and consistently maintained by the author. In addition to narrating the essential events of the work (justifying the status of *narrator*), the speaker may also introduce other aspects of his or her knowledge, and may express judgments and opinions. Often the character of the speaker is of as much interest in the story as the *actions* or *incidents*. 000

specific language Words referring to objects or conditions that may be perceived or imagined; distinguished from *general language*. 000

speeches See *dialogue*.

spondee A two-syllable *foot* consisting of successive, equally stressed words or syllables (e.g., *SLOW TIME, MEN'S EYES*). 000

sprung rhythm or **accentual rhythm** A method of accenting, developed by Gerard Manley Hopkins, in which major stresses are "sprung" from the poetic line, as in "DAP - ple - DAWN - DRAWN FALcon, in his RID - ing . . ." from "The Windhover." 000

stage business See *business*.

stage convention See *convention*.

stage directions A playwright's instructions concerning *blocking*, movement, *action*, tone of voice, entrances and exits, *lighting*, *scenery*, and the like. 000

stanza A group of *poetic lines* corresponding to paragraphs in prose; stanzaic *meters* and *rhymes* are usually repeating and systematic. 000

stasimon (plural **stasima**) A *choral ode* separating the *episodes* in Greek tragedies. Because of the word's derivation, it would seem that the chorus remained stationary in the orchestra and watched during the episodes, and then stood before speaking or chanting its designated odes. 000

static character A character who undergoes no change, a *flat character*; contrasted with a *dynamic character*. 000

stereotype A character who is so ordinary and unoriginal that he or she seems to have been cast in a mold; a *representative character*. 000

stichomythy In ancient Greek drama, dialogue consisting of one-line speeches designed for rapid interchanges between characters. 000

stock character A *flat character* in a standard role with standard *traits*, such as the irate police captain, the bored hotel clerk, or the sadistic criminal; a *stereotype*. 000, 000

story A *narrative*, usually fictional, and short, centering on a major character, and rendering a complete action. 00

stress The emphasis given to a syllable, either strong or light. See also *accent*. 000

strong-stress rhythm See *heavy-stress rhyme* or *rising rhyme*.

structuralist critical approach An interpretive literary approach that attempts to find relationships and similarities among elements that might originally appear to be separate and discrete. 0000

structure The arrangement and placement of materials in a work. 00, 000–000, 000

style The manipulation of language; the placement of words in the service of content. 000–000

subject The topic that a literary work addresses, such as love, marriage, war, death, and social inequality. 000

subplot A secondary line of action in a literary work that often comments directly or obliquely on the main plot. See also *multiple plot*. 000

substitution A variant poetic *foot* within a poem in which a particular metrical foot is dominant. *Formal substitution* is the use of an actual variant foot within a line, such as an *anapest* being used in place of an *iamb*. *Rhetorical substitution* is the manipulation of the caesura to create the effect of a series of differing *feet*. 000

suspended rhyme See *inexact rhyme*.

syllable A separately pronounced part of a word (e.g., the *sing* and *ing* parts of "singing"; the *sub, sti, tu,* and *tion* parts of "substitution"). Some words consist of only one syllable (e.g., *a, an, man, girl, the, when, screeched*), and other words have many syllables (*antidisestablishmentarianism, Aldeborontiphoscophornio*). 000

symbol, symbolism A specific word, idea, or object that may stand for ideas, values, persons, or ways of life. 00, 000, 000–000, 000–000, 000, 000

symbolic character A character whose primary function is symbolic, even though the character also retains normal or *realistic* qualities. 000

symbolic critical approach See *archetypal approach*.

synecdoche A *figure of speech* in which a part stands for a whole, or a whole for a part. 000

synesthesia A *figure of speech* uniting or fusing separate sensations or feelings; the description of one type of perception or thought with words that are appropriate to another. 000

syntax Word order and sentence structure. A mark of style is a writer's syntactical patterning (regular patterns and variations), depending on the rhetorical needs of the literary work. 000

syzygy See *dipody*.

tactile imagery *Images* of touch and responses to touch. 000

tenor (figure of speech) The ideas conveyed in a *metaphor* or *simile*. See also *vehicle*. 000

tense Besides embodying reports of actions and circumstances, verbs possess altering forms—*tenses*—that signify the times when things occur, whether past, present, or future. Perfect and progressive tenses indicate completed or continuing activities. Tense is an important aspect of *point of view* because the notation of time influences the way in which events are perceived and expressed. Narratives are usually told in the past tense, but many recent writers of fiction prefer the present tense for conveying a sense of immediacy. No matter when a sequence of actions is presumed to have taken place, the introduction of *dialogue* changes the action to the present. See *point of view*. 000

tercet or **triplet** A three-line unit or stanza of *poetry*, usually rhyming *a a a, b b b,* etc. 0, 000

terza rima A three-line *stanza* form with the interlocking rhyming pattern *a b a, b c b, c d c,* etc. 000

tetrameter A *line* of four metrical *feet*. 000

theater In ancient Athens a theater was a "place for seeing." Today it is the name given to the building in which plays and other dramatic productions are performed. It is also a generic name for local or national drama in all its aspects, as in "Tonight we're going to the theater," and "This play is the best of the New York theater this year." 000, 000

Theater of Dionysus The ancient Athenian outdoor amphitheater at the base of the Acropolis, where Greek drama began. 000

theater-in-the-round See *arena stage* and *platform stage*.

theme (1) The major or central idea of a work. (2) An essay, a short composition developing an interpretation or advancing an argument. (3) The main point or idea that a writer of an essay asserts and illustrates. 00, 000–000, 000

theos apo mechanes See *deus ex machina*.

thesis sentence or **thesis statement** An introductory sentence that names the topics and ideas to be developed in the body of an *essay*. 00

third-person objective point of view See *dramatic point of view*.

third-person point of view A third-person method of *narration* (i.e., *she, he, it, they, them*, etc.), in which the *speaker* or *narrator* is not a part of the story, unlike the involvement of the narrator of a *first-person point of view.* Because the third-person speaker may exhibit great knowledge and understanding, together with other qualities of *character*, he or she is often virtually identified with the author, but this identification is not easily decided. See also *authorial voice, omniscient point of view.* 00, 000, 000

three unities Traditionally associated with Aristotle's descriptions of drama as expressed in the *Poetics*, the three unities are those of action, place, and time. The unities are a function of *verisimilitude*—the creation of literary works that are as much like reality as possible. Therefore a play should dramatize a single major *action* that takes place in a single place during the approximate time it would take for completion, from beginning to end. During the Renaissance, some critics considered the unities to be essential aspects, or *rules*, of *regular drama.* Later critics considered the unity of action important, but minimized the unities of place and time. See also *regular play.* 000

thrust stage See *apron stage.*

tiring house An enclosed area in an Elizabethan theater in which *actors* changed *costumes* and awaited their cues, and in which stage *properties* were kept. The word *tiring* is derived from *attire* (e.g., clothing or costumes). 000

tone The techniques and modes of presentation that reveal or create attitudes. 00, 000–000, 000–000, 000

topic sentence The sentence determining or introducing the subject matter of a paragraph. 00

topical/historical critical approach An interpretive literary approach that stresses the relationship of literature to its historical period. 0000

tragedy A drama or other literary work that recounts the fall or misfortune of an individual who, while undergoing suffering, deals responsibly with the situations and dilemmas that he or she faces, and who thus demonstrates the value of human effort and human existence. 000, 000–0000

tragic flaw See *hamartia.*

tragicomedy A literary work—*drama* or *story*—containing a mixture of *tragic* and *comic* elements. 000

trait A typical mode of behavior; the study of major traits provides a guide to the description of *character.* 000

trilogy A group of three literary works, usually related or unified. For the ancient Athenian festivals of Dionysus, each competing tragic dramatist submitted a trilogy (three *tragedies*), together with a *satyr play.* 000

trimeter A line of three metrical *feet*, as in "To-DAY / I WENT / to SCHOOL." 000

triplet See *tercet.*

trochaic (double) rhyme Rhyming trochees such as *FLOWER* and *TOWER.* 000

trochee, trochaic A two-syllable *foot* consisting of a heavy *stress* followed by a light stress (e.g., *RUN-ning, SING-ing, EAT-ing*). Sometimes called a *choree.* 000

trope A short dramatic dialogue inserted into the church mass during the early Middle Ages. 000

Tudor interlude Tragedies, comedies, or historical plays performed by both professional actors and students during the reigns of Henry VII and Henry VIII (i.e., the first half of the sixteenth century). The Tudor interludes sometimes featured abstract and allegorical characters and provided opportunities for both music and farcical action. 000

unaccented syllable A syllable receiving a *light stress.* 000

unchanging character See *flat character.*

understatement A *figure of speech* by which details and ideas are deliberately underplayed or undervalued in order to create emphasis—a form of *irony.* 000, 000

unit set A series of platforms, rooms, stairs, and exits that form the locations for all of a play's actions. A unit set enables scenes to be changed rapidly, without the drawing of a curtain and the placement of new sets. 000

unities See *three unities*.

universal (public) mythology Widely known mythic systems that have been well established over a long period of time, such as Greco-Roman mythology and Germanic mythology. 00, 000

universal symbol See *cultural symbol*.

unreliable narrator A speaker who through ignorance, self-interest, or lack of capacity may tell lies and distort details. Locating the truth in an unreliable narrator's story requires careful judgment and not inconsiderable skepticism. 000

unstressed syllable See *light stress*.

value, values The attachment of worth, significance, and desirability to an *idea* so that the idea is judged not only for its significance as thought but also for its importance as a goal, ideal, or standard. 000

vehicle The image or reference of figures of speech, such as a *metaphor* or *simile*; it is the vehicle that carries or embodies the *tenor*. 000

verbal irony Language stressing the importance of an idea by stating the opposite of what is meant. 00, 000, 000, 000

verisimilitude (i.e., "like truth") A characteristic whereby the *setting*, circumstances, *characters*, *dialogue*, *actions*, and outcomes in a work are designed to seem true, lifelike, real, plausible, and probable. See also *realism*. 00, 000

versification See *prosody*.

villanelle A *closed-form* poem of nineteen lines, composed of five *tercets* and a concluding *quatrain*. The form requires that whole lines be repeated in a specific order and that only two rhyming sounds occur throughout. See also *tercet*. 0, 000

virgule A slash mark (/) used in poetic *scansion* to mark the boundaries of poetic *feet*. A double virgule (//) is commonly used to indicate the placement of a *caesura*. 000

visual imagery Language describing visible objects and situations. 000

visual poetry Poetry written so that the lines form a recognizable shape, such as a pair of wings or a geometrical figure. Also called *concrete poetry* or *shaped verse*. 000

voice See *point of view* and *speaker*.

voiced and **voiceless sounds** Consonants that are voiced are made with the full vibration of the vocal chords, as in *b*, *z* and *v*. Consonants that are voiceless are made without the use of the vocal chords, as in *p*, *s* and *f*. These two sets of consonants are formed identically, the only difference being that one set is *voiced* whereas the other is *voiceless*, or whispered. Normally, all vowels are voiced. 000

vowel rhyme The use of nonrhyming vowel sounds in rhyming positions, as in *DAY* and *SKY*, or *KEY* and *PLAY*. 000

vowel sounds or **vowel segments** Meaningful sounds produced by the continuant resonation of the voice in the space between the tongue and the top of the mouth, such as the *ee* in "feel," the *eh* in "bet," and the *oo* in "cool." 000

well-made play (*la pièce bien faite*) A form developed and popularized in nineteenth-century France by Eugène Scribe (1791–1861) and Victorien Sardou (1831–1908). Typically, the well-made play is built on both secrets and the timely arrivals of new characters and threats. The protagonist faces adversity and ultimately overcomes it. Ibsen's *A Dollhouse* exhibits many characteristics of the well-made play. 0000, 0000

words The spoken and written signifiers of thoughts, objects, and actions—the building blocks of language. 000–000

CREDITS

LITERARY

"Night Talkers" from *The Dew Breaker* by Edwidge Danticat, copyright © 2004 by Edwidge Danticat. Used by permission of Alfred A. Knopf, a division of Random House, Inc.

"A Rose for Emily," copyright 1930 and renewed 1958 by William Faulkner, from *Collected Stories of William Faulkner* by William Faulkner. Used by permission of Random House, Inc.

"The Things They Carried" from *The Things They Carried* by Tim O'Brien, copyright © 1990 by Tim O'Brien. Reprinted by permission of Houghton Mifflin Company. All rights reserved.

"Everyday Use" from *In Love & Trouble: Stories of Black Women*, copyright © 1973 by Alice Walker, reprinted by permission of Houghton Mifflin Harcourt Publishing Company.

"A Worn Path," from *A Curtain of Green and Other Stories*, copyright 1941 and renewed 1969 by Eudora Welty, reprinted by permission of Harcourt, Inc.

PHOTO

Marketing Walkthrough: p. v (*top*) Larry Riley/Miramax/Picture Desk, Inc./Kobal Collection; p. v (*bottom*) © Universal International Pictures/Photofest.

Part I: p. 5 Time/Life Pictures/Getty Images.

Chapter 1: p. 65 Dan Piraro/King Features Syndicate; p. 66 From *Maus II: A Survivor's Tale/And Here My Trouble Began* by Art Spiegelman, © 1986, 1989, 1990, 1991, by Art Spiegelman. Used by permission of Pantheon Books, a division of Random House, Inc.; p. 71 Culver Pictures, Inc.; p. 77 AP Wide World Photos; p. 89 CORBIS/Bettmann; p. 95 Jerry Bauer; p. 105 Getty Images/Hulton Archive Photos; p. 108 AP Wide World Photos; p. 114 AP Wide World Photos.

Appendix I: p. 1908 Missouri Historical Society; p. 1911 *The New York Times*, July 2007.

Alphabetical List of Authors Included in *Literature*, Ninth Edition

Aesop, ca. 600 BCE
Agüeros, Jack, b. 1934
Albee, Edward, b. 1928
Aldiss, Brian W., b. 1925
Angelou, Maya, b. 1928
Arnold, Matthew, 1822–1888
Atwood, Margaret, b. 1939
Auden, W. H., 1907–1973
Baldwin, James, 1924–1987
Bambara, Toni Cade, 1939–1995
Berry, Wendell, b. 1934
Bierce, Ambrose, 1842–1914?
Bishop, Elizabeth, 1911–1979
Blake, William, 1757–1827
Bogan, Louise, 1897–1970
Bontemps, Arna, 1902–1973
Bradstreet, Anne, 1612–1672
Brewster, Elizabeth, b. 1922
Brontë, Emily, 1818–1848
Brooks, Gwendolyn, 1917–2000
Browning, Elizabeth Barrett, 1806–1864
Browning, Robert, 1812–1889
Bryant, William Cullen, 1794–1878
Burns, Robert, 1759–1796
Carroll, Lewis, 1832–1898
Carruth, Hayden, b. 1921
Carter, Jimmy, b. 1924
Carver, Raymond, 1939–1989
Chekhov, Anton, 1860–1904
Chioles, John, b. 1940
Chopin, Kate, 1851–1904
Cisneros, Sandra, b. 1954
Clampitt, Amy, 1920–1994
Clifton, Lucille, b. 1936
Clough, Arthur Hugh, 1819–1861
Cohen, Leonard, b. 1934
Coleman, Anita Scott, 1890–1960
Coleridge, Samuel Taylor, 1772–1834
Collins, Billy, b. 1941
Conrad, Joseph, 1857–1924
Cornford, Frances, 1886–1960
Cowper, William 1731–1800
Crane, Stephen, 1871–1900
Creeley, Robert, 1926–2005
Cummings, E. E., 1894–1962
Danticat, Edwidge, b. 1969
Davison, Peter, 1928–2004
Dennis, Carl, b. 1939
Dickinson, Emily, 1830–1886
Donne, John, 1572–1631
Dryden, John, 1631–1700
Dubus, Andre, 1936–1999
Dunbar, Paul Lawrence, 1872–1906
Dunn, Stephen, b. 1939
Durem, Ray, 1915–1963
Eberhart, Richard, 1904–2005
Edelman, Bart, b. 1951
Eliot, T. S., 1888–1965
Ellison, Ralph, 1914–1994
Elizabeth I (Elizabeth Tudor, Queen Elizabeth I), 1533–1603
Emanuel, James, b. 1921
Emanuel, Lynn, b. 1949
Emerson, Ralph Waldo, 1803–1882
Evans, Abbie Huston, 1881–1983
Evans, Mari, b. 1923
Farrar, John Chipman, 1896–1974
Faulkner, William, 1897–1962
Field, Edward, b. 1924
Forché, Carolyn, b. 1950
Francis, Robert, 1901–1987
Frost, Robert, 1874–1963
Gardner, Isabella, 1915–1981
George, Chief Dan, 1899–1981
Gilman, Charlotte Perkins, 1860–1937
Ginsberg, Allen, 1926–1997
Giovanni, Nikki, b. 1943
Glaspell, Susan, 1882–1948
Glück, Louise, b. 1943
Graham, Jorie, b. 1951
Graves, Robert, 1895–1985
Gray, Thomas, 1716–1771
Greenberg, Joanne, b. 1932
Griffin, Susan, b. 1943
Hacker, Marilyn, b. 1942
Halpern, Daniel, b. 1945
Hamod, H. S. (Sam), b. 1936
Hardy, Thomas, 1840–1928
Harjo, Joy, b. 1951
Harper, Frances E. W., 1825–1911
Harper, Michael S., b. 1938
Hass, Robert, b. 1941
Hawthorne, Nathaniel, 1804–1864
Hayden, Robert, 1913–1980
Heaney, Seamus, b. 1939
Hemingway, Ernest, 1899–1961
Henley, Beth, b. 1952
Henley, William Ernest, 1849–1903
Herbert, George, 1593–1633
Herrick, Robert, 1591–1674
Heyen, William, b. 1940
Hirsch, Edward, b. 1953
Hirshfield, Jane, b. 1953
Hollander, John, b. 1929
Hope, A. D., 1907–2000
Hopkins, Gerard Manley, 1844–1889
Hospital, Carolina, b. 1957
Housman, A. E., 1859–1936
Hughes, Langston, 1902–1967
Ibsen, Henrik, 1828–1906
Ingham, John Hall, 1860–ca. 1931
Jackson, Shirley, 1919–1965
Jacobsen, Josephine, 1908–2003
Jarrell, Randall, 1914–1965
Jeffers, Robinson, 1887–1962
Jonson, Ben, 1573–1637
Joyce, James, 1882–1941
Justice, Donald, 1925–2004
Kafka, Franz, 1883–1924
Keats, John, 1795–1821
Keller, Betty, b. 1935
Kennedy, X. J., b. 1929
Kenny, Maurice, b. 1929
Kenyon, Jane, 1947–1990
King, Henry, 1592–1669
Kincaid, Jamaica, b. 1949
Kinnell, Galway, b. 1927
Kizer, Carolyn, b. 1925
Komunyakaa, Yusef, b. 1947
Kooser, Ted, b. 1939
Larkin, Philip, 1922–1985
Larson, Katherine, b. 1977
Laurents, Arthur, b. 1918
Laux, Dorianne, b. 1952
Lawrence, D. H., 1885–1930
Layton, Irving, 1912–2006
Lazarus, Emma, 1849–1887
Lee, Li-Young, b. 1957
Lehman, David, b. 1948
Levertov, Denise, 1923–1998
Levine, Philip, b. 1928
Lewis, C. Day, 1904–1972
Lightman, Alan, b. 1948
Lincoln, Abraham, 1809–1865
Lochhead, Liz, b. 1947
Longfellow, Henry Wadsworth, 1807–1882
Lorde, Audre, 1934–1992
Lowell, Amy, 1874–1925
Lowell, Robert, 1917–1977
Luke (St. Luke), fl. ca. 90 CE
Lux, Thomas, b. 1946
MacLeish, Archibald, 1892–1982
MacNeice, Louis, 1907–1963
Mansfield, Katherine, 1888–1923
Marlowe, Christopher, 1564–1593
Marvell, Andrew, 1621–1678
Masefield, John, 1878–1967
Maupassant, Guy de, 1850–1893
McHugh, Heather, b. 1948
McKay, Claude, 1890–1948
Mankiewicz, Herman J., 1897–1953
Melville, Herman, 1819–1891
Merwin, W. S., b. 1927
Millay, Edna St. Vincent, 1892–1950
Miller, Arthur, 1915–2005
Milton, John, 1608–1674
Minty, Judith, b. 1937
Molière (Jean Baptiste Poquelin), 1622–1673
Momaday, N. Scott, b. 1934
Montale, Eugenio, 1896–1981
Moore, Lorrie, b. 1957
Moore, Marianne, 1887–1972
Mora, Pat, b. 1942
Mueller, Lisel, b. 1924
Munro, Alice, b. 1931
Nash, Ogden, 1902–1971
Nemerov, Howard, 1920–1991
Neruda, Pablo, 1904–1973
Northrup, Jim, b. 1943
Nye, Naomi Shihab, b. 1952
O'Brien, Tim, b. 1946
O'Connor, Flannery, 1925–1964
O'Connor, Frank, 1903–1966
O'Neill, Eugene, 1888–1953
Oates, Joyce Carol, b. 1938
Olds, Sharon, b. 1942
Oliver, Mary, b. 1935
Olsen, Tillie (Lerner), 1913–2007
Orozco, Daniel, b. 1957
Ortiz Cofer, Judith, b. 1952
Ortiz, Simon, b. 1941
Owen, Wilfred, 1893–1918
Ozick, Cynthia, b. 1928
Parédes, Americo, 1915–1999
Parker, Dorothy, 1893–1967
Pastan, Linda, b. 1932
Peacock, Molly, b. 1947
Petronius (Gaius Petronius Arbiter), d. 66 CE
Piercy, Marge, b. 1934
Pinsky, Robert, b. 1940
Pirandello, Luigi, 1867–1936
Plath, Sylvia, 1932–1963
Poe, Edgar Allan, 1809–1849
Pope, Alexander, 1688–1744
Porter, Katherine Anne, 1890–1980
Pound, Ezra, 1885–1972
Prunty, Wyatt, b. 1947
Quasimodo, Salvatore, 1901–1968
Radnóti, Miklós, 1909–1944
Ralegh, Sir Walter, 1552–1618
Randall, Dudley, 1914–2000
Ransom, John Crowe, 1888–1974
Raven, John, b. 1936
Reed, Henry, 1914–1986
Rich, Adrienne, b. 1929
Ridler, Anne, 1912–2001
Rilke, Rainer Maria, 1875–1926
Ríos, Alberto, b. 1952
Robinson, Edwin Arlington, 1869–1935
Roethke, Theodore, 1907–1963
Rossetti, Christina, 1830–1894
Rückert, Friedrich, 1788–1866
Rukeyser, Muriel, 1913–1980
Russell, George William (Æ), 1867–1935
Salinas, Luis Omar, b. 1937
Sanchez, Sonia, b. 1934
Sandberg, Carl, 1878–1967
Sarton, May, 1912–1995
Sassoon, Siegfried, 1886–1967
Schnackenberg, Gjertrud, b. 1953
Scott, Virginia, b. 1938
Seeger, Alan, 1888–1916
Serotte, Brenda, b. 1946
Sexton, Anne, 1928–1974
Shakespeare, William, 1564–1616
Shapiro, Karl, 1913–2000
Shelley, Percy Bysshe, 1792–1822
Shore, Jane, b. 1947
Silko, Leslie Marmon, b. 1948
Smith, Dave, b. 1942
Smith, Stevie, 1902–1971
Snyder, Gary, b. 1930
Sophocles, 496–406 BCE
Soto, Gary, b. 1952
Spender, Sir Stephen, 1909–1995
Stafford, William, 1914–1993
Steinbeck, John, 1902–1968
Stern, Gerald, b. 1925
Stevens, Wallace, 1879–1955
Strand, Mark, b. 1934
Swenson, May, 1919–1989
Swift, Jonathan, 1667–1745
Tan, Amy, b. 1952
Tate, James, b. 1943
Tennyson, Alfred, Lord, 1809–1892
Terranova, Elaine, b. 1939
Thomas, Dylan, 1914–1953
Tobin, Daniel, b. 1958
Toomer, Jean, 1894–1967
Twain, Mark (Samuel Clemens), 1835–1910
Twichell, Chase, b. 1950
Ulisse, Peter, b. 1944
Updike, John, b. 1932
Van Duyn, Mona, 1921–2004
Villanueva, Tino, b. 1941
Viorst, Judith, b. 1931
Voigt, Ellen Bryant, b. 1943
Wagner, Shelly, b. 1948
Wagoner, David, b. 1926
Walker, Alice, b. 1944
Waller, Edmund, 1606–1687
Webb, Charles Harper, b. 1952
Webb, Phyllis, b. 1927
Weigl, Bruce, b. 1949
Welles, Orson, 1915–1985
Welty, Eudora, 1909–2001
Wheatley, Phillis, 1754–1784
Whitecloud, Tom, 1914–1972
Whitman, Walt, 1819–1892
Whittier, John Greenleaf, 1807–1892
Whur, Cornelius, 1782–1853
Wilbur, Richard, b. 1921
Williams, C. K., b. 1936
Williams, Tennessee, 1911–1983
Williams, William Carlos, 1883–1963
Wilson, August, 1945–2005
Wojahn, David, b. 1953
Wordsworth, William, 1770–1850
Wright, James, 1927–1980
Wyatt, Sir Thomas, 1503–1542
Yeats, William Butler, 1865–1939
Zimmer, Paul, b. 1934